Rural
and small town
Canada

Rural and small town Canada

Ray D. Bollman, Editor

TEP

THOMPSON EDUCATIONAL PUBLISHING, INC.

Published by Thompson Educational Publishing, Inc. in cooperation with Statistics Canada and the Canada Communications Group-Publishing, Supply and Services Canada.

Additional copies of this book may be obtained from the publisher.

Orders may be sent to:

United States	or	Canada
269 Portage Road		11 Briarcroft Road
Lewiston, New York		Toronto, Ontario
14092		M6S 1H3

For faster delivery, please send your order by telephone or fax to:
Tel. (416) 766-2763 / FAX (416) 766-0398

Canadian Cataloguing in Publication Data

Bollman, Ray D.
   Rural and small town Canada

Includes bibliographical references.
ISBN 1-55077-041-1
1. Canada - Rural conditions. 2. Canada - Economic conditions - 1991 - .* 3. Canada - Social conditions - 1971- .* I. Title.

HC113..   1993   330'.0971   C92-094720-4

76763

Photos: Industry, Science and Technology Canada.
Cover photos (clockwise): Gull Lake, Saskatchewan; Moose Jaw, Saskatchewan; Chemainus, British Columbia; Lunenburg, Nova Scotia; Carstairs, Alberta.

Printed in Canada   1 2 3 4   95 94 93 92

Table of contents

Introduction

Business linkages

Rural labour markets

Rural well-being

Does rural matter?

Preface

In the four years from 1986 to 1990, one half of Canadian census divisions lost population. These are the rural census divisions (Map 1). Rural and small town Canada is declining. In 1988, a group of researchers and policy analysts formed the Agriculture and Rural Restructuring Group (ARRG) to foster research, discussion and debate on the future of rural populations. Researchers and policy analysts felt there was no rural information available. I undertook to show there is a wealth of information collected and stored in Statistics Canada's databases. I invited 20 colleagues each to prepare a paper to inform the rural policy debate. Each chapter in this book represents merely a glimpse of the available information.

Thanks are due to many. First, a major thanks to each author. In addition, I wish to thank Tony Fuller for foresight and energy in organizing ARRG; Jacob Ryten and George Andrusiak for taking the risk on this endeavour; Judy Buehler for organizing the conference where these papers were first presented; Colleen Briggs and Sylvie Blais for hours of technical editing; and Danielle Baum for designing and preparing the manuscript in the two languages. The final thanks is to Betty Lorimer for the music.

Ray D. Bollman
July, 1992

MAP 1
Net migration, 1986-1990

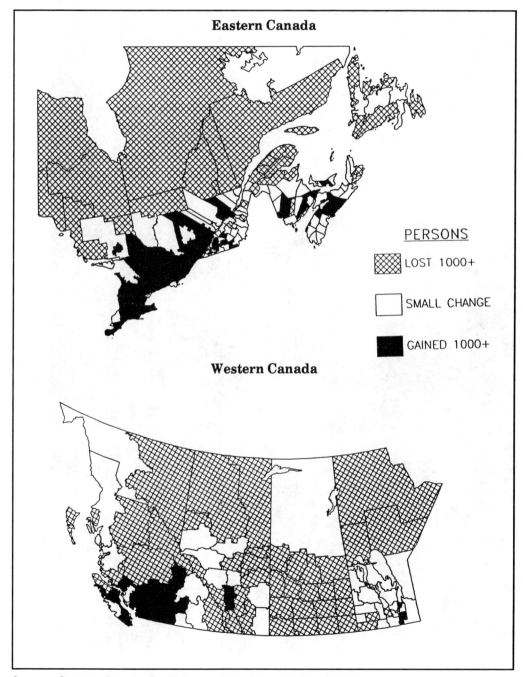

Source: Statistics Canada. Small Area and Administrative Data Division.

Pembroke, Ontario

1

Rural and small town Canada: an overview

Ray D. Bollman and Brian Biggs

Summary

Global restructuring of commodity and financial markets, rapid technological change and policy responses to this changing environment will continue to influence rural and small town Canada. This paper provides an overview of the demographic features, the labour market characteristics, and some indicators of well-being for rural and small town Canada.

The paper highlights that the rural population is increasing, small town population is constant and that rural growth rates lag urban growth rates. The farm population became a minority in rural Canada by 1956. Our migration patterns reveal that more people move urban to rural than rural to urban.

Although slight growth has occurred in rural and small town employment, the rural share of employment growth is declining. Labour force participation rates are lower in rural and small towns but labour force participation rates are highest among the male and female farm population. The rural and small town labour force is more concentrated in the goods-producing industries than the urban labour force; however, nearly 60% of the rural and small town labour force is in the service-performing industries.

Families in small towns have the lowest average income. Rural and small towns have the lowest incidence of families with incomes below Statistics Canada's low income cut-offs. Rural families receive more social transfers and pay less taxes than do other Canadians. Compared to large urban areas, rural and small towns have lower education levels and lower literacy and numeracy skills. More people volunteer their time in rural and small town communities than in urban areas.

Table of contents

Rural and small town Canada: an overview

Ray D. Bollman and Brian Biggs

1. Introduction

Rural populations in Canada are facing changes brought about by fundamental continuing and cumulating trends. Increasingly, capital substitutes for labour in a world where real prices continue to fall for products of primary resource industries. Variability and uncertainty increase as commodity and financial markets become global. Employment growth is concentrated in urban centres.

This overview will document some fundamental trends in rural and small town Canada. This is a national overview. With some exceptions, we have lumped together the wide diversity of rural and small town Canada. Fuller et al. (1990), among others, have argued that rural Canada shows *macro diversity and micro specialization*. Rural Canada consists of a diverse set of small areas, each quite specialized. This overview represents the necessary beginning for future research.

Few information compendia on rural Canada exist today. Some would point to the collection of studies edited by Marc-Adélard Tremblay and Walt Anderson (1966) as the most recent. More recent volumes do exist (Hodge and Qadeer 1983; Basran and Hay (ed.) 1988; Dasgupta 1988).

To present an overview of some of the conflicting forces present in rural Canada, we shall address three general themes:

Demography-the number and characteristics of the population affect, and are affected by, changes in economic and social structure.

Labour markets-many problems identified in rural areas may be classified as labour market issues and many of the solutions proposed for development of rural areas may be classified as labour market initiatives.

Indicators of economic well-being–the level of well-being of rural populations is often used as the justification of public policy for rural areas.

The concept of rural

Before 1921, our population was predominantly rural. Our natural resource base was, and continues to be, primarily rural. Small towns provided the commercial and trade links between resource-endowed rural communities and larger centres, and were the focus for the cultural and social life of rural Canada.

Over the past few decades, technological advances in transportation and communication have contributed to a growing similarity of rural and urban lifestyles. Television, radio, and satellite transmissions, now available in even remote areas, provide common cultural experiences. Improved transportation lessens the physical isolation imposed by great distances.

This convergence of lifestyles has prompted some researchers to consider space and distance as the remaining distinctive feature of rural areas (Gilford et al. 1981). However, the influence of space on rural life is not uniform across Canada. Rural areas in close proximity to large urban centres are less affected by the constraints of distance than the remote hinterland.

The heterogeneity of rural Canada is reinforced by the variation in climate and resources. Different resource bases generate different economic and social conditions associated with their exploitation. Consider the conditions associated with a tourist area in cottage country as opposed to a mining community in northern British Columbia. The growing similarity of rural and urban lifestyles coupled with the heterogeneity of rural areas may make the distinctions between urban and rural more misleading than informative.

Definitions

Before summarizing the data, a brief discussion of definitions is necessary. The general definition used by the census of population classifies a settlement of 1,000 or more population as 'urban' and the remaining population as 'rural'. The limitation of this definition is that it leads to boundary cases where remote towns with populations barely exceeding 1,000 people are classified with metro Toronto as urban. The detailed definition[1] of 'rural' and 'urban' over time is summarized in Table 1.

TABLE 1
History of population definitions

Census year(s)	Definitions
1931, 1941	The population residing within the boundaries of incorporated cities, towns and villages, regardless of size, was classified as urban and the remainder as rural.
1951	The urban population includes all persons residing in cities, towns and villages of 1,000 and over, whether incorporated or unincorporated as well as the population of all parts of census metropolitan areas. All others were classified as rural farm or rural non-farm.
1956	The urban population definition is the same as in 1951 except that the fringe parts of urban areas that were not census metropolitan areas were classified as urban. These were areas around cities with populations between 30,000 and 100,000 and which possessed similar economic, geographic and social relationships.
1961, 1966, 1971	The urban areas included persons living in (1) incorporated cities, towns and villages with a population of 1,000 or more, (2) unincorporated places of 1,000 or more having a population density of at least 1,000 per square mile, and (3) the urbanized fringe of (1) and (2) where a minimum population of 1,000 and a density of at least 1,000 per square mile existed.
1976	The urban population density was 1,000 persons per square mile with a maximum discontinuity of 1 mile.
1981, 1986	Persons living in continuously built-up areas having a population concentration of 1,000 or more and population density of 400 per square kilometre, based on the previous census, were classified as urban.

Source: Statistics Canada. Censuses of Population

---

1.   Statistics Canada definitions are a result of two conflicting considerations. First is the concern that continual redefinition of concepts inhibits the comparability of statistics over time. Second is the desire to accommodate these definitions to a changing socioeconomic reality to maintain some relevance. Over the past 60 years, definitional changes have increasingly added a spatial dimension to account for urban sprawl. Today urban areas are not only defined by number of residents (as was the case in 1931) but by population density and geographical proximity to an urban core. As well, the rural/urban dichotomy has transformed (at the census metropolitan area and census agglomeration level) into urbanized core, urban fringe and rural fringe categories to reflect the varying degrees of social and economic integration of regions adjacent to major cities.

2.   Demographic features

2.1   Rural population trends

The number of people living in rural Canada has increased continuously since Confederation except for a slight decline in the early 1950s and the 1960s (Figure 1). In 1986, nearly 6 million Canadians lived in rural areas. However, the more rapid growth of the urban population over time has resulted in marked trend towards urbanization over the past 125 years[2]. The share of the population designated as rural has fallen from 87% in 1851 to 23% in 1986. The last national rural majority was in 1921. By 1931, rural Canadians were the minority.

The rural population became a minority at varying times in the different provinces. As expected, the rural population became a minority first in the provinces which are the most urbanized today. Rural populations were a minority in Ontario, Quebec, and British Columbia before 1921 (Table 2). The rural population is still in the majority in Prince Edward Island.

TABLE 2

Rural minority, by province

1911	Ontario
1921	Quebec
1921	British Columbia
1951	Nova Scotia
1951	Manitoba
1956	Alberta
1961	Newfoundland
1966	New Brunswick*
1971	Saskatchewan
??	Prince Edward Island

*   The rural population of New Brunswick returned to a (slim) majority in 1986.

Source: Statistics Canada. Censuses of Population

2.   Since the rural population is measured as a residual, changes to urban definitions necessarily have an effect on rural population figures. An examination of these definitional changes (documented in Table 1) suggests that, collectively, they have not added a uni-directional bias to the trend towards urbanization. For example, the 1951 changes reclassified large unincorporated towns as urban thereby increasing urban population while the 1961 definitional changes had the opposite effect by setting stricter criteria for the urban classification.

FIGURE 1

Population trends: Canada
Rural minority in 1931

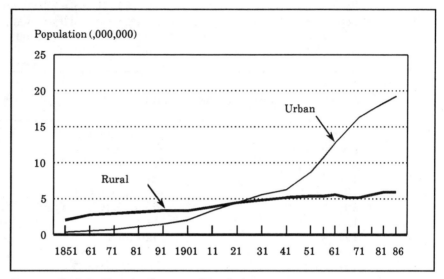

Source: Statistics Canada. Censuses of Population.

FIGURE 2

Rural population: Canada
Farmer minority in rural Canada in 1956

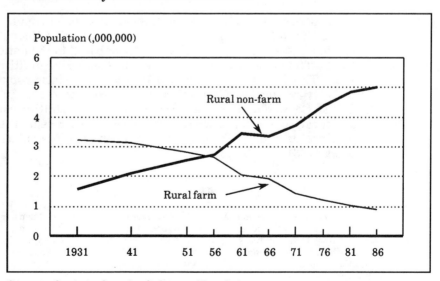

Source: Statistics Canada. Censuses of Population.

2.2   Trends in rural farm and rural non-farm population

The farm population[9] now represents 15% of the population living in rural areas[4]. The farm population, now under 1 million persons, had become a minority in rural areas by 1956 (Figure 2). As with the rural population, the farm population became a minority at varying times in different provinces. The farm population did not become a rural minority in the Prairie provinces until the 1970s (Table 3).

TABLE 3

Farmer minority in rural population

always	Newfoundland
always	British Columbia
1941	Nova Scotia
1941	Ontario
1951	New Brunswick
1961	Prince Edward Island
1961	Quebec
1971	Manitoba
1976	Alberta
1976	Saskatchewan

Source: Statistics Canada. Censuses of Population.

The rural non-farm population shows an opposite but equally uniform trend. It has increased from 1.6 million (1931) to 5 million (1986) and now represents 85% of the rural population.

In 1986, Saskatchewan had the largest rural farm population relative to both its total population (16% compared to 4% at the national level) and to its total rural population (41% compared to the national level of 15%). The farm population was a rural minority in all provinces in 1986. This is in sharp contrast to 1931 when the farm population was a majority in rural areas in all but two provinces—Newfoundland and British Columbia. One dramatic example of the shifting composition of the rural population occurred in Prince Edward Island (still a rural province) where the farm component of the rural population fell from 81% in 1931 to 13% in 1986.

---

3.   The definition of the farm population has also changed over time. In 1986, the farm population was all individuals living in a rural household where an operator of a census-farm lived. The 1976 farm population is defined for individuals living in households of an operator of all agricultural holdings of $50 or more. Thus, the definition is consistent with the 1971 definition. Note that published 1976 farm population refer to census-farms of $1,200 or more gross farm sales. The Northwest Territories and the Yukon are excluded.

4.   We continue to define "rural" population as individuals living outside settlements of 1,000 or more.

2.3   Rural population growth rates

The rural population grew faster than the urban population only during
1971-1976. The trend towards urbanization in Canada in the context of
(generally) positive rural growth rates was uninterrupted from 1861 to
the early 1970s. Census data for 1971-1976 showed a reversal of this
trend when the rural population growth rate exceeded the urban
population growth rate (Figure 3).

FIGURE 3

Population growth rates: Canada
Rural growth rates exceeded urban only in 1971-1976

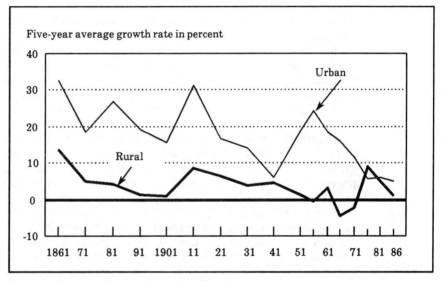

Source: Statistics Canada. Censuses of Population.

The interruption of the urbanization trend, which also occurred in the
U.S. and other developed nations, sparked speculation of a rural
renaissance and gave rise to research into the reasons for such a
turnaround. This literature, as it pertains to Canada, may be
summarized as follows:

a.   A significant net migration occurred within Canada to rural
      areas during the 1970s (Field 1988). Its effect on urbanization
      was largely offset by the influx of immigrants to urban areas.

b.   A cyclical pattern of growth rates exists for the rural non-farm population—mainly because areas were reclassified from rural to urban[5].

c.   A considerable proportion of rural population growth occurred in areas close to major urban centres, suggesting some growth could be attributed to urban sprawl (Joseph, Keddie, and Smit 1988).

Rural growth rates were again below urban growth rates during 1976-1981 and 1981-1986. The turnaround of the urbanization trend was short-lived. Nevertheless, the small differences between rural and urban growth rates since 1971 suggest that while the trend towards urbanization is not reversing, it is slowing markedly.

Between 1981 and 1986, approximately three quarters of total population growth occurred in the urban core regions. During the same period, rural population growth was primarily located in the rural fringe areas that surround large urban centres (Figure 4). By 1986, 23% of Canada's population was classified as rural; however, one third of this rural population (7% of Canada's total population) was located in the rural fringe of urban areas (Mitchell 1989: chart 4).

In Prince Edward Island, the trend towards urbanization halted in 1976, but by 1986 urban growth rates had once again exceeded rural growth rates. New Brunswick and Nova Scotia were the only two provinces where rural exceeded urban growth rates during 1981-1986.

Between 1981 and 1986, British Columbia, Newfoundland, Alberta, Saskatchewan and Quebec experienced a decline in rural populations. In Quebec, this slight decline followed a period (1971-1981) of considerable rural population growth, both in number and relative to urban rates. This growth was prevalent in both rural fringe and more remote areas (Joseph and Keddie 1991b).

---

5.   Rapid population growth in rural areas adjacent to urban areas leads to reclassification through a) urban boundary expansion, b) fringe populations achieving urban density thresholds and c) rural communities attaining urban population levels. Reclassification is part of the natural process of urban expansion and its effects are included in Statistics Canada data. However, higher rural than urban growth rates should not be interpreted as a significant back-to-the-land movement during a period of time given these reclassification effects (Keddie and Joseph 1990a). By imposing the rural/urban designations of one census on the data from previous censuses, an estimate of population growth within geographical boundaries is obtained. Given that reclassification is increasingly redefining rural areas to be urban, this method will yield a smaller estimate of the "rural" population for previous census years and hence higher "rural" population growth rates compared to measurements that do not adjust the previous designations of rural/urban areas. When 1986 boundaries are applied to 1981 data, 160,000 rural residents are reclassified as urban. As a consequence, the adjusted rural growth rate is 3 percentage points higher than the unadjusted rate. If reclassification is viewed as part of the natural growth process of urban centres, this method which defines rural areas in terms of unchanging geographical entities will overstate rural population growth (Keddie and Joseph 1991a).

FIGURE 4

Composition of population growth, 1981-1986
One-fifth of growth is rural fringe of urban

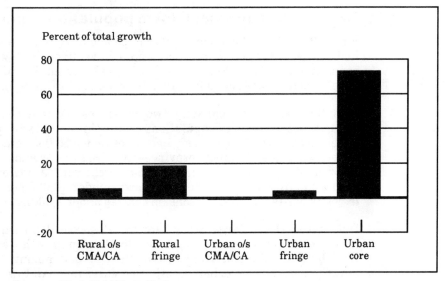

Source: Mitchell, 1989: Table 6.

FIGURE 5

Population by urbanization class
Constant population in small towns

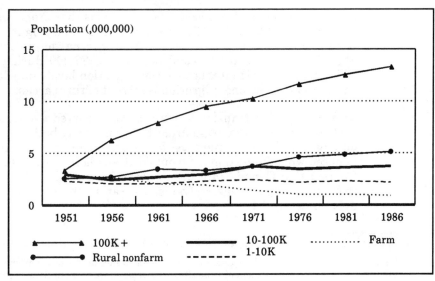

Source: Statistics Canada. Censuses of Population.

Saskatchewan has reported a rural population minority since 1971 and an uninterrupted trend towards urbanization since 1956. Moreover, Saskatchewan has experienced a decline in rural population in every five-year period since 1941.

2.4   Rural and small town population trends

Since 1951, about the same number of people have lived in small towns in Canada. About 2.3 million people have lived in towns[6] with a population of 1-10,000 since 1951. Similarly, about 3.5 million people have lived in centres of 10,000-100,000 since 1951 (Figure 5).

Less than 40 years ago only two provinces, British Columbia and Ontario, had a minority population residing in centres with populations under 10,000. In 1986, persons in centres under 10,000 remained in the majority in the Atlantic provinces and Saskatchewan. Hence, in Newfoundland, Nova Scotia and Saskatchewan, a majority of the population lives in rural and small towns under 10,000 persons, but no majority exists for rural persons (in centres under 1,000).

During 1951-1986, large urban growth rates exceeded rural and small town growth rates in every province. Small town growth was highest in British Columbia and Alberta (which also had among the highest growth rates in large urban areas). Decreases in small town population occurred in Manitoba and Quebec. During 1981-1986, 6 provinces had declining small town and rural populations; the largest decreases were in Western Canada.

2.5   Rural-urban mobility

More people moved from *urban to rural* areas than from *rural to urban* areas during 1971-1976, 1976-1981 and 1981-1986 (Figure 6). The net population transfer to rural areas from internal migration peaked at 256,000 during 1976-1981 and declined to 77,000 during 1981-1986. This decline is attributable to lower migration levels into rural regions rather than increasing migration levels out of rural areas.

This net positive transfer to rural areas occurred even though urban centres were the more popular destination among both rural and urban outmigrants[7]. The preference for urban regions is even more pronounced when migration from outside Canada is considered. Migration from outside Canada into urban areas is more than 10 times higher than into rural areas. The same ratio for internal migrants is approximately 3:1.

---

6.   Towns with a population of 1,000-10,000 were considered small towns by Hodge and Qadeer (1983).

7.   A higher proportion of both urban and rural migrants prefer urban destinations. However, in absolute terms the small proportion of urbanites who prefer rural destinations is greater than the larger proportion of rural residents who prefer urban destinations. Hence, internal migration has a positive impact on the population of rural Canada.

FIGURE 6

Urban-rural mobility, Canada, 1966-1986
Urban to rural exceeds rural to urban

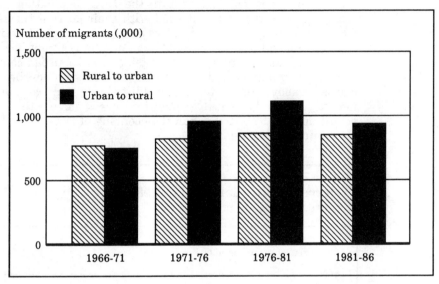

Source: Statistics Canada. Censuses of Population.

Using data derived from the 1976 census, Field (1988) found that only rural areas and medium sized urban areas (population of 30,000-100,000) had gained population as a result of internal migration. Moreover, the rural sector had the largest net transfer of population of any urban category during 1971-1976. This exchange of population from urban to rural areas was more a result of lower rural outmigration rates than a rural/urban differential ability to attract newcomers. Outmigration rates were inversely related to urban size with the highest rates found in unincorporated settlements with populations less than 1,000[8]. Population transfers to rural areas were widespread across regions (only Quebec had rural population losses from migration) and across urban size categories.

---

8.   Field (1988) classified unincorporated settlements with under 1,000 population separately from rural residents which explains his findings of low rural outmigration but high outmigration from "settlements with under 1,000 population".

2.6   Preferred residential location

Individuals prefer to reside in rural areas. Only 41% of residents of urban core areas want to stay; the remaining 59% prefer to move to less urbanized areas (Figure 7). This level of dissatisfaction among urban core residents is not apparent in the rural population. Rural farm residents were the most satisfied with their current residency status: 89% of farm residents prefer to live on a farm; only 11% prefer an urban setting. As well, more than 85% of Canadians living in remote rural areas (i.e., more than 100 miles outside a major urban centre) want to remain in rural Canada. These preferences underlie the results discussed above: urban-to-rural mobility is greater than rural-to-urban mobility and the rural population grew faster than the urban population in 1971-1976 when the economy of rural Canada made this economically feasible.

FIGURE 7

Preferred residential location, 1989
Rural residences are preferred

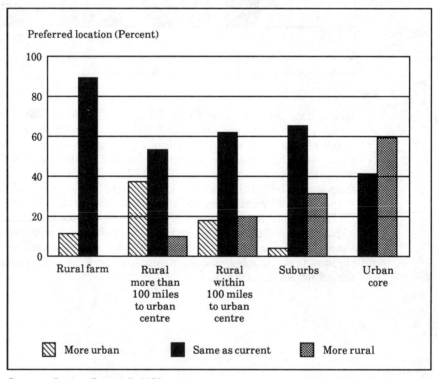

Source: Decima Research, 1989.

2.7   Population dependency ratios

Dependency rates are highest in small towns (Figure 8)[9]. Interestingly, small towns have both high proportions of older persons and high proportions of younger persons per person in the 15 to 64 age category. The dependency ratio for the farm population was lower than all urban size classes except for those with populations greater than 500,000. Across all urban size classes, the population under 15 years of age was the largest component of the "dependent" population. Youth dependency was most pronounced among rural residents.

FIGURE 8

Dependency rates: Canada, 1986

Dependency rates highest in small towns

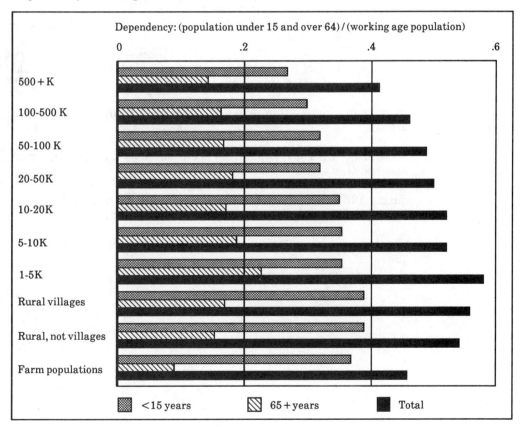

Source: Statistics Canada. Census of Population, 1986.

---

9.   The population dependency ratio is defined here as the sum of the population under 15 years of age plus the population 65 years of age and over divided by the remainder of the population. It is an estimate of the population not eligible for labour market participation relative to the population that is.   Hence "dependency" is defined in terms of belonging to an age category in which active involvement in the labour market is subject to social or legal restrictions.

From 1921 to 1986, the dependency ratio followed a similar pattern in urban and rural Canada. Throughout this period, rural dependency ratios were above those of the urban population. The recent decline in the dependency ratio has slowed for both the rural and urban population.

2.8   To summarize

The following are the main findings from our overview of the demographics of rural and small town Canada:

a.   the population in rural Canada is continuing to increase;

b.   the rural population became a minority before 1931;

c.   within the rural population, the farm population became a minority before 1956;

d.   the growth rate of the rural population exceeded the growth rate of the urban population only during 1971-1976;

e.   more people move from urban to rural than from rural to urban areas;

f.   one third of the rural population is classified as the rural fringe of metropolitan areas;

g.   during 1981-1986, 73% of the population growth was in the urban core and 19% was in the rural fringe of metropolitan areas;

h.   the aggregate population of small towns has been stable since 1951.

3.   Labour market characteristics

3.1   Trends in employment

The level of employment[10] in rural and small town Canada (R&ST) has remained stable since 1976 (Figure 9). The level of employment was 2.4 million in 1976 and grew[11] marginally to 3.0 million in 1989. In contrast, the level of employment in towns and cities (T&C)[12] grew from 7.0 million in 1976 to 8.0 million in 1981; declined to 7.7 million in 1982-1983; and grew to 9.4 million in 1989. The same pattern is observed in most provinces. However, in Saskatchewan, R&ST employment has declined by 4% since 1987.

Thus, in absolute terms, employment growth is becoming more concentrated in T&C. During 1976-1980, R&ST employment grew by nearly 400,000, representing 30% of total employment growth. During 1985-1989, this figure fell: the R&ST employment growth of 250,000 was only 20% of total growth in employment.

During the early 1980s, British Columbia and Alberta had the greatest relative decreases in both R&ST and T&C employment. New Brunswick, Ontario, Manitoba and Saskatchewan had employment gains in T&C but employment losses in R&ST. During 1985-1989, growth in R&ST and T&C employment was evident in most provinces. R&ST growth rates were highest in British Columbia and New Brunswick. Above average growth rates in R&ST employment also occurred in Newfoundland, Nova Scotia and Quebec. However, during the same period, R&ST employment growth in absolute terms was concentrated in Ontario and Quebec.

---

10. Most of the labour market data presented here are obtained from the Labour Force Survey. At one level, the survey classifies areas into self-representing units (SRU) and non-self-representing units (NSRU). SRUs are in the sample of the Labour Force Survey each month and, in this sense, are "self-representing". NSRUs are only included randomly and thus when one is included, it may be considered to be representing more than itself. While the guidelines vary from province to province, the SRUs are generally urban areas with populations in excess of 10,000. Consequently, NSRUs constitute rural areas and small urban centres. Nationally, over 60% of the NSRU population are rural residents (in centres under 1,000 persons) and the NSRUs in the Atlantic region are the most representative of rural areas (80%). While SRU/NSRU does not correspond exactly to the urban/rural distinction, NSRU data is suited to provide insights into the labour market of rural and small town Canada. The Labour Force Survey was redesigned in 1985 which included refinements in estimation and sampling methods. As a result, some caution should be exercised in the comparison of pre-and post-1985 data.

11. The concept of employment growth and job creation are not identical. Job creation deals exclusively with labour demand. Employment growth measures changes in the number of persons who have accepted employment at the existing wage levels. This differs from the number of jobs created by i) disregarding job gains or losses among multiple jobholders and ii) including job gains or losses that result from an increased labour supply. For example, an influx of immigrants from less developed nations may exploit job opportunities that previously existed but were refused by the domestic labour force.

12. R&ST will refer to the NSRU data and T&C will refer to the SRU data, as defined in footnote (10).

FIGURE 9

FIGURE 9

Trends in employment, 1976-1989
Slight growth in rural and small town employment

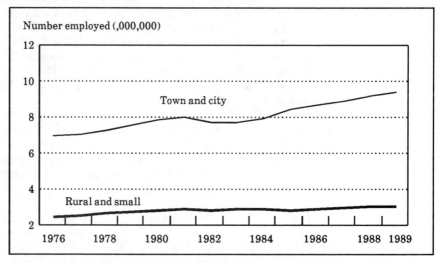

Source: Statistics Canada. Labour Force Survey.

3.2   Employment ratio

Throughout the 1980s, the R&ST employment ratio[13] was lower than the T&C employment ratio. However, there is little difference in the trends in the employment ratios between R&ST and T&C. For both areas, the male employment ratio declined slightly during the decade while the female employment ratio fell but recovered after the recession to surpass 1981 levels by 5 percentage points. Despite the relative gains in female employment, a lower proportion of women were employed[14] in R&ST. The female employment ratio was approximately 65% of the male employment ratio in R&ST and 80% in T&C.

The national pattern of a stable R&ST employment ratio and a declining then increasing T&C ratio was, in the main, replicated provincially. The employment ratio was lowest in the Maritime provinces. In 1989, Alberta had both the highest R&ST employment ratio and the highest T&C ratio. Above average differences between the R&ST and T&C ratio occurred in the Maritime provinces (with the exception of Prince Edward Island) while the smallest differences were evident in the Prairies.

---

13. The employment ratio is the ratio of employment to total population 15 years of age and older. A trend analysis of this ratio will partially control for changes in employment that result when a segment of the population reaches the age of labour force eligibility.

14. "Employed" includes paid workers, self-employed workers, and unpaid family workers.

3.3   Labour force participation rates

Throughout the 1980s, the labour force participation rate[15] in R&ST
was lower than in T&C. This pattern of R&ST rates being below T&C
rates was true for both men and women. The R&ST participation rate
was generally 5 percentage points below the T&C rate for males and 8
percentage points below for females. Male participation rates showed
little variation during the period. Female rates showed an upward
trend with R&ST participation increasing at a slightly greater rate
than T&C.

Urbanization class data derived from the 1986 census indicate that the
farm population had the highest female and male labour force
participation rate (Figure 10). The lowest participation rates were in
rural settlements and small urban centres.

FIGURE 10

Labour force participation rate, 1986
Lowest in small towns

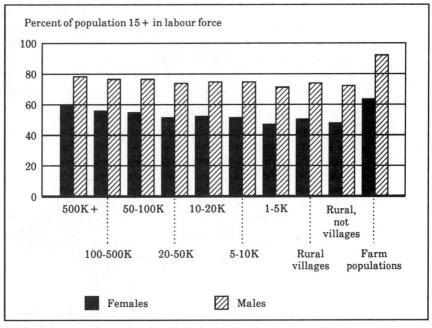

Source: Statistics Canada. 1986 Census of Population.

---

15. The labour force participation rate is the percent of the population, 15 years of age and over, in the
labour force. The labour force consists of individuals employed as paid workers, self-employed
workers, and unpaid family workers plus individuals classified as unemployed.

Provincial data generally replicate the national labour force participation rate trends. In Prince Edward Island, participation rates across the R&ST and T&C classification were roughly equal while elsewhere trends followed the national pattern with R&ST rates below T&C rates by a significant but decreasing margin. The lowest R&ST labour force participation rate was in Newfoundland while Alberta had the highest participation rates across both gender and residence categories.

3.4   Unemployment rates[16]

R&ST unemployment rates were consistently above T&C rates during 1976-1989 (Figure 11). Unemployment rates have fluctuated between 7% and 12%. R&ST rates increased more slowly during the recessionary period of the early 1980s. In 1983 the unemployment rate differential between R&ST and T&C was non-existent. Beginning in 1984, the R&ST and T&C rates tended to diverge reflecting regional-specific economic expansion. By 1989, the R&ST unemployment rate was 8.8%. This was 24% higher than T&C unemployment rate of 7.1% (Figure 12).

FIGURE 11

Unemployment rate, 1976-1989
Rate is higher in rural and small towns

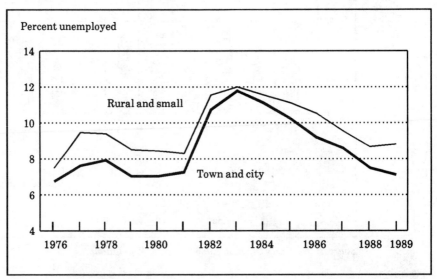

Source: Statistics Canada. Labour Force Survey.

---

16.   The unemployment rate is the percent of the labour force that is classified as unemployed.

FIGURE 12

Rural and small town unemployment
Is 24% above town and cities in 1989

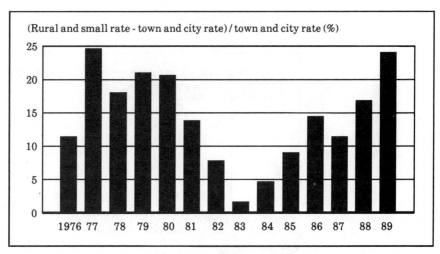

During the recession in the early 1980s, the female unemployment rate increased more slowly than the male unemployment rate for both R&ST and T&C areas. However, since 1984, the gap between the female and male unemployment rate has widened with R&ST trends mirroring T&C trends. This relative increase in female unemployment can only partially be explained by the increase in the female labour force. The drop in T&C female employment relative to male employment suggests that the economic expansion enhanced job opportunities for males to a greater degree.

The three Prairie provinces were the only provinces to have lower R&ST than T&C unemployment rates throughout the decade. This is, in part, because a large proportion of their rural population resides on farms. The farm population generally has lower unemployment rates because the decision to leave farming is usually accompanied with a change of residence. Also, self-employed farmers did not qualify for unemployment insurance benefits. Consequently, there exists a greater incentive for this population to undertake a job search immediately after becoming unemployed.

3.5   Employment by industry

In 1971, 24% of the labour force in rural[17] Canada was in agriculture (Figure 13). However, by 1981, the share of rural employment in agriculture had declined to 16%. The predominant employment category was 'services'. By 1986, 24% of rural employment was in the service sector.

---

17. "Rural" continues to refer to the population in centres of less than 1,000 population.

FIGURE 13

Labour force distribution by industry,Canada, 1971-1986

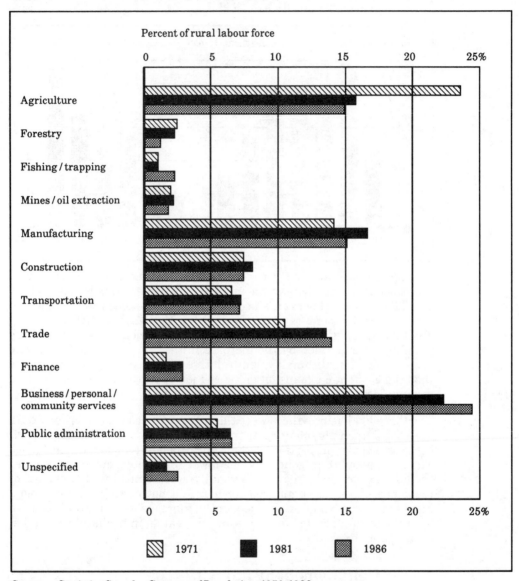

Source: Statistics Canada. Censuses of Population, 1971-1986.

The continuing decline in agriculture relative to other industrial sectors (and more recently, also an absolute decline) and the continuing growth in the service sector is indicated by annual data for R&ST.[18] Throughout 1976-1989, the service industries constituted the largest sector <u>and</u> the service sector provided the largest growth in R&ST employment (Figures 14 and 15). In 1976, 539,000 R&ST workers (22%) were employed in the broadly-defined service sector[19] and by 1989, R&ST employment in the service sector had increased to 833,000 (28%). In 1976, the agricultural sector was the second largest sector but declined in absolute and relative terms by 1989. In 1976, 422,000 R&ST workers (17%) were employed in agriculture and this declined to 346,000 (12%) in 1989.

In R&ST areas, absolute and relative growth occurred in manufacturing employment, retail and wholesale trade, finance, insurance and real estate (FIRE) and construction industries during 1985-1989.

FIGURE 14

Employment in four largest sectors
Rural and small town, Canada, 1976-1989

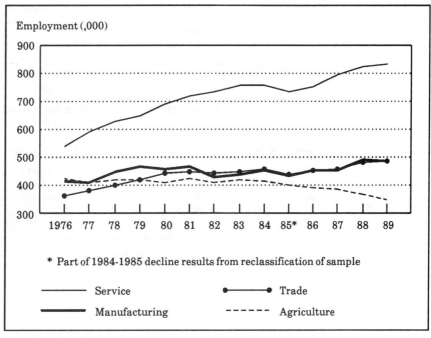

* Part of 1984-1985 decline results from reclassification of sample

	Service		Trade
	Manufacturing		Agriculture

Source: Statistics Canada. Labour Force Survey.

---

18. This discussion of Rural and Small Town (R&ST) Canada reverts to the non-self representing units from the Labour Force Survey, as discussed in footnote (10).

19. The broadly-defined "service sector" encompasses the health/medical sector, educational services, real estate, hospitality industry, and various personal and business services.

The R&ST share of employment growth has declined since the late 1970s. Employment growth, broken down by industry, shows that the R&ST share of growth increased in only two sectors—manufacturing and construction. Employment growth in the primary and service-related industrial sectors has become more a phenomenon of T&C areas in the late 1980s.

FIGURE 15

Employment in five smallest sectors
Rural and small town, Canada, 1976-1989

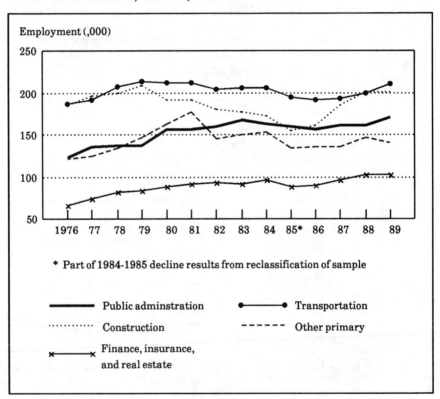

* Part of 1984-1985 decline results from reclassification of sample

——— Public adminstration   ●——● Transportation

⋯⋯⋯ Construction   – – – – Other primary

×——× Finance, insurance,
and real estate

Source: Statistics Canada. Labour Force Survey.

3.6   Location quotients[20]

In 1986, workers who lived in centres of under 5,000 population were
35% more concentrated in the goods-producing sector[21] compared to
workers in larger centres. This concentration has changed little during
1971-1986 (Figure 16).

FIGURE 16

Goods industries, location quotients

Areas <5,000 population are 35% more intensive in goods

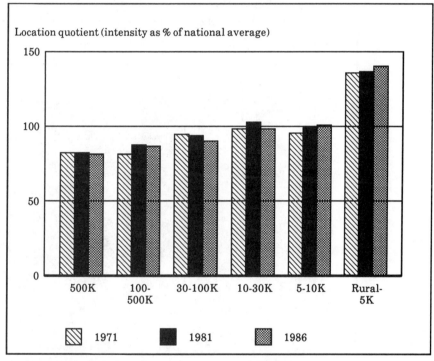

Source: Statistics Canada. Censuses of Population, 1971-1986.

20. The location quotient is a commonly used index of regional specialization. For example, see Coffey
     (1987). It is the ratio of the relative employment in an industry at the regional level to the relative
     employment in the same industry on a national scale. A number greater than 100 indicates that a
     particular region is more intensive (in terms of employment) in a particular activity compared to the
     national average. The LQ for industry i in region j located in national economy n is $((E_{ij} / E_j) / (E_{in} / E_n)) * 100$ where
     E_{ij} = employment for industry i in region j
     E_j = total employment in region j
     E_{in} = employment for industry i in national economy n
     E_n = total employment in the national economy n.

21. The "goods-producing sector" includes agriculture, forestry, mining and oil wells, manufacturing and
     construction. The data are labour force data from the Census of Population.

Conversely, workers who lived in centres of 5,000 or more were relatively concentrated in the service-performing sector.[22] A steep gradient of concentration in the service-performing sector is not evident, however as larger urbanization classes are examined (Figure 17). In 1986, workers who lived in centres under 5,000 persons were 15% less intensive in the service industries than were Canadians in larger centres.

FIGURE 17

Service industries, location quotients
Areas <5,000 population are 15% less intensive in services

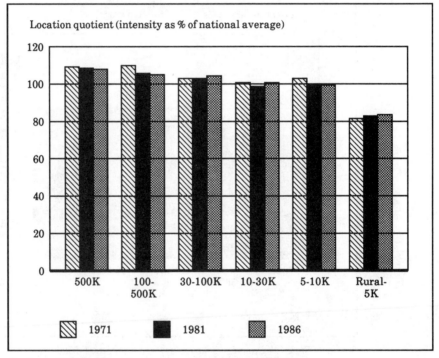

Location quotient (intensity as % of national average)

Source: Statistics Canada. Censuses of Population, 1971-1986.

The location quotients (LQ) based on Labour Force Survey data suggest R&ST specialization in agriculture and the other primary industries (Figure 18). The construction industry was also concentrated within R&ST regions. The LQs of the remainder of the industrial classifications indicate T&C specialization.

---

22. The "service-performing" sector includes transportation, communication, wholesale and retail trade, finance, insurance and real estate plus government, education, health and accommodation services. The data are labour force data from the Census of Population.

FIGURE 18

Location quotients: employment
Rural and small town Canada: 1976, 1985 and 1989

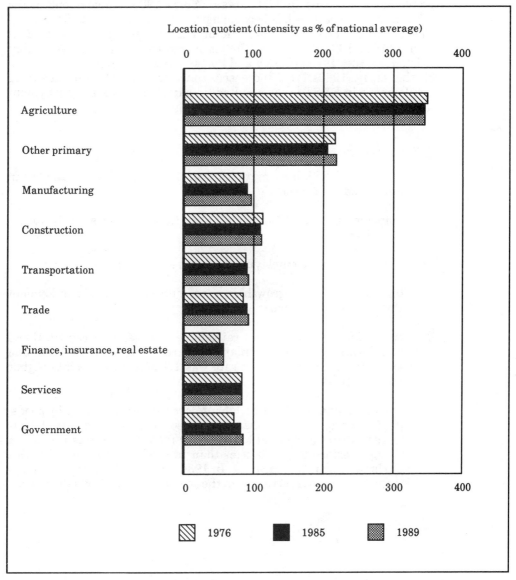

Source: Statistics Canada. Labour Force Survey.

Changes in the sectoral LQs (measured by the difference in LQs taken at different years) reflect relative changes in the concentration of employment. Since 1976, agricultural employment has become less concentrated in R&ST areas—a joint result of the declining agricultural workforce in R&ST regions and the increased incidence of agricultural employment residing in T&C areas. Since 1985, employment in the other industrial sectors has become more concentrated in R&ST areas.[23] The declining T&C specialization in manufacturing that is evident during 1981-1984 and 1985-1989 is a continuation of a trend that existed in the 1970s (Coffey and Polèse 1988). During the recession of the early 1980s, the increased concentration of manufacturing employment in R&ST areas resulted, in part, from greater employment losses in T&C than in R&ST manufacturing.

3.7   To summarize

Our overview of the labour market in rural and small town Canada can be summarized as follows:

a.   employment in rural and small town Canada grew slightly during 1976-1989;

b.   the rural share of employment growth is declining;

c.   during 1985-1989, growth in rural and small town employment was primarily in Quebec and Ontario;

d.   since 1983, unemployment rates have diverged between rural and small town areas and town and city areas. In 1989, the rural and small town unemployment rate was 1.7 percentage points higher than in towns and cities;

e.   the rural and small town labour force is concentrated in goods-producing industries when compared to town and city labour forces. Rural and small town labour force growth was greater in service-performing industries than in goods-producing industries during the past two decades. In 1986, nearly 60% of the rural and small town labour force was in the service-performing industries.

---

23. Some sectors have had a declining share of employment growth and increases in their LQs. Changes in shares of employment growth depend only on employment changes in a single sector while changes in LQs also depend on changes in the proportion of the total employment (i.e., sum of employment in each sector) in the region.

4.   Indicators of well-being

To conclude our overview of rural and small town Canada, we present a brief comparative survey of selected rural and urban indicators of well-being.

4.1   Elements of economic well-being[24]

4.1.1   Average family incomes

Since 1983, the average income of economic families[25] plus unattached individuals has been lowest in centres of 1,000-30,000 population[26] (Figure 19). The average income of rural residents (in centres under 1,000 people) was slightly higher than the 1,000-30,000 population class during 1983-1989. The average income of economic families and unattached individuals in urban centres of 100,000 or more population has been about $4,000[27] higher than rural and small town families throughout 1980-1989.

No clear pattern emerged in the 1980s for growth rates of average family and unattached individual income across urbanization classes. In terms of average income growth rates, small urban and rural areas were the most adversely affected by the recession of the early 1980s. Rural income growth resumed by 1984 and in 1987, the rural population had the highest growth rate across all urbanization classes. While rural average incomes grew during 1988, large urban centres (of 100,000 or more population) showed the greatest increase.

---

24. A thorough comparison of the economic well-being of urban and rural residents necessarily would involve the examination of the level of social and economic benefits experienced by each population. Since the comparison would be based on groups of individuals, such an analysis would take into account the distribution of these benefits both across individuals at a single time and across generations. A study of this type is beyond the scope of this paper. The data presented here deal only with the elements of well-being that are captured by family and individual income.

25. The income-based approach to the measurement of well-being has the family or the household as its unit of analysis. In economic theory, the household is defined in terms of the level of organization at which consumption decisions are made. This concept is implemented by presenting data for "economic families". An economic family is defined as a group of two or more persons who live in the same dwelling and are related to each other by blood, marriage, or adoption.

26. Two caveats should be remembered when imputing changes in economic well-being from trends in family income. Firstly, family size may not be constant over the period of study. In fact, from 1971 to 1986 the average size of a census family declined 14% in urban areas and nearly 20% in rural areas. Given the relative decline in urban family size, reductions in family income differentials between rural and urban areas during this time may not signal increases in rural well-being. Secondly, income data are market valuations. Hence, no account is given to the decreased amount of leisure or non-market production within the household that may be associated with increases in employment income. Moreover, rural-urban comparisons of family income do not account for social and environmental heterogeneity of the two regions that could compensate for differentials in income. These difficulties should be kept in mind when interpreting the following data in terms of well-being.

27. In constant 1981 dollars.

FIGURE 19

Average family income ($1981)
Lowest incomes in small towns (1-30K)

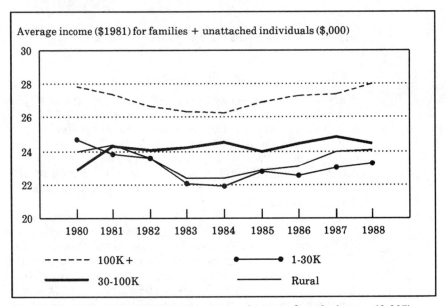

Source: Statistics Canada. Income distributions by size in Canada, (cat. no. 13-207).

4.1.2   Incidence of low incomes

By 1988, the incidence of families with low income was similar across
all urbanization classes. In 1973, the highest incidence of families with
low incomes was 17% in centres of under 30,000 population (Figure 20).
The incidence of low income for this group followed a downward trend
from 1973 to 1988. By 1988, this urbanization class reported the lowest
incidence (6%) of families below Statistics Canada's low income cut-off
(LICO)[28].

During 1973-1988 low income families became more concentrated in
urban areas with populations in excess of 500,000 and less concentrated
in rural areas. By 1988 over 45% of low income families resided in large
metropolitan areas while approximately 15% lived in rural regions. In
1973, the proportion of low income families was highest in rural areas
at 17%. The rural proportion fell to 7% by 1988 and was the lowest
across urbanization classes. The general pattern of a decreasing rural
incidence of low incomes also holds for unattached individuals.

---

28. Low income families spend on average 62% or more of their income on food, shelter and clothing. The
    low income cut-off (LICO) is defined for different urbanization classes and family sizes. Thus, the
    impact of differing costs among urbanization classes and the impact of differing family structures (not
    accounted for in the comparison of average family incomes above) are accounted for in the comparison
    of low family incomes shown in Figure 20.

FIGURE 20

Incidence of low income families
Lowest incidence in rural since 1983

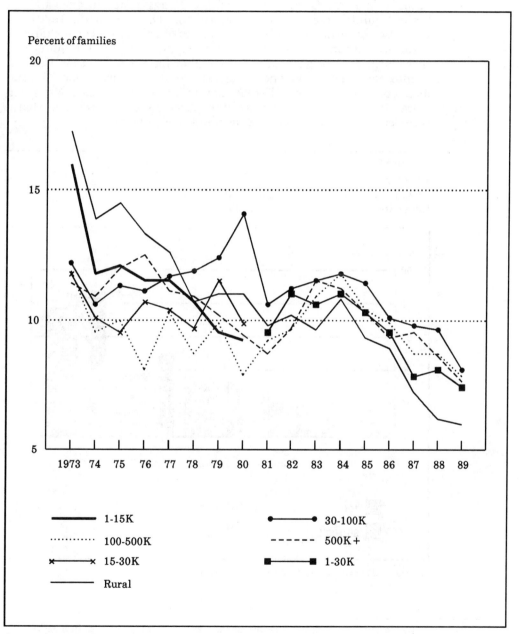

Source: Statistics Canada. Income distributions by size in Canada, (cat. no. 13-207).

4.1.3   Quintile data and Gini coefficients[29]

An equal income distribution among quintiles (groups composed of one fifth of the population that are ranked in terms of income shares) would exist if each quintile received 20% of total income. In 1988, the lowest quintile in rural Canada received 6% of aggregate income and the highest quintile received 41% (Figure 21). Throughout the 1980s, the lower two quintiles fared better in terms of relative income shares in rural areas than in large urban centres. As well, the top quintile in these large centres generally had a higher income share than its rural counterpart. This evidence suggests that a more equal income distribution exists in rural areas than in large urban areas. Moreover, since 1986 this rural/metropolitan discrepancy in income shares received by both the lowest and top quintile is growing.

FIGURE 21

Income shares: 1988
Income is less concentrated in rural Canada
(more in low 20%, less in top 20 %)

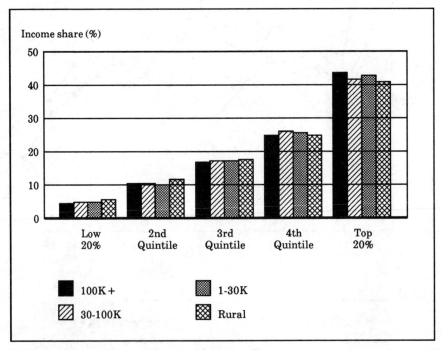

Source: *Statistics Canada. Survey of Consumer Finances.*

---

29. These inequality measures deal with money income (e.g., salaries, net investment income, transfer payments). They do not provide information on the distribution of elements of economic welfare such as wealth, income-in-kind, leisure, and capital gains. These measures are applied to the set of economic families and unattached individuals.

FIGURE 22

Income inequality
Lower in rural Canada and decreasing in rural Canada

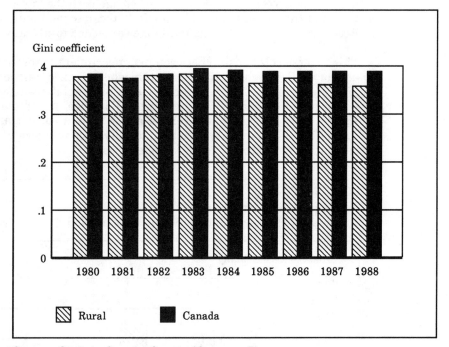

Source: Statistics Canada. Survey of Consumer Finances.

The Gini coefficient is another commonly used measure of inequality. The Gini index is constructed such that higher values are associated with greater income inequality[30]. The Gini evidence reinforces the quintile evidence of lesser income inequality in rural Canada (Figure 22). As with the quintile data, there is a suggestion of lessening income inequality in rural Canada as its Gini coefficient has decreased since 1986.

---

30. A brief description of the Gini coefficient is in Osberg (1981, 12- 17). A value of 1 indicates "perfect inequality".

4.1.4   Taxes paid and transfers received by rural families

In 1986, the combined effects of provincial and federal governments on family income (i.e., total taxes-total transfers) shows that rural and small urban area residents are favourably treated compared to families in large urban centres[31]. Rural families had both the lowest average tax load and the highest level of transfer[32] income per family (Figure 23). Across all population strata, total taxes exceeded total transfers.

This inverse relationship between net government transfers and size of area of residence shows little variation when specific transfers (or taxes) are considered. However, federal and provincial transfer payments which are universal such as family allowance or old age security showed only marginal differences across urban-rural classifications. The effect of commodity taxes on family incomes was stable across population strata compared to income taxes.

FIGURE 23

Taxes paid and transfers received
Rural families receved more and paid less in 1986

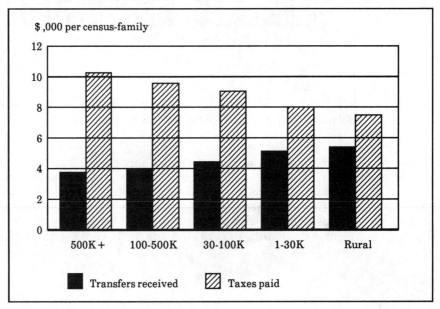

Source: Statistics Canada. SPSD/M.

31. An assessment of government impact on family incomes across rural-urban designations requires data on not just transfer payments but on the spatial distribution of total expenditures. A more complete analysis would examine the time series of tax and expenditure distributions between urban and rural areas. This section uses data from the Social Policy Simulation Data Base/Model, Statistics Canada.

32. In this case, transfer income refers to social transfers (e.g. family allowances, unemployment insurance, government pensions). It does not include agricultural or other business subsidies.

4.2   Other indicators of well-being

Numerous non-pecuniary indicators of well-being are available. We present a selection that truly reflects the generic title of 'other'!

4.2.1   Education levels

Educational levels represent one indicator of development or the capacity to participate in the 'knowledge-intensive' growth sectors. Across the urbanization gradient, the level of persons 20 years or older with some postsecondary education falls 7 percentage points, from 32% for large metropolitan centres to 25% for the population in centres of 1,000-5,000 and for the rural non-farm population (Figure 24). Similarly, the proportion of the population 15 years and over with less than a Grade 9 rises 7 percentage points across the gradient, from a low of 14% in large urban centres to over 21% for the population in centres of less than 5,000 (Figure 25).

FIGURE 24

Postsecondary education
For population 20+ years, Canada, 1986

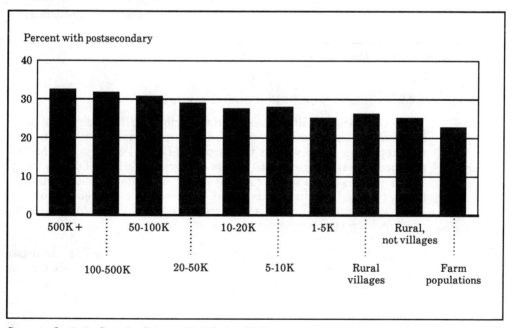

Source: Statistics Canada. Census of Population, 1986.

FIGURE 25

Less than grade 9 education

For population > 15 years, Canada, 1986

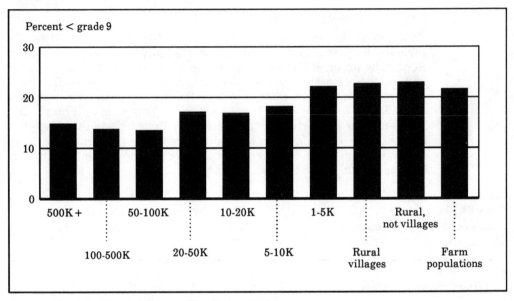

Source: Statistics Canada. Census of Population, 1986.

4.2.2   Literacy skills and numeracy skills

When the actual ability to read and to perform arithmetic calculations
is examined, the gradient from urban to rural areas is similar. In 1989,
the proportion of individuals that attained Level 4[33] on the literacy test
declined 7 percentage points across the gradient, from 64% in larger
urban centres to 57% for rural areas of less than 1,000 population
(Figure 26). It is instructive that attained levels of education and
literacy ability each show a 7 percentage point differential between
rural and larger urban centres.

The results for the numeracy test in 1989 were very similar. In urban
areas, 64% achieved the highest level[34] and 55% achieved this level in
rural and small town regions (Figure 27).

---

33.   In 1989, Statistics Canada surveyed the literacy skills of the adult population (ages 16 to 69).
      Respondents are categorized into four literacy skill levels according to their ability to comprehend
      and use the written word. Respondents assigned to the highest level (Level 4) demonstrated a
      capacity to "meet most everyday reading demands" while those classified to Level 1 were unable to
      process information from simple text.

34.   The 1989 survey also assesses the numeracy skills of Canadians. Three levels are used in this
      classification. The highest level, 3, indicates that respondents can "perform simple sequences of
      numerical operations which enable them to meet everyday demands".

FIGURE 26

Literacy skills, Canada, 1989

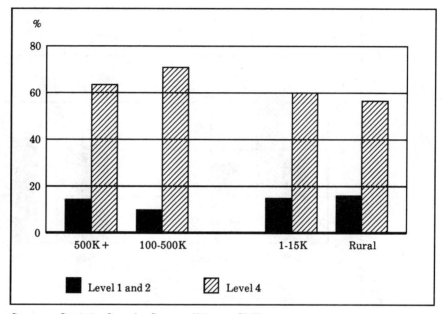

Source: Statistics Canada. Survey of Literacy Skills.

4.2.3   Crime rates

Statistics from 1988 suggest there is little variation across urban size groups in the rate of total offenses[35] reported by the police (Figure 28). However, rates of criminal offenses were lowest in small urban centres of less than 10,000 population and in rural communities. Violent crime rates in metropolitan areas were over 15 percentage points higher than rates in small urban and rural communities.

During 1980-1988, communities of less than 2,500 population had the smallest increase in rates of both total Criminal Code violations and violent crimes. As well, the rate of total offenses declined by almost 20% in these communities.

---

35.   Crimes excluding traffic offenses per 100,000 population.

FIGURE 27
Numeracy skills, Canada, 1989

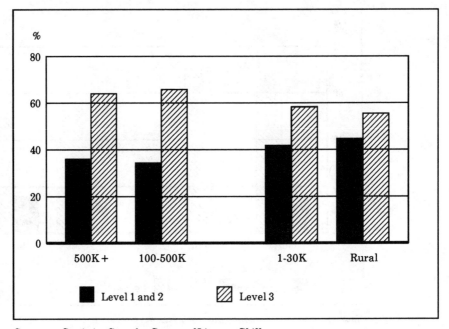

Source: Statistics Canada. Survey of Literacy Skills.

4.2.4   Expenditure patterns

In a consumer-oriented society, an analysis of consumption patterns may be useful in discerning lifestyle differences across urbanization classes. Consumer-good innovations in rural households appears to lag behind urban centres[36]. The presence of such recent innovations as the compact disk player and video recorders is positively correlated with urban size. In contrast, consumption of more established goods such as radio and television shows little variation across urbanization classes. Several factors could account for the slower diffusion of these new products into rural areas including the lower average household income present in rural Canada; the availability of both the products and complimentary consumption goods such as compact disks and repair services; and perhaps even a different social milieu which assigns less status to those who purchase new consumption goods.

---

36.   This information is derived from <u>Household Facilities by Income and Other Characteristics</u>. Statistics Canada cat. no. 13-218 (1989).

A relationship between the degree of urbanization and certain housing characteristics also exists. The large majority of rural households (87%) own the dwellings in which they reside as opposed to large urban areas where only 56% of households have ownership title. The relatively small number of renters in rural regions is also reflected in statistics on dwelling type as single detached homes are more popular among rural (87%) than large urban households (47%). The abundance of space in rural Canada clearly lessens the need for the high density housing that is associated with rental accommodation.

4.2.5 Volunteer and community work

Volunteer activity is more common among residents of rural and small urban areas (population less than 15,000). Within each educational group, there was a general increase in the share of population involved in community work as area population size decreased (Figure 29). While this relationship is not as strong across religious categories, the highest volunteer rates were generally found in rural and small urban areas. These results are consistent with the intuitive notion that smaller centres possess a greater sense of community than the less socially cohesive "big city".

FIGURE 28
Crime rates in Canada, 1988
Small towns: similar crime rates, lower criminal offenses

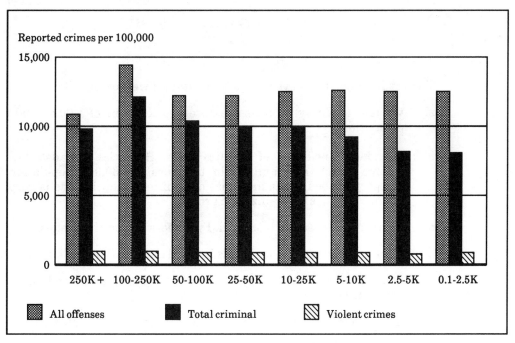

FIGURE 29

Volunteer and community work
More volunteers in rural and small town Canada

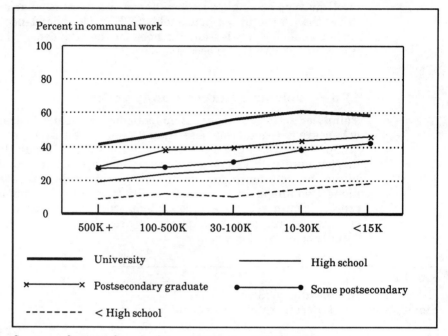

Source: Statistics Canada. Survey of Volunteer Activity, 1987.

4.3   To summarize

The key findings in our overview of indicators of well-being follow:

a.   the lowest family incomes are observed in towns of 1,000-30,000 population;

b.   the lowest incidence of families below Statistics Canada's low income cut-off are families in the rural to 30,000 population category, although the incidence of families in low income is very similar among all urbanization groups;

c.   rural families receive more social transfers and pay less taxes;

d.   there are lower education levels in rural and small town Canada;

e.   there are lower literacy and numeracy skills in rural and small town Canada;

f.   there is a lower incidence of criminal offenses in small towns;

g.   there are more volunteers in rural and small town Canada.

Conclusion

The diverse data presented here are difficult to summarize. Signs of convergence between rural and urban populations are evident in socioeconomic indicators such as distribution of labour forces by industry; and yet, divergence is evident in indicators such as unemployment rates. Convergence could be associated with the redistribution of the non-urban population. A trend of declining populations on rural farms and in small towns continues, while rural communities, especially those located near large urban centres, experience increases in population. Signs of divergence are primarily found in economic variables. While the economy of rural and small town Canada has grown since the early 1980s (at least in terms of labour market variables), it has not kept pace with urban Canada in such areas as labour force growth rates, share of employment growth, and decreases in unemployment rates.

Overall, we were surprised that trends in rural Canada were essentially level. In one sense, this is alarming because we know some communities are closing down. In another sense, a flat national average suggests that if some communities are declining, others must be growing. This overview has provided a national context in which trends in specific regions can be analyzed. Essential questions remain: for example, which communities are declining and which communities are progressing? And why?

The definition of rural and the definition of small town changed throughout the paper. We did not dwell on the question, "What is rural?" Recognize, however, that the rural population (individuals living outside of settlements of 1,000 or more) represents 23% of the national population, but that one third of this rural population is classified as the fringe of a census metropolitan area or a census agglomeration. If you were thinking 'remote' when you were reading 'rural', you may wish to reread parts of this paper.

The word 'rurban' has been suggested by some to denote the population within a given distance of an urban centre. In some respects, television and airplanes have made us all close to an urban centre. In other respects, the space and distance of remote rural Canada is very real. The choice of rural definition will depend upon the issue being addressed. Perhaps a typology that classifies small areas along an urban to rural continuum would be appropriate.[37]

---

37. Statistics Canada databases can be used to define and tabulate data according to a multitude of ideas formulated by analysts.

Rural Canada endures, is enduring and will endure. Our natural resources are still rural-based, but the employment in resource-based sectors is not growing. In rural Canada, the broadly-defined service sector is growing in relative and absolute terms. This appears to be the sector for analysts to monitor, for activists to activate, and for historians to assess whether rural Canada seized or missed an opportunity.

Ray D. Bollman & Brian Biggs
Agriculture Division
Statistics Canada
Ottawa K1A 0T6

References

Basran, G.S. and D.A. Hay, ed. 1988. The Political Economy of Agriculture in Western Canada. Toronto: Garamond Press

Biggs, Brian, Ray D. Bollman and Michael McNames. 1990. Trends and Characteristics of Rural and Small Town Canada. Agriculture Working Paper, Agriculture Division. Ottawa: Statistics Canada.

Coffey, William J. and Mario Polèse. 1988. Locational shifts in Canadian employment 1971-81: decentralization v. decongestion. The Canadian Geographer, 32(3): 248-256.

Coffey, William J. 1987. Structural changes in the Canadian space economy. In Still Living Together: Recent Trends and Future Directions in Canadian Regional Development, edited by William J. Coffey and M. Polèse. Montreal: Institute For Research on Public Policy.

Dasgupta, Satadal. 1988. Rural Canada: Structure and Change. Kingston: E. Mellon Press.

Decima Research. 1989. Decima Quarterly Report: Executive Summary, 10(3): 45-56.

Department of Regional and Economic Expansion. 1979. Single-Sector Communities. Ottawa: Supply and Services.

Economic Council of Canada. 1990. From the Bottom Up: The Community Economic-Development Approach. Ottawa: Economic Council of Canada.

Field, Neil C. 1988. Migration through the rural-urban hierarchy: Canadian patterns. Canadian Journal of Regional Science, 11(1): 33-56.

Fuller, Tony, Philip Ehrensaft and Michael Gertler. 1990. Sustainable rural communities in Canada: issues and prospects. In Sustainable Rural Communities in Canada, edited by Michael E. Gertler and Harold R. Baker. Proceedings of Rural Policy Seminar #1. Saskatoon: Agriculture and Rural Restructuring Group.

Gilford, D., G. Nelson and L. Ingram, ed. 1981. Rural America in Passage: Statistics for Policy. Washington, D.C.: National Academic Press.

Hodge, Gerald and M.A. Qadeer. 1983. Towns and Villages in Canada: The Importance of Being Unimportant. Toronto: Butterworth & Co.

Joseph, A., P. Keddie and B. Smit. 1988. Unravelling the
    population turnaround in rural Canada. <u>The Canadian
    Geographer</u>, 32(1): 17-30.

Joseph, A., and P. Keddie. 1991a. Reclassification and
    the rural-versus-urban population change in Canada, 1976-81: a
    tale of two definitions. <u>The Canadian Geographer</u>, 35 (4): 412-420.

Joseph, A., and P. Keddie. 1991b. The turnaround of
    the turnaround?: rural population change in Canada, 1976 to 1986.
    <u>The Canadian Geographer</u>, 35 (4): 367-379.

Martin, F. 1976. <u>Regional Aspects of the Evolution of Canadian
    Employment</u>. Ottawa: Economic Council of Canada.

Mitchell, Rick. 1989. <u>Canada's Population from Ocean to Ocean</u>,
    Statistics Canada cat. no. 98-120. Ottawa: Statistics Canada.

Osberg, Lars. 1981. <u>Economic Inequality in Canada</u>. Toronto:
    Butterworth & Co.

Reid, J. Norman. 1990. Economic change in the rural U.S.:
    a search for explanations. Paper presented at the "Europe 1993:
    Implications For Rural Areas" seminar. Douneside, Scotland: The
    Arkleton Trust.

Statistics Canada. 1989. <u>Household Facilities by Income and
    Other Characteristics</u>, Statistics Canada cat. no. 13-218. Ottawa:
    Statistics Canada.

Tremblay, Marc-Adélard, and Walton J. Anderson. 1966.
    <u>Rural Canada in Transition: A Multidimensional Study of the
    Impact of Technology and Urbanization on Traditional Society</u>.
    Ottawa: Agricultural Economics Research Council of Canada.

Vanderkamp, John and E.K. Grant. 1988. Canadian internal
    migration statistics: some comparisons and evaluations. <u>Canadian
    Journal of Regional Science</u>, 11(1): 9-32.

2

Falling farther behind:
current conditions in rural America

David Freshwater and Kenneth Deavers

Summary

Rural areas are falling farther behind. The gap has been growing at a slower rate in the last few years as the business cycle matured and the economy approached full employment. However, it would seem that both cyclical forces and long term trends adversely affect rural America. If rural employment drops first in an economic downturn and recovers last, this will result in each business cycle starting rural people from a point farther back and giving them less time to make up lost ground.

In addition, longer term trends in the nature of employment suggest that high wage jobs in expanding sectors will be under represented in rural areas, both because of inadequate skills of the rural labour force and because rural areas are not well suited to attract the growth sectors. Economic growth will require identifying niche markets that match rural areas' comparative advantages.

Riceton, Saskatchewan

Falling farther behind: current conditions in rural America

David Freshwater and Kenneth Deavers

Perceptions of high levels of rural economic and population growth in the United States in the 1970s led to the decade being described as the "Rural Renaissance". Conversely, the subsequent decade has been a form of rural Dark Ages. A renewed interest in rural studies has provided a large amount of new information about the nature of rural America over the last few years. Unfortunately, our increased knowledge has not been translated into improved policy, or into improved conditions for rural people. Our intent in this paper is to present basic material on the structure of rural areas in the United States. This material will be used to introduce some important trends that will affect the future pattern of rural development.

The growing interest in rural conditions came after an economic collapse that could not be ignored. In the early 1980s agriculture, mining and forestry all declined as a result of weak domestic and international demand, high interest rates, and an overvalued dollar. Rural manufacturing faced the same set of problems and, in addition, had to deal with increased competition from developing countries. Income and employment levels fell further behind metro levels (Figures 1 and 2). These forces reversed much of the progress made in rural areas in the previous decade and led to poverty rates that were once again comparable to those found in the inner cities (Table 1) (Barancik 1990).

One major event that became evident during the 1980s was the decoupling of agricultural conditions from rural conditions. Since rural policy in the United States has been seen, and justified, primarily as an adjunct of farm policy this decoupling has important implications for the future. While both agriculture and rural areas experienced major disruptions in the early 1980s, government support for farmers did little for the broader rural economy, including communities in farm dependent areas.

FIGURE 1

Non - metro per capita income as a percentage of metro per capita income

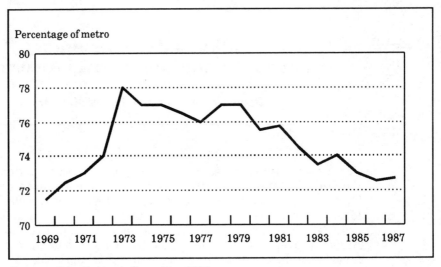

Source: Joint Economic Committee, 1989.

FIGURE 2

Difference in unemployment rates (metro and non - metro, 1976 - 1987)

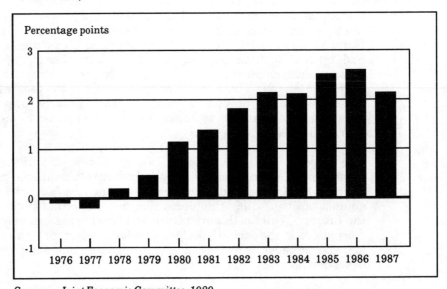

Source: Joint Economic Committee, 1989.

TABLE 1
Non - metro and metro poverty rates, 1970 - 1987

	Non-metro	Total metro* Percent	Central city
1970	16.9	10.2	14.2
1971	17.2	10.4	14.2
1972	15.3	10.3	14.7
1973	14.0	9.7	14.0
1974	14.2	9.7	13.7
1975	15.4	10.8	15.0
1976	14.0	10.7	15.8
1977	13.9	10.4	15.4
1978	13.5	10.4	15.4
1979	13.8	10.7	15.7
1980	15.4	11.9	17.2
1981	17.0	12.6	18.0
1982	17.8	13.7	19.9
1983	18.3	13.8	19.8
1984	**	**	**
1985	18.3	12.7	19.0
1986	18.1	12.3	18.0
1987	16.9	12.5	18.6

* includes both central city and suburban areas.

** data not available.

Source: Barancik.

The basic structure

In September, 1985, the U.S. Department of Agriculture (USDA) released *The Diverse Social and Economic Structure of Nonmetropolitan Areas* (Bender et al. 1985). The report set out a typology for classifying rural areas based on 1979 data that changed the way many people thought about rural areas. By focusing on the predominant characteristics of rural counties, the wide diversity of conditions in the nation were made easy to understand. Bender et al. identified the following categories (Figures 3-9):

> farming dependent — agriculture contributed at least 20% of total labour and proprietor income during 1975-1979.

> manufacturing dependent — manufacturing contributed 30% or more of total labour and proprietor income in 1979.

mining dependent — mining contributed 20% or more of total labour and proprietor income in 1979.

persistent poverty counties — per capita family income was in the lowest quintile in each of the years, 1950, 1959, 1969 and 1979.

retirement destination counties — counties where during 1970-1980, net inmigration rates of people 60 years or older were 15% or more of the 1980 population of persons 60 or older.

specialized government counties — government contributed at least 25 per cent of total labour and proprietor income in 1979.

federal lands — land owned by the federal government represented at least 33% of the total land area in the county in 1979.

FIGURE 3
Farming-dependent counties in non - metro areas, 1979

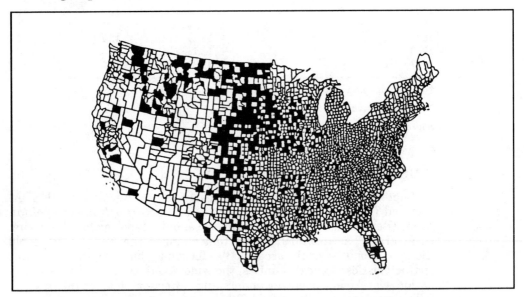

Source: USDA, Economic Research Service.

FIGURE 4

Manufacturing-dependent counties in non - metro areas, 1979

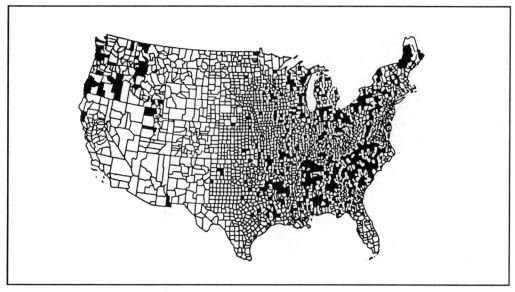

Source: USDA, Economic Research Service.

FIGURE 5

Mining-dependent counties in non - metro areas, 1979

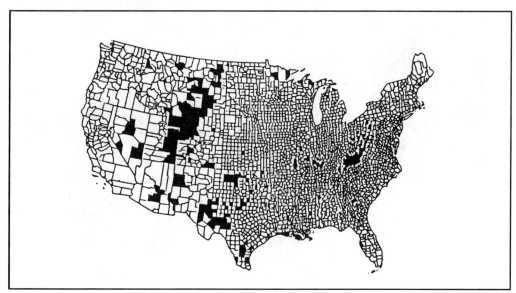

Source: USDA, Economic Research Service.

FIGURE 6

Persistent poverty counties in non - metro areas, 1979

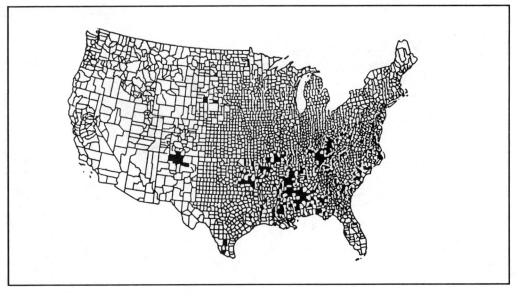

Source: USDA, Economic Research Service.

FIGURE 7

Retirement-dependent counties in non - metro areas, 1979

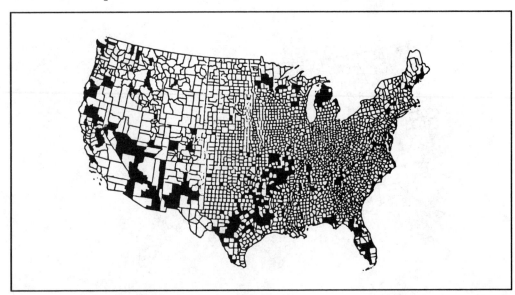

Source: USDA, Economic Research Service.

FIGURE 8

Government-dependent counties in non - metro areas, 1979

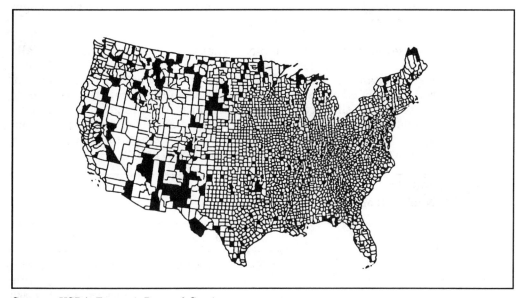

Source: USDA, Economic Research Service.

FIGURE 9

Federal lands counties in non - metro areas, 1979

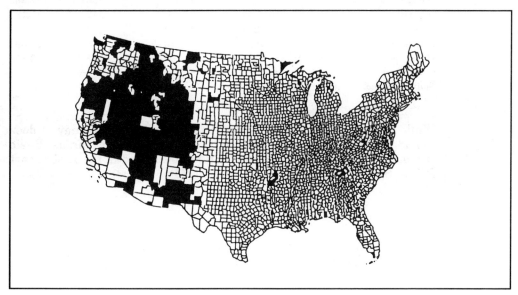

Source: USDA, Economic Research Service.

In 1990, USDA released an update of the report showing that between 1979 and 1986, conditions had changed in some of the county types (Hady and Ross 1990). The two reports present snap-shots of conditions during the boom of the 1970s and the depression of the 1980s. Consequently, they are useful in depicting the nature of the changes that occurred in rural areas.

The seven categories are not exhaustive, nor are they mutually exclusive. In the 1985 report there were 370, out of 2,443, non-metropolitan counties that did not fall into any category. In addition, some 22% of counties satisfied the criteria for two county types, while 6% of the classified counties fell into three or more groups. The rural population is not uniformly distributed among the categories. Non-metropolitan manufacturing counties have the highest population and farming counties have the lowest population (Table 2).

TABLE 2
Non-metropolitan county types

	1979		1986	
	Number of counties	Population (,000)	Number of counties	Population in 1979 (,000)
Farming	716	11,107	516	8,617
Manufacturing	621	36,680	577	35,117
Mining	155	21,901	124	20,724
Government	233	32,334	358	27,981
Poverty	242	15,180	242	15,180
Federal lands	247	22,084	247	22,084
Retirement	515	27,490	515	27,490
Ungrouped	370	29,798	542	29,158

Source: Bender et al. and Hady and Ross.

While the county typology does not follow a uniform taxonomy, it does provide a useful organization and characterization of rural areas. Basic characteristics of the various county types described in the 1985 report follow (Bender et al. 1985):

Farming	– concentrated in the Great Plains, along the Mississippi, and in parts of the Southeast and Pacific Northwest, – remote from metro areas and regional population centres, – large population losses in the 1960s followed by below average gains in the 1970s, – uneven income distribution characterized by high average per capita incomes but low median family incomes, – slightly lower than average proportions of labour and proprietor income from the services sector, – slightly above average proportions of people over 65.
Manufacturing	– concentrated in counties east of the Mississippi, – larger urbanized populations and relatively close to metro centres, – greater than average population increases in the 1960s followed by average gains in the 1970s, – larger than average black populations, particularly in the southeast, – slightly below average proportion of income from the services sector.
Mining and Oil Extraction	– concentrated in the Appalachian region, the oil patch states and the Northern Plains, – generally remote from major metro areas but with average levels of urban population in the county, – high rates of population increase in the 1970s following declines in the 1960s, – high income levels, – below average levels of service sector income.
Government	– fairly evenly distributed throughout the nation, – slightly above average proportions of urban population, – high rates of population increase, – lower than average incomes, – low wage activities more prevalent than on average.

Persistent Poverty	– concentrated in Appalachia, the Southeast and scattered through the West,
	– very sparse settlement patterns with below average urban populations,
	– low income levels,
	– a large proportion of the labour force is disadvantaged,
	– most counties also fall into another county type (82%).
Federal Lands	– concentrated in the West,
	– remote from metro areas,
	– population concentrated in towns rather than dispersed through the county,
	– rapid population increases in the 1970s,
	– average levels of service income.
Retirement	– concentrated from east Texas to the eastern mountain ranges, in Florida, in the upper Great Lakes, along the Pacific coast and in the lower Southwest,
	– high population growth rates in both the 1960s and 1970s,
	– remote from major metro areas,
	– large share of income from transfer payments,
	– above average service sector.

What did Hady and Ross find that had changed by 1986? Their data only allowed them to determine changes for the first 4 economic categories. Declines in the number of farming, manufacturing and mining dependent counties reflect the events of the last decade. In a geographic sense the losses were quite uniform with the exception of mining and oil extraction where losses were concentrated in the West. Growth in government specialized counties was uniformly distributed. Hady and Ross also found an increase in the number of counties that remained unclassified and a slight increase in the number of counties that met more than one set of criteria. This suggests continued decline in specialization, both within rural areas in aggregate and within individual counties. Evidence from other sources suggests that growth also occurred in retirement counties over the period (Reeder and Glasgow 1990).

Hady and Ross initially held the distribution of metro and non-metro counties constant for their analysis. This allowed them to isolate the effects of population change which moved some counties from non-metro to metro status over the decade. Incorporating the effects of population change over time produces shifts in the metro non-metro classification, as well as movements among county types. Between 1979 and 1986, 134 counties moved from non-metro to metro status, as a result of a 1983 reclassification by the Office of Management and Budget, while 48 moved from metro to non-metro (Table 3).

TABLE 3

County changes in metro / non-metro status, 1974 to 1983

	Non-metro in 1974	Non-metro to metro	Metro to non-metro	Non-metro in 1983
Farming	516	4	0	512
Manufacturing	577	45	21	553
Mining	124	1	1	124
Government	358	23	12	347
Retirement	515	35	0	480
Poverty	242	3	0	239
Federal lands	247	11	7	243
Unclassified	542	37	14	519
Number of counties [a]	2,443	134	48	2,357

a. Columns sum to more than these numbers because some counties are in more than one category.

Source: Hady and Ross.

The data suggest that in aggregate, the basic structure of rural America is stable. The concentrations of activity did not move a great deal over the period. However, at a local government level there is considerable flux. Long term trends continue to move the broad patterns of activity in the same direction, but levels of individual welfare can vary considerably over time and between places.

Early results from the 1990 Census confirm the decline in population of rural areas. It appears that the rural population may have fallen by 1.4 million over the decade, a larger decline than had been expected. In regional terms, it appears that growth continued in the Sun Belt, but rather than being in smaller communities, as in the 1970s, it tended to be concentrated in coastal urban areas. This suggests a continuation of the trend to an increasingly urbanized country.

New dimensions

Just as the last decade differed from the previous one, so we should expect the 1990s to differ from the 1980s. We identify what we believe are three key trends that will help shape the evolution of rural America. Other factors will also be important, but these three trends point out the broad nature of the types of changes we see as important:

- growing divergence of real earnings between rural and urban areas that suggests rural areas are becoming a marginal part of the economy;

- growing conflicts between urban and rural interests over allowable forms of activity in rural areas that reflects different values, particularly over preservation of the environment;

- limits on the ability of the rural populace to participate in technological advances which places rural areas at a disadvantage in terms of economic competitiveness and quality of life.

Rural areas have had lower labour force participation rates and lower levels of per capita income since these statistics have been collected. However, during the 1970s it appeared that a convergence was taking place as rural incomes grew faster than urban incomes. Convergence would suggest that internal labour markets are functioning; either by employers seeking lower wage areas to locate their operation, or by people moving to areas where job opportunities are greater[1]. Through the 1980s this process has, at best, stopped and may have reversed (Figures 1- 2).

Why did this change occur? One explanation comes from the changing nature of the labour market in the nation. There has been considerable debate over the types of jobs that are being created in the U.S. economy. Following the 1981-1982 recession, concern that the structure of labour markets had changed materialized. While job creation was taking place it tended to be in the service sector, rather than manufacturing. Analysis of income data suggested that real earnings were falling, even though labour markets were tightening. Arguments were advanced that this was the result of a shift to a service economy that emphasized low wage, low skill, part time jobs (Bluestone and Harrison 1986).

In addition, there was concern that economic growth was robust in only certain parts of the country. In particular, the notion of a bi-coastal economy was advanced, pointing out that states on the two coasts accounted for the vast bulk of economic growth in the mid 1980s[2] (Joint Economic Committee 1987).

---

1.   The significance of convergence as an equalization mechanism has been an important area of research in Canada in the past twenty five years. Important studies by the Economic Council of Canada and John Vanderkamp have looked at regional labour flows as a factor in assessing the effects of unemployment assistance and regional equalization payments.

2.   Once again similar concerns exist in Canada, particularly in the context of an economic boom in the Toronto area and stagnation in many other parts of the country.

These two arguments have important rural dimensions. McGranahan (1988) argues that the structure of the rural economy results in over representation of low wage, low skill jobs (Figure 10), and the rural population tends to be more concentrated in the middle of the country. Uniform distribution of employment would result in 21% of each job class being in rural areas, since 21% of the labour force is rural. The county specialization maps indicate the bulk of the rural population is in the centre of the country. Thus, both trends suggest rural residents did not participate fully in the economic recovery. Rural incomes recovered at a slower rate than did urban following the recession, and rural unemployment rates fell slower than urban rates.

FIGURE 10

Non-metro share of jobs in production sector by type of industry, 1986

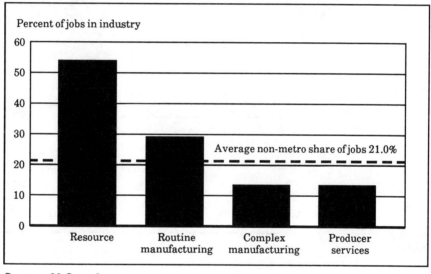

Source: McGranahan.

Examining the growth sectors of the U.S. economy during this period shows that growth was strongest in advanced services (banking, insurance, health care) and in advanced manufacturing (electronics, aerospace). These are primarily urban activities, and are found mainly on the coasts. In activities that take place in both rural and urban areas, employment growth has been significantly slower. Finally, traditional rural industries had the slowest rates of growth[3] (Figure 11). More recent data for 1988 and 1989 show higher rates of employment growth for rural workers in all sectors as the business cycle matures and full employment limits are reached (Table 4).

---

3. Growth rates in manufacturing must be interpreted with caution since, during 1979-1986, rural manufacturing lost over 400,000 jobs.

FIGURE 11

Non-traditional rural industries biggest gainers

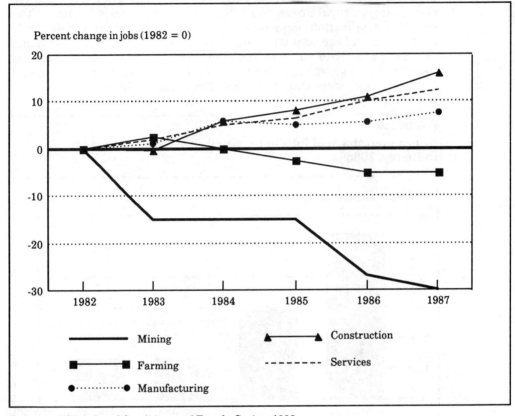

Source: USDA, Rural Conditions and Trends, Spring, 1990.

These data are consistent with a changing structure of the economy, where rural production is the first to be reduced in softening markets and the last to be brought back in a recovery. The composition of jobs in rural areas, and the sensitivity of rural production and income to fluctuations in the world economy, suggest that rural America will experience both shorter periods of economic growth, and greater variability in income and employment than the national average.

TABLE 4

Annual average employment change

	1979 to 1986	1986 to 1989	1988 to 1989
		Percent	
U.S. total	10.9	7.0	2.0
Metro	12.9	7.2	2.0
Non-metro	3.8	6.5	2.1
Region:			
Northeast	8.9	7.6	1.8
Midwest	-2.8	5.6	1.5
South	6.3	6.2	1.8
West	9.0	8.4	4.3
County type:			
Agricultural	-3.4	3.4	.8
Manufacturing	2.9	6.7	1.6
Mining	-9.6	-.5	1.7
Retirement	17.8	10.5	2.8
Urban-rural continuum codes:			
Adjacent	6.1	7.1	2.1
Urban	7.9	7.5	1.6
Less urban	4.5	6.7	1.9
Rural	7.9	8.3	2.6
Non-adjacent	1.7	5.8	2.1
Urban	4.4	6.5	2.8
Less urban	.5	5.7	1.8
Rural	.3	4.8	1.5

Source: USDA, Rural Conditions and Trends, Summer, 1990.

The **second new dimension** is a growing conflict between rural and urban interests. The focus of the conflict is differing values for economic activities and environmental concerns. Urban interests see preservation of the environment as an important option. From their perspective, lower employment and more expensive local services in rural areas are minor issues compared to preservation of the environment. Conversely, rural residents are generally willing to trade some portion of the environment for jobs and income.

These controversies attract national attention, as in the case of the spotted owl in the Pacific Northwest where preservation of the habitat for an endangered species threatens employment in the forest industry. In the process, local interests are overwhelmed by the voices of parties thousands of miles away. Those remote from the community do not experience any adverse effects; hence, a reduction in logging may be an acceptable price to pay to protect the spotted owl.

The most obvious case in Kentucky involves an existing textile factory, the Union Underwear plant in Jamestown. The factory wants to pipe effluent directly into Lake Cumberland instead of into a creek that feeds into the lake. At issue is preservation of the lake as a recreation and tourist attraction versus retention and expansion of manufacturing jobs at Union Underwear. Behind this main issue is the question of where public policy decisions are made. Local sentiment tends to favour the pipeline, since the manufacturing jobs are vital to the Jamestown economy, while sentiment in the state tends toward protecting the environment (Louisville Courier Journal 1990). The environmental conflict is becoming an urban-rural conflict as the urban majority imposes standards of environmental quality on rural areas.

Another example is the environmental ballot initiative in California known as Big Green. This initiative would restrict pesticide use, limit forestry and tighten a host of other environmental regulations with significant effects on rural areas. In Canada, the controversy over completion of the Alameda and Rafferty dams in Saskatchewan is a corresponding example of urban and rural conflicts over development and environmental protection.

A fourth example involves the different level of burden associated with meeting uniform health and safety standards. The U.S. federal government now requires, as part of the Safe Drinking Water Act, that all municipal water systems filter water, rather than chlorinate it, unless they have adequate watershed protection programs. The change results from concern about giardiasis, an uncommon problem which causes flue-like intestinal disturbances. For small water systems the cost of constructing a filtration plant may be so high that they shut down. As a result, people revert to wells which expose them to more serious health hazards. Larger communities can spread the costs of a filtration system over a large base of users; but small, rural communities lack the resources to comply with the law.

These examples reflect growing conflicts between local economic development interests and broader public policy. An increasingly urban population with minimal links to the rural economy is moving public policy in a direction that will increasingly burden rural areas. In general, increased restrictions on rural areas are not accompanied by any form of compensation for lost property rights. All these instances share the common feature that, in areas with few alternatives, local employment and income are placed at risk. Consequently, a disproportionate share of the burden of developing a cleaner environment falls upon the shoulders of the rural population.

The **third new dimension** involves the effect of changing technology on rural areas. Changes in technology are rarely neutral in their effects and they tend to induce outmigration from rural areas. The two most interesting technological changes for rural areas in the future involve telecommunications and health care.

Advanced telecommunications, or the Information Age Society, is seen by some as the potential salvation of rural areas (Parker et al. 1989). They argue that telecommunication technology reduces the effects of distance and dispersion by allowing instantaneous communication among people in all regions. This, in combination with the shift to a service economy and the rise of small business, would provide an opportunity for rural residents to become more fully integrated into the mainstream economy.

They argue that economic growth will be predicated on access to advanced telecommunications networks that can support computers, fax machines and data transfer. Without the network rural areas will be unable to attract or retain business. Rural telecommunications advocates support a new Federal policy to help provide the infrastructure to upgrade and support telecommunications in rural areas.

Two important points must be raised about the role of telecommunications in rural areas. First, is the absence of telecommunications the limiting factor in economic growth? Do we know that if these systems are put in place that rural areas will be able to attract the business to make use of them? Can rural areas provide the other elements: skilled labour, support services, amenities and so forth, that leading edge businesses require? Secondly, with scarce government funds, is the creation of a rural telecommunications network a major policy priority? The relatively small number of rural people and the limited public benefits from such an investment suggest it is not.

Even if we fail to accept the proposition that rural areas can benefit greatly from advanced telecommunications, the converse is almost certainly true. The absence of advanced telecommunications systems will reduce current rates of growth of rural areas. More business is conducted by electronic means each day. Fax machines and computerized data systems are important parts of business communications. If a rural area is not part of the network it will most certainly face slow economic growth.

The second example of how technology affects rural areas is in health care. New medical techniques and technology have improved the quality of health care. However, these techniques involve large outlays on specialized equipment and personnel. Small hospitals in rural areas are unable to afford much of the new technology. At the same time improved transportation systems often make it possible to move patients to more advanced facilities in urban areas. In many cases rural residents have the means and an incentive to bypass their local hospital.

In addition, the high proportion of Medicaid and Medicare clients in rural hospitals adds to the financial burden facing the hospital, since federal payments for these patients often do not cover the cost of providing services (Joint Economic Committee 1990). As a result, rural hospitals are closing because they cannot attract a sufficient number of patients to cover their costs, and because of rising costs.

When a hospital closes, facilities to provide emergency care may not be available which severely affects the community and surrounding area. Even where there is an adequate volume of patients to support a hospital, rural communities face a growing problem of attracting people. Doctors and nurses are increasingly reluctant to move to rural areas where they have limited support services, little time off, little opportunity for professional development, low income and few cultural attractions.

The lack of a hospital affects the economic development opportunities of a community. Not only are direct jobs lost, but the attractiveness of the community as a place to start a business and live is reduced. Without ready access to at least emergency health care, a community will find it hard to grow.

Conclusion

Rural areas are falling farther behind. The gap grew at a slower rate in the last few years as the business cycle matured and the economy approached full employment. However, it would seem that both cyclical forces and long term trends adversely affect rural America. If rural employment drops first in an economic downturn and recovers last, the result in each business cycle is that rural people start from a point farther back and have less time to make up lost ground.

In addition, longer term trends in the nature of employment suggest that high wage jobs in expanding sectors will be under represented in rural areas because of the rural labour force's inadequate skills and because rural areas are not well suited to attract the growth sectors. Economic growth will require that niche markets be identified to match rural areas' comparative advantages.

At the same time the traditional economic base of rural areas is declining in absolute and relative terms, and rural residents are falling behind in income and employment levels. In part, the decline reflects structural shifts in the national and global economies that have made foreign products more competitive with traditional rural activities. It also reflects a growing mismatch between rural workers' skills and those required for new job opportunities.

Beyond market forces there are adverse effects from changing institutions. A growing urban interest in environmental protection and health and safety regulation is limiting traditional rural activities and raising the cost of providing basic services in rural areas. These decisions are made on the basis of national priorities, not local ones.

Changing technology also has an urban bias. Advances in telecommunications and health care are not scale neutral. With a high volume of use they have low unit costs, but this does not help rural areas. As new technology becomes the defacto minimum standard—in telecommunications and health care for example—rural areas become uncompetitive by failing to adapt, or by adapting and incurring higher costs.

Little evidence exists to suggest that market forces or current policy will reverse these long term trends. During the 1980s the level of government support to rural areas was reduced in all sectors but agriculture, compounding the difficulty of adjustment. In principle, growing differences between urban and rural areas should lead to pressures for convergence, but there are a large number of rigidities and market imperfections to limit this process.

As a result, arguments can be made for place-specific government policy. First, there are major inefficiencies in the labour market—resulting from persistent unemployment and underemployment in rural areas—that reduce aggregate production. Second, a "taking-issue" occurs whenever national decisions preclude local opportunities for economic development, as environmental regulations frequently do. Finally, there is an equity issue about equal access to social services, be they medical or telecommunications.

Unfortunately the odds of this sort of policy being adopted are not good. Limited political influence, a splintered rural constituency and other pressing claims on scarce resources are major impediments. As a result, rural areas in the U.S. will likely experience a trend of greater divergence from urban areas in terms of economic and social indicators. This trend will be punctuated by brief periods of improvement at the end of each business cycle as rural resources are brought into production.

David Freshwater
Dept. of Agricultural Economics
University of Kentucky
Lexington, Kentucky
40526-0276

Kenneth Deavers
Ag. & Rural Econ. Div.
U.S. Dept. of Agriculture
Washington, D.C.
20005-4789

References

Barancik, Scott. 1990. The Rural Disadvantage. Washington: Center on Budget and Policy Priorities.

Bender, Lloyd D. et al. 1985. The Diverse Social and Economic Structure of Nonmetropolitan America. RDRR-49. Economic Research Service. Washington: U.S. Department of Agriculture.

Bluestone, Barry and Bennett Harrison. 1986. The Great American Jobs Machine. Study prepared for the Joint Economic Committee of Congress. Washington: unpublished mimeo.

Economic Council of Canada. 1977. Living Together: A Study of Regional Disparities. Ottawa: Minister of Supply and Services.

Economic Council of Canada. 1978. Recent trends in regional income differentials in Canada. In Regional Economic Policy: The Canadian Experience, edited by N.H. Lithwick. Toronto: McGraw Hill.

Hady, Thomas and Peggy Ross. 1990. An update: the diverse social and economic structure of nonmetropolitan America. AGES 9036. Economic Research Service. Washington: U.S. Department of Agriculture.

Joint Economic Committee. 1987. The Bicoastal Economy. Staff study prepared for the Joint Economic Committee. Washington: unpublished mimeo.

Joint Economic Committee. 1989. Towards Rural Development Policy for the 1990s: Enhancing Income and Employment Opportunities, (Senate print, 101-150). Washington: Government Printing Office.

Joint Economic Committee. 1990. Better Health Care for Rural America. Joint Economic Committee Hearing, (Senate print, 101-595). Washington: Government Printing Office.

Louisville Courier Journal. 1990. Lake pipeline opposed by large majority. Louisville Courier Journal. Thursday Oct. 11, 1990.

McGranahan, David. 1988. Rural workers in the national economy. In Rural Economic Development in the 1980's, edited by David Brown et al. RDRR-69. Economic Research Service. Washington: U.S. Department of Agriculture.

Parker, Edwin B. et al. 1989. Rural America In The Information Age. Lanham, Maryland: Aspen Institute and University Press of America.

Reeder, Richard J. and Nina L. Glasgow. 1990. Nonmetro retirement counties' strengths and weaknesses. <u>Rural Development Perspectives</u>, 6(2).

United States Department of Agriculture (USDA). 1990. <u>Rural Conditions and Trends</u>, 1(1,2).

Vanderkamp, John. 1968. Interregional mobility in Canada: a study of the time pattern of migration. <u>Canadian Journal of Economics</u>, 1(3): 595-608.

Vanderkamp, John. 1970. The effect of out-migration on regional employment. <u>Canadian Journal of Economics</u>, 3(4): 541-549.

Vanderkamp, John. 1976. The role of population size in migration studies. <u>Canadian Journal of Economics</u>, 9(3): 508-517.

Vanderkamp, John. 1977. Industrial mobility: some further results. <u>Canadian Journal of Economics</u>, 10(3): 462-472.

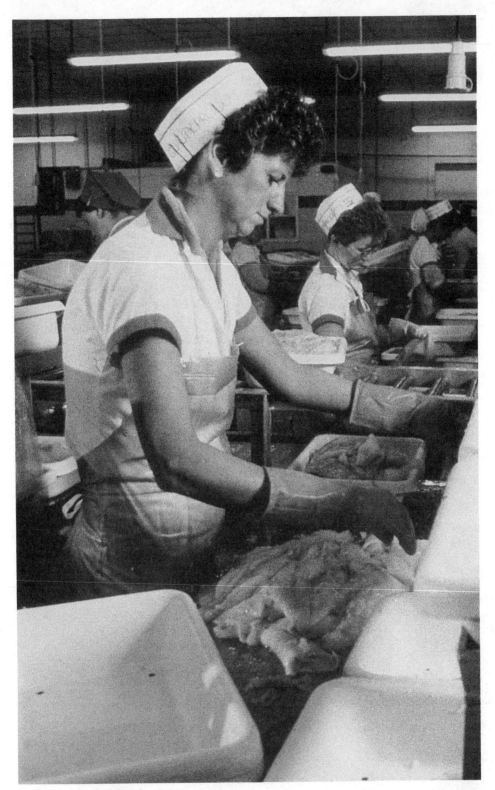

St. John's, Newfoundland

3

Products and competitiveness of rural Canada

Michael Trant and George Brinkman

Summary

Competitiveness has emerged as a worldwide concern in the past decade. The easing of trade restrictions is expected to benefit some sectors of the economy and some parts of the country and to disadvantage others. Labour force growth in rural areas during 1971-1986 ranked a distant second to growth in large metropolitan centres. Labour force growth during 1971-1986 was a phenomenon of the largest metropolitan centres (over 500,000 population) for 8 of 11 industry groups. Rural areas (under 5,000 population) ranked second in labour force growth for 7 of 11 industry groups. In other words, during 1971-1986, rural labour force growth was generally stronger than in any urbanization class between 5,000 and 499,999 population. A detailed analysis of the manufacturing sector, which employs 16% of rural residents and 17% nationally, indicates that the major rural manufacturing sectors (wood-paper, and food-beverage) maintained employment levels <u>and</u> posted productivity gains that were above the national average. However, rural manufacturing as a whole reported no productivity gains during 1981-1986.

Continuous pressure to improve competitiveness and to compete in world markets suggests further substitution of capital for labour in the traditional rural industries. The question remains—can this scenario sustain rural communities as we know them? Strategies to encourage people to remain in the community and to attract new people are needed to provide the critical mass to support local business and consumer services. This appears to be the key to sustaining rural communities as we now know them.

Table of contents

Products and competitiveness of rural Canada[1]

Michael Trant and George Brinkman

---

1.   Introduction

Competitiveness has emerged as a worldwide concern in the past decade. The Canada-United States Trade Agreement and the ongoing Uruguay Round of the General Agreement on Tariffs and Trade (G.A.T.T.) have focused the attention in Canada. The easing of trade restrictions is expected to benefit some sectors of the economy and some regions of the country and to disadvantage others. This paper will discuss the competitiveness of Canada's rural economy by detailing employment trends by industry and by comparing productivity changes in terms of value added per hour of labour across urbanization classes.

Competitiveness is the result of a complex set of domestic and international factors. All sectors of the domestic economy compete for and use the country's resources and are affected by changes in technology, productivity, input costs, consumer preferences and exchange rates. Government policies and programs also affect competitiveness by offering loan guarantees or regional economic incentives. Most studies on competitiveness have focused on international trade considerations with applications both in theory and economic modelling. Examples of recent studies include Durand and Giorno (1987), Hazledine (1991), Klein (1988), Rugman (1985), and O.E.C.D. (1988).

One way a nation can maintain or improve its competitiveness is by devaluing its currency regardless of domestic labour costs and productivity. However, when productivity does not improve (measured for instance by value added per hour of labour), a decline in the exchange rate reduces the country's standard of living. A better concept for measuring competitiveness would be to measure productivity growth. Improvements in domestic productivity improve a nation's ability to trade in the world market, to maintain a healthy trade balance and to improve its citizens' standard of living.

---

1.   The authors wish to acknowledge the contributions of Gerry Welsh, Brian Biggs and Bernard Houle of Statistics Canada for all the assistance they provided.

International efforts through G.A.T.T. and the development of stronger economic relationships among countries in Europe, Asia and North America have dismantled protectionist economic policies and barriers to trade. The result is global economic competition freeing the movement of capital, technology and labour. For Canada's rural regions, this implies changes in the economic base as it strives to remain competitive. One very real possibility is that excess resources, including labour, may be removed from rural Canada unless new strategies for net job creation can be developed.

Competition can be successfully confronted in a number of ways but, as mentioned above, one of the fundamental methods is to improve productivity. In agriculture over the past two decades, technology has substantially improved annual productivity in most if not all of the developed world. Expectations are that productivity increases will continue and given a slower increase in effective demand, resources and labour will shift out of agriculture. With the prospect of depressed commodity prices, only increased public funding will maintain farm family incomes and keep labour in agriculture.

In the forestry, oil and gas, mining, and fishing sectors, technological change over the past decade has also resulted in rising productivity and greater output for the inputs of labour, energy and materials. Competition from substitute products such as plastics plus technological advances in production methods and machinery for harvesting and extraction make it unlikely that there will be an increase in employment in these sectors, with the possible exception of oil and gas (Galston 1987).

In the manufacturing sector, competition means continued pressure for marketing and productivity improvements. In rural Canada, manu-facturing output should be able to maintain or increase productivity levels but it will likely be through decreased labour input.

2.   Methodology

Definitive empirical evidence of the competitiveness of the output and employment of rural areas is hard to establish. Little information is available to compare the cost and revenue structure of Canadian firms in various regions. As a result, this study will use employment as a proxy for measuring competitiveness. The employment approach is often referred to as survivor analysis. The existence of an industry as measured by employment numbers is used as evidence that it is competitive. This approach is based on the premise that businesses are profit-oriented, and with the exception of public services, a business will be operated as long as it is profitable. The existence of an economic activity implies it is profitable and competitive in the domestic or export market. The approach, however, does ignore the possible effect of government policies to support industry in a particular region and the differential effects of municipal, provincial and federal taxes. As current public policies and programs do not specifically target rural areas, they are unlikely to play a major role.

For the manufacturing sector, additional data were available for value added per hour of labour by city size. These data from the 1981 and 1986 Censuses of Manufactures provide more detail and insight for manufacturing industries than is possible with census data.

Identifying the products and competitiveness of rural Canada requires data on economic activity which can be disaggregated by geographic area. Three Statistics Canada databases can provide such comprehensive information:

1.   the quinquennial Census of Population;

2.   the annual Census of Manufactures (up to 1986); and

3.   experimental databases of taxation data. For preliminary results, see McVey (1992), Meyers (1992) and Picot and Heath (1992) in this volume.

Economic analysis of "rural competitiveness" using employment statistics raises three difficult questions:

1.   How do we define rural Canada?

2.   Which geographic areas (e.g. county, enumeration area) do we classify as rural or urban?

3.   How do we relate the definition of economic activity to a standard industrial classification for analysis?

To facilitate analysis, standard geographic areas called census subdivisions[2] were used as building blocks. The labour force was assigned to population size categories according to the population size of the census subdivision in which the individual resided.

Census subdivisions were classified into 6 population categories, based upon a classification structure developed by Hodge and Qadeer (1983).

Residence category	Population		
Rural areas and small towns	under		5,000
Towns	5,000	-	9,999
City	10,000	-	29,999
	30,000	-	99,999
Metropolis	100,000	-	499,999
	over		500,000

2.   Census subdivisions are municipalities, Indian reserves, Indian settlements and unorganized territories. In Newfoundland, Nova Scotia and British Columbia, CSDs can also be geostatistical areas created by Statistics Canada in co-operation with the provinces, as equivalents for municipalities (Statistics Canada 1988: 74).

Consideration was also given to applying an alternative, more sophisticated sorting procedure which classified the geographic areas bordering large urban centres by the population of the urban centre rather than by the population of the geographic area itself. The rationale for this approach is that these peripheral areas are essentially part of the urban area even though they may have been classified rural. This modified classification was examined but it had no significant impact on the results of the study and consequently was not used.

Economic activity for the study has been classified by the 1970 Standard Industrial Classification (SIC) system. The 1970 SIC was selected as it was the only system which could be applied to data from the 1971, 1981 and 1986 Censuses.

3.   Observations

This paper presents only national observations. Analytic tables were prepared for each province but, because of the volume of information, they have not been included in this report. However, they are available from the authors upon request.

3.1   Population

In 1986, rural parts of Canada (including towns and villages with less than 5,000 people) had a population of 7.4 million or almost 30% of Canada's population (Table 1). Rural Canada is home to a substantial proportion of Canadians. Although Canada is becoming increasingly urbanized, the number of people in rural areas has remained surprisingly stable since 1931. The rural population has however changed in composition. Fewer people now live on farms. In 1986 only 16% of the rural population lived on farms, a significant decrease from 1956 when almost 50% of rural residents lived on farms.

TABLE 1

Labour force by industry and urbanization class, Canada, 1986

Industry	Under 5,000	5,000 to 9,999	10,000 to 29,999	30,000 to 99,999	100,000 to 499,999	500,000 and over	Total
				Urbanization class			
Goods producing (subtotal)	1,394,710	110,905	217,240	281,290	352,470	1,375,215	3,731,830
Agriculture	434,780	6,720	10,300	13,515	11,475	27,450	504,240
Forestry	77,715	4,790	9,420	6,730	3,870	6,860	109,385
Fishing / trapping	36,010	985	2,195	965	1,010	2,890	44,055
Mines / oil wells	74,180	12,945	27,015	14,295	10,340	49,475	188,250
Manufacturing	531,765	64,885	130,130	186,725	252,505	987,950	2,153,960
Construction	240,260	20,580	38,180	59,060	73,270	300,590	731,940
Service performing (subtotal)	2,015,095	266,560	537,945	784,160	1,034,740	4,413,125	9,051,625
Transportation	243,525	27,460	54,135	79,030	92,800	461,795	958,745
Trade and commerce	478,925	64,505	134,570	192,035	235,845	990,995	2,096,875
Finance / insurance / real estate	101,995	13,680	29,050	48,170	73,500	402,090	668,485
Health / education / recreation	849,825	113,655	238,535	350,285	477,340	1,935,940	3,965,580
Public administration	223,015	35,270	58,475	81,620	115,040	436,690	950,110
Other	117,810	11,990	23,180	33,020	40,215	185,615	411,830
Total labour force	3,409,805	377,465	755,185	1,065,450	1,387,210	5,788,340	12,783,455
Total population	7,389,920	797,260	1,584,505	2,174,160	2,694,425	10,669,060	25,309,330

Source: Statistics Canada. 1986 Census of Population, unpublished tabulation.

3.2   Labour force by industry and location

Measured in terms of the labour force[3], the service sector was more than twice the size of the goods producing sector in 1986. Approximately 13 million people were in the labour force with 9 million in the service sector and 4 million in the goods producing sector (Table 1). Economic activity in rural Canada is significant as over 3 million (27%) of the labour force resided in rural areas[4].

---

3.   All numbers in this section on labour force by industry and location refer to people in the labour force. The text interchanges the terms "number of employed", "number in the labour force", and "number of jobs" whereas, strictly, the "labour force" is defined as the sum of the "employed" and the "unemployed".

4.   Census data classify workers to the place where they live, not to the urbanization class of the place where they work.

TABLE 2

Percent distribution of labour force by industry within each urbanization class, Canada, 1986

Industry	Under 5,000	5,000 to 9,999	10,000 to 29,999	30,000 to 99,999	100,000 to 499,999	500,000 and over	Total
			Urbanization class				
Goods producing (subtotal)	**40.9**	**29.4**	**28.8**	**26.4**	**25.4**	**23.8**	**29.2**
Agriculture	12.8	1.8	1.4	1.3	.8	.5	3.9
Forestry	2.3	1.3	1.3	.6	.3	.1	.9
Fishing / trapping	1.1	.3	.3	.1	.1	.1	.3
Mines / oil wells	2.2	3.4	3.6	1.3	.8	.9	1.5
Manufacturing	15.6	17.2	17.2	17.5	18.2	17.1	16.9
Construction	7.1	5.5	5.1	5.5	5.3	5.2	5.7
Service performing (subtotal)	**59.1**	**70.6**	**71.2**	**73.6**	**74.6**	**76.2**	**70.8**
Transportation	7.1	7.3	7.2	7.4	6.7	8.0	7.5
Trade and commerce	14.1	17.1	17.8	18.0	17.0	17.1	16.4
Finance / insurance / real estate	3.0	3.6	3.9	4.5	5.3	7.0	5.2
Health / education / recreation	24.9	30.1	31.6	32.9	34.4	33.5	31.0
Public administration	6.5	9.3	7.7	7.7	8.3	7.5	7.4
Other	3.5	3.2	3.1	3.1	2.9	3.2	3.2
Total labour force	**100.0**	**100.0**	**100.0**	**100.0**	**100.0**	**100.0**	**100.0**

Source: Statistics Canada. 1986 Census of Population, unpublished tabulation.

In rural areas and towns with less than 5,000 population, the goods producing sectors of the economy are more important than they are in more urbanized areas (Table 2). In rural areas, 1.4 million people (41%) were employed in the goods producing sector. As in urban areas, the rural service performing sector is becoming an increasingly important source of employment. In 1986, 2 million people (59%) were employed in the rural service performing sectors.

In cities, the services sector is clearly the dominant source of employment employing 71% of the labour force in the towns of 5,000 to 9,999 people and increasing to 76% in the cities of over half a million. Trade and commerce; finance, insurance, real estate; health, education, recreation; and public administration are the occupational service sectors where urban areas differ most in comparison to rural areas. The goods sector is the reverse to the services sector. In towns of 5,000 to 9,999, 29% of the 400,000 jobs were in the goods sector while in the largest cities of over 500,000, less than 24% of the 5.8 million person labour force was employed in that sector.

Agriculture accounts for 13% of the rural labour force. Another 5% of the labour force in rural areas is employed in other traditionally rural occupations such as forestry, fishing, trapping, mining, and oil and gas extraction. Primary industry, by its nature, is rural based. Jobs in the primary industries indeed provide employment opportunities to people in rural areas that are not available in more urbanized parts of the country. If the jobs in agriculture, for instance, did not exist, the profiles for employment between the goods and service sectors in rural Canada would look similar to the pattern in the more urbanized parts of the country.

TABLE 3

Labour force by industry and urbanization class, Canada, 1981

Industry	Under 5,000	5,000 to 9,999	10,000 to 29,999	30,000 to 99,999	100,000 to 499,999	500,000 and over	Total
Goods producing (subtotal)	**1,401,715**	**118,335**	**239,430**	**287,805**	**354,655**	**1,398,740**	**3,800,680**
Agriculture	423,350	6,235	8,615	10,450	10,345	22,280	481,275
Forestry	72,440	4,660	9,350	5,110	3,290	5,915	100,765
Fishing / trapping	29,395	900	1,835	835	1,210	2,690	36,865
Mines / oil wells	85,535	14,945	31,570	14,850	13,785	49,340	210,025
Manufacturing	540,660	68,335	146,895	192,275	256,080	1,015,130	2,219,375
Construction	250,335	23,260	41,165	64,285	69,945	303,385	752,375
Service performing (subtotal)	**1,845,390**	**254,125**	**497,510**	**678,045**	**930,715**	**3,990,855**	**8,196,640**
Transportation	229,055	28,985	54,600	75,400	87,850	459,680	935,570
Trade and commerce	449,610	62,415	126,990	174,380	217,170	927,015	1,957,580
Finance / insurance / real estate	95,485	13,870	28,390	42,705	69,395	371,270	621,115
Health / education	743,685	100,130	211,365	291,925	410,845	1,641,490	3,399,440
Public administration	205,755	37,360	52,780	71,840	106,815	412,050	886,600
Other	121,800	11,365	23,385	21,795	38,640	179,350	396,335
Total labour force	**3,247,105**	**372,460**	**736,940**	**965,850**	**1,285,370**	**5,389,595**	**11,997,320**

Source: Statistics Canada. 1981 Census of Population, unpublished tabulation.

The situation in 1981 was similar to that of 1986 (Table 3). The total labour force was smaller by 800,000 people in 1981 and a higher proportion were employed in the goods sector (37%) compared to 1986 (Table 4). Rural employment patterns experienced a similar change. In 1981, 150,000 fewer people worked in rural areas an a higher proportion (43%) were employed in the goods sector.

TABLE 4
Distribution of labour force, Canada, 1971-1986

	Rural areas, under 5,000 population			All areas		
Urbanization class	1971	1981	1986	1971	1981	1986
	Percent					
Goods producing	47	43	41	34	32	29
Service performing	53	57	59	66	68	71
Total	100	100	100	100	100	100

Source: Statistics Canada. 1971-1986 Censuses of Population, unpublished tabulation.

TABLE 5
Labour force by industry and urbanization class, Canada, 1971

	Urbanization class						
Industry	Under 5,000	5,000 to 9,999	10,000 to 29,999	30,000 to 99,999	100,000 to 499,999	500,000 and over	Total
Goods producing (subtotal)	1,124,815	103,890	226,605	254,320	398,120	857,850	2,965,600
Agriculture	444,850	5,005	10,885	4,950	7,945	7,560	481,195
Forestry	55,960	3,310	6,350	2,670	2,645	3,445	74,380
Fishing / trapping	21,380	435	1,305	300	595	1,425	25,440
Mines / oil wells	62,460	12,375	24,405	13,395	18,005	8,395	139,035
Manufacturing	364,065	63,445	145,550	188,090	276,770	669,415	1,707,335
Construction	176,100	19,320	38,110	44,915	92,160	167,610	538,215
Service performing (subtotal)	1,279,715	213,665	446,325	524,880	1,024,020	2,172,705	5,661,310
Transportation	164,545	24,950	52,410	58,915	103,335	266,900	671,055
Trade and commerce	278,490	47,760	102,300	120,975	227,180	492,585	1,269,290
Finance / insurance / real estate	46,385	9,395	22,185	26,230	66,875	186,980	358,050
Health / education	438,495	78,770	166,955	204,605	390,315	762,250	2,041,390
Public administration	143,470	28,415	52,525	56,105	134,010	225,055	639,580
Other	208,330	24,375	49,950	58,050	102,305	238,935	681,945
Total labour force	2,404,530	317,555	672,930	779,200	1,422,140	3,030,555	8,626,910

Source: Statistics Canada. 1971 Census of Population, unpublished tabulation.

In 1971, the Canadian labour force was 8.6 million people, 3.3 million less than the 12 million person labour force of 1981 (Table 5). In 1971, employment in the goods producing sector accounted for 3 million people (34%). The service sector employed the remaining 5.7 million (66%). In 1971, 1.1 million people (47%) in rural Canada held jobs in the goods producing sector. Rural Canada, in 1971, had almost as many people employed in the goods producing sector as in services. In 1971, there were only 1.3 million people employed in the service sector representing 53% of the employment in rural areas.

Since 1971 the proportion of the labour force employed in the goods producing sector has declined. At the national level it was 34% in 1971, 32% in 1981 and 29% in 1986. In contrast, the share of the labour force in the service performing sector has increased from 65% in 1971 to over 70% in 1986. In the rural parts of Canada the rate and direction of change have been similar. In 1971, the rural labour force was almost evenly split between the goods and services sectors of the economy. By 1986 the goods sector had dropped to 41% while the service sector increased to 59% of the labour force in rural areas.

Much of the change in rural employment patterns was caused by the rapid growth in the service sector—employment in the goods producing industries grew during 1971-1981 but remained almost unchanged during 1981-1986. Goods sector employment in rural areas increased only 7,000 between 1981 and 1986. In contrast, there was substantial growth in employment in the rural services sector, an increase of 170,000 service sector jobs.

TABLE 6

Percent change in labour force by industry by urbanization class, Canada, 1971 to 1986

Industry	Under 5,000	5,000 to 9,999	10,000 to 29,999	30,000 to 99,999	100,000 to 499,999	500,000 and over	Total
			Percent change, 1971 to 1986				
Goods producing (subtotal)	24	7	-4	11	6	60	26
Agriculture	-2	34	-5	173	44	263	5
Forestry	39	45	48	152	46	99	47
Fishing / trapping	68	126	68	222	70	103	73
Mines / oil wells	19	5	11	7	-43	489	35
Manufacturing	46	2	-11	-1	-9	48	26
Construction	36	7	0	31	-21	79	36
Service performing (subtotal)	57	25	21	49	1	103	60
Transportation	48	10	3	34	-10	73	43
Trade and commerce	72	35	32	59	4	101	65
Finance / insurance / real estate	120	46	31	84	10	115	87
Health / education / recreation	94	44	43	71	22	154	94
Public administration	55	24	11	45	-14	94	49
Other	-43	-51	-54	-43	-61	-22	-40
Total labour force	42	19	12	37	-2	91	48

Source: Statistics Canada. 1971 and 1986 Censuses of Population, unpublished tabulation.

The service sector is not only significant when measured by the increase in the number of jobs but also when measured by rates of growth. In Canada between 1971 and 1986, employment in the service sector increased 60%, an annual average growth rate of 4% (Table 6). The increase during 1981 to 1986 was 900,000 or 2% annually.

In the service sector the leading growth areas nationally were in the health, education, recreation, accommodation and food services industries. Employment doubled from 2 million jobs in 1971 to 4 million in 1986. That was an annual growth rate of over 6% for the period. The finance, insurance and real estate sector, employing just over half a million people in 1986, was the next fastest growth sector increasing at the annual rate of almost 6% between 1971 and 1986. Third in terms of growth was the trade and commerce sector with an average annual growth rate of over 4% (65% over the 15 year period). The trade and commerce industries are the second largest category of jobs in the services sector.

The ability of the service sector to outperform the goods producing industries is somewhat discouraging for the economies of rural areas as the service performing industries are largely urban based. Rural Canada is not sharing in the benefits resulting from the rapid increase in employment in the service sector in comparison to urban parts of the country because rural Canada has a larger share of its employment in the slower growing goods sector.

In comparison to the service sector, the goods producing industries grew by 800,000 employees or only 2% per year between 1971 and 1986. During 1981-1986, jobs were lost from the goods sector at a rate of 0.4% per year. The loss of jobs was greatest in the manufacturing industries followed by oil, gas, mining and construction industries. Employment continued to grow in forestry and fishing at 3.6% per year during 1971 to 1986. Employment in agriculture was stable during the period, increasing 1,000 people per year on average.

To summarize the growth rates among the various industries and urbanization classes, it is instructive to consider which urbanization class experienced the highest growth rates within each industry. Between 1971 and 1986, the highest growth rates were in cities with populations over 500,000 for all industries except forestry, fishing and finance-insurance-real estate (Table 7). The urbanization class of under 5,000 population ranked second for seven industries and ranked first for finance-insurance-real estate. We acknowledge that part of the growth of the labour force in areas smaller than 5,000 results from growth in the number of workers who live in small census subdivisions who commute to nearby urban centres. However, a significant share is attributable to employment growth in areas not adjacent to urban centres.

TABLE 7

Urbanization classes ranked by size of growth in the labour force within each industry, Canada, 1971-1986

Industry	Rank of urbanization class, in terms of percent growth of labour force, 1971 to 1986					
	#1	#2	#3	#4	#5	#6
Goods producing, subtotal	500K+	<5K	30-100K	5-10K	100-500K	10-30K
Agriculture	500K+	30-100K	100-500K	5-10K	<5K	10-30K
Forestry	30-100K	500K+	10-30K	100-500K	5-10K	<5K
Fishing and trapping	30-100K	5-10K	500K+	100-500K	<5K	10-30K
Mines and oil wells	500K+	<5K	10-30K	30-100K	5-10K	100-500K
Manufacturing	500K+	<5K	5-10K	30-100K	100-500K	10-30K
Construction	500K+	<5K	30-100K	5-10K	10-30K	100-500K
Service performing, subtotal	500K+	<5K	30-100K	5-10K	10-30K	100-500K
Transportation	500K+	<5K	30-100K	5-10K	10-30K	100-500K
Trade and commerce	500K+	<5K	30-100K	5-10K	10-30K	100-500K
Finance, insurance, real estate	<5K	500K+	30-100K	5-10K	10-30K	100-500K
Health and education	500K+	<5K	30-100K	5-10K	10-30K	100-500K
Public administration	500K+	<5K	30-100K	5-10K	10-30K	100-500K
Other	500K+	30-100K	<5K	5-10K	10-30K	100-500K
Total	**500K+**	**<5K**	**30-100K**	**5-10K**	**10-30K**	**100-500K**

Source: Statistics Canada. 1971 and 1986 Censuses of Population.

3.3   Manufacturing industries

Currently, little detailed data on the cost and revenue structure of Canadian industry can be manipulated to provide statistics classified by city size. The exception is the annual census of manufactures, but because of program changes, 1986 is the last year the data can be classified and tabulated by city size (see Statistics Canada 1990).

Census of manufactures data are collected from Canadian manufacturers and census of population data are collected from households. The definitions and concepts are not the same for the two surveys. The census of manufactures consistently records employment[5] figures lower than those estimated by the census of population (Table 8). It is not clear exactly why the differences exist or why there is so much variation among provinces.

---

5.   The employment figures in this section on manufacturing industries represent the number of people employed as reported by manufacturers on the Census of Manufactures.

Table 8
Comparison of estimates of the labour force in manufacturing activities, census of population and census of manufactures. Canada, 1986

	Manufacturing labour force		
	Census of population, by place of residence (1)	Census of manufacturing, by plant location (2)	(2) as percent of (1) (3)
Newfoundland	35,700	16,737	47
Prince Edward Island	5,825	3,374	58
Nova Scotia	50,655	34,338	68
New Brunswick	45,660	30,429	67
Quebec	597,325	481,977	8
Ontario	1,047,385	885,557	85
Manitoba	65,150	51,058	78
Saskatchewan	28,190	18,333	65
Alberta	99,906	69,518	70
British Columbia	176,895	126,752	72
Canada	**2,153,970**	**1,718,412**	**80**

Sources: Statistics Canada. 1986 Census of Manufactures, and 1986 Census of Population.

The census of manufactures data however confirm the findings from the census of population that the goods producing industries, of which manufacturing is a significant sector, are a slow growth area. It is also a sector that is under pressure from global competition.

TABLE 9

Total number of employees by manufacturing activity by urbanization class of plant location, Canada, 1981 and 1986

Manufacturing activity	Urbanization class of plant location						
	Under 5,000	5,000 to 9,999	10,000 to 29,999	30,000 to 99,999	100,000 to 499,999	500,000 and over	Total
Food / beverage							
1986	41,383	18,050	24,129	33,265	49,534	43,647	210,008
1981	40,223	17,004	25,864	35,480	50,033	54,086	222,690
Clothing							
1986	20,000	10,699	17,934	33,216	23,272	86,073	191,194
1981	19,232	11,368	28,670	33,230	23,391	89,308	205,199
Wood / paper							
1986	71,176	37,595	58,111	69,006	85,775	74,458	396,121
1981	70,802	38,308	68,058	70,640	71,783	73,309	392,900
Metal							
1986	16,335	14,702	34,793	68,495	81,207	29,291	244,823
1981	19,116	18,540	39,657	79,693	81,081	36,247	274,334
Machinery / electric							
1986	27,812	14,399	59,439	95,741	159,659	50,181	407,231
1981	24,756	14,450	58,816	96,925	137,364	55,013	387,324
Petro / chemical							
1986	11,584	11,012	28,143	37,829	42,430	20,722	151,720
1981	15,405	12,344	31,424	33,882	38,394	19,262	150,711
Other							
1986	9,949	7,861	14,080	24,727	35,564	25,124	117,305
1981	9,007	8,352	15,103	23,687	32,704	27,577	116,430
Total							
1986	198,239	114,318	236,629	362,279	477,441	329,496	1,718,402
1981	198,541	120,366	267,592	373,537	434,750	354,802	1,749,588

Source: *Statistics Canada. 1981 and 1986 Censuses of Manufactures.*

In the context of total Canadian economic activity, manufacturing in 1986 employed 17% of the labour force at the national level and 16% in rural areas (Table 1). Although a significant source of rural employment, manufacturing reflects the overall population distribution and is essentially an urban activity. Over 80% of all manufacturing takes place in cities with more than 10,000 people and almost 50% in cities of over 100,000 people.

In 1986, employment in manufacturing in rural Canada amounted to almost 200,000 jobs or 12% of all the jobs in the manufacturing sector (Table 9). The majority of rural manufacturing jobs were in industries normally associated with rural areas. Jobs in wood, paper and allied industries accounted for 35% of the manufacturing employment in rural areas and represented almost 20% of all the manufacturing jobs in the wood and paper sector. Not surprisingly, the food and beverage industry, which is closely associated with agriculture, employed 20% of the rural labour force in manufacturing and 20% of all jobs in the food and beverage industry.

TABLE 10

Percent change in number of employees by manufacturing activity and urbanization class of plant location, Canada, 1981-1986

Manufacturing activity	<5K	5-10K	10-30K	30-100K	100-500K	500K+	Total
			Urbanization class of plant location				
Food / beverage	2.9	6.2	-6.7	-6.2	-1.0	-19.3	-5.7
Clothing	4.0	-5.9	-37.4	.0	-.5	-3.6	-6.8
Wood / paper	.5	-1.9	-14.6	-2.3	19.5	1.6	.8
Metal	-14.5	-20.7	-12.3	-14.1	.2	-19.2	-10.8
Machinery / electric	12.3	-.4	1.1	-1.2	16.2	-8.8	5.1
Petro / chemical	-24.8	-10.8	-10.4	11.6	10.5	7.6	.7
Other	10.5	-5.9	-6.8	4.4	8.7	-8.9	.8
Total	-.2	-5.0	-11.6	-3.0	9.8	-7.1	-1.8

Source: Statistics Canada. 1981-1986 Censuses of Manufactures.

Manufacturing is not a growth sector. National employment levels have remained essentially unchanged during 1981-1986 (Table 10). In rural areas the pattern is similar as gains in some manufacturing industries compensated for losses in others. Rural jobs in the petro-chemical and metal fabricating industries have been lost. The loss in metal fabricating has been felt across the industry regardless of plant location. In the petro-chemical sector, jobs have been lost in the rural areas and small towns under 30,000 in population. The petro-chemical industry job losses in the rural areas were offset for the most part by increases in the number of jobs in more urban parts of the country. Industries manufacturing machinery and electrical products showed modest growth in employment of about 5% during 1981-1986.

3.4   Productivity of manufacturing industries

A critical indicator of the competitiveness of an industry is its productivity. We measure productivity in terms of value added per hour of labour. The data are tabulated and classified by the size of the city where the plants are located.

TABLE 11

Productivity of Canadian manufacturing activity by urbanization class of plant location, Canada, 1981 and 1986

	<5K	5-10K	10-30K	30-100K	100-500K	500K+	Total

	<5K	5-10K	10-30K	30-100K	100-500K	500K+	Total
Food / beverage							
1986	27.84	34.41	59.73	60.20	53.64	47.05	46.78
1981	23.07	29.84	43.40	49.69	45.61	41.91	39.22
Clothing							
1986	16.37	22.38	20.00	22.76	17.47	17.08	18.53
1981	16.38	19.44	20.57	21.64	20.84	17.72	19.08
Wood / paper							
1986	29.58	39.07	43.17	35.81	34.94	37.32	36.08
1981	26.93	35.28	33.12	30.92	33.58	36.25	32.67
Metal							
1986	30.40	35.09	41.36	33.82	34.35	30.89	34.53
1981	29.56	28.90	34.03	35.69	32.87	32.98	33.47
Machinery / electric							
1986	28.50	32.90	38.83	35.78	39.39	31.94	36.53
1981	31.91	29.45	34.90	35.59	35.54	37.16	35.19
Petro / chemical							
1986	49.58	60.97	78.07	69.81	57.39	53.02	63.32
1981	69.76	59.07	74.56	76.69	52.13	51.29	64.49
Other							
1986	33.10	34.01	34.77	30.68	34.75	26.00	31.76
1981	32.24	33.23	34.16	31.29	36.34	28.77	32.62
Total							
1986	28.96	36.99	44.52	39.01	38.94	31.05	36.87
1981	29.08	33.34	37.55	37.63	36.25	31.74	34.77

Urbanization class of plant location — value added per person-hour of labour, constant 1986 dollars

Source: Statistics Canada. 1981 and 1986 Censuses of Manufactures. The deflator to convert to constant dollars is Statistics Canada's GDP implicit price index, 1986 = 100.

Productivity of all Canadian manufacturers, measured in constant dollars increased from $34.77 to $36.87 per hour of labour during 1981-1986 (Table 11). This is a modest 6% increase (Table 12) or just over one percent per year during the period. At the same time there was almost a 2% reduction in employment in manufacturing even though there were almost 7% more manufacturers in 1986 than in 1981.

TABLE 12

Percent change in value-added per person hour of labour by manufacturing activity and urbanization class of plant location, Canada, 1981 to 1986

| | Urbanization class of plant location | | | | | | |
	<5K	5-10K	10-30K	30-100K	100-500K	500K+	Total
	Percent change, 1981 to 1986						
Food/beverage	21	15	38	21	18	12	19
Clothing	0	15	-3	5	-16	-4	-3
Wood/paper	10	11	30	16	4	3	10
Metal	3	21	22	-5	5	-6	3
Machinery/electrical	-11	12	11	1	11	-14	4
Petro/chemical	-29	3	5	-9	10	3	-2
Other	3	2	2	-2	-4	-10	-13
Total	0	11	19	4	7	-2	6

Source: Statistics Canada. 1981 and 1986 Censuses of Manufactures.

In contrast to productivity growth nationally, the rural parts of Canada recorded no productivity gains overall. The value added per hour of labour, in constant dollars, remained at $29 in 1986, virtually the same as it was in 1981. Productivity gains in 'typical' rural manufacturing sectors (food-beverages, and wood-paper) were counterbalanced by small gains or losses elsewhere. The food and beverage industry enjoyed a 21% increase or 4% per year and the wood and paper industries experienced a 10% increase or 2% per year. The productivity increases for those two industries were essentially the same nationally.

The Canadian metal fabricating and clothing industries experienced little change in productivity over 1981 to 1986. The clothing industry in fact slipped 3% and the metal fabricating industries increased 3%.

The only other significant source of manufacturing jobs in rural areas, the petro-chemical industry did not fare well during 1981-1986. Abundant supplies and weak prices have had a marked effect on the industry. Employment in the industry has remained almost unchanged and productivity in terms of value added per person hour of labour has slipped by 2% nationally and almost 29% in the plants in rural Canada.

In summary, Canada level productivity gains in manufacturing have been an unspectacular 1% annually and manufacturing industry located in rural communities showed no measurable change during 1981-1986. The lack of productivity improvements in the rural manufacturing sector is of concern to rural communities.

4.   Conclusion

Modest employment growth in the rural goods and service industries indicates that rural communities continue to make a substantial contribution to the economic activity in the country. Alarmingly though, rural employment growth falls short of growth rates in urban Canada. The quickly expanding service sector is underdeveloped in rural Canada in comparison to urban areas. It appears that the traditional rural industries—agriculture, forestry, natural resource extraction and manufacturing—will remain the economic base in rural Canada for some years yet.

The modest productivity improvement achieved by Canadian manufacturers raises some concerns about the ability of the manufacturing sector to continue contributing to the economic well-being of rural communities. The manufacturing sector has been a significant source of employment for people in rural communities in the past. The lack of any measurable improvements in the productivity of manufacturing facilities in rural communities compared to more urbanized areas requires attention.

A competitive industrial base is important to the health of rural communities but it is not the only requirement. Continuous pressure to improve competitiveness suggests further substitution of capital for labour. This observation confronts the other basic factor in the rural development debate. Population growth is critical to maintaining the viability of rural communities. Strategies to encourage people to remain in the community and to attract new people are needed. Increasing population densities provide the critical mass to support local business and consumer services. This appears to be the key to sustaining rural communities as we now know them (Galston 1987).

Michael Trant
Agriculture Division
Statistics Canada
Ottawa, Ontario
K1A 0T6

George Brinkman
School of Agricultural
Economics and Business
University of Guelph
Guelph, Ontario N1G 2W1

References

Brinkman, G. L. 1987. The competitive position of Canadian agriculture. Canadian Journal of Agricultural Economics, 35(2): 263-288.

Coffey, W. J. and J. J. McRae. 1989. Service Industries in Regional Development. Montréal: Université du Québec à Montréal, Département d'étu de urbaines.

Coffey, W. J. and Mario Polèse. 1987. Trade and location of producer services: a Canadian perspective. Environment and Planning, 19: 597-612.

Durand, M. and G. Giorno. 1987. Indicators of international competitiveness. Conceptual aspects and evaluation. O.E.C.D. Economic Studies. Paris: 147-183.

Galston, W. 1987. U.S. rural economic development in a competitive global economy. Agriculture and Beyond. College of Agricultural and Life Sciences. Madison: University of Wisconsin.

Hazledine, Tim. 1991. Productivity in Canadian food and beverage industries: an interpretive survey of methods and results. Canadian Journal of Agricultural Economics, 39(1): 1-34.

Hodge, G. and A. M. Qadeer. 1983. Towns and Villages in Canada, The Importance of Being Unimportant. Toronto: Butterworths.

Klein, L. R. 1988. Components of competitiveness. Science, 241: 308-313.

McVey, John. 1992. Growth of small and medium size business: a rural-urban comparison. Chapter 4 in this volume. Rural and Small Town Canada. Toronto: Thompson Educational Publishing Inc.

Meyer, Bruce. 1992. Population, income and migration characteristics for urban-rural areas and farm/non-farm families in Saskatchewan. Chapter 15 in this volume. Rural and Small Town Canada. Toronto: Thompson Educational Publishing Inc.

Organization for Economic Co-operation and Development. 1988. O.E.C.D. Economic Outlook. Paris: December, no.44.

Picot, Garnett and John Heath. 1992. Small communities in Atlantic Canada: Industrial structure and labour market conditions in the early 1980s. Chapter 8 in this volume. Rural and Small Town Canada. Toronto: Thompson Educational Publishing Inc.

Rugman, A. M. 1985. A Canadian strategy for international competitiveness. <u>Business Quarterly</u>, 50(3): 18-21.

Statistics Canada. 1991. Special tabulations from the 1971, 1981 and 1986 Census of Population. Ottawa: Statistics Canada.

Statistics Canada. 1991. Special tabulations from the 1981 and 1986 Census of Manufactures. Ottawa: Statistics Canada.

Statistics Canada. 1988. <u>Census Handbook</u>, (cat. no. 99-104). In the 1986 Census of Population series. Ottawa: Statistics Canada.

Statistics Canada. 1990. <u>Manufacturing industries of Canada, sub-provincial areas, 1986</u>, (cat. no. 31-209). Ottawa: Statistics Canada.

Oliver, British Columbia

4

Growth of small and medium size business: a rural-urban comparison

J.S. McVey

Summary

Small and medium size enterprises (SMEs) in Canada account for 53% of aggregate sales by all incorporated firms in Canada. Unincorporated businesses and large corporate firms (with sales of $50 million or more) were not included in this study.

Relative to the distribution of population, SME sales are more concentrated in centres with a population of 100,000 or more. SME sales in these centres showed more growth during 1981-1987 compared to SMEs in smaller centres. Although SMEs in larger centres were more profitable in both 1981 and 1987, SME profitability bounced back more in centres with population under 100,000. "Newly identified" firms between 1981 to 1987 accounted for a large share of sales in centres of all sizes. However, since "no longer identified" firms were less frequent in centres of 10,000 or less, the turnover had a significant and positive impact on business activity in these small centres. SMEs in larger centres were more concentrated in the service sector and this sector grew more in larger centres during 1981-1987.

Growth of small and medium size business: a rural-urban comparison

J.S. McVey

Introduction

Mainstream economics has always paid little attention to geographic considerations. At least as far back as 1776, when Adam Smith published his monumental "Inquiry Into the Nature and Causes of the Wealth of Nations", the emphasis has always been on these artificial entities known as nations. Nations differ greatly, however, in their geographic expanse and in urban composition. They are made up of urban areas of widely varying number and size.

Like most modern industrialized developed nations, Canada's population is clustered in large urban centres. In 1986 slightly over 60% of the population was located in 27 centres of over 100,000 people. A further 151 mid-size cities and towns with populations between 10,000 and 100,000 accounted for almost another 20% of the population. Therefore, 178 medium and large towns and cities represented almost 80% of Canada. Yet the other fifth of Canada's population, an important component of more than 5 million people, lived in 4,235 centres of less than 10,000. Unfortunately, most statistics are available at the national, provincial, or at most, for a small handful of major metropolitan areas.

This paper's objective is to shed new light on the development and experiences of all urban areas in Canada over the 1980s, regardless of size, to understand Canadian economic development. To do so, taxation data and record linkage techniques will be used. This paper represents only a partial first step in such an undertaking, but the approach employed opens up the possibility of many more detailed and wider ranging analyses.

The paper presents new findings on the distribution and growth of small and medium size business by town size. It looks at how much of Canada's small and medium size business is conducted in smaller centres and if these businesses are growing faster, slower or turning over more than in larger centres. Statistics are analyzed for the various regions of Canada. It examines the size of the service sector in relation to the goods sector in smaller centres and in larger centres. It locates Canada's small and medium size firm manufacturing and shows in which areas it is growing fastest. This paper provides evidence from the 1980s on these important issues. After a brief description of the data and methodology, the analysis is presented. A concluding section notes some possible extensions.

Methodology

The analysis employs administrative personal taxation data (for the self-employed unincorporated component) and corporate taxation data and several different types of record linkage. Corporate tax files for 1981 and 1987 have mailing addresses, as do the 1981 and 1988 personal tax files. The postal codes on these files are matched to the Statistics Canada Postal Code Conversion File[1] to assign codes for census metropolitan and other urban agglomeration areas. Census of population estimates for 1986 (Statistics Canada 1988a, 1988b) are also obtained for these same urban areas to assign town sizes. Smaller towns with no separate Census urban code are based on their postal codes. The rural "fringes" surrounding large centres have been treated as part of these large centres in this study. A total of 4,413 urban centres were used in this study, with a population of 24.9 million or 99.6% of Canada's estimated non-institutional 1986 population. These 4,413 centres were grouped into two different town sizings: 0-4K, 5-9K, 10-29K, 30-99K, 100-499K, 500K+ and 0-9K, 10-99K, 100K+. These groupings were used by Hodge and Qadeer (1983).

The personal taxation files contain records for all taxpayers each year including self employment income from fishing, farming, business, professional, commission, and rental sources[2]. In 1988, 2.6 million people reported self employment income compared to 2.2 in 1981. Since postal codes were introduced in the late 1970s, more 1981 records had uncoded postal codes. However, to facilitate inter-year comparisons, terminal year locations were used for both continuing personal and corporate taxfilers. About 12,000 records in 1988 (less than 1%) and 100,000 records in 1981 (about 5%) could not be linked to towns via postal codes. Further work using town name could lower this number.

The corporate tax files for 1981 contain 517,000 records, and 643,000 records for 1987 (Statistics Canada 1984, 1990). There were 6,854 records, with sales of $57 billion, unlinked to the towns file in 1981. There were 1,402 records, with sales of $42 billion (this was only 4% of the total 1987 sales) unlinked in 1987. Most of these were small foreign controlled branches with foreign mailing addresses.

---

1. See Detailed User Guide Postal Code Conversion File, January 1990 version for more information. This is available from Statistics Canada's Geography Division.

2. See Taxation Statistics, various years, Revenue Canada Taxation, Ottawa for more information.

To assess the impact of using terminal year locations for continuing records, it was found that 12% of the 1.2 million continuing self-employed taxfilers had changed towns, while only 5% of the 304,000 continuing corporate taxfilers had changed towns possibly because they changed taxation numbers when they changed location.

Businesses in towns fall into three main types: unincorporated self-employed businesses, small and medium size incorporated firms operating in one location, and large incorporated firms operating in several locations. The large numbers of small unincorporated businesses were not considered further. They will require a separate analysis. When using corporate taxation records, there is no way of splitting these large firms into the towns in which they operate, so they are excluded from the analysis. If they were coded to the headquarter's mailing address they would erroneously inflate activity in the headquarter's town and erroneously undercount the other towns in which they operate. As a result, an arbitrary size of $50 million sales in 1981 was picked as the cut-off for the large firm size boundary. Firms entering since 1981 are sized using their 1987 sales deflated to 1981 dollars. This was done by crudely assuming an average annual inflation rate of 5% over this period.

Overall, 1,306 large firms were excluded in 1987, which accounted for $473 billion revenue or 47% of total corporate revenues (Table 1). However, the study was still left to analyze 639,977 small and medium firms in 1987 with combined revenues of $541 billion or 53% of total corporate revenues[3]. Finally, franchise and parent-subsidiary relationships have not been accounted for in this study.

TABLE 1
Firms by sales size[a], Canada, 1987

Firm sales size $ million	Number of firms	Aggregate sales	
		$ billion	%
0 - 49	639,977	541	53
50 +	1,306	473	47
Total	641,283	1,014	100

a. Firms are sized as of 1981 except those newly identified which are sized as of 1987 but in 1981 dollars.

Source: Statistics Canada. Small Business and Special Surveys Division.

---

3. This study only includes forms with valid SIC codes, sales greater than $25,000 and assets greater than $50,000.

Another strand of analysis tracks all small and medium size corporations longitudinally between 1981 and 1987[4]. This is accomplished by using their taxation identification numbers. Firms in 1987 with I.D. numbers not present in 1981 are termed "newly-identified" and represent newly created firms or firms formed by merger. Conversely, firms in 1981 with I.D. numbers not present in 1987 are termed "no-longer-identified" and represent firms that have gone out of business or that have been acquired. Among those firms present in both years, a further breakdown is noted between those with growing or declining *real* sales between 1981 and 1987. These four categories of firm life status are analyzed by region and town size.

Analysis

Distribution of small and medium firms by town size, 1987 and change from 1981

Are small and medium size firms distributed among town sizes proportionately to the population located in these towns? Have small and medium enterprises (SMEs) grown evenly in all town sizes since 1981? Sales of SMEs in 1987 are over represented among the largest town-size group relative to their share of Canada's population and under represented in the two smaller town size groups (Figure 2 and Table 2). Towns over 100,000 had 60% of total population and 75% of SME sales, a 15 percentage point higher share. The smallest towns, those less than 10,000 population accounted for 22% of the population but only a 11% share of SME sales, a 11 percentage point difference.

TABLE 2

Distribution of small and medium size firms[a] and population[b] by town size[c], Canada, 1987

Town size	Towns			Firms		
		Population			Sales	
(,000)	Number	(,000)	%	Number	$ billion	%
0 - 9	4,235	5,534	22	98,602	59	11
10 - 99	151	4,415	18	105,068	76	14
100 +	27	15,144	60	436,307	406	75
Total	4,413	25,093	100	639,977	541	100

a. Firms are sized as of 1981 except those newly identified which are sized as of 1987 but in 1981 dollars; small and medium firms are those with sales less than $50,000,000.
b. Population is from 1986 Census of Population.
c. Towns are sized using 1986 Census of Population.

Source: Statistics Canada. Small Business and Special Surveys Division.

4. This approach was used when analyzing payrolls of firms longitudinally between 1978 and 1984; see cat. no. 18-501, Developing a Longitudinal Database on Businesses in the Canadian Economy: An Approach to the Study of Employment, Statistics Canada, Ottawa, 1988.

FIGURE 2

Distribution of SME sales and population by town size, Canada, 1987

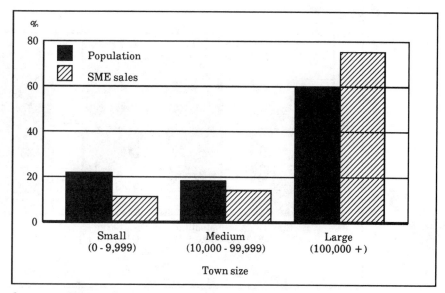

Source: Statistics Canada. Small Business and Special Surveys Division.

The growth of SME sales by town size between 1981 and 1987 is not only distributed unevenly in favour of the largest town size group, but SME sales of the largest towns grew about 16 percentage points more than those of the two smaller town size groups (Figure 3 and Table 3). Large town SME sales grew 77% between 1981 and 1988, whereas smaller town SME sales grew only about 60% over the same period.

TABLE 3

Small and medium size firms[a] by town size[b], Canada, 1981 and 1987

Town size (,000)	1987			1981			Sales growth, 1981 to 1987
	Number of firms	Sales		Number of firms	Sales		
		$ billion	%		$ billion	%	
0 - 9	98,602	59	11	75,998	37	12	61
10 - 99	105,068	76	14	89,040	48	15	59
100 +	436,307	406	75	343,641	230	73	77
Total	**639,977**	**541**	**100**	**508,679**	**315**	**100**	**72**

a. Firms are sized as of 1981 except those newly identified which are sized as of 1987 but in 1981 dollars; small and medium firms are those with sales less than $50,000,000.
b. Towns are sized using 1986 Census of Population.

Source: Statistics Canada. Small Business and Special Surveys Division.

FIGURE 3

SME sales growth by town size, Canada, 1981-1987

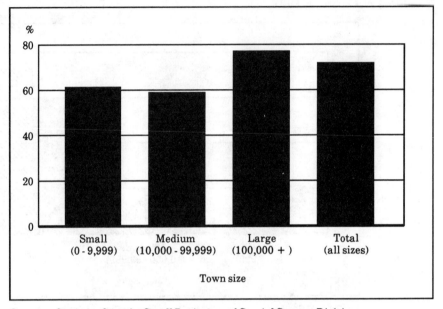

Town size

Source: Statistics Canada. Small Business and Special Surveys Division.

Small and medium size firm profitability by town size

Are SMEs located in smaller towns more or less profitable than those in large towns and has there been any change in the pattern between 1981 and 1987? A consistent pattern is evident between town size and SME profitability measured as the rate of profits before tax to sales (Figure 4a and Table 4). SMEs in larger towns are more profitable than those in smaller towns. In 1987, the SMEs of towns over 100K had profitability of 8% of sales compared with 6% for the medium size towns and only 5% in the smallest towns. Profits, while generally lower in 1981, still showed the same pattern as 1987.

FIGURE 4a

SME profitability levels by town size, Canada, 1987 and 1981

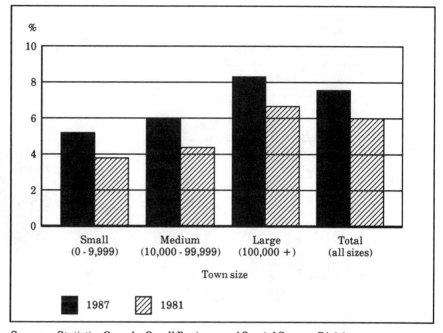

Source: Statistics Canada. Small Business and Special Surveys Division.

TABLE 4

Profitability[a] of small and medium size firms[b] by town size[c], 1981 and 1987

Town size (,000)	1987			1981			1987/1981 Profitability change %
	Sales $ billion	Profits $ billion	Profits /Sales %	Sales $ billion	Profits $ billion	Profits /Sales %	
0 - 9	59.3	3.1	5.2	36.8	1.4	3.8	37
10 - 99	75.5	4.5	6.0	47.6	2.1	4.4	36
100 +	406.0	33.9	8.3	229.7	15.3	6.7	24
Total	**540.8**	**41.5**	**7.7**	**314.1**	**18.8**	**6.0**	**28**

a. Profits are before tax and profitability is profits per dollar of sales.
b. Firms are sized as of 1981 except those newly identified which are sized as of 1987 but in 1981 dollars; small and medium firms are those with sales less than $50,000,000.
c. Towns are sized using 1986 Census of Population.

Source: Statistics Canada. Small Business and Special Surveys Division.

However, profitability grew faster (or bounced back more) between 1981 and 1987 for the two smaller town sizes than for the largest town size (Figure 4b). Profitability grew 37% for small towns and 36% for medium towns between 1981 and 1987, but only 24% for large towns.

FIGURE 4b

SME profitability growth by town size, Canada, 1981 to 1987

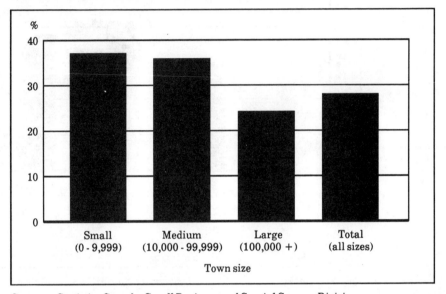

Source: Statistics Canada. Small Business and Special Surveys Division.

Small and medium size firm turnover by town size

As was outlined in the methodology section, each SME was matched between 1981 and 1987 to determine its life status over this period. Firms were assigned one of three statuses: continuing, newly-identified or no-longer identified. Those assigned continuing status were further subdivided according to whether their 1987 sales (converted to 1981 dollars) increased or declined from their 1981 sales. For example, the total block at the bottom of Table 5 shows that 303,633 firms existed in both years. These firms represented 63% of all SME sales in 1987 and 69% in 1981. While only 66,163 of these 303,633 (about 20%) experienced rising real sales over this period, this group nevertheless accounted for almost 72% of the whole continuing firm group's sales in 1987.

There were 336,344 firms newly-identified since 1981 and still active in 1987. Note that other firms that were created since 1981 and disappeared before 1987 are not reflected in these numbers. These 336,344 new firms accounted for 37% of 1987 sales. Counterbalancing this, 205,046 firms in 1981, representing 28% of 1981 sales disappeared before 1987. The last two columns of Table 5 show that, on balance, continuing firms accounted for 52% of the sales growth between 1981 and 1987 and that the combined newly-identified and no-longer-identified group accounted for the other 48%.

The aggregate sales of new firms (measured in terms of 1987 total sales) were slightly higher in large towns, at 39% of total sales, than those in small and medium size towns, which were each 36% of total sales (Figure 5a and Table 5). Looking at rates of firm disappearance by town size, large towns also had the highest rates at 33% of 1981 sales, while the medium town rate was 27% and the small town rate was 24%.

Even though large towns had the highest rates of newly and no-longer-identified firms, small towns had the highest net turnover rate differential (12 percentage points), compared to medium towns, (9 percentage points) and large size towns (6 percentage points). Thus although large towns have the highest turnover rates of both new and no-longer-identified firms, small towns have the largest net contribution from the turnover process.

FIGURE 5a

Importance of firm turnover by town size, Canada, 1987

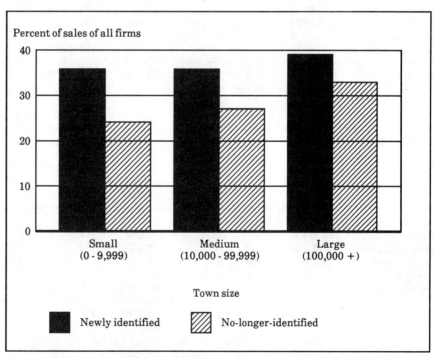

Source: Statistics Canada. Small Business and Special Surveys Division.

Growth of small and medium size business:
a rural-urban comparison

TABLE 5

Turnover of small and medium size firms[a] by town size[b], Canada 1981 and 1987

Town size (,000) and life status of firm	1987				1981				Sales change, 1981 to 1987	
	Number of firms	Sales $ billion	%	%	Number of firms	Sales $ billion	%	%	$ billion	%
0 - 9										
Continuing firms	50,517	38	64	100	50,517	29	76	100	9	43
– increasing sales[c]	9,809	22	37	58	9,809	9	24	31	13	-
– decreasing sales	40,708	16	27	42	40,708	20	52	69	-4	-
Newly identified	48,085	21	36	-	-	-	-	-	21	57
No-longer-identified	-	-	-	-	25,481	9	24	-	-9	-
Total	**98,602**	**59**	**100**	-	**75,998**	**38**	**100**	-	**21**	**100**
10 - 99										
Continuing firms	54,520	49	64	100	54,520	35	73	100	14	50
– increasing sales[c]	11,123	31	41	63	11,123	12	25	34	19	-
– decreasing sales	43,397	18	23	37	43,397	23	48	66	-5	-
Newly identified	50,548	27	36	-	-	-	-	-	27	50
No-longer-identified	-	-	-	-	34,520	13	27	-	-13	-
Total	**105,068**	**76**	**100**	-	**89,040**	**48**	**100**	-	**28**	**100**
100 +										
Continuing firms	198,596	246	61	100	198,596	153	67	100	93	53
– increasing sales[c]	45,231	174	43	71	45,231	59	26	38	115	-
– decreasing sales	153,365	72	18	29	153,365	94	41	62	-22	-
Newly identified	237,711	160	39	-	-	-	-	-	160	47
No-longer-identified	-	-	-	-	145,045	77	33	-	-77	-
Total	**436,307**	**406**	**100**	-	**343,641**	**230**	**100**	-	**176**	**100**
All town sizes										
Continuing firms	303,633	333	63	100	303,633	217	72	100	116	49
– increasing sales[c]	66,163	227	40	64	66,163	80	25	34	147	-
– decreasing sales	237,470	106	23	36	237,470	137	47	66	-31	-
Newly identified	336,344	208	37	-	-	-	-	-	208	51
No-longer-identified	-	-	-	-	205,046	99	28	-	-99	-
Total	**639,977**	**541**	**100**	-	**508,679**	**316**	**100**	-	**225**	**100**

a. Firms are sized as of 1981 except those newly identified which are sized as of 1987 but in 1981 dollars; small and medium firms are those with sales less than $50,000,000.

b Towns are sized using 1986 Census of Population.

c. Increasing and decreasing sales life status are computed using 1987 sales converted to 1981 dollars.

Source: Statistics Canada. Small Business and Special Surveys Division.

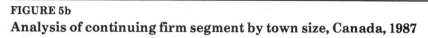

FIGURE 5b

Analysis of continuing firm segment by town size, Canada, 1987

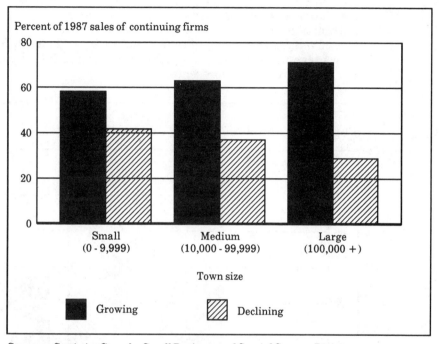

Source: Statistics Canada. Small Business and Special Surveys Division.

Looking at the relative contribution to overall sales growth of continuing versus the net turnover process (the right column of Table 5), each contributed roughly half to overall sales growth for all three town sizes. Also of note within the continuing firm group itself, that although increasing sales firms were fewer in number than the decreasing sales group, they nevertheless represented much higher sales shares in 1987 in all three town sizes (Figure 5b). This result increases with town size; in 1987 firms with increasing sales accounted for 58% of the sales of all continuing firms in small towns, 63% in medium towns and 71% in large towns.

The perspective is different however if 1981 is chosen to compare these firms. In 1981 these increasing sales firms accounted for only 31% in small towns, 34% in medium and 38% in large towns. Overall this just seems to illustrate the underlying upheaval within this continuing group of firms. Again this growth and decline can result from internal growth or decline, acquisition or divestiture activity.

Small and medium size firms by region and town size

To see if the national results are consistent across Canada, the country was divided into four broad regions[5]. Atlantic Canada had 9% of all population but only 5% of SME activity in 1987, while Quebec had 25% population and 26% SME activity, Ontario had 37% population and 43% SME activity and Western and Northern Canada had 29% population and 26% SME activity (Figure 6a and Table 6). Thus Ontario had a 6 percentage point greater share of SME activity, while the Atlantic and the West were under represented.

FIGURE 6a

Population and SME sales by region, 1987

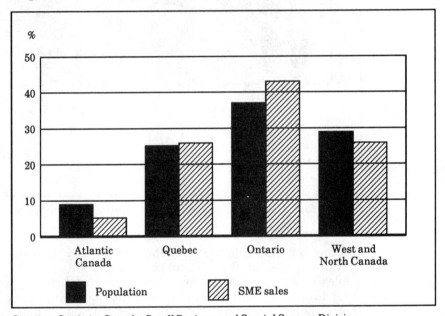

Source: *Statistics Canada. Small Business and Special Surveys Division.*

As for Canada, in each of the four regions' large towns, SME activity outweighs population, while the reverse (not shown graphically) is true for small towns. Of the four regions, Ontario had the highest portion of SME activity in large towns at 83% and Atlantic Canada had the lowest SME activity in large towns at 41%.

---

5.   This database can be tabulated into any geographic subsets that are of analytic interest.

TABLE 6

Small and medium size firms[a] and population[b] by region and town size[c], 1987

Region and town size(,000)	Towns			Small and medium size firms			SME sales per capita
		Population			Sales		
	Number	(,000)	%	Number	$ billion	%	($,000)
Atlantic Canada							
0 - 9	738	898	40	11,109	8	28	8.5
10 - 99	23	609	28	11,653	9	31	14.9
100 +	4	707	32	12,968	12	41	16.4
Total	765	2,214	100	35,730	29	100	12.8
Quebec							
0 - 9	978	1,420	23	26,111	18	13	12.7
10 - 99	3	1,016	16	23,591	19	14	26.3
100 +	5	3,823	61	104,164	101	73	26.3
Total	1,016	6,259	100	153,866	138	100	22.0
Ontario							
0 - 9	761	1,246	14	20,783	16	7	12.4
10 - 99	45	1,377	15	26,735	24	10	17.6
100 +	11	6,558	71	174,637	195	83	29.7
Total	817	9,181	100	222,155	235	100	25.5
West and North Canada							
0 - 9	1,758	1,790	25	40,600	18	13	10.1
10 - 99	50	1,413	19	43,089	23	16	16.3
100 +	7	4,056	56	144,538	99	71	24.5
Total	1,815	7,259	100	228,227	140	100	19.4
Canada							
0 - 9	4,235	5,354	26	98,603	60	15	10.9
10 - 99	121	3,400	20	105,068	75	18	18.8
100 +	27	15,144	55	436,307	407	67	24.2
Total	4,413	24,913	100	639,978	542	100	19.9

a. Firms are sized as of 1981 except those newly identified which are sized as of 1987 but in 1981 dollars; small and medium firms are those with sales less than $50,000,000.
b. Populations from 1986 Census of Population. (This accounts for 98.3 % of total official count of 25,300,000.)
c. Towns are sized using 1986 Census of Population.

Source: Statistics Canada. Small Business and Special Surveys Division.

FIGURE 6b

Population and SME sales for large towns by region, 1987

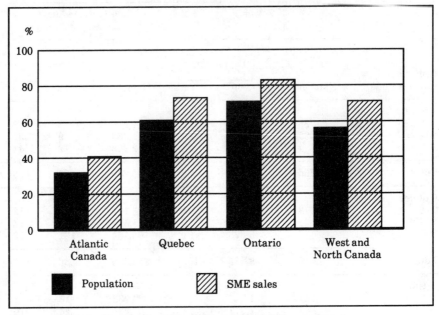

Source: *Statistics Canada. Small Business and Special Surveys Division.*

From a growth perspective, Ontario's large town SME sales growth was fully 20 percentage points higher than medium and small town growth (Figure 7 and Table 7). There was not much difference in SME growth between town sizes in the other three regions. Western and Northern Canada had considerably weaker growth than all other three regions over this period.

FIGURE 7

SME sales growth by region and town size, 1981 to 1987

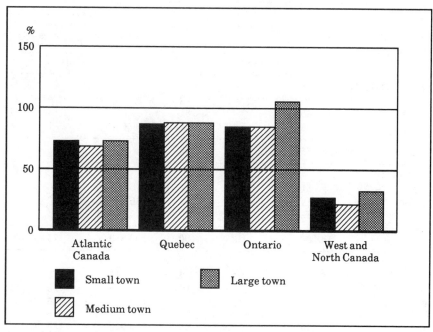

Source: *Statistics Canada. Small Business and Special Surveys Division.*

TABLE 7

Small and medium size firmsa by region and town sizeb, 1981 and 1987

Region and town size (,000)	1987			1981			Sales growth, 1981 to 1987
	Number of firms	Sales		Number of firms	Sales		
		$ billion	%		$ billion	%	%
Atlantic Canada							
0 - 9	11,109	8	28	8,342	4	25	73.0
10 - 99	11,653	9	31	9,672	5	31	69.0
100 +	12,968	12	41	10,609	7	44	73.0
Total	**35,730**	**29**	**100**	**28,623**	**16**	**100**	**72.0**
Quebec							
0 - 9	26,110	18	13	15,508	10	13	87.0
10 - 99	23,591	19	14	15,189	10	14	88.0
100 +	104,164	101	73	69,646	54	73	88.0
Total	**153,865**	**138**	**100**	**100,343**	**74**	**100**	**87.0**
Ontario							
0 - 9	20,783	16	7	15,588	8	7	85.0
10 - 99	26,735	24	10	21,225	13	11	85.0
100 +	174,637	195	83	133,103	95	82	105.0
Total	**222,155**	**235**	**100**	**169,916**	**116**	**100**	**101.0**
West and North Canada							
0 - 9	40,600	18	13	36,560	14	13	27.0
10 - 99	43,089	23	16	42,954	19	18	22.0
100 +	144,538	99	71	130,283	74	69	33.0
Total	**228,227**	**140**	**100**	**209,797**	**108**	**100**	**31.0**
Canada							
0 - 9	98,602	60	15	75,998	36	15	68.0
10 - 99	105,068	75	18	89,040	47	19	66.0
100 +	436,307	407	67	343,641	230	67	74.8
Total	**639,977**	**542**	**100**	**508,679**	**314**	**100**	**72.8**

a. Firms are sized as of 1981 except those newly identified which are sized as of 1987 but in 1981 dollars; small and medium firms are those with sales less than $50,000,000.
b. Towns are sized using 1986 Census of Population

Source: Statistics Canada. Small Business and Special Surveys Division.

Small and medium firms by industry and town size

Each firm in this database is coded industrially at the three-digit level
of the 1970 Standard Industrial Classification (Statistics Canada 1970).
However, for the purposes of the present study this detail is too fine and
firms have been split into just two broad sectors—the goods-producing[6]
industries and the service-producing[7] industries. As well, the
manufacturing sector was singled out for separate analysis because of
its importance.

Beginning with the goods-service analysis, 1987 SME output was split
2/3 in services and 1/3 in goods industries both at the national level and
roughly over all town sizes (Figure 8A and Table 8). Services are more
important the larger the town size, varying from 60% in small towns,
63% in medium to 67% in large towns.

FIGURE 8a

SME sales by industry and town size, Canada, 1987

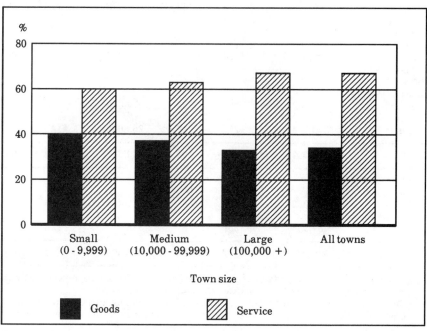

Source: *Statistics Canada. Small Business and Special Surveys Division.*

---

6.   Goods-producing industries covers Agriculture, Forestry, Fishing, Mining, Manufacturing,
     Construction and Major Group 4 of Division 7 (Electric Power, Gas and Water Utilities).

7.   Service-producing industries comprise the other 3 Major Groups of Division 7 namely Transportation,
     Storage and Communication as well as Retail and Wholesale Trade, Finance, Insurance and Real
     Estate and the Community, Business and Personal Service Industries. Public Administration and
     Defence is not covered in this study.

110
Growth of small and medium size business:
a rural-urban comparison

TABLE 8

Small and medium size firmsᵃ by industry sectorᵇ and town sizeᶜ, Canada, 1981 and 1987

Town size (,000) and Industry sector	1987			1981			Sales growth, 1981 to 1987
	Number of firms	Sales		Number of firms	Sales		
		$ billion	%		$ billion	%	%
0 - 9							
Goods-producing industry	33,991	24	40	26,311	15	41	58
Service-producing industry	64,611	36	60	49,687	22	59	64
Total	**98,602**	**60**	**100**	**75,998**	**37**	**100**	**61**
10 - 99							
Goods-producing industry	26,238	28	37	23,102	18	38	51
Service-producing industry	78,830	48	63	65,938	29	62	64
Total	**105,068**	**76**	**100**	**89,040**	**47**	**100**	**59**
100 +							
Goods-producing industry	91,803	134	33	74,039	83	36	63
Service-producing industry	344,504	272	67	269,602	147	64	85
Total	**436,307**	**406**	**100**	**343,641**	**230**	**100**	**77**
All towns in Canada							
Goods-producing industry	152,032	186	34	123,452	116	38	60
Service-producing industry	487,945	356	67	385,227	198	62	79
Total	**639,977**	**542**	**100**	**508,679**	**314**	**100**	**73**

a. Firms are sized as of 1981 except those newly identified which are sized as of 1987 but in 1981 dollars; small and medium firms are those with sales less than $50,000,000.
b. Goods-producing industries include primary, mining, manufacturing, construction and the utilities group of Division 7 (1970 SIC basis). Service-producing industries includes the remaining industries except public administration.
c. Towns are sized using 1986 Census of Population.

Source: Statistics Canada. Small Business and Special Surveys Division.

Service industries grew faster than goods industries in all three town sizes between 1981 and 1987 (Figure 8b). Note also that the growth differential rises with town size: 6 percentage points for small towns, 13 percentage points for medium towns and 22 percentage points for large towns.

FIGURE 8b

SME sales growth by industry and town size, Canada, 1981 to 1987

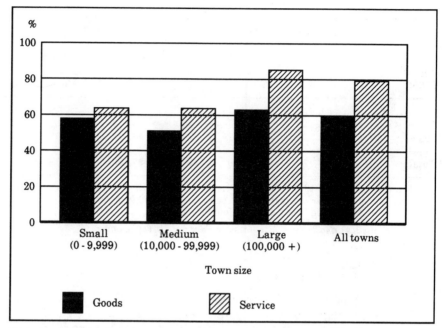

Source: Statistics Canada. Small Business and Special Surveys Division.

Manufacturing firms of all sizes had revenues of $315 billion in 1987. SMEs accounted for $110 billion of this revenue or about 1/3 of the total. The distribution of SME manufacturing activity among the three different town size groups is an almost exact mirror image of the all-industry SME distribution, 11% in small towns, 14% in medium towns, and 75% in large towns (Tables 3 and 9). Between 1981 and 1987 SME manufacturing grew 58% in both small and medium size towns, but grew 63%, or 5 percentage points faster in large towns.

TABLE 9

Small and medium size manufacturing firms[a] by town size[b], Canada,1981 and 1987

| Town size (,000) | 1987 | | | 1981 | | | Sales growth, 1981 to 1987 |
| | Number of firms | Sales | | Number of firms | Sales | | |
		$ billion	%		$ billion	%	%
0 - 9	6,371	12	11	5,134	8	12	58
10 - 99	6,442	16	14	5,414	10	14	58
100 +	33,257	82	75	26,645	51	74	63
Total	46,070	110	100	37,193	69	100	179

a. Firms are sized as of 1981 except those newly identified which are sized as of 1987 but in 1981 dollars; small and medium firms are those with sales less than $50,000,000.
b. Towns are sized using 1986 Census of Population.

Source: Statistics Canada. Small Business and Special Surveys Division.

Conclusion

Small and medium size enterprises (SMEs) in Canada account for 53% of aggregate sales by all incorporated firms in Canada. Unincorporated businesses and large corporate firms (with sales of $50 million or more) were not included in this study.

Relative to the distribution of population, SME sales are more concentrated in centres with a population of 100,000 or more. SME sales in these centres showed more growth during 1981-1987 compared to SMEs in smaller centres. Although SMEs in larger centres were more profitable in both 1981 and 1987, SME profitability bounced back more in centres with population under 100,000. "Newly identified" firms from 1981 to 1987 accounted for a large share of sales in centres of all sizes. However, since "no-longer-identified" firms were less frequent in centres of 10,000 or less, the turnover had a significant and positive impact on business activity in these small centres. SMEs in larger centres were more concentrated in the service sector and the service sector in larger centres grew more during 1981-1987.

The databases used in this study are ideally suited for both small area and longitudinal analysis. Further work could focus on the fastest and slowest growing towns or the fastest growing industries in small towns. Numerous recent reports on rural and small town Canada suggest that such research would be warranted (Leitch 1990; Science Council of Canada 1990a and 1990b; Morris 1990; Economic Council of Canada 1990).

J.S. McVey
Small Business and Special Surveys Division
Statistics Canada
Ottawa K1A 0T6

References

Economic Council of Canada. 1990. From the Bottom-up The
  Community Economic Development Approach (22 170). Ottawa:
  Economic Council of Canada.

Leitch, Carolyn. 1990. Tech in the towns. Globe and Mail,
  Sept. 11: B7.

Morris, Chris. 1990. The move is out: small towns' lifestyle benefits
  targeted at corporate Canada. The Citizen, Oct. 7: B10.

Science Council of Canada. 1990a. Firing up the Technology
  Engine: Stategies for Community Economic Development.
  Ottawa: Supply and Services Canada.

Science Council of Canada. 1990b. Grassroots Initiatives, Global
  Success. Ottawa: Supply and Services Canada.

Hodge and Qadeer. 1983. Towns and Villages in Canada: The
  Importance of Being Unimportant. Toronto: Buttersworth.

Statistics Canada. 1970. Standard Industrial Classification Manual.
  Revised 1970 (cat. no. 12-501). Ottawa: Statistics Canada.

Statistics Canada. 1984. Corporation Financial Statistics 1981,
  (cat. no. 61-207). Ottawa: Statistics Canada.

Statistics Canada. 1988a. Urban and Rural Areas, Canada,
  Provinces and Territories, Part 1. In the 1986 Census of Canada
  series, (cat. no. 94-129). Ottawa: Statistics Canada.

Statistics Canada. 1988b. Census Metropolitan Areas and
  Census Agglomerations, Part 2. In the 1986 Census of Canada
  series, (cat. no. 94-128). Ottawa: Statistics Canada.

Statistics Canada. 1990. Corporation Financial Statistics 1987,
  (cat. no. 61-207). Ottawa: Statistics Canada.

5

The importance of the agriculture sector to the Canadian economy: an input-output analysis

Paul J. Thomassin

Summary

The Statistics Canada input-output model indicates that both the agriculture and food processing sectors have strong linkages to other sectors of the economy.

A $100 million increase in final demand for primary agriculture products would result in an increase of industrial output by $185.4 million, GDP at factor cost by $85.7 million, and employment by 2,850 jobs. A change in demand for food process products of $100 million would result in an increase of industrial output by $205.6 million, GDP at factor cost by $83.6 million, and employment by 1,848.

Gull Lake, Saskatchewan

The importance of the agriculture sector to the Canadian economy: an input-output analysis

Paul J. Thomassin

Introduction

The Canadian economy is made up of many industrial sectors which produce goods and services. These goods and services are used either as inputs into the production of other goods and services (intermediate demand) or are consumed by individuals or industries as final demand. The flow of goods and services between industrial sectors and final demand categories provides a means of investigating the relationship between industrial sectors in the economy. These inter-industry transactions can be used to measure the importance of a particular industrial sector to the economy.

This paper uses the input-output framework to investigate the inter-industry relationships between agriculture and the food processing industries with other industries in the economy. The following section of the paper introduces the 1986 input-output model which is used in the analysis. The next section estimates the importance of the agriculture and food processing sectors to the Canadian economy. Their importance is measured by industrial output, gross domestic product (GDP) at factor cost[1], and employment. The linkages between industrial outputs and inputs going into the agriculture and food processing sectors are also analyzed. The next section estimates the impact on the Canadian economy of an exogenous change in the demand for commodities produced by the agriculture and food processing sectors.

---

1. Gross domestic product at factor cost, or value added, is equal to total sales (gross output) less inputs of goods and services that were purchased (intermediate inputs). The term "gross" indicates that costs associated with the depletion of capital assets (buildings, machinery and equipment) have not been netted out. The expression "at factor cost" means that production is valued at the cost of the factors such as labour and capital, excludes indirect taxes but includes subsidies.

The input-output model framework

Input-output models are based on a set of accounting data. The data estimate three relationships: the value of inputs used in the production process; the value of output produced by each industrial sector; and the value of goods and services consumed by final demand categories. For example, the model estimates the value of all inputs going into the agriculture industry, such as feed, fuel, and seed. The value of agriculture output (grains, live animals, and other agriculture products) is also estimated. The output produced by the agriculture industry is either sold to other industrial sectors, as an input into their industrial process, or is consumed by final demand categories. For example, the grain produced by the agriculture sector is sold to industrial sectors, such as feed mills or the flour industry as an intermediate input, or is exported to the world market. The model measures the dollar flows for each of the industrial inputs and outputs. These flows estimate the degree of inter-industry relationship among the industrial sectors.

The model used in the analysis is the 1986 Statistics Canada medium level input-output model (Statistics Canada 1990). It uses a rectangular framework of commodities and industries to measure the inter-industry relationships. The number of commodities is larger than the number of industries. This allows any industrial sector to produce more than one commodity. This type of accounting framework is particularly useful for the agriculture industry because this industry produces more than one commodity. The rectangular accounting framework is also useful for identifying the various commodities used as inputs into the production process.

The values in the input-output model are in producer prices. These prices estimate the value of the commodity at the industry gate or farm gate for agriculture. They do not include any margins for retail, wholesale, storage, etc. Seven margins are included in the model as separate commodities. Given this relationship, the producer prices plus the value of the margins is equal to purchaser prices. Purchaser prices would be equivalent to prices paid by the consumer.

The Statistics Canada medium level model contains 100 commodities and 50 industrial sectors. It has one agriculture sector and three food and beverage processing sectors; three primary agriculture commodities (grains, live animals, and other agriculture products) and twelve processed food commodities.

The agriculture and food and beverage processing sectors

The agriculture sector produced $23.6 billion of industrial output in 1986. The GDP at factor cost from this industrial output was $11.1 billion (Table 1) which represents approximately 3% of the total GDP of the economy. The agriculture and food processing sectors combined account for approximately 8% of the industrial output, 6% of GDP at factor cost, and 8% of employment in the Canadian economy.

TABLE 1

Industrial output, GDP at factor cost, and employment for selected industries in the Canadian economy, 1986

	Industrial output ($ Billion)	GDP at factor cost ($ Billion)	Employment (number of jobs) (,000s)
Agriculture	23.6	11.1	488.8
Food processing	35.2	9.5	194.4
Beverage industry	5.4	2.3	31.7
Tobacco industry	1.7	0.6	7.0
Total ag-food system	65.9	23.5	721.9
Canadian economy	783.2	367.8	8,561.7

Source: Statistics Canada. *The Input-Output Structure of the Canadian Economy 1986*. (cat. no. 15-201).

The agriculture sector's contribution to the economy is evident in the inter-industry relationships with other industrial sectors. Of the three primary agriculture commodities in the model the agriculture sector produced 100% of the grains and live animals and 99% of the other agriculture products. The agriculture sector produced $6 billion of grain products. Twenty two percent of this commodity was used as an input by the agriculture sector and an additional 19% was used by the other food and beverage processing industries. In total approximately 41% of the grain output is used as intermediate demand in the Canadian economy. The remaining grain output is used by final demand categories of which exports are the major component (Table 2).

TABLE 2

Supply and disposition of the primary agriculture commodities, 1986. (Values are in producer prices)

	Make (Supply)	Intermediate use		Final demand categories			Other final demand	Total
		Agric.	Ag-food[a] system	Con-sumer expend.	Ex-ports	Im-ports		
		($ Billions)						
Grains	6.03	1.30	1.16	0.00	2.57	-0.11	1.08	6.00[b]
Live animals	6.62	0.47	5.48	0.18	0.35	-0.17	-0.02	6.29[b]
Other agriculture products	9.89	2.88	4.28	2.72	0.99	-1.73	0.36	9.50[b]

a. The ag-food system includes the following industries: food processing, beverage, and tobacco industries.

b. Difference between the make values and the total use values are the intermediate demand for these commodities by other industrial sectors.

Source: Statistics Canada. The Input-Output Structure of the Canadian Economy 1986. (cat. no. 15-201)

The intermediate demand for live animals is larger than for grain products. Almost 84% of the live animal output is used by the agriculture sector or the food and beverage sectors. The major use of live animals by the agriculture sector is as feeder cattle, starter pigs, and broilers. The food system uses live animals in such industries as the meat and poultry processing industries. The exports of live animals is the largest use by the final demand categories. It accounts for approximately 5% of the total output value of live animals (Table 2).

Approximately 72% of the output of "other agriculture products" is used by the intermediate demand of the agriculture and food and beverage sectors. This again indicates a strong link between the agriculture sector and other sectors in the economy. The large value of imports of these commodities can be explained by the imports of fruit and vegetables (Table 2).

The supply and disposition of the agriculture sector's output indicates strong ties between agriculture and other sectors in the Canadian economy. These ties are particularly strong with the food and beverage processing sectors. This would suggest that the inter-industry linkages between the two are important for analyzing the impact of an increase or decrease in the demand for the products produced by these industries.

The agriculture and food and beverage industries allocate a larger percent of their total costs to intermediate inputs than the average for the Canadian economy (Table 3). Intermediate inputs are purchases from other industrial sectors. Primary inputs include the value added elements of the economy such as wages and salaries, and net income to unincorporated businesses. The large share of the agriculture and food sectors' intermediate costs emphasizes the magnitude of inter-industry relationships between the agri-food sectors and other sectors in the economy.

TABLE 3

Allocation of input costs for selected industries, 1986. (As a percent of total costs)

	Intermediate inputs	Primary inputs
Agriculture	0.59	0.41
Food processing	0.70	0.27[a]
Beverage industry	0.52	0.46[a]
Tobacco industry	0.61	0.38[a]
Canadian economy (average)	0.48	0.50[a]

a.   The sum of the rows do not add to 1.0 because of suppressed confidential data.

Source: *Statistics Canada.* *The Input-Output Structure of the Canadian Economy 1986.* *(cat. no. 15-201).*

Impact on the Canadian economy of an increase in the demand for commodities produced by the agriculture and food system

The input-output model is useful for estimating the macroeconomic impact of an increase in the demand for commodities. The model uses the accounting framework to estimate the inter-industry relationships within the economy (see Appendix 1). This allows the analyst to estimate the impact on the economy of an increase in one industry's output.

Macroeconomic impacts are measured as direct and indirect effects. The direct effect measures the change in demand for the original industrial sector. The indirect effect measures the increase in industrial output by all other industries needed to satisfy the increase in demand for intermediate inputs by the original industrial sector. For example, an increase in the demand for bread (a direct effect) requires the bakery industry to buy more flour from the milling industry. The milling industry would purchase more wheat from the agriculture sector, which would purchase additional inputs such as fertilizer to grow the wheat. The model estimates the direct increase in bread output plus the indirect impact of this increase in industrial output on the economy.

The model was used to estimate the impact of an increase in demand for two scenarios[2]. The first scenario estimated the impact of an increase in the final demand for primary agriculture products while the second scenario estimated the impact of an increase in final demand for food products. The demand vectors are given in Table 4. Each of the demand vectors were converted from purchaser prices to producer prices before the model was used to estimate the impacts.

The final demand vectors were estimated taking into consideration the current consumption by final demand categories of primary agriculture and food products. The increase in demand for grains and live animals would be from the export markets. While the demand for other agriculture products, such as fruits and vegetables, would be from personal expenditures. The second demand vector indicates an increase in the demand for processed food products. Most of this increased demand would be from the domestic market from consumer expenditures.

TABLE 4

Increase in final demand vectors for scenario one and two

		Scenario 1[a] Primary agriculture products	Scenario 2[a] Food products
Commodities:		($ Millions)	
1.	Grains	59	0
2.	Live animals	6	0
3.	Other agriculture products	35	0
14.	Meat products	0	34
15.	Dairy products	0	23
17.	Fruit and veg. preparations	0	12
18.	Feeds	0	2
20.	Breakfast cereals and bakery	0	13
22.	Miscellaneous food products	0	6
Total hypothesized increase in demand		**100**	**100**

a. The values given in the table are in purchaser prices. These were converted to producer prices before the model was used to estimate the impact.

The impact on the Canadian economy of an increase in final demand from these two scenarios is given in Table 5. The direct plus indirect effect on the economy of scenario one was an increase in industrial output by $185.4 million, GDP at factor cost by $85.7 million, and employment by 2,850 jobs. The impact of the change in final demand for food products was an increase in industrial output by $205.6 million, GDP at factor cost by $83.6 million, and employment by 1,848 jobs. The

2. The impact matrix used to estimate the impacts of the two scenarios was published in Statistics Canada (1990).

impact on industrial output was larger for the change in food products than for primary agriculture commodities because a larger amount of inter-industry transaction exists for the food processor sector. The food processing industry allocates 70% of its costs to intermediate inputs (Table 3). In comparison, the agriculture sector allocates 59%. This suggests that the food processing sector purchases more inputs to produce its output than does the agriculture sector.

TABLE 5

Macroeconomic impact on the Canadian economy of a $100 million increase in the final demand for products of the agriculture and food system, scenarios one and two

	Industrial output ($ Millions)	GDP at factor cost ($ Millions)	Employment[a] (number of jobs)
Scenario 1 Direct + indirect effects	185.4	85.7	2,850
Scenario 2 Direct + indirect effects	205.6	83.6	1,848

a.   Includes self-employed, paid and unpaid family workers.

The impact on GDP at factor cost was larger for the agriculture sector than the food processing sector because the agriculture sector allocates more of its costs to primary inputs (such as labour) than does the food processing sector (Table 3).

The employment figures are significantly higher for the primary agriculture vector compared to the process food final demand because the employment estimates include self-employed, paid and unpaid family workers. The agriculture sector has the highest number of unpaid workers in the economy. If the estimates included only paid employment the number of jobs created with the primary agriculture impact would be 1,456. The paid employment with the increase in final demand for food products was 1,359. These estimates indicate that no significant difference in the paid employment impact exists between the two scenarios.

The estimated impacts include only the direct and indirect effects on the economy. They do not include the impact of increased consumer spending as industrial output is increased. This increase in consumer spending is the induced effect. Since the direct plus indirect effects do not take the induced effect into account, the impacts presented should be considered as an under estimate.

Conclusion

The Statistics Canada medium level input-output model is useful for investigating the inter-industry relationships in the Canadian economy. This model indicates that both the agriculture and food processing sectors have strong linkages to other industrial sectors. These linkages would suggest that increases in the industrial output produced by the agri-food sectors would have positive impacts on the other industrial sectors in the economy.

A $100 million increase in final demand for primary agriculture products resulted in the following increases: industrial output by $185.4 million, GDP at factor cost by $85.7 million, and employment by 2,850 jobs. A change in demand for food process products of $100 million resulted in the following increases: industrial output by $205.6 million, GDP at factor cost by $83.6 million, and employment by 1,848. A large increase in employment occurred in the primary agriculture scenario because the employment numbers included self-employed, paid and unpaid family workers. Including only paid jobs would decrease this number by 1,376 jobs.

The input-output model provides a framework to estimate the inter-industry linkages in the economy. The model can be improved to better address questions related to agriculture policy and rural development. The one agriculture sector could be expanded to consider the diversity of farm types. This would enable a detailed examination of the inter-industry linkages between farm types and other sectors in the economy. To better indicate the impact on the rural economy, the information on industrial sectors could be expanded. The information could include the number of firms in each sector located in either rural or urban areas. This could be used to indicate where the economic growth would take place. Finally, input-output models could be developed for provincial and sub-provincial regions. These models would be useful to estimate the impact of changes in final demand on a regional and rural basis. The impacts would measure changes in industrial output, GDP at factor cost, and employment. Such models would be extremely helpful for assessing the impact of rural development policies.

Paul J. Thomassin
Department of Agricultural Economics
McGill University
Ste. Anne de Bellevue, Québec
H9X 1C0

Appendix 1

The rectangular input-output model and accounting framework

A detailed description and derivation of the model can be found in Statistics Canada (1984) and chapter 5 of Miller and Blair (1985). A rectangular accounting framework is used for the model where the number of commodities is larger than the number of industries.

The accounting framework documents the supply and disposition of commodities in the economy and is composed of five matrices (Figure 1):

U	-	the intermediate input matrix by industry
YI	-	the primary input matrix by industry
V	-	the make or output matrix
F	-	the final demand matrix
YF	-	the primary inputs going into final demand

FIGURE 1

The Input-Output Tableau

	Commodities	Industries	Final demand	Total
COMMODITIES		U	F	q
INDUSTRIES	V			g
PRIMARY INPUTS		YI	YF	
TOTAL	q'	g'		

Where:

NC	=	number of commodities
NI	=	number of industries
NY	=	number of primary inputs
NF	=	number of final demand categories
V	=	is a NI * NC order matrix showing the value of gross domestic output of industries by commodities
U	=	is a NC * NI order matrix showing the value of commodities used by industries as current inputs
F	=	is a NC * NF order matrix showing the value of commodities used by the final demand categories
YI	=	is a NY * NI order matrix showing the value of primary inputs used by industries

YF = is a NY * NF order matrix showing the value of primary inputs used in final demand categories

q = is a NC * 1 vector which shows the values of total commodity outputs

g = is a NI * 1 vector which shows the values of total industrial outputs

Manipulation of the accounting framework

The accounting framework provides a number of relationships which can be used to estimate the total impact on the economy of a change in demand for goods produced. The first outlines the disposition of commodities by industry in the production process and by categories of final demand.

| The value of total commodity outputs | = | Value of intermediate demand for commodities | + | Value of final demand for commodities |

(1) $q = U \cdot i + F \cdot i$

The second relationship outlines the domestic supply of commodities by industry.

| The total value of industrial outputs | = | The summation of the value of the industrial outputs by commodity |

(2) $g = V \cdot i$

The following assumptions were made concerning the industrial technology or industrial processes used in the model. The first is that inputs used by each industry are proportional to the output produced by that industry.

(3) $U = B\hat{g}$ where: B is a NC * NI matrix of technical coefficients relating inputs to output.

The second assumption is that the demand for domestically produced commodities is allocated among industries according to fixed market shares. This can be defined by:

(4) $V = D\hat{q}$ where: D is a NI * NC matrix of market share coefficients.

Taking these relationships, (1) through (4), it is possible to estimate the industrial output required for a given level of final demand.

Taking equation   (2) $g = V{\cdot}i$ Substituting for $V{\cdot}i$, eq. (4):

                      (5) $g = Dq$ Substituting for q, eq. (1):

                      (6) $g = D(U{\cdot}i + F{\cdot}i)$ Substituting for U, eq. (3):

                      (7) $g = D(Bg + F{\cdot}i)$ Rewriting:

                      (8) $g = (I\text{-}DB)^{-1} DF{\cdot}i$

Equation 8 provides an estimate of the industrial sector's output needed to satisfy the final demand.

Leakages in the economy

In the above development of the model, the final demand for commodities is treated as a single matrix (F). This matrix can be disaggregated into a number of categories.

$$(9) \quad F = f + E + X - A - W - Y$$

Where:

f = is a NC * 1 vector of the values of final demand excluding exports, re-exports, imports, government production and withdrawals from inventory

E = is a NC * 1 vector of the value of re-exports

X = is a NC * 1 vector of the value of commodity exports

A = is a NC * 1 vector of the value of commodity imports

W = is a NC * 1 vector of the value of inventory withdrawals

Y = is a NC * 1 vector of the value of government production of commodities.

Leakages in the economy will occur when imports, inventory withdrawals and government production are used to supply commodities into the intermediate inputs and final demand sectors of the economy. To take these leakages into account, the following assumption was made: that the amount of each commodity represented by imports, withdrawals from inventory and government production is a fixed proportion of the domestic commodities demanded. Putting this assumption into matrix notation:

128
The importance of the agriculture sector to the Canadian economy:
an input-output analysis

$$(10) \quad A = \hat{\mu} \ (Bg + f + E)$$
$$(11) \quad W = \beta \ (Bg + f + X)$$
$$(12) \quad Y = \alpha \ (Bg + f + X)$$

Where:

$\hat{\mu}$ = is a NC * NC diagonal matrix of coefficients whose elements are a ratio of imports to commodity used

β = is a NC * NC diagonal matrix of coefficients whose elements are a ratio of inventory withdrawals to commodity used

α = is a NC * NC diagonal matrix of coefficients whose elements are a ratio of government production to commodity use

It is now possible to determine the industry impacts of changes in final demand for commodities produced in the economy taking into account the leakages which occur.

From equation $\qquad$ (7), $\quad g = D(Bg + F \cdot i)$

Substituting for F, A, W, and Y.

$$(13) \ g = [I - D(I - \hat{\mu} - \beta - \alpha) B]^{-1} D[(I - \hat{\mu} - \beta - \alpha) f + (I - \hat{\mu}) E + (I - \beta - \alpha)X]$$

Equation 13 estimates the industrial output which would be required to satisfy the change in final demand for the economy.

References

Miernyk, W.H. 1965. The Elements of Input-Output Analysis. New York: Random House.

Miller, R.E. and P.D. Blair. 1985. Input-Output Analysis: Foundations and Extensions. Englewood Cliffs, New Jersey: Prentice-Hall Inc.

Statistics Canada. 1984. The Input-Output Structure of the Canadian Economy 1971-80, (cat. no. 15-201). Ottawa: Statistics Canada.

Statistics Canada. 1990. The Input-Output Structure of the Canadian Economy 1986, (cat. no. 15-201). Ottawa: Statistics Canada.

Syed, Aftab. 1985. The input-output structure of agriculture in Canada. In Agricultural Sector Models for Policy Analysis, edited by Z. Hassan and H.B. Huff. Ottawa: Agriculture Canada.

6

Workers in the urban shadow

Robert Parenteau and Louise Earl

Summary

One third of the rural population in Canada lives in the rural fringe of Census Metropolitan Areas (CMAs) and Census Agglomerations (CAs). The population living in the rural fringes of the 5 CMAs considered in this study showed strong growth between 1971 and 1986.

The proportion of women aged 15 and older in white-collar jobs is high, with a strong predominance of "clerical support" jobs. As a result, the proportion of women aged 15 and older in the blue-collar category is very low (often under 6%).

The female to male earnings ratio in white-collar occupations is the same as in blue-collar occupations, except in the Windsor metropolitan area where unions have a stronger influence in closing the gap between women's and men's earnings. However, there is a marked disparity between women's average incomes in the urbanized core and the rural fringe, with the situation of women relatively better in the urbanized core than in the rural fringe.

Turning to education, the percentage of women with some postsecondary education in the urbanized core is 6 to 8 percentage points higher than in the rural fringe. In general men living in the urbanized core have more education (i.e. some postsecondary training) than men living in the rural fringe.

Family income is higher for families living in the urbanized core than for families living in the rural fringe; female lone-parent families are an exception.

Table of contents

Workers in the urban shadow

Robert Parenteau and Louise Earl

1.   Introduction

An article titled "Le monde rural se reprend en main" in the Le Droit on September 19, 1990 said:

> Rural decline requires that we take control of our affairs...We must clearly recognize the decline in our way of life; however, rural residents are excluded from the benefits of this knowledge and prosperity. (Adaptation)

Does this gloomy outlook apply to all of Canada's rural population or only to the rural farm population?

Census data indicate that the rural farm population is shrinking; the rural non-farm population is growing; 80% of total population growth is occurring in urban areas; and one third of the rural population lives in the rural fringes of urban areas.

This paper will study a sample of the population living in the rural fringes of specific urban centres. The information is from the 1971, 1981 and 1986 Censuses of Population databases. The 1976 Census is not included because it lacks the question on income.

It proved extremely difficult to analyze the rural fringe population of all large urban centres. Therefore, 5 large urban centres were selected, based on a study of the proportion of the population aged 15 and older living in the rural fringes of each census metropolitan area (CMA)[1]. The 5 CMAs are St. John's, Newfoundland; Halifax, Nova Scotia; Chicoutimi-Jonquière, Québec; Windsor, Ontario and Sudbury, Ontario.

---

1.   A CMA is the main labour market area of an urban area (the urbanized core) of at least 100,000 population, based on the previous census. Smaller labour market areas, centred on urbanized cores of at least 10,000 population are census agglomerations (CAs).

TABLE 1

Distribution of population, (aged 15 and older) living in CMAs, by urbanized core, urban fringe and rural fringe 1971, 1981 and 1986

	Urbanized core			Urban fringe			Rural fringe		
	1971 %	1981 %	1986 %	1971 %	1981 %	1986 %	1971 %	1981 %	1986 %
St. John's	76.6	72.4	82.2	3.7	13.2	5.8	19.7	14.4	11.8
Halifax	86.8	81.3	81.7	4.4	1.5	0.4	8.8	17.2	17.9
Saint John	85.6	82.2	75.9	6.4	1.8	1.9	8.0	16.0	22.2
Chicoutimi- Jonquière	82.9	82.7	81.4	11.4	1.1	1.8	5.7	16.2	16.8
Québec	87.0	91.8	90.6	10.2	0.3	0.3	2.8	7.9	9.1
Sherbrooke	100.0	86.2	83.0	--	--	--	--	13.8	17.0
Trois-Rivières	96.8	93.6	83.3	21.0	--	1.6	1.2	6.4	15.1
Montréal	93.2	94.2	97.0	5.8	3.4	0.6	1.0	2.4	2.4
Ottawa-Hull	90.1	86.8	88.3	4.4	3.6	1.2	5.4	9.7	10.5
Oshawa	92.8	95.0	86.5	4.5	--	1.7	2.7	5.0	11.7
Toronto	90.7	95.5	92.4	7.8	1.4	2.6	1.6	3.1	5.0
Hamilton	86.3	92.5	92.6	7.1	--	--	6.6	7.5	7.4
St. Catharines- Niagara	40.2	91.0	84.9	59.8	1.4	4.4	--	7.6	10.6
Kitchener	66.9	92.8	93.2	27.7	2.8	2.8	5.4	4.4	4.1
London	78.1	92.1	89.3	11.6	--	0.6	10.3	7.9	10.1
Windsor	84.7	88.1	87.0	5.1	2.4	2.3	10.2	9.5	10.7
Sudbury	64.2	75.8	83.1	22.5	14.7	7.6	15.4	9.6	9.4
Thunder Bay	97.0	90.8	89.5	--	--	--	3.0	9.2	10.5
Winnipeg	98.0	96.6	95.3	0.2	--	--	1.8	3.4	4.7
Regina	99.1	99.0	94.2	--	--	1.4	0.9	1.0	4.4
Saskatoon	100.0	100.0	89.6	--	--	2.7	--	--	7.8
Calgary	100.0	100.0	95.2	--	--	2.0	--	--	2.8
Edmonton	92.4	91.7	88.2	3.4	2.8	2.8	4.1	5.5	9.0
Vancouver	86.6	90.4	91.6	6.1	4.4	3.8	7.4	5.2	4.6
Victoria	84.9	90.4	91.6	4.1	4.3	1.3	10.9	5.3	7.0

Source: Statistics Canada. Censuses of Population 1971, 1981 and 1986.

2.   Geographic concepts

The "main labour market" concept was first used to delineate CMAs in the 1971 Census. The main labour market corresponds to an area of daily migration (i.e. an area from which a large number of residents may travel daily to a workplace located in the main built-up area). Since no data on commuting were available in 1971, labour market areas were delineated using other criteria.

Beginning with the 1976 Census, commuting data have been used for CMA delineation. In the 1981 Census, delineation criteria were unchanged from 1976, except for conversion to the metric system. A few changes were made to CMA boundaries to reflect new municipal limits. In the 1986 Census, although the basic concept was the same, there were sweeping changes in the way the criteria were applied.

We did not compare data on the geographical limits of a single reference year; the populations of the 5 selected CMAs are examined on the geographical limits used to define the CMA in each Census year.

A CMA may consist of three parts: urbanized core, urban fringe and rural fringe, defined as follows.

Urbanized core: Large urban area around which a CMA is delineated.

Urban fringe: Urban area within a CMA, but outside of the urbanized core.

Rural fringe: All territory within a CMA lying outside of the urban areas.

"Urban areas" are continuously built-up areas with a population of 1,000 or more and a population density of 400 or more per square kilometre based on the previous census. A "rural area" is any territory outside urban areas.

3.   Population in the 5 selected CMAs

In 1971, in the 5 selected CMAs, 11% of the population aged 15 and older lived in the rural fringe; in 1986 the comparable figure was close to 14%. Women as a percentage of total population are similar for both the rural fringe and urban core (51% of the total population).

The total population of the 5 selected CMAs increased almost 13% between 1971 and 1986, composed of an 18% increase for the urbanized cores, a 35% increase for the rural fringes and a drop of more than 61% for the urban fringes. The change in definition of a CMA is obviously an important factor. During the same period, total land area nearly doubled (Table 2).

TABLE 2
Area of selected CMAs, 1971, 1981 and 1986

CMA	1971 (km²)	1981 (km²)	1986 (km²)
St. John's	838.0	1,127.5	1,130.0
Halifax	692.7	2,508.1	2,508.1
Chicoutimi-Jonquière	421.7	1,132.5	1,723.3
Windsor	820.8	768.9	861.7
Sudbury	1,531.2	2,379.8	2,612.1

Source: Statistics Canada. Censuses of Population, 1971, 1981 and 1986.

For the rural fringe of the St. John's CMA, both the male and female population declined in percentage between 1971 and 1986 (Table 3). Only the group aged 25-34 registered an increase. In contrast to the situation in the St. John's metropolitan area, the Halifax CMA population in the rural fringe rose sharply and the urbanized core registered population growth for all age groups (Table 4). The Chicoutimi-Jonquière CMA was similar to Halifax in that the rural fringe population increased very rapidly (Table 5). In the Windsor area, the population remained stable between 1971 and 1986 (Table 6). However, population figures for the younger age groups fell in all parts of the Windsor CMA, with the exception of men in the rural fringe.

Of the 5 CMAs studied, only Sudbury registered population decreases in both the urban and rural fringes for all age groups (except the 65 and older group in the rural fringe) (Table 7). The Sudbury population aged 15-24 declined everywhere except in the urbanized core. The senior population of the Sudbury area is growing rapidly.

TABLE 3

Percent change in population within each age and gender group, St. John's, 1971 to 1986

	15+	15-24	25-34	35-64	65+
CMA					
T	36.4	12.0	67.3	36.8	48.9
M	34.7	14.4	60.1	34.8	45.9
F	38.0	9.9	74.9	38.7	51.0
Urban core					
T	46.6	21.9	74.7	47.6	63.3
M	45.8	25.5	67.8	46.0	64.5
F	47.4	18.6	81.9	49.1	62.1
Urban fringe					
T	112.0	78.4	227.7	97.1	75.0
M	117.0	101.1	219.7	95.0	74.4
F	107.4	57.7	242.1	97.7	78.4
Rural fringe					
T	-18.0	-37.6	11.6	-16.5	-21.2
M	-20.7	-38.1	4.1	-17.5	-29.3
F	-15.0	-37.2	19.5	-15.4	-14.3

T = Total population   M = Males   F = Females

Source: Statistics Canada. Censuses of Population, 1971 and 1986.

TABLE 4

Percent change in population within each age and gender group, Halifax, 1971 to 1986

	15+	15-24	25-34	35-64	65+
CMA					
T	48.1	19.4	81.7	46.7	69.8
M	47.2	23.4	74.4	45.6	70.3
F	48.9	15.6	89.3	47.8	69.3
Urban core					
T	39.4	14.3	76.7	34.6	61.1
M	38.2	18.0	69.6	33.0	60.3
F	40.5	10.7	84.1	36.1	61.6
Urban fringe					
T	-87.5	-88.6	-92.3	-85.4	-69.0
M	-87.1	-85.7	-94.4	-84.5	-65.5
F	-87.8	-90.7	-90.6	-86.5	-69.0
Rural fringe					
T	201.3	124.5	226.1	236.5	211.6
M	196.5	129.3	214.1	227.1	202.8
F	206.3	119.9	237.0	247.7	219.7

T = Total population   M = Males   F = Females

Source: Statistics Canada. Censuses of Population, 1971 and 1986.

TABLE 5

Percent change in population within each age and gender group, Chicoutimi-Jonquière, 1971 to 1986

	15+	15-24	25-34	35-64	65+
CMA					
T	32.4	-14.5	62.6	45.9	92.3
M	30.9	-13.8	61.3	46.4	73.2
F	33.9	-15.3	63.9	45.6	109.9
Urban core					
T	29.9	-15.2	53.4	42.5	108.5
M	27.9	-13.6	52.5	41.2	86.5
F	31.9	-16.8	54.2	43.7	128.2
Urban fringe					
T	-79.6	-85.8	-62.0	-82.2	-85.8
M	-78.5	-87.0	-59.3	-79.4	-88.0
F	-80.5	-84.5	-64.2	-85.3	-84.0
Rural fringe					
T	292.9	121.9	422.9	378.4	356.0
M	275.8	105.7	397.4	386.7	283.9
F	312.7	143.7	449.5	369.4	440.0

T = Total population   M = Males   F = Females

Source: Statistics Canada. Censuses of Population, 1971 and 1986.

TABLE 6

Percent change in population within each age and gender group, Windsor, 1971 to 1986

	15+	15-24	25-34	35-64	65+
CMA					
T	8.4	-8.4	26.0	9.8	13.0
M	6.8	-7.5	22.3	9.3	5.2
F	9.9	-9.4	29.8	10.3	19.2
Urban core					
T	11.3	-5.7	32.7	11.3	15.8
M	9.4	-5.1	28.4	10.8	7.5
F	13.1	-6.5	37.2	11.7	22.5
Urban fringe					
T	-51.7	-63.4	-45.9	-50.1	-40.4
M	-53.2	-61.9	-48.6	-51.6	-47.7
F	-50.1	-64.8	-43.0	-48.4	-35.3
Rural fringe					
T	14.3	-2.2	11.0	26.2	16.4
M	15.1	1.8	10.6	25.4	15.3
F	13.5	-6.5	11.1	27.3	18.1

T = Total population   M = Males   F = Females

Source: Statistics Canada. Censuses of Population, 1971 and 1986.

TABLE 7

Percent change in population within each age and gender group, Sudbury, 1971 to 1986

	15+	15-24	25-34	35-64	65+
CMA					
T	9.9	-18.8	3.8	22.2	94.7
M	2.5	-23.7	-8.6	17.1	83.4
F	18.1	-13.4	17.9	27.8	105.0
Urban core					
T	42.3	7.9	43.5	53.2	123.2
M	32.6	1.5	23.7	48.5	105.2
F	52.8	14.7	66.9	58.0	138.6
Urban fringe					
T	-63.0	-76.5	-71.3	-52.4	-10.8
M	-64.0	-75.7	-73.6	-54.9	-1.2
F	-61.8	-77.4	-69.2	-49.5	-18.3
Rural fringe					
T	-22.9	-42.3	-35.3	-6.4	31.0
M	-27.8	-47.5	-42.4	-11.9	45.6
F	-17.8	-36.4	-27.5	0.4	18.0

T = Total population   M = Males   F = Females

Source: Statistics Canada. Censuses of Population, 1971 and 1986.

4.   Occupations

For this study, we grouped occupations into two main categories: white-collar and blue-collar[2]. Unstated occupations are not included in the two main categories but they are included in the total figures for all occupations.

During 1971-1986, the proportion of women with white-collar occupations increased steadily in the St. John's CMA reaching over 95% in 1986 for rural fringe and urbanized core (Table 8). The proportion of men with white-collar occupations grew 20 percentage points to 60% in the rural fringe.

The earnings gap between men and decreased between 1971 and 1986 for all occupations, white-collar and blue-collar. In white-collar occupations, the earnings gap was lower in the rural fringe than in the urbanized core. The situation for blue-collar workers is the reverse, except for 1971.

In the Halifax CMA, the proportion of women in white-collar occupations is high, and shows a steady increase over the years (from about 90% in 1971 to 94% in 1986) (Table 9). The proportion is high for the rural fringe and for the urbanized core as well. The figures for men are lower and have changed very little over time.

Between 1971 and 1986, women's earnings in proportion to men's earnings, for all occupations increased for both the rural fringe and urbanized core, reaching 65% in 1986. White-collar worker catch-up has been less significant, and the average earnings of women in the category has risen very little relative to the earnings of men. The trend in blue-collar occupations is different: the earnings gap decreased between 1971 and 1981, and then widened again between 1981 and 1986 for the CMA and the urbanized core. The situation has changed very little for the rural fringe.

---

2.   White-collar occupations include: managerial, natural sciences, social sciences, religion, teaching, medicine, artistic, clerical, sales and service (including related sectors-occupations).

Blue-collar occupations include: primary occupations, processing, machining, product fabricating, construction, transport, material handling, equipment operating, and occupations not elsewhere classified (including related sectors).

TABLE 8

White-collar and blue-collar workers and women's earnings as a percent of men's earnings, St. John's, 1971, 1981 and 1986

	All occupations		Percent white-collar		Percent blue-collar		Women's earnings as percent of men's earnings		
	M No.	F No.	M	F	M	F	All occ.	White-collar	Blue-collar
1971									
CMA	20,115	8,760	57.6	86.1	35.7	3.2	52.0	47.7	48.5
Urban core	15,880	7,175	62.4	87.4	31.1	2.4	50.8	47.4	45.3
Rural fringe	3,690	1,370	39.7	79.6	53.1	7.7	58.2	54.0	55.1
1981									
CMA	24,720	13,880	66.2	93.4	31.7	2.8	61.7	57.5	64.2
Urban core	18,175	10,710	70.4	93.6	27.5	2.5	60.0	56.4	63.1
Rural fringe	3,430	1,715	56.4	93.0	41.3	3.8	66.6	62.1	62.5
1986									
CMA	24,975	16,075	69.2	95.2	28.7	2.9	64.7	60.0	67.6
Urban core	20,870	13,505	71.4	95.3	26.6	2.7	64.5	59.8	69.0
Rural fringe	2,720	1,700	59.7	95.0	38.6	4.1	65.7	61.5	65.0

Source: Statistics Canada. Censuses of Population, 1971, 1981 and 1986.

TABLE 9

White-collar and blue-collar workers and women's earnings as a percent of men's earnings, Halifax, 1971, 1981 and 1986

	All occupations		Percent white-collar		Percent blue-collar		Women's earnings as percent of men's earnings		
	M No.	F No.	M	F	M	F	All occ.	White-collar	Blue-collar
1971									
CMA	41,830	17,120	67.5	89.5	27.7	3.7	54.9	52.6	48.2
Urban core	35,985	15,390	69.6	89.5	25.6	3.7	54.3	52.2	47.3
Rural fringe	3,660	1,100	51.4	87.7	44.5	3.6	59.6	57.9	54.9
1981									
CMA	53,050	28,715	67.6	94.1	30.6	3.6	62.3	58.8	61.8
Urban core	42,920	24,410	71.1	94.3	27.1	3.2	62.0	58.8	64.4
Rural fringe	9,290	3,960	53.1	92.8	45.1	5.9	62.8	58.8	53.2
1986									
CMA	58,095	34,025	68.6	93.8	28.9	4.1	65.1	61.6	58.5
Urban core	46,950	28,560	71.5	93.9	26.0	3.8	65.1	61.8	60.2
Rural fringe	11,010	5,380	56.5	92.8	41.3	5.5	64.9	60.6	54.0

Source: Statistics Canada. Censuses of Population, 1971, 1981 and 1986.

TABLE 10

White-collar and blue-collar workers and women's earnings as a percent of men's earnings, Chicoutimi-Jonquière, 1971, 1981 and 1986

	All occupations		Percent white-collar		Percent blue-collar		Women's earnings as percent of men's earnings		
	M No.	F No.	M	F	M	F	All occ.	White-collar	Blue-collar
1971									
CMA	20,125	5,880	47.4	81.5	44.2	3.3	59.0	57.0	54.6
Urban core	16,545	5,170	48.2	82.0	43.8	3.3	58.4	56.2	51.3
Rural fringe	1,415	205	46.3	70.7	42.0	9.8	67.8	63.1	160.1
1981									
CMA	21,740	7,990	53.5	94.4	43.4	1.8	66.7	62.6	74.0
Urban core	17,980	6,750	56.6	94.7	40.4	1.7	65.5	61.6	68.6
Rural fringe	3,615	1,055	38.9	91.9	57.4	1.7	72.5	73.7	130.5
1986									
CMA	24,765	9,915	55.9	90.0	41.3	3.5	62.1	60.7	59.7
Urban core	20,120	8,440	58.0	91.4	39.4	3.2	61.2	60.1	62.4
Rural fringe	4,035	1,390	44.5	86.0	53.5	6.5	64.6	63.8	55.0

Source: Statistics Canada. Censuses of Population, 1971, 1981 and 1986.

TABLE 11

White-collar and blue-collar workers and women's earnings as a percent of men's earnings, Windsor, 1971, 1981 and 1986

	All occupations		Percent white-collar		Percent blue-collar		Women's earnings as percent of men's earnings		
	M No.	F No.	M	F	M	F	All occ.	White-collar	Blue-collar
1971									
CMA	41,435	14,900	45.4	82.6	49.4	9.3	56.3	53.0	54.6
Urban core	34,400	12,950	47.6	83.1	47.2	8.6	55.9	52.9	54.9
Rural fringe	4,710	1,300	32.9	75.8	61.7	15.0	58.7	52.6	53.0
1981									
CMA	34,075	19,410	53.4	87.4	44.5	10.3	61.3	56.8	69.6
Urban core	29,545	17,205	54.8	87.5	43.0	10.1	60.9	56.7	71.6
Rural fringe	3,680	1,705	43.2	84.5	55.8	12.9	64.3	56.9	55.2
1986									
CMA	47,345	23,100	42.1	84.0	55.3	13.7	63.1	56.7	72.8
Urban core	40,550	20,255	43.4	84.0	54.1	13.7	63.4	57.1	73.4
Rural fringe	5,660	2,355	32.9	82.6	64.8	15.1	61.3	51.1	67.5

Source: Statistics Canada. Censuses of Population, 1971, 1981 and 1986.

TABLE 12

White-collar and blue-collar workers and women's earnings as a percent of men's earnings, Sudbury, 1971, 1981 and 1986

	All occupations		Percent white-collar		Percent blue-collar		Women's earnings as percent of men's earnings		
	M No.	F No.	M	F	M	F	All occ.	White-collar	Blue-collar
1971									
CMA	28,590	7,155	31.7	85.3	60.9	3.7	53.8	49.9	58.7
Urban core	18,010	5,290	36.7	86.2	56.7	3.6	53.3	48.3	58.1
Rural fringe	3,905	655	24.1	76.3	65.8	8.4	55.9	58.1	64.4
1981									
CMA	25,875	9,970	41.5	94.8	56.5	3.6	62.4	58.2	62.8
Urban core	18,845	7,925	44.2	95.5	53.8	3.0	62.3	57.9	65.4
Rural fringe	2,620	835	31.9	88.6	65.5	8.4	65.6	61.0	55.0
1986									
CMA	22,180	11,160	48.5	94.1	49.3	4.3	63.6	60.5	54.3
Urban core	18,385	9,635	50.0	94.3	47.9	4.1	63.8	60.3	55.7
Rural fringe	2,070	890	43.0	90.4	54.3	6.2	67.1	64.5	56.8

Source: Statistics Canada. Censuses of Population, 1971, 1981 and 1986.

Between 1971 and 1981, the proportion of women with white-collar jobs increased 12 percentage points in the Chicoutimi-Jonquière CMA and in the urbanized core. In the rural fringe, the proportion rose by 20 percentage points to virtually the same level as for the urbanized core (95%) (Table 10). However the trend did not continue between 1981 and 1986, slipping more than 4 percentage points for the CMA and the rural fringe, and 3 percentage points for the urbanized core. There were no major changes for men: the percent of men with white-collar jobs is about half the proportion reported by women.

The proportion of men in blue-collar jobs has changed little over time. The figures are higher for the rural fringe, where over 50% of men report blue-collar jobs, except in 1971. The proportion of women in blue-collar jobs is low.

For 1971, 1981, and 1986, women's earnings relative to men's earnings is higher in the rural fringe than in the urbanized core for all occupations (white-collar and blue-collar), with the exception of blue-collar jobs in 1986. In 1971 and 1981, women's earnings relative to men's earnings are very high for blue-collar occupations because of the low representation of women in this category.

Except for 1981, the Windsor CMA and its urbanized core had fewer than 48% of male workers in the white-collar category; the comparable figure for the rural fringe is 33% (Table 11). In 1981 and 1986, the proportion of women in white-collar occupations was above 82% for both the rural fringe and the urbanized core.

In 1971, women's earnings as a percent of men's earnings was similar for white-collar and blue-collar workers. In 1981 and again in 1986, women with blue-collar occupations gained relative to men.

In Sudbury more women held white-collar jobs in 1981 and 1986 than in 1971 (Table 12). More than 90% of all jobs held by women are white-collar.

In Sudbury, the proportion of men with blue-collar jobs is the highest of all the CMAs studied, with the exception of Windsor in 1986 (near 60% in 1971 and 50% in 1986). The figures for women in the urbanized core and the rural fringe changed very little between 1971 and 1986.

Women's earnings as a percent of men's earnings is higher in the rural fringe than in the urbanized core (except for blue-collar jobs in 1981). Women with blue-collar occupations had earnings closer to men's earnings in 1971 and 1981 whereas women with white-collar occupations were closer to men's earnings in 1986.

In 1986 over 80% of the jobs held by women were in the white-collar category for the 5 CMAs, with predominance in the urbanized cores. The proportion of blue-collar jobs held by women remained fairly low (close to 4% for the urbanized core and 6% for the rural fringe), except in the Windsor CMA (14% for the urbanized core and 15% for the rural fringe).

St. John's and Halifax, both provincial capitals and regional headquarters for many federal government departments, register the highest percentages of "clerical and related" jobs held by women. The figures for jobs in this group held by men are almost all under 10%.

More men than women work in the "sales" occupations—typically a male job sector where earnings are traditionally higher.

Female representation in "managerial, administrative and related" occupations is very low. For 1971, only 4% of jobs held by women were in this occupation group, in both the rural fringe and urbanized core. In 1981, figures range between 4% and 9%, and in 1986, figures were between 7% and 10%. The proportion of these jobs held by men did go down, with the exception of St. John's and Halifax. Partly because of the strong government presence, both CMAs show a high percentage of men in "managerial and administrative" occupations, with the largest proportion in the urbanized core.

In the Chicoutimi-Jonquière CMA, aluminium plants and a number of paper plants result in 10%-15% of jobs held by men being in the "processing and machining" occupation group. For 1971, 1981, and 1986, the proportion of processing and machining jobs held by women is never above 2%. There is little difference in distribution between the rural fringe and the urbanized core.

In 1986 in Windsor, a car manufacturing city, over 7% of the female population held jobs in the "product fabricating, assembling and repairing" group. Windsor also registered the greatest level of women's earnings relative to men's earnings (73% for the urbanized core and 68% for the rural fringe). The higher relative earnings of women may be attributable to the high unionization rate in Windsor. In the other regions, the proportion of jobs in the product fabricating group held by women was low (often under 2%); percentages are similar for the urbanized core and the rural fringe. In "transport", another blue-collar group examined, the presence of women is virtually non-existent.

5.   Income of individuals and families

Examination of average employment income (in 1985 dollars) shows the disparity between the average employment incomes of men and women, in both urbanized cores and rural fringes. For the 5 selected CMAs, comparison of average employment income of men and women aged 15 and older shows that, in 1971, 1981, and 1986, women consistently earned less than men, in both the urbanized core and the rural fringe. Very few women earned more than $25,000. The majority of women held jobs in the lowest income brackets ($10,000 to $14,999 and $15,000 to $19,999), while the average income earned by men was in the $25,000 to $29,999 and $30,000 to $34,999 brackets.

A second important factor is the disparity in average employment income between urbanized core and rural fringe. In 1971 the average employment income for men in the urbanized core was between $20,000 and $34,999; in the rural fringe, the range was between $15,000 and $34,999. Distribution between urbanized core and rural fringe remained stable from 1981 to 1986 ($20,000 to $34,999). For women there is little difference between average employment income figures for the urbanized core and the rural fringe (between $15,000 and $24,999).

For those aged 35-64, the majority of average employment income figures for women are under $25,000; for men, they are over $25,000, with the sole exception in the 1971 figures for the rural fringe (between $20,000 and $29,999). The disparity between urbanized core and urban fringe is also a factor for those aged 35-64. For men in the urbanized core, 1971 average employment income figures fall into the $20,000 to $34,999 bracket; in the rural fringe, most figures fall into the $20,000 to $29,999 bracket. Average employment income figures for women range between $10,000 and $19,999. In 1981 and 1986, those aged 15 and older had similar results to 1971.

As a group, census families living in the rural fringes of the 5 selected CMAs had larger average incomes than did their provincial rural census families (Table 13). The census families living in the urbanized cores of the CMAs had far higher average incomes than did families living in the rural fringes.

TABLE 13
Average income of census families, 1985

	St. John's	Halifax	Chicoutimi-Jonquière	Windsor	Sudbury
			$		
Provincial total	37,827	32,938	34,582	41,692	41,692
Provincial rural population	24,039	30,435	29,765	34,484	34,484
CMA	36,849	39,729	33,949	41,045	36,516
Urbanized core	37,360	40,007	34,515	40,573	36,410
Rural fringe	35,160	38,806	31,662	45,083	35,936

Source: Statistics Canada. 1986 Census of Population.

Within a study of workers it is also important to briefly portray the non-workers. Some of these non-workers include census families relying upon government transfer payments for their income. Government transfer payments are composed of unemployment benefits, old age security payments, family allowances, Canada and Québec pension plans, and other income from government sources.

TABLE 14
Percent of female lone-parent families that had government transfer payments as their principal source of income

	St. John's	Halifax	Chicoutimi-Jonquière	Windsor	Sudbury
			Percent		
1971					
Urban core	32.9	26.6	44.0	32.0	23.7
Rural fringe	38.3	26.9	40.0	24.6	43.3
1986					
Urban core	35.0	31.0	45.6	33.8	40.4
Rural fringe	41.9	29.3	45.9	25.3	52.0

Source: Statistics Canada. Censuses of Population, 1971 and 1986.

Between 1971 and 1986 the percentage of female lone-parent families that relied upon government transfer payments for income increased (Table 14). The highest percentage of such families was in the rural fringe of Sudbury (1986) at 52%. Female lone-parent families living in the rural fringe of Chicoutimi-Jonquière had the second highest reliance at 46%.

The average income of female lone-parent families living in the rural fringes of the CMAs in 1986 ranged between $14,560 (Sudbury) and $26,775 (Windsor). Also female lone-parent families living in the rural fringes who relied on government transfer payments for their financial support had much lower incomes; ranging from $7,938 (Sudbury) to $9,427 (St. John's). This income range is higher than for female lone-parent families living in the urbanized cores in 1986, perhaps reflecting the concentration of female lone-parent families in the urbanized cores. In 1986 the income range for female lone-parent families living in the urbanized cores was between $7,472 (Sudbury) and $8,516 (Chicoutimi-Jonquière).

In 1986, the low income cut-off for a two-person family living in rural areas was $9,891. This figure suggests that the average female lone-parent family living in the CMAs whose major source of income was government transfer payments was living in difficult circumstances. In 4 of the 5 rural fringes studied, the average male lone-parent family lived slightly above the low income cut-off for a two-person family in a rural area. Note that these comparisons are broad generalizations as the average size of the families has not been calculated and the income figures presented are averages.

6.   Educational attainment

The levels of educational attainment of the target populations are important in a study of labour markets as the information is relevant to the formal training that certain professions and job categories require. Between 1971 and 1986, the percentage of women and men aged 15 and older who had attained some postsecondary qualifications increased (Tables 15 and 16). However, the postsecondary educational attainment of those aged 15 and older living in the rural fringes was still between 6 to 8 percentage points lower than for the population of the urbanized cores in 1986. Interestingly though, for the CMAs of St. John's and Halifax in 1986, the percentages of men and women with some postsecondary qualifications, in the rural fringes and the urbanized cores, are almost identical.

When making comparisons for Windsor, Sudbury and Chicoutimi-Jonquière, the occupational composition of the metropolitan areas must be considered in the educational attainment of residents. These 3 metropolitan areas are traditionally thought to be heavily industrial and blue collar.

In 1986, the proportion of the female population aged 15 and older living in the rural fringes of these 3 CMAs with some postsecondary education ranged from 14% to 31%, which is much lower than the rural fringe of Halifax or St. John's. For the male population aged 15 and older, the range, although still lower than in the Atlantic CMAs, remains higher than the percentages for females at between 28% to 35%. Also, on the whole, men living in the urbanized cores had attained more education than those living in the rural fringes within the same CMAs.

The population aged 65 and older with some postsecondary qualifications has increased in all 5 CMAs. However, the largest proportion of this population remained within the grade 13 or less category of educational attainment (Tables 17 and 18). Note again, for this population the more rapid shift towards attaining postsecondary qualifications in St. John's, Halifax and Windsor than in Chicoutimi-Jonquière and Sudbury. Social support services when working with the elderly in the rural fringes of CMAs should be aware of the lower educational attainment of these populations, ranging between 79% and 93% with grade 13 or less education.

The female population aged 25-34 is important to study as this population has the following general demographic characteristics:

the population has completed its educational pursuits;

working women are beginning their careers; and

women are within their childbearing years.

The percentages of women aged 25-34 with some postsecondary qualifications in all 5 CMAs has increased sharply from 1971 to 1986 (Tables 19 and 20). Again among the CMAs, St. John's and Halifax show the higher percentages in 1971 and 1986. The St. John's rural fringe showed an impressive 40 percentage point increase between these census years; in 1986, 60% of women reported some postsecondary education. In Sudbury, the more significant growth of women aged 25-34 with some postsecondary education was in the rural fringe. Chicoutimi-Jonquière showed the lowest percentages of women aged 25-34 with postsecondary education for both census years and the lowest increase among any of the CMAs in both the rural fringe and the urbanized core.

In St. John's and Sudbury, a larger share of women than men aged 25-34 living in the rural fringes have some postsecondary education; and in Windsor, the percentages for the sexes are almost equal. However, for the other CMAs and the urbanized cores, a larger share of males in this age group have some secondary education.

These tendencies show that the younger populations living in the rural fringes of the 5 selected CMAs are attaining postsecondary qualifications that should permit them better access to more challenging employment.

TABLE 15

Women aged 15 and older, by level of education, 1971 and 1986

		1971		1986	
		Grade 13 or less	Some post-secondary	Grade 13 or less	Some post-secondary
		Percent			
St. John's	Urban core	75.3	24.7	53.9	46.1
	Rural fringe	85.7	14.3	59.1	40.9
Halifax	Urban core	68.2	31.8	49.0	51.0
	Rural fringe	78.9	21.1	57.4	42.6
Chicoutimi-Jonquière	Urban core	87.3	12.7	65.4	34.6
	Rural fringe	77.0	23.0	69.3	30.7
Sudbury	Urban core	79.2	20.8	63.4	36.6
	Rural fringe	87.0	13.0	70.1	29.9
Windsor	Urban core	92.2	7.8	82.5	17.5
	Rural fringe	91.9	8.1	85.9	14.1

Source: Statistics Canada. Censuses of Population, 1971 and 1986.

TABLE 16

Men aged 15 and older, by level of education, 1971 and 1986

		1971		1986	
		Grade 13 or less	Some post-secondary	Grade 13 or less	Some post-secondary
		Percent			
St. John's	Urban core	72.9	27.1	54.3	45.7
	Rural fringe	84.4	15.6	60.0	40.0
Halifax	Urban core	69.3	30.7	48.5	51.5
	Rural fringe	87.3	12.7	56.6	43.4
Chicoutimi-Jonquière	Urban core	75.0	25.0	59.2	40.8
	Rural fringe	81.5	18.5	65.5	34.5
Sudbury	Urban core	78.0	22.0	64.8	35.2
	Rural fringe	87.6	12.4	71.8	28.2
Windsor	Urban core	76.1	23.9	59.4	40.6
	Rural fringe	81.6	18.4	65.9	34.1

Source: Statistics Canada. Censuses of Population, 1971 and 1986.

TABLE 17

Women aged 65 and older, by level of education, 1971 and 1986

		1971		1986	
		Grade 13 or less	Some post-secondary	Grade 13 or less	Some post-secondary
		Percent			
St. John's	Urban core	94.3	5.7	82.6	17.4
	Rural fringe	97.4	2.6	90.4	9.6
Halifax	Urban core	84.7	15.3	72.6	27.4
	Rural fringe	94.9	5.1	78.6	21.4
Chicoutimi-Jonquière	Urban core	96.5	3.5	88.2	11.8
	Rural fringe	95.0	5.0	90.6	9.4
Sudbury	Urban core	93.8	6.2	90.7	9.3
	Rural fringe	100.0	--	91.7	8.3
Windsor	Urban core	92.2	7.8	82.5	17.5
	Rural fringe	91.9	8.1	85.9	14.1

Source: Statistics Canada. Censuses of Population, 1971 and 1986.

TABLE 18

Men aged 65 and older, by level of education, 1971 and 1986

		1971		1986	
		Grade 13 or less	Some post-secondary	Grade 13 or less	Some post-secondary
		Percent			
St. John's	Urban core	93.5	6.5	82.0	18.0
	Rural fringe	95.9	4.1	93.3	6.7
Halifax	Urban core	86.3	13.7	68.4	31.6
	Rural fringe	97.2	2.8	85.3	14.7
Chicoutimi-Jonquière	Urban core	93.3	6.7	89.0	11.0
	Rural fringe	93.5	6.5	90.8	9.2
Sudbury	Urban core	93.3	6.7	85.4	14.6
	Rural fringe	98.5	1.5	88.9	11.1
Windsor	Urban core	91.7	8.3	78.6	21.4
	Rural fringe	95.5	4.5	86.8	13.2

Source: Statistics Canada. Censuses of Population, 1971 and 1986.

TABLE 19

Women aged 25-34, by level of education, 1971 and 1986

		1971		1986	
		Grade 13 or less	Some post-secondary	Grade 13 or less	Some post-secondary
		Percent			
St. John's	Urban core	66.1	33.9	36.0	64.0
	Rural fringe	80.2	19.8	39.6	60.4
Halifax	Urban core	56.0	44.0	35.1	64.9
	Rural fringe	66.1	33.9	44.3	55.7
Chicoutimi-Jonquière	Urban core	72.3	27.7	53.9	46.1
	Rural fringe	75.3	24.7	62.3	37.7
Sudbury	Urban core	69.0	31.0	48.2	51.8
	Rural fringe	79.3	20.7	55.3	44.7
Windsor	Urban core	70.1	29.9	49.5	50.5
	Rural fringe	72.0	28.0	52.7	47.3

Source: Statistics Canada. Censuses of Population, 1971 and 1986.

TABLE 20

Men aged 25-34, by level of education, 1971 and 1986

		1971		1986	
		Grade 13 or less	Some post-secondary	Grade 13 or less	Some post-secondary
		Percent			
St. John's	Urban core	59.3	40.7	36.2	63.8
	Rural fringe	72.4	27.6	44.0	56.0
Halifax	Urban core	57.6	42.4	34.7	65.3
	Rural fringe	69.6	30.4	40.6	59.4
Chicoutimi-Jonquière	Urban core	60.9	39.1	48.2	51.8
	Rural fringe	70.2	29.8	56.4	43.6
Sudbury	Urban core	65.6	34.4	45.9	54.1
	Rural fringe	80.9	19.1	60.0	40.0
Windsor	Urban core	62.1	37.9	43.8	56.2
	Rural fringe	70.2	29.8	52.6	47.4

Source: Statistics Canada. Censuses of Population, 1971 and 1986.

7.   Conclusion

One third of the rural population in Canada lives in the rural fringe of Census Metropolitan Areas (CMAs) and Census Agglomerations (CAs). The population living in the rural fringes of the 5 CMAs considered in this study showed strong growth between 1971 and 1986.

The proportion of women aged 15 and older in white-collar jobs is high, with a strong predominance of "clerical support" jobs. As a result, the proportion of women aged 15 and older in the blue-collar category is very low (often under 6%).

Women's earnings as a percent of men's earnings are similar across white-collar and blue-collar jobs, except in the Windsor metropolitan area where unions have a stronger influence on workers' salaries. However there is a marked disparity between average employment income in the urbanized core and the rural fringe, with the situation of women relatively better in the urbanized core than in the rural fringe.

Turning to education, the percentage of women with some post-secondary education in the urbanized core is 6 to 8 percentage points higher than in the rural fringe. In general men living in the urbanized core have more education (i.e. some postsecondary training) than men living in the rural fringe.

Family income is higher for families living in the urbanized core than for families living in the rural fringe. Female lone-parent families are an exception: a higher percentage in the urbanized core depend on government programs for income.

These indicators partly support the quotation from Le Droit which maintains that rural residents (living in the rural fringe) have no part in prosperity. We have found that residents in the rural fringe are somewhat disadvantaged. What is the situation of "true rural residents" who live far from large urban centres?

Robert Parenteau
Geography Division
Statistics Canada
Ottawa K1A 0T6

Louise Earl
Census Operations Division
Statistics Canada
Ottawa K1A 0T6

References

Statistics Canada. 1972. Dictionary of the 1971 Census Terms, (cat. no. 12-540). Ottawa: Minister of Industry, Trade and Commerce.

7

Are single industry towns diversifying? An examination of fishing, forestry and mining towns

Heather Clemenson

Summary

A community was defined as a single industry community if 30% or more of its labour force was employed in a single industry or a single sector. The average population size of the sample communities was 3,400 people in 1976.

From 1976 to 1986, there was more change in the industrial composition of the labour force in mining and wood-based communities than in fishing communities. By 1986, only 4 of the 38 fishing communities were not classified as "single industry communities" as their labour force in fishing had fallen to below 30% of the total community labour force. In mining communities, 30 out of 54 reduced their labour force concentration in mining to less than 30% by 1986, mainly because of an absolute decline in employment in mining. Similarly, over half of the 80 wood-based communities reduced their labour force concentration on wood, but in 17 cases this was accompanied by an increase in total community labour force and a proportional shift in employment to other industries.

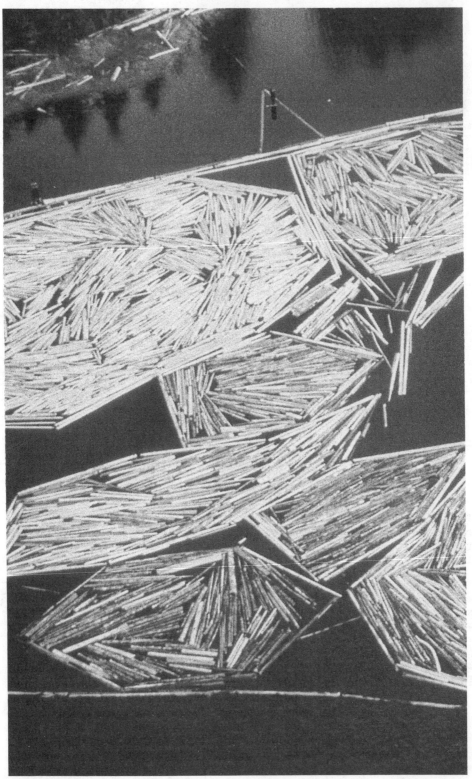

Vancouver Island, British Columbia

Are single industry towns diversifying? An examination of fishing, forestry and mining towns

Heather Clemenson

Introduction

Single industry or single sector communities are characteristic of much of remote and rural Canada. Many are based on resource industries that have been and continue to be a major component of the Canadian economy. The recession in the early 1980s had a significant impact on employment in resource dependent communities across Canada and it refocused attention on the future of many of these communities. At issue is their long-term sustainability. If the economic base of a single industry community is threatened, whether by changes in the market (domestic or international), by depletion of a resource base, product substitution, technological change or other factors, the future of the entire settlement can be at risk.

Definitions

The term "single industry town" has been widely used in Canadian settlement studies, but despite its frequent use, there is no universal definition.

One way of defining these communities is to establish a threshold of dependency based on a measure of employment. Such a measure was used by the former Department of Regional and Economic Expansion (DREE) in a research study in the 1970s (DREE 1979). The communities selected for this paper are taken from a list of single sector communities identified in the DREE study for the census year 1976.

The communities were selected on the basis that 30% or more of their labour force was in a single industry or a single sector.

> A single-industry community: is a centre where 30% or more of its labour force is in a single standard industrial classification (SIC).

154

Are single industry towns diversifying?
An examination of fishing, forestry and mining towns

> A single-sector community: is a centre which depends on one resource or one type of activity and may combine a number of different SIC groups into one sector (for example, the wood-based sector includes logging, sawmills and pulp and paper mills, all with different SIC codes).

The standard 1986 Census geo-coding system was used to define community boundaries. The size of community selected was also restricted to a maximum population of 20,000 in 1976. However, the average size of community in the final study group was just under 3,400 in 1976.

Study objective

The study objective is not to redefine or identify the precise number of single sector communities in Canada, but to examine some of the changes that have taken place in a group of these communities from 1976 to 1986; particularly to assess how many have become either more dependent on a single resource or more industrially diversified. It is a "where are they now" look at a group of small towns in Canada.

The very nature of communities—their origin, location, social structure, the industries on which they depend, and many other factors—gives each a unique set of characteristics. However, for this analysis communities have been grouped on the basis of their major industrial dependence as identified in the DREE study.

TABLE 1

Single sector communities—study group and SIC* codes

Type of community	Number of communities	SIC codes
Fish and fish processing	38	041, 045, 102
Metal mining, non-metal mining and refining	54	051-059, 061-064, 071-099 291, 294, 295, 365, 369
Wood-based	80	031-039, 251-274
Total communities	**172**	

*   Standard Industrial Classification, 1970.

Source: Department of Regional and Economic Expansion (DREE), 1979.

The 38 fishing communities are all in the Atlantic provinces, the vast majority in Newfoundland. The 54 mining communities are more widely scattered, but the majority are in the provinces of Quebec, Ontario and British Columbia. The 80 wood-based communities are mainly located in the provinces of New Brunswick, Quebec, Ontario and British Columbia. Most of the communities are isolated; few are in close proximity to alternative employment opportunities in large urban areas.

Are single industry towns diversifying?
An examination of fishing, forestry and mining towns

155

Population

The median population size for all three types of community in 1976 was from 1,000 to 2,000; close to 40% of all the communities were in this range (Figure 1). Two thirds had less than 3,000 inhabitants while over 80% had a population below 5,000.

FIGURE 1

Communities by population size, Canada, 1976

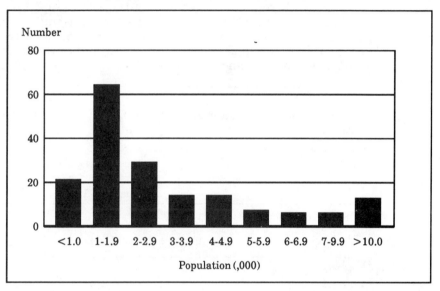

Net population growth during 1976-1986 shows some broad differences between the three types of community, though it should be emphasized that net change reveals nothing about the population flows into and out of each community during the ten-year period[1]. The most stable in terms of net population growth or decline from 1976 to 1986 were the fishing communities; over 80% gained or lost less than 15% of their population. The most volatile in terms of population change were the mining communities. Few had a small percentage change in population: most changes were quite dramatic. Close to 30% lost more than a quarter of their population; whereas at the other extreme, close to 20% had an increase in population of more than 25%.

---

1. Changes in census subdivision boundaries between census periods also account for some of the changes that appear to have taken place.

Two thirds of the 80 wood-based communities had a lower population in 1986 than in 1976: though most lost less than 10% of their population.

Labour force and industry

Communities were selected for this study because at least 30% of their labour force worked in one natural-resource sector (fishing, mining or wood-based) in 1976[2].

One way of examining change is to see what proportion of the total labour force in each community remained in fishing, mining or wood-based industries over time. For each community the percentage of the labour force working in the appropriate natural-resource sector was estimated for 1981 and 1986 (Table 2).

TABLE 2

Number of study communities by percent of labour force remaining in a single sector, Canada, 1981 and 1986

	Percent of labour force in a single sector		
	>30%	15-29%	<15%
38 Fishing communities			
1981	33	5	0
1986	34	4	0
54 Mining communities			
1981	42	11	1
1986	24	22	8
80 Wood-based communities			
1981	52	27	1
1986	37	40	3

Source: Statistics Canada. Census of Population, 1981 and 1986.

Fishing communities are the most stable in terms of the proportion of their labour force remaining in the industry: 33 of the 38 communities still had over 30% of their labour force in fishing in both 1981 and 1986; only 4 or 5 communities had a slight reduction in their fishing labour force to less than 30% and in no case had the proportion fallen below 15%.

2. Though the list was selected from the 1979 publication in which the population figures and data for each community were for 1976, where possible, the community data was checked for 1971 to see if 30% or more of the labour force was in the single sector at that date. The 1976 census contained no data on industry that would permit this type of verification.

Mining communities showed more change. In 1981, 42 of the 54 communities still had over 30% of their labour force in mining, but by 1986 the number was reduced to 24. By 1986, more than half of the communities could no longer be considered as predominantly mining in terms of labour force, in 22 cases the proportion was between 15% and 29%, while in 8 communities less than 15% of the labour force remained in the mining sector.

In 1981, 52 of the 80 communities of the wood-based communities still had over 30% of their labour force in the industry. By 1986, the comparable figure was 37 of the 80. Half of the communities, however, still had between 15% and 29% of their labour force in wood-based industries.

It is tempting to conclude that in communities in which the resource-sector labour force dependency has dropped, there was an increase in industrial diversity. Certainly, there was a change in the proportional distribution of the labour force, but such a simple calculation cannot be used to conclude that these communities have in any way diversified their industrial base.

A proportional reduction in an industry's labour force relative to the total community labour force can occur for many reasons. It does not necessarily imply that new industry has come into a community, that other industries have expanded, or that the major industry has in fact reduced its actual labour force.

A simple framework can be used to identify the direction of change in a community labour force by industry (Figure 2). This framework helps to more clearly establish which of the study communities have potentially diversified and are in a stable or growth situation, and which may be more vulnerable in terms of a declining labour force or an increasing dependence on a single sector.

The framework indicates whether the total community labour force has increased or decreased and whether the labour force in the major resource sector (fishing, mining and wood-based) has similarly increased or decreased. It is used only as a preliminary sorting device since the allocation to each category is based on absolute numbers and does not provide any indication of the magnitude of change. Each community can, however, be placed in one of four categories based on the relative changes in its labour force from 1981 to 1986[3]:

1. An increase in the total community labour force and a decrease in the single sector labour force—among this group are those communities that have, in some way, diversified.

---

3. For some communities, the magnitude of change is so small that the community could be classed as stable. In all cases, however, at least one of the two elements changed. In cases where the community labour force was the same for both years the community was placed in the plus category; if the single sector labour force was stable it too was placed in the plus category.

158

Are single industry towns diversifying?
An examination of fishing, forestry and mining towns

FIGURE 2
Labour force change, 1981 to 1986

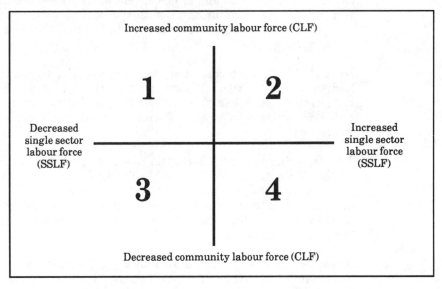

2. An increase in both the total community labour force and the single sector labour force—depending on the size of the respective increases, some of these communities may have either diversified or increased dependency on a single sector.

3. A decrease in both the total community labour force and the single sector labour force—again depending on the size of the respective decreases, some of these communities may have increased their dependence on a single sector or may have changed their labour force structure. They are, however, in a situation of a declining total labour force.

4. A decrease in total community labour force but an increase in the single sector labour force—the small number of communities in this group may have become more dependent on a single sector despite a reduction in their total labour force.

The most solid case for increased industrial diversity is in those communities where the total community labour force has increased, but the labour force in the major resource sector has decreased to less than 30% of the total.

Few cases of this type exist in either fishing communities or mining communities.

Fishing communities

In 1977, Canada extended its fisheries jurisdiction from 12 to 200 miles. The outcome was an increase in employment, investment and incomes in the Atlantic fisheries. In the early 1980s a major financial crisis occurred in the industry caused by the economic recession, high interest rates, high oil costs, and weak product prices. Major fish processing firms had serious financial difficulty and, largely with government assistance, the industry refinanced and restructured during 1983-1985 (Fisheries and Oceans 1989).

The number of fish plants in Atlantic Canada has almost doubled in the last decade from about 500 in 1977 to about 900 in 1988[4]. The numbers employed in fish processing in Atlantic Canada increased rapidly after 1977, declined in 1983 with the rationalization of the major processing plants, but grew rapidly in the mid-1980s, peaking at the equivalent of 30,580 full-time jobs in 1988 (APEC 1990).

FIGURE 3

38 Fishing communities, 1981 to 1986

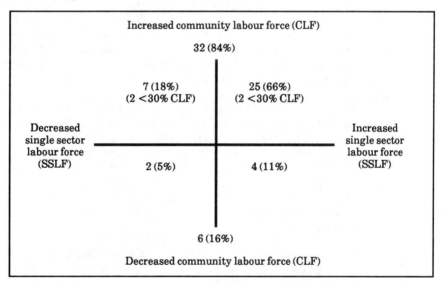

The employment growth is reflected in the study data which indicate that in 32 of the 38 fishing communities, the total community labour force either remained stable or increased during 1981-1986 (Figure 3).

1.   In 7 of these communities the labour force in fishing declines slightly over the period, but in only 2 was the dependency on fishing reduced to less than 30% of the total labour force.

---

4.   This number includes licensed fish processing plants in Quebec.

160

Are single industry towns diversifying?
An examination of fishing, forestry and mining towns

2. Of particular note is that 25 of the communities increased both their total community labour force and their labour force in fishing during 1981-1986, and in only two cases did the labour force in fishing fall below 30% in 1986. In all other communities the proportion was in excess of 30% and in the majority of cases was higher in 1986 than in 1981. For most of these communities, therefore, labour force dependency on the single sector has increased.

Only 6 of the fishing communities recorded a net decline in total labour force over the period, but in no case did sector dependency fall below 30%.

For the 38 study communities, little change occurred in labour force dependency on fishing by 1986. Not only did the vast majority still have 30% or more of their labour force in the industry, but any increase in a community labour force during 1981-1986 also appears to have gone into the fishing industry.

Dependence on fishing continues to be a major concern in Atlantic Canada. The industry still accounts for over 10% of all jobs, and it directly employs over 100,000 people in more than 1,300 communities (APEC 1990). Since 1989, the industry has faced another cycle of low fish prices and declining fish stocks. Reduced quotas in 1989 and 1990 forced a number of large fish processing plants to close or gear down leaving thousands out of work.

In response to the crisis in the industry, the federal government announced, in May 1990, a five-year $584 million Atlantic Fisheries Adjustment Program. The program is aimed at ensuring a viable fishery in the long-term for Atlantic Canada by rebuilding fish stocks, and promoting economic diversity within the fishing industry. Part of the initiative, including a $90 million Fisheries Alternatives Program, is to provide alternative employment opportunities and economic diversification within fisheries dependent communities (Government of Canada 1990).

One of the study communities is Canso, Nova Scotia. In 1986, this community of approximately 1,300 people had over 52% of its labour force in fishing. The town's major employer closed its fish processing plant in March 1990 as part of the company's rationalization of processing and production facilities. This decision put approximately 750 people out of work. The company sold the plant and production resumed in late 1990, though at a lower level of employment than previously.

Major plant closures have also taken place in at least four other communities in the study group: Trepassey, Gaultois, Grand Bank and Lockeport. Along with Canso, these communities now form part of a group of seven communities which receive support from a $30 million community development fund financed by the Atlantic Canada

Opportunities Agency (ACOA) and delivered through the Community Futures Program of Employment and Immigration Canada.

Mining communities

From 1981 to 1986, in just over a third of the 54 mining communities the total community labour force remained stable or increased.

1. In 13 there was a decline in the mining labour force, but in only 8 did the dependency on mining fall below 30%.

2. In 6 communities the labour force in mining and the total community labour force increased; in 2 cases, however, mining no longer accounted for over 30% of the total community labour force by 1986.

FIGURE 4

54 Mining communities, 1981 to 1986

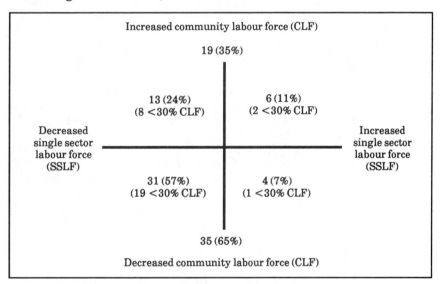

It is the 10 communities with less than 30% of their labour force in mining and an increase in total community labour force that have potentially diversified.

The predominant situation in the 54 mining communities, however, has been one of decline in the total community labour force. Two thirds of the mining communities had a smaller total labour force in 1986 than in 1981[5].

5. The "stages of growth" concept for single industry towns suggests that in the early growth stage the labour force may be inflated because of transient labour employed in construction projects. As some mining communities are new settlements, their total community labour force in the mid to late 1970s may have been higher because of the transient labour.

3.   Of these, in 31, or close to 60% of the study group, the labour force
      in mining also dropped and in 19 cases it represented less than
      30% of the total by 1986.   This illustrates a change in the
      composition of the labour force in these communities but in a
      declining situation.

The 1981-82 recession had a devastating impact on employment in
mining communities. "At the height of the recession in late 1982, close
to half of the Canadian mining sector was shut down temporarily for
periods varying from a few days to several months... The recession also
precipitated the permanent closure of the main employer in some
communities, resulting in severe social readjustment and relocation for
most of their residents and businesses" (E.M.R. 1985).

Within the study group are clear examples of the dramatic changes that
occurred in the early 1980s. The community of Schefferville, located in
the Quebec-Labrador iron-ore mining region is one such case. In 1982,
the Iron Ore Company of Canada closed the Schefferville mine and
closed the townsite in mid-1983. The town had a population of close to
3,500 in 1976. By 1986, 320 residents remained and less than 3% of the
labour force was in mining. The fate of Gagnon in the same region was
even more drastic. In 1976, the town had a population of over 3,400;
fewer than five residents remained in Gagnon by 1986.

Though closure also occurred in Buchans (Newfoundland) this
community is looking for a long-term future. The copper-zinc mine in
Buchans had a work force of 550 in 1979, by 1982 only 12 miners were
employed and the mine was permanently closed in 1984.   The
community had planned for the eventual closure of the mine and
produced an Area Development Strategy in 1984 identifying potential
areas for economic development. Many of the former mine workers
chose to remain in the community. The older workers (aged 55-64) were
able to receive an income maintenance allowance until they became
reemployed or they reached the age of 65. The community has taken
over the infrastructure of the abandoned mine site in its efforts to
attract new industry.

A number of communities, including Atikokan and Ear Falls in
Ontario, Fraser Lake and Granisle in British Columbia, have shifted
their primary employment dependence to another resource base. They
have shifted from mining communities to communities either largely
dependent on wood industries or communities with a dual resource
dependency. By 1986, 29% of the Atikokan labour force and 31% of the
Fraser Lake labour force were in wood-based industries and only 1%
and 4% respectively remained in mining. The relative proportions for
Ear Falls and Granisle are 26% and 34% (wood industries) and 12% and
26% (mining industries).   Both Ear Falls and Granisle had a dual
dependency on primary resources by 1986.

The recession of the early 1980s was a major cause of employment
decline in some communities, but other factors need to be considered.

For example, technological development has also led to a change in the demand for labour. Increased substitution of capital for labour may mean that, even though an industry remains important to a community, a reduced number of workers are employed and there may be little prospect of employment growth.

The mining sector will undoubtedly continue to be one of boom and bust and much concern exists about future growth and community planning. A number of arrangements have evolved ranging from the fly-in/fly-out sites with no permanent settlement to fully planned, more centralized communities which serve a number of mines. The fully planned communities have a larger population base for service provision and a more diversified employment structure. An example of this type of settlement is the planned community of Tumbler Ridge in British Columbia.

Wood-based communities

Wood-based industries also suffered during the recession of the early 1980s: in the forestry industry, for example, employment fell from over 300,000 in 1980 to below 260,000 in 1982.

Some of the labour force changes in wood-based industries, similar to the mining sector, are the result of increased capitalization and rationalization of the industry. In this process some communities have benefitted while others have suffered.

In the case of the 80 wood-based communities in this study, over 50% had a stable or a higher total community labour force in 1986 than in 1981 (Figure 5).

1. In 24 of these communities the labour force in wood-based industries declined and, in 17 cases, no longer accounted for over 30% of the total labour force. This represents the most significant potential change towards diversification among the three types of community.

There are examples of increased diversity in wood-based communities that have also resulted in a dual dependence on wood and mining. Marathon, Ontario is a case in point. This community has long been associated with pulp and paper; in 1981 over 50% of its labour force was still in wood-based industry. By 1986, the proportion had dropped to 22%. From 1981 to 1986 the labour force increased from over 1,200 to more than 1,800. Marathon is still dependent on natural resource industries, but now has a dual dependency on pulp and paper and gold mining. By 1986, over 20% of Marathon's labour force was employed in mining. The potential for tourism and recreation development has also been recognized. The location of the community on the shores of Lake Superior and in close proximity to Pukaskwa National Park are assets in this regard.

164
Are single industry towns diversifying?
An examination of fishing, forestry and mining towns

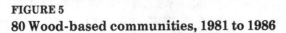

FIGURE 5
80 Wood-based communities, 1981 to 1986

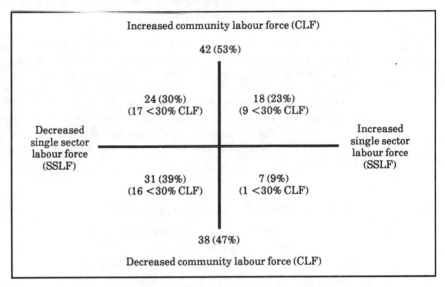

2.   In 18 communities the labour force increased both in total and in the wood-based industry, but in 9 communities, the wood-based industry no longer accounted for over 30% of the total labour force by 1986.

In 38, or a close to half of the wood-based communities, the total community labour force fell during 1981-1986.

3.   In 17 of these communities the wood-based labour force also declined to less than 30% of the total community labour force by 1986.

Conclusion

This study of single industry communities showed that more change occurred in the industrial composition of the labour force in mining and wood-based communities than in fishing communities. During 1981-1986, some fishing communities, in fact, increased their dependency on a single resource. In all three sectors, those communities which have experienced major growth or decline stand out clearly; for the remainder the changes are more subtle.

Many other factors still need to be considered in examining change in these communities. The basic sorting of communities based on the size of their single sector and total community labour forces indicates nothing about labour force activity, the level of employment or unemployment, whether employment is predominantly for men or

Are single industry towns diversifying?
An examination of fishing, forestry and mining towns

165

women, and whether the jobs are full time or part time. These and many other aspects of the labour force and changing industrial composition in the study communities are the present research focus.

As the Canadian economy enters another period of recession, what lies in the future for small resource-dependent communities? Many residents of these small communities have a history of coping with hard times and have developed a kinship and strength to fight for their community. For others community attachment may not be so strong. More than in the past, there appears to be a growing concern for community sustainability which, in the long term, implies some element of economic diversification. Problems of diversification and alternative employment opportunities for many of these communities may, however, be magnified because of their small size and remoteness.

Economic diversification in many of these communities is now taking place through the work of local municipalities, the Canadian Association of Single Industry Towns (CASIT), the Community Futures Program, and other government and organizational initiatives. Many single industry communities are examining alternatives to continued dependence on one resource and are seeking new ways to ensure their future.

Heather Clemenson
Program Evaluation Division
Agriculture Canada
Ottawa, Ontario
K1A 0C5

166

Are single industry towns diversifying?
An examination of fishing, forestry and mining towns

References

Atlantic Canada Opportunities Agency (ACOA). 1990.
Fisheries alternative program announced. News Release, Nov. 29.

Atlantic Provinces Economic Council (APEC). 1990.
The Atlantic fishery in the 1990s: background to crisis. Atlantic
Report, 25(2): 3-20.

Centre for Resource Studies. 1983. Mining communities:
hard lessons for the future. Proceedings of the 12th CRS
Discussion Seminar. Kingston, Ontario: Sept.

Department of Regional and Economic Expansion (DREE). 1977.
Single Industry Communities. Occasional Papers. Ottawa:
Government Publishing Centre.

Department of Regional and Economic Expansion (DREE). 1979.
Single Sector Communities. Occasional Papers. Ottawa:
Government Publishing Centre.

Employment and Immigration Canada. 1987. Canada's Single
Industry Communities: A Proud Determination to Survive.
Ottawa: Canada Employment and Immigration Advisory Council.

**Energy, Mines and Resources (EMR), Canada and the
Department of Energy and Mines, Manitoba. 1985.** New
Financial Mechanisms For Addressing Mining Community
Problems. Ottawa: Government Publishing Centre.

Fisheries and Oceans. 1989. Today's Atlantic Fisheries. Ottawa:
Fisheries and Oceans, Communications Directorate.

Fisheries and Oceans. 1990. Status of Atlantic Fisheries Adjustment
Program. Backgrounder, October (B-HQ-90-13E).

Government of Canada. 1990. Atlantic Fisheries Adjustment
Program. News Release, May 7.

Pharand, N.L. 1988. Forest-Sector Dependent Communities in
Canada: A Demographic Profile. Information Report DPC-X-23,
Labour Market Development Branch, Canadian Forestry Service.
Ottawa: Canadian Forestry Service.

8

Small communities in Atlantic Canada: their industrial structure and labour market conditions in the early 1980s

Garnett Picot and John Heath

Summary

The natural resource sector in Atlantic Canada declined during the recession of the mid 1980s. Communities based on natural resource industries tend to be smaller on average and they 'appeared' to become more diversified during 1981-1986, but this results from a decline in natural resource employment, not from an expansion in the other sectors.

The labour market experiences of individual workers differ by size of community and by the industry mix of employment in the community. Workers in smaller communities experienced a decline in real earnings whereas workers in larger ones experienced an increase in real earnings. Among the smaller communities, the real earnings of workers declined the most in natural resource-based communities.

Workers in smaller communities were more likely to move compared to workers in larger communities. However, among the smaller communities, mobility in the natural resource communities was the lowest— lower than mobility in diversified or public sector communities, even though labour market conditions were inferior in the resource-based towns.

When the dominant industry in a community declines, one might expect all workers in the community to be affected. However, within smaller natural resource communities, the real earnings of workers in the goods sector declined whereas the real earnings of workers in the commercial or public service sectors increased. And, workers in the goods sector still reported a lower rate of mobility out of the community than workers in other industrial sectors.

Earnings of workers appear tremendously volitile. Few individuals experience the calculated average change in earnings. The average change in earnings for a group of workers masks a tremendous variability in the experiences of individual workers. For example, the average Atlantic Canada worker with earnings of more than $6,600 in 1981 and with some earnings in 1986 experienced a 1% increase in earnings. This masks that 61% of the workers experienced a gain in real earnings that averaged 27%, and 39% of the workers experienced a decline in real earnings that averaged 33%.

Table of contents

Small communities in Atlantic Canada: their industrial structure and labour market conditions in the early 1980s

Garnett Picot and John Heath

Introduction and objective

The impact of economic cycles on small natural resource towns and their workers can be severe. In Atlantic Canada, natural resource communities depend mainly on fishing, forestry, mining and their related processing industries. During the recession of the early 1980s employment in the natural resource sector[1] fell by about 9% in Atlantic Canada (Figure 1). There was some recovery during 1986-1989, but the impact of the cyclical downturn on towns with high dependency on these industries must have been significant[2].

Other events besides a downturn in the economic cycle can negatively influence natural resource communities. These include:

1. the depletion of a mine or some other natural resource connected with the town;

2. structural (or long term) changes in the demand for a natural resource or related manufactured commodities which may result in a permanent decline in employment opportunities in a town;

3. shifts in international prices for natural resource commodities which render plants unprofitable and candidates for closure. Commodity prices over the early and mid 1980s were declining in many cases, and a price index of 33 commodities (excluding energy) fell 25% from 1981 to 1986 (Economic Council 1990).

---

1. Including primary industries plus the processing industries in manufacturing directly dependent on natural resources such as pulp and paper, wood industries, and fish processing.

2. Like any study with a focus on a particular period, these findings are determined by the economic events of the period. The 1981 to 1986 period was chosen because 1981 preceded the recession and the recovery was underway by 1986. Also, it was helpful to compare the data with census of population data for the two periods. This database facilitates cross-section (ie. one point in time) and annual longitudinal analysis of workers and firms at the municipal level. Analysts are invited to contact the author concerning the availability of data for their research projects.

FIGURE 1

Index of employment in Atlantic Canada by industry, 1978-1989

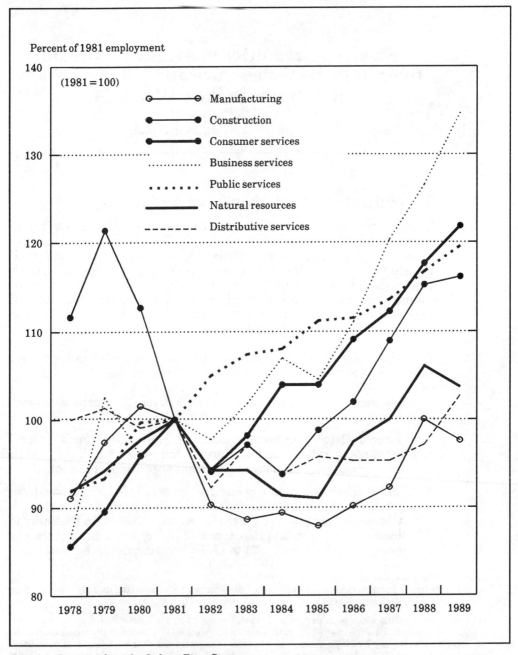

Percent of 1981 employment

(1981 = 100)

○———○ Manufacturing
●———● Construction
●———● Consumer services
.... Business services
•••••••• Public services
———— Natural resources
- - - - - - Distributive services

Source: *Statistics Canada. Labour Force Survey.*

These forces may negatively influence any town and its workers, but communities with a large proportion of their payroll in the natural resources sector may be particularly vulnerable to such economic forces. Single industry (usually small, natural-resource) communities, and the plight of their workers during economic downturns is of longstanding interest in Canada, especially as up to one-quarter of the rural worker population lives in such communities with fragile economies. Although the communities have been the subject of various reports (e.g. CEIC 1987; CEIC 1988; Royal Commission of Employment and Unemployment 1986), little information is available on the impact on workers. In particular, little work looks at the experience of natural resource communities and their workers within a context. Comparisons with other types of communities are necessary to do this.

Of course, the major concern to small resource communities is the vulnerability of their economies and the resulting effect on the labour market conditions for workers. Unemployment rises, and workers and their families may be forced to move.

To assess the effect on the workers requires longitudinal data. How flexible is the labour market in these areas and do workers move to locate new employment in the face of a very tight labour market in their community? And when they move does adjustment occur quickly, or do their earnings remain depressed and unemployment high? And do conditions in the community improve so that remaining workers secure employment and higher earnings? Two requirements are needed to answer such questions. First, longitudinal <u>data</u> on the workers are needed to determine what happens to earnings and unemployment over a number of years. Second, a benchmark, or point of comparison is needed to determine if the labour market conditions faced by workers from these communities were significantly different from the conditions encountered by workers from communities. Even when special surveys are conducted to track workers from resource communities over time, there is rarely a "control group" against which to compare the surveys. The experimental data source in this work provides both longitudinal data and data on comparison groups because virtually all workers in the Atlantic area are included in the database.

If adjustment policies are intended for workers in particular types of industries affected by structural change, it may be necessary to consider the type of community (labour market) where they are located. Workers in large, diversified communities face very different labour market conditions than those in smaller, concentrated labour markets. To assess such targeting, comparisons of the adjustment experiences of workers in various labour markets are necessary.

The industrial structure of a town is important. Diversified or public service communities would experience less impact from an economic cycle than natural resource dominated communities given the patterns of employment change (Figure 1). To achieve this characteristic of employment and economic stability, communities seek diversification.

Recent work by the Economic Council and others discuss how single industry communities can foster development strategies to encourage growth and diversification from within (Economic Council 1990; Decter 1989). Diversified communities, and workers in them, should show more stable employment patterns, less variation in earnings and perhaps less mobility than workers from natural resource communities.

But size is also important. Many natural resource communities are small and isolated, adding to their vulnerability when the dominant industry declines. Larger communities tend to have larger service sectors. The Economic Council Report (1990) observed that financial, business, transportation and communication services tended to locate in larger centres such as Halifax. Such service firms need access to a number of features found in larger centres, such as highly skilled labour, head offices, financial institutions, services other than their own, and a larger market. These industries are highly dependent upon access to information and face-to-face contact, which is lost in small communities isolated from the market. Service firms, unlike goods-producing firms, generally service clients face to face, and do not "ship" output nearly as often (although some do).

An interaction between size and industrial structure is apparent: larger communities tend to develop larger service sectors than smaller communities. Employment growth in general has been in the services sector, tending to favour middle size and larger communities and perhaps, augmenting regional disparities. Smaller communities are more likely to be single industry dependent and have more difficulty attracting jobs in the business service and distributive service sectors in particular. Workers laid off in a small natural resource town would have less opportunity for employment in a small concentrated labour market, making it likely that they would have to move to find other employment. They may also have longer breaks in earnings, and a decrease in income over time. In medium and large communities, laid off workers may have more opportunities in other industrial sectors, and may not have to resort to geographic mobility.

This paper will use an experimental data source being developed in Statistics Canada to address a number of questions about the issues described above:

1. How heterogeneous—in terms of industrial structure—are communities in Atlantic Canada, and in particular, what differentiates small from large communities?

2. Did the resource communities develop a more diversified industrial structure during 1981-1986?

3. In general, did workers from small communities face more difficult labour market conditions over the early 1980s than workers from large communities? (How important is community size in determining the manner in which workers adjust?).

4.   Did the labour market experiences of workers in small natural
     resource towns differ significantly from those of workers in other
     small communities?

5.   Four communities of different size, industrial structure and
     economic history are selected to determine how their workers fared
     compared to workers in general in Atlantic Canada over the same
     period. The four communities are Corner Brook, Newfoundland;
     Labrador City, Newfoundland; Summerside, P.E.I.; and Halifax,
     Nova Scotia.

Methodology

The following is a brief outline of the methodology. More detail is given
in Appendix I, and in a paper describing the database construction
(Heath 1990).

Geographical information on both the workers (postal codes from
Revenue Canada files) and the firms where the workers are employed
(postal codes for firms from Statistics Canada's business register) is
used to allocate workers to a community. The geographical location
refers to the worker's place of employment, not necessarily the place of
residence. Information on annual income, unemployment insurance
benefits, age, gender, and industry for each worker in any year comes
from Revenue Canada and business register data files. This information is available for workers for each year, and hence a longitudinal
microdata source is created (i.e. information on the same worker over
time) for 1981 to 1986. In this study, information is used only for the
end points of this period, in most cases.

The industrial distribution of the payroll in a particular community is
calculated simply by adding the annual payroll of all workers employed
in that community (not necessarily resident there) during any year
(e.g. 1981 and 1986). Payroll is a good indicator of the industrial
structure of a community because it measures an industry's contribution to the community through the paycheque. All communities in
Atlantic Canada are classified according to three sizes—small (700 to
5,000 workers), medium (5,000 to 20,000 workers) and large (more than
20,000 workers)—and four types of industrial structure: natural
resource, public service, diversified and other. Quartiles are used to
allocate the towns to types of industrial structure. Within each size
class, the one-fourth of all towns which have the highest share of payroll
in the natural resource sector are classified as natural resource
communities. Similarly, one-quarter are allocated to the public service
sector, and the one-quarter most diversified (as measured by the
Herfindal index based on industrial distribution of payroll) are called
diversified communities. The remaining one-quarter are left in the
"other" category. The change in industrial structure (i.e. industrial
distribution of payroll) is measured for communities during 1981-1986.

Four indicators of labour market conditions for workers are developed and used:

1. the change in annual employment earnings,

2. the proportion of workers with earnings in 1981 but not 1986,

3. the unemployment insurance benefits received by the workers (as a proxy for unemployment) and,

4. the proportion of workers migrating.

These measures are described in more detail later.

The major interest in this paper is how the labour market conditions changed for workers with a strong labour market attachment. A large volume of workers with low ($1,000 to $5,000) annual earnings result from partial attachment to the labour force. Hence, the four labour market indicators outlined above were calculated only for workers with labour market earnings of more than $6,600 in 1981 (the annual earnings for a full-time worker in a job paying the minimum wage). The industrial payroll in the communities, however, was calculated using the earnings of all workers in that community.

The industrial structure of small and large towns

The industrial structure of small communities differs from that of large communities in two ways. First, small towns are more dependent on natural resources[3] than their larger counterparts. And second, large communities develop distributive services (transportation, communications, wholesale trade) and business services (financial services, consulting, etc.) sectors which smaller communities do not possess to the same degree. In 1986, 26% of the payroll in larger communities came from these industries, compared to only 12% in small communities (Table 1 and Figure 2). This has implications for workers. Because of cyclical downturns such as the early 1980s and as a result of longer term structural changes occurring in the economy, the natural resource and other goods-producing sectors' share of jobs has declined. The natural resource sector's share of total payroll in Atlantic Canada fell from 14% in 1981 to 11% in 1986. This naturally affected the resource-dependent communities, and in particular the small communities where the dependence on natural resources is greater.

---

3. Natural resources here includes both primary industries, plus natural resource manufacturing industries (i.e. pulp and paper, wood, fish processing, utilities and petroleum and coal industries).

TABLE 1

Industrial distribution of payroll, by community type, Atlantic communities, 1981 and 1986

Community type	Natural resouces	Other manufact- uring	Distri- butive services	Consumer services	Business services	Public services	Constr- uction	Total	No. commu- nities	No. workers >$6,600
	%	%	%	%	%	%	%	%		(,000)
Natural resource*										**1981**
Small	61.3	3.1	3.8	9.0	2.1	17.9	2.8	100.0	27	18.2
Medium	40.3	3.5	9.2	18.8	3.5	20.8	3.9	100.0	5	38.1
Large	29.0	3.3	10.5	13.8	5.9	32.5	5.1	100.0	1	30.6
Total	40.9	3.3	8.5	15.1	4.0	24.0	4.1	100.0	33	86.9
Public service										
Small	9.8	7.1	8.4	11.4	3.3	55.6	4.3	100.0	27	24.4
Medium	6.4	4.6	6.6	13.7	3.9	59.6	5.1	100.0	5	21.9
Large	7.1	5.0	8.9	15.9	8.7	49.6	4.9	100.0	1	22.1
Total	7.8	5.6	8.0	13.6	5.3	54.8	4.8	100.0	33	68.4
Other										
Small	16.7	7.7	17.0	17.5	2.7	31.6	6.7	100.0	27	16.5
Medium	8.7	8.1	23.3	13.8	5.4	36.6	4.2	100.0	5	25.6
Large	5.0	7.3	14.8	13.8	10.6	43.4	5.1	100.0	4	167.1
Total	6.2	7.4	16.0	14.1	9.4	41.7	5.1	100.0	34	209.3
Diversified										
Small	21.2	11.2	11.5	14.7	4.7	31.3	5.5	100.0	27	27.7
Medium	13.2	15.3	14.5	15.5	5.5	30.7	5.2	100.0	6	34.5
Large	8.0	14.5	20.7	13.5	9.3	27.6	6.4	100.0	2	104.7
Total	11.2	14.2	18.0	14.1	7.8	28.8	6.0	100.0	37	166.9
Total										
Small	25.9	7.7	10.0	13.1	3.4	35.2	4.8	100.0	108	86.8
Medium	20.4	7.9	13.1	16.0	4.5	33.5	4.5	100.0	21	120.2
Large	8.2	9.1	15.9	13.8	9.6	37.8	5.5	100.0	8	324.5
Total	13.7	8.6	14.4	14.2	7.5	36.4	5.2	100.0	137	531.6
Natural resource*										**1986**
Small	54.9	2.7	3.3	10.5	1.9	23.7	3.0	100.0	27	
Medium	32.2	4.3	7.3	12.4	4.4	34.1	5.4	100.0	5	
Large	20.0	3.4	14.4	15.5	5.0	36.0	5.7	100.0	1	
Total	32.4	3.6	9.0	13.1	4.1	32.8	5.0	100.0	33	
Public service										
Small	8.0	6.8	8.2	14.2	2.9	54.3	5.6	100.0	27	
Medium	6.2	4.9	6.6	13.5	4.1	61.0	3.7	100.0	5	
Large	7.1	5.5	8.0	14.3	5.8	48.8	4.8	100.0	1	
Total	7.1	5.5	8.0	14.3	5.8	54.5	4.8	100.0	33	
Other										
Small	16.1	10.1	12.2	15.2	2.9	38.5	5.0	100.0	27	
Medium	7.5	8.6	11.6	16.2	5.6	46.6	4.0	100.0	5	
Large	4.9	6.7	14.8	14.4	12.0	41.8	5.5	100.0	4	
Total	5.9	7.2	14.2	14.6	10.7	42.1	5.3	100.0	34	
Diversified										
Small	18.6	10.3	9.1	16.7	4.5	36.2	4.7	100.0	27	
Medium	12.6	15.7	11.1	15.8	6.0	34.8	4.1	100.0	6	
Large	9.7	12.7	16.5	15.0	7.6	33.6	4.9	100.0	1	
Total	11.2	14.2	18.0	14.1	7.8	28.8	6.0	100.0	37	
Total										
Small	22.5	7.7	8.3	14.5	3.3	39.1	4.7	100.0	108	
Medium	16.6	8.6	9.1	14.4	5.1	41.9	4.4	100.0	21	
Large	6.8	8.1	16.0	14.5	10.3	39.0	5.4	100.0	8	
Total	11.2	8.1	13.4	14.5	8.1	39.6	5.1	100.0	137	

* Including primary industries plus resource and other manufacturing (wood, pulp and paper, fish processing, utilities)

Source: Statistics Canada. Business and Labour Market Analysis Group.

Overall, small communities in Atlantic Canada lost ground over the early 1980s largely because the natural resources sector declined. The value (in constant dollars) of payroll in the natural resource sector in small communities fell by 16% during 1981-1986 although there was some recovery in employment in that sector in 1987 and 1988 (Figure 1). Nonetheless, as a result of this large decline in natural resource payroll in these small towns, their industrial structure became more concentrated in the public sector (Figure 2). The proportion of payroll in the public sector increased slightly from 35% to 39%, and the Herfindal index of concentration[4] increased from .227 to .240 during 1981-1986, indicating increased concentration.

FIGURE 2

Distribution of payroll by industry, 1981 and 1986

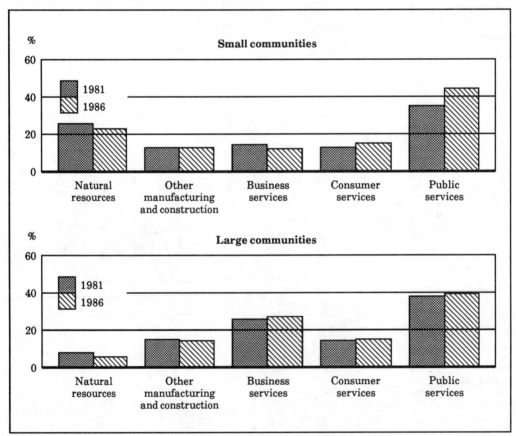

Source: Statistics Canada. Business and Labour Market Analysis Group.

---

4.   Simply the sum across all industries of the square of the payroll share (or proportion) in each industry.

Thus, small communities in general lost ground, largely because of the downturn in natural resources. As a result, their payroll became more concentrated in the public services sector.

The heterogeneous nature of small communities

Small Atlantic communities are not a homogeneous group; their industrial structure varies dramatically (Figure 3). An equal number of the 108 small communities were allocated to each of four categories: natural resource, public sector, diversified and other. The one-quarter of the small towns which are most dependent on natural resources had fully 61% of their payroll in that sector in 1981. But the same number of small communities depended equally on the public sector (health, education and government). These 27 communities had, on average, 56% of their payroll from that sector. Similarly, the one-quarter most diversified communities have a relatively flat distribution of payroll across industrial structure. This clearly has implications for the stability of the local economy and labour market conditions for workers. This paper is focusing on small, resource-based communities. Like small towns in general, they lost substantial ground over this period. Their share of total payroll in Atlantic Canada (as a proxy for employment) fell from 3.4% in 1981 to 2.9% in 1986. The natural resource sector declined as the value (in constant dollars) of payroll fell by 20% over the period in small resource towns. This decline made it look as if these communities became more diversified, as the dependence in natural resources seemed to decline and the Herfindal index of concentration fell from .420 to .372. However, little expansion of other industrial sectors in these communities occurred as the total payroll (in constant dollars) fell in all industries except for the public services, where it rose 3% annually. Thus, diversification came mainly as a result of the decline in the major industrial sector, not because of growth in other sectors.

FIGURE 3

Distribution of payroll, small community types, 1981 and 1986

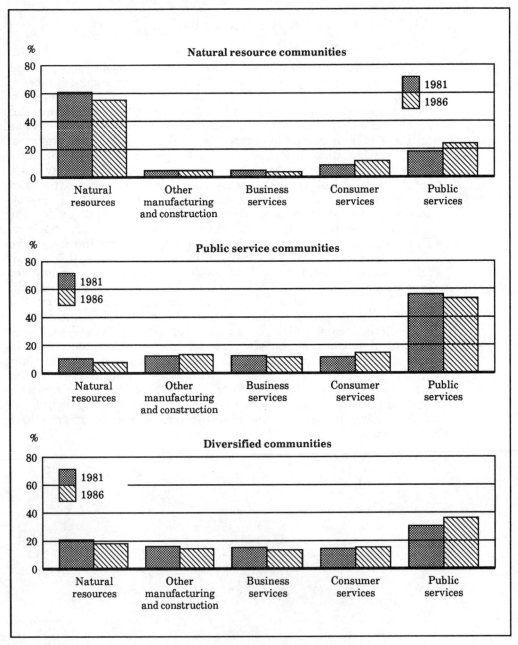

Source: Statistics Canada. Business and Labour Market Analysis Group.

With this background on the industrial structure of these communities, the labour market experiences of workers are now considered.

Labour market experiences of workers from different communities

The interest in the vulnerability of small resource towns' economies comes in part from the effect that it has on labour market conditions, earnings and unemployment. That effect is addressed by using longitudinal data on workers during 1981-1986. Workers who had a strong labour force attachment in 1981 are of key interest. Those workers who earned only a few thousand dollars during the year because of their weak attachment to the labour force were excluded. Only persons earning more than $6,600 in 1981 are included in the analysis (approximately annual earnings for a full-time worker at minimum wage).

Four indicators assess workers' labour market experiences:

1. change in annual employment earnings for workers who have earnings in both 1981 and 1986. This change can result from a change in hours worked or wages paid, but it is a good measure of the overall earnings the labour market generated during the year.

2. the proportion of workers with earnings in 1981 but no earnings in 1986. The absence of employment earnings in 1986 may be caused by retirement, emigration from Canada, death, or unemployment. The proportion of workers with no earnings in 1986 is tabulated for those 25-44 to eliminate the impact of retirement or death. Emigration from Canada is quite small for all age groups.

3. the unemployment insurance benefits received by workers in any group during a given year as a proportion of all employment earnings for that group during the year. This is used as an indicator of unemployment.

4. the proportion of workers[5] (in any group) who were in the same community in both 1981 and 1986. This is a measure of the geographical mobility of a group of workers.

---

5. For workers who had earnings in both years, since if no tax form is filed, the place of residence cannot be established.

There are four major observations using these indicators.

A. **Workers from small communities generally faced less favourable labour markets than workers in large communities and outmigration is generally higher from small communities.**

In small communities, workers' earnings declined by 3% on average between 1981 and 1986 (in real dollars), while those in large communities increased by 3% (Table 2). Of course, information on the change in cost of living would be needed to completely assess these differences, but while the cost of living may be lower in small towns, the change in the cost of living is likely to be similar in both small and large communities.

Much of this difference may be an industry effect, since the natural resource sector is more significant in smaller communities. To control for the industry mix in each community, a regression analysis was conducted. In addition to the industry mix, other variables taken into account were the age and gender composition of the worker population, earnings in 1981[6], and industrial and geographic mobility. After the contribution of all these variables were taken into account, there still remained a significant difference in the rate of change of earnings for workers from small and large communities over this period.

These findings are supported by the UI benefits results. Unemployment insurance benefits were 6% of total employment earnings among workers from small towns, compared with 3% among those from large centres, suggesting more unemployment in small towns.

Geographic mobility declined as size of community increased; 70% of workers in small towns were still there in 1986, compared to 80% of workers in medium size towns, and 90% of workers from large communities. This is not surprising, since the broader range of job opportunities in a large city means that when workers want to, or are forced to change jobs, they are more likely to be able to remain in a large centre to do so than in a small community.

B. **Among different types of small communities, workers from natural resource towns encountered the most difficult labour market, but this did not result in higher outmigration rates in those towns.**

---

6. The ln $\left(\frac{\text{earning } 86}{\text{earning } 81}\right)$ was the dependent variable. The log of earnings in 1981 were included as a dependent variable because workers with low earnings tend to have more rapid increases than those with high earnings.

As mentioned earlier, small communities have heterogeneous industrial structures, and hence the labour market outcomes of their workers is also likely to vary considerably. The labour market experiences of workers from the three community types (natural resource, diversified and public service) were of interest. Over this period, the more prevalent the public service sector in the community, the better the labour market for the workers—the more prevalent the natural resources sector, the worse the labour market.

Average earnings <u>declined</u> almost 5% among workers from small natural resource towns, while they remained the same among workers in small public service communities. UI benefits usage supports the differential (benefits were 8% of earnings in small natural resource communities compared to 4% in small public service communities) as did the proportion of workers with earnings in 1981 but none in 1986 (9% compared to 6%). But in spite of these differences, the proportion remaining in the community was if anything, highest in the small natural resource towns[7] (Table 2).

C. **Within small, natural resource communities, workers in the goods-producing industry encountered a much more difficult labour market than those in the commercial or public services.**

Another issue of interest is whether all workers are affected equally when a small community faces a downturn. One might argue that as the major industry declines, there is a sort of negative multiplier effect. As the purchasing power of workers in the affected sector decreases, jobs in other sectors of the community are also affected.

While this is likely the case, these indicators suggest a very significant difference in the impact on the earnings and unemployment on various workers. Those in the goods sector saw their earnings <u>fall</u> on average 7%, while those in the public services in the same small natural resource towns had an average <u>increase</u> of almost 2% in earnings. The earnings and employment of the public service workers are not as dependent on immediate market conditions as workers in the private sector. The UI usage supports this, as it was 10% (as % of earnings) among goods sector workers and only 3% among public sector workers, indicating much more unemployment in these small resource towns among the goods workers. The labour market conditions for commercial service sector workers were between those for the goods and public sector workers: the weaker the economic link to the goods sector, the better the workers in these towns did in earnings gain and employment.

---

7. The very low rate in the public service communities is likely related to high mobility among Armed Forces personnel.

TABLE 2

Outcome on the four indicators for workers from communities of different sizes, 1981-1986

	Small	Medium	Large
Average % change in earnings (those with earnings in both years)	-2.6	-0.6	2.7
UI benefits received (as a % of earnings over 6 years for all workers)	5.8	4.1	2.9
% with no earnings in 1986 (25-44 years olds)	6.9	6.2	7.5
% of workers remaining in community*	70	80	90

Outcomes for workers from different types of small communities, 1981-1986

	Natural resource	Diver- sified	Public service
Average % change in earnings (those with earnings in both years)	-4.9	-2.4	-0.2
UI benefits received (as a % of earnings over 6 years for all workers)	8.1	5.3	4.4
% with no earnings in 1986 (25-44 year olds)	8.7	6.7	5.7
% of workers remaining in community*	74	70	65

Outcomes for workers in small natural resource communities, by industrial sector of employment, 1981-1986

	Goods- producing	Commercial service	Public service
Average % change in earnings (those with earnings in both years)	-7.1	-3.9	1.8
UI benefits received (as a % of earnings over 6 years for all workers)	10.2	6.5	2.7
% with no earnings in 1986 (25-44 year olds)	8.4	8.0	4.4
% of workers remaining in community*	75	62	71

Note: For workers earning more than $6,600 in 1981. The community size refers to the community in which the workers worked in 1981.

* % of workers with earnings in both 1981 and 1986, since place of residence is determined from tax records and it is necessary for the worker to have employment earnings in both 1981 and 1986 to be included in these tabulations.

Source: Statistics Canada. Business and Labour Market Analysis Group.

In spite of this difference in labour market conditions, the goods sector workers were no more likely to move than other workers. The percent of workers (with earnings in both years) remaining in the community was highest among the goods sector workers. While no attempt is made in this exploratory study to determine why this is the case, it may be related to a many factors:

1. Educational attainment of workers and job opportunities.
    Workers in the goods sector in small communities often have relatively low levels of education, making it difficult for them to locate work elsewhere. As a result, job opportunities may be very limited in other communities.

2. Potentially large financial losses when selling fixed assets.
   A decline in the value of large fixed assets, particularly a house, would discourage many from selling and moving.

3. Social and family ties.
   Many workers may have lived in the communities for a considerable time, and social and family ties may be very strong.

4. A spouse holding employment.
   As more and more families become dual-income families, one spouse losing a job does not necessarily imply zero employment earnings for the family. The cushion of the second income may retard migration.

5. Workers' expectation about recovery.
   In boom and bust communities workers likely witness downturns and recoveries over their working lives. The expectation that conditions will improve (in some cases a false expectation) may discourage workers from moving to other communities, particularly when the upturn would provide a high-wage job relative to what the worker might earn in other communities or industries.

6. Effect of unemployment insurance and other transfer payments.
   Unemployment insurance benefits may discourage worker mobility, especially in combination with the items listed here.

7. The relative importance of migration to other jobs versus migration away from unemployment.
   In many communities, "pull" migration is much more important then "push" migration. In the public service communities in particular, a great portion of the migrants may be people leaving jobs to move to better jobs or people transferring jobs. This may be a significant portion of migration in some communities. In natural resource communities, this type of migration may be much lower. Thus, the aggregate outmigration rate in a resource town may be lower than, say, in public sector towns, even if the "push" outmigration (leaving because of unemployment) is higher.

Some or all of these factors may help explain the outmigration rates observed in this work. However, it is beyond the scope of this exploratory work to attempt to determine the relative importance of each factor.

Labour market experiences of workers from four communities

Having portrayed some baseline information, we now focus on four specific communities. Knowledge of general trends in different types of communities is necessary to place findings for a specific community within a context, or to make general statements about the effect of structural change on different types of communities. However, the real advantage of our database is its ability to look at specific communities and types of workers within these communities. Three medium sized and one large community are selected to demonstrate this aspect of the database. These communities were selected to validate this experimental data source. Data from both the census and the experimental source were readily available for these communities:

1. Corner Brook, Newfoundland
    This city of around 30,000 was growing at about 1% per year during 1981-1986. The pulp and paper and the forestry industry were important in the community. During the early 1980s a very large mill made major renovations which resulted in productivity gains and many displaced workers. In fact, this community is quite diversified (Table 3). Although the natural resource sector is relatively large, the distributive services sector (transportation, communications, wholesale trade) is also above average in size. Nonetheless, there was substantial unemployment in this area during the early 1980s.

2. Labrador City, Newfoundland
    This community of around 13,000 is a classic single industry town as it is almost totally dependent upon the iron ore mining industry. During the 1960s and 1970s this was a major centre, but as the U.S. steel industry declined in the 1980s, the mining industry here and in nearby communities had major closures. The community shrank at a rate of about 4% annually during 1981-1986. The average earnings of workers in this community were extremely high ($34,300 in 1981) compared to most other communities ($20,000 to $25,000).

3. Summerside, P.E.I.
    Largely dependent on the public services sector (including defence), this community of about 13,000 grew about 1% per year during 1981-1986. The industrial base of this town is radically different from the first two.

4. Halifax, Nova Scotia
    Chosen as a reference point, this large centre (255,000 in 1981) grew at 1% per year over the period. While quite diversified, this city is also highly dependent on the public service sector (e.g. defence, provincial government, university, health) as 43% of payroll comes from that sector (Table 3). It also has an above average size business service sector and distributive service sector. It has a relatively small natural resource sector.

TABLE 3
Industrial distribution of payroll in four Atlantic communities, 1981 and 1986

	Corner Brook, Newfoundland		Labrador City, Newfoundland		Summerside, P.E.I.		Halifax, Nova Scotia	
Population								
1981	29,400		13,000		13,600		255,000	
Growth, 1981 to 1986	+1%/year		-4.4%/year		+0.7%/year		+1.3%/year	
Industrial distribution of payroll (%)	1981	1986	1981	1986	1981	1986	1981	1986
Natural resource	25	20	70	61	4	4	5	4
Other manufacturing	4	7	2	2	6	8	8	7
Construction	6	4	2	4	6	5	5	6
Distributive services	26	12	6	6	9	9	14	14
Construction services	25	15	7	9	17	17	14	14
Business services	5	6	2	2	5	6	11	11
Public services	29	36	12	16	52	52	44	42
Average 1981 ($) earnings of workers with strong labour force attachment*	24,100		34,300		21,300		24,800	

*   i.e. earning more than $6,600 in 1981.

Source: Statistics Canada. Business and Labour Market Analysis Group.

A comparison of the labour market conditions

Workers remaining in Corner Brook over the period experienced more difficult labour market conditions than those from other communities, notably compared to those in Halifax or regional workers in general. Corner Brook workers who stayed in the community saw their earnings fall by almost 5% on average compared to a 2% increase for all workers in the region (Table 4). Their UI benefits were 5% of earnings, compared to 3% for all workers and 2% for Halifax workers remaining in the community. Furthermore, this 5% loss in earnings masks the fact that 53% of workers remaining in Corner Brook saw their earnings fall by an average 27% in real terms over the period.

Workers who left Labrador City—likely because of job loss in that single industry community—generally did not encounter favourable labour market conditions compared to other workers. The vast majority of them (77%) took pay cuts, and among all workers the annual earnings decreased by an average 35%. (The 77% taking pay cuts saw their annual earnings fall 50% in real terms). This left the workers with an average pay below that of other workers (at $19,300 compared to $21,700), although their 1981 earnings had been well above that of other workers. And UI benefits among this population (averaged over all six years) were 11% of earnings, compared to 7% for all workers who moved in Atlantic Canada. Thus, the 25% of workers leaving this classic single industry community and moving within Atlantic Canada did not face favourable labour market conditions. Workers who managed to continue working in Labrador City did better even though their earnings declined on average.

TABLE 4
Labour market conditions for workers from four communities during 1981-1986

All workers	Corner Brook	Labrador City	Summerside	Halifax	All workers in Atlantic Canada
No.of Workers earning more than $6,600 in 1981 (,000)	9.5	6.2	5.2	112.8	531.6
Average earnings in 1981 ($)	24,100	34,700	21,400	25,200	23,600
No earnings in 1986, population aged 25-44 (%)	5.6	6.3	5.1	7.9	7.1
Change in earnings, 1981-1986 (%)	-3.8	-17.2	3.7	6.5	1.2
UI benefits as % of earnings (over all six years)	5.6	4.9	3.8	2.4	3.6
Workers remaining in community*					
% of all workers who remain	83.0	59.0	64.0	82.0	78.0
Change in earnings, 1981-1986 (%)	-4.9	-11.9	1.5	6.7	1.5
Average earnings in 1986 ($)	23,100	33,300	20,600	25,900	24,400
UI benefits as % of earnings (over all six years)	4.7	2.3	3.2	1.7	3.1
Workers moving in Atlantic Canada*					
% of all workers who move within Atlantic Canada	11.0	25.0	21.0	8.0	14.0
Change in earnings, 1981-1986 (%)	-3.1	-35.0	0.5	3.9	-5.3
Average earnings in 1986 ($)	22,200	19,300	22,200	22,200	21,700
UI benefits as % of earnings (over all six years)	7.0	11.0	5.2	4.9	6.8

* percent of workers with earnings in both 1981 and 1986, since without employment earnings their geographic location is not known.

Source: Statistics Canada. Business and Labour Market Analysis Group.

Workers from the mainly public sector community of Summerside, and the larger diversified city of Halifax in general experienced less difficulty. Earnings among Summerside workers rose 4%, and among Halifax workers 7%, compared to a 1% rise for workers in general in Atlantic Canada. They also experienced relatively little unemployment (as indicted by UI benefits received).

Not surprisingly, workers in different communities encountered different labour market conditions during 1981-1986.

The large variance in change in annual earnings

The average change in earnings for a group of workers masks a tremendous variability in the experiences of individual workers. There is a surprisingly large variation in the annual earnings of individual workers, even among males aged 25-44.

For workers selected in this study for Atlantic Canada, average earnings rose 1% (for workers earning more than $6,600 in 1981 and with earnings in both years). But this masks that the 61% of workers who gained real earnings saw their earnings rise by 27% on average, and the 39% whose earnings fell experienced an average 33% loss.

Some of this decline could have been related to retirement, workers dropping out of the labour force to raise children, or for other reasons. However, even when the earnings variability of males aged 25-44 are considered, the result is much the same.

TABLE 5

Volatility of earnings for males 25-44

	Corner Brook	Labrador City	Sum- merside	Halifax	All workers in Atlantic Canada
Average earnings in 1981 ($)	27,800	39,000	24,600	29,400	27,800
Average % change in earnings 1981-1986 (workers with earnings in both years)	-6.1	-18.9	2.8	3.8	3.2
Gainers					
% with earnings gain	47	25	70	69	60
Average gain (%)	26	20	20	27	24
Losers					
% with earnings loss	53	75	30	31	40
Average loss (%)	-26	-25	-30	-27	-28

Source: Statistics Canada. Small Business and Labour Market Analysis Group.

For males 25-44, the gainers and losers in real income for the four Atlantic communities and all Atlantic Canada (earning >$6,600) is shown in Table 5. While the average earnings change was 3% among these workers in Atlantic Canada, 60% of them experienced a gain of 24%, while 40% lost 28% in real earnings. There is a tremendous amount of variance in earnings change, and the average masks substantial variations.

Conclusion

The natural resource sector in Atlantic Canada declined during the recession of the early 1980s, and by 1986 had not recovered to its pre-recession level. Communities based on natural resource industries tend to be smaller on average and they appeared to become more diversified during 1981-1986. However, a decline in natural resource employment is responsible, not an expansion in other sectors.

The labour market experiences of individual workers differs by size of community and by the industry mix of employment in the community. Workers in smaller communities experienced a decline in real earnings whereas workers in larger towns experienced an increase in real earnings. Among the smaller communities, the real earnings of workers declined the most in natural resource communities.

Workers in smaller communities were more likely to move compared to workers in larger communities. However, among the smaller communities, mobility in the natural resource communities was the lowest.

Within smaller natural resource communities, the real earnings of workers in the goods sector declined whereas the real earnings of workers in the commercial or public service sectors increased. However, workers in the goods sector still reported a lower mobility rate out of the community.

The average change in earnings for a group of workers masks a tremendous variability in the experiences of individual workers. For example, the average Atlantic Canada worker with earnings of more than $6,600 in 1981 and with some earnings in 1986 experienced a 1% increase in earnings. This masks the fact that 61% of the workers experienced a 27% gain in real earnings and 39% of the workers experienced a 33% decline in real earnings.

Like any study with a focus on a particular period, these findings are determined by the economic events of the time. The 1981 to 1986 period was chosen because 1981 preceded the recession and the economy had recovered by 1986. Also, it was helpful to compare the data from this experimental data source with the census of population for the two periods. This database facilitates cross-section (i.e. one point in time) and annual longitudinal analysis of workers and firms at the municipal level. Development of the database is continuing.

Garnett Picot
John Heath
Business and Labour Market
   Analysis Group
Statistics Canada
Ottawa, K1A 0T6

Appendix I

Classifying the communities

One of the strengths of this data source is its wide coverage of virtually all workers and communities. To take advantage of the wide coverage, all communities in Atlantic Canada which had more than 700 workers (137 communities) were included in the analysis.

For communities greater than roughly 10,000 population, geographical boundaries of the municipalities were determined by Statistics Canada's postal code conversion file, which converts postal codes to municipal areas for census agglomerations (CAs typically have a population between 10,000 and 100,000) and census metropolitan areas (CMAs have populations over 100,000). Commuters living outside the municipality in the surrounding rural postal code areas but working in the community were included in the municipality counts (see Heath 1990). For communities under approximately 10,000 in population, the rural postal code area for the town is used. Hence, the geographical unit of observation for the small communities is not necessarily the municipal boundaries, but rather the rural postal code area to which the community belongs. Fairly large areas can encompass more than the community itself, but the areas are usually very sparsely populated outside the smaller community.

The communities were classified by size and industrial structure as of 1981. This year was selected to ascertain the type of community in which workers resided at the beginning of the period. Three size classes were used, 700-4,999 workers in 1981, 5,000-19,999 and 20,000 or more workers. This roughly converts to groups based on population of 1,200 to 8,500, 8,500 to 35,000, and over 35,000. Industrial structure was measured by the distribution of the town's total payroll across a seven industry classification. Payroll is a better measure than employment because of the wide variation among industries in hours worked (share of part-time employment). It is useful as well because the amount of money an industry contributes to the local economy through paycheques is of interest to communities. It must be remembered, however, that the distribution of payroll may differ significantly from the distribution of employment, particularly for sectors which have above average wage rates (e.g. public service) or hours of work which differ significantly from the average (e.g. consumer services). For this classification, primary industries (excluding agriculture, which was dropped from the study) were combined with natural resource manufacturing industries to form the natural resource sector. Any economic event which affected the primary sector would also directly affect the processing industries directly dependent on the natural resources.

This work did not attempt to classify single industry communities. That requires some sense of an absolute measure of dependence on an industry, and it is difficult to know at what level of industrial concentration a town becomes a single industry community. Rather a relative measure of industrial dominance was used. Thus the most natural resource towns could be compared to the most public service towns, and so on.

Four types of community structure are used: natural resource communities, public service communities, industrially diversified communities, and communities classified to an "other" category. Within each size class towns were divided into quartiles based on their industrial structure. Hence, one-quarter of the communities were allocated to each industrial structure class.

The natural resource dominant communities include the 25% of communities (within each size class) that are the most dependent upon the natural resource sector for the town's payroll. This is different then identifying single industry communities where the absolute dependence of the community in a single sector must be identified. Similarly, the public service sector includes the 25% of communities with the largest public service sectors. The diversified group contains the 25% of communities which have the most diversified industrial structure (based on the distribution of payroll) as measured by the Herfindal index, a commonly used measure of diversification (or concentration). The remaining 25% of communities within each size class is the "other" category. This group has a work force which is neither among the most concentrated in natural resources or public services, nor the most diversified.

This classification method results in 108 small communities divided equally among the four industrial classifications (27 in each), 21 medium-sized communities with approximately 5 in each industrial class, and 8 large communities.

The quartile approach used to classify the community resulted in cut-off points being established by the method. These cut-off points are the following: all small communities with more than 40% of the payroll in the natural resources sector were identified as natural resource communities. This cut-off for medium and large communities was 27% because they have larger service sectors than smaller communities. For the public service sector, communities with greater than 44% of payroll in the sector were said to be public service dominant. And finally, communities for which the Herfindal index was less than .27 (for small), and .21 (medium) and .23 for large were said to be diversified. This difference in the cut-offs indicates that small communities generally have more concentrated industrial structures than large.

References

Atlantic Provinces Economic Council. 1987. Atlantic Canada
Today. Halifax: Formac Publishing Ltd.

Beale, E.J. 1989. Regional Development in Atlantic Canada. An
Overview and a Case Study of the Human Resources Development
Agency , Local Development Paper #3. Ottawa: Economic
Council of Canada.

Decter, M.B. 1989. Diversification and Single Industry Communities:
The Implications of a Community Economic Development
Approach , Local Development Paper #10. Ottawa: Economic
Council of Canada.

Economic Council of Canada. 1990. From the Bottom Up, the
Community Economic Development Approach. Ottawa: Economic
Council of Canada.

Employment and Immigration Canada. 1987. Canada's Single-
Industry Communities: A Proud Determination to Survive.
Ottawa: Canada Employment and Immigration Advisory Council.

Employment and Immigration Canada. 1988. Canada's Single-
Industry Communities: In Search of a New Partnership. Hull,
Quebec: Canada Employment and Immigration Advisory Council.

Heath, J. 1990. Developing a Small Area Business and Labour
Database. Business and Labour Market Analysis
Group,(mimeo).Ottawa: Statistics Canada.

Locke, Wade. 1986. Lets recycle our throwaway communities and
disposable workers: policies for dealing with mining communities.
Background Report. St. John's, Newfoundland: Royal Commission
on Employment and Unemployment.

Robson, R. 1986. Canadian Single Industry Communities:
A Literature and Annotated Bibliography. Rural and Small Town
Research Studies Programme, Department of Geography.
Sackville, New Brunswick: Mount Allison University.

Newfoundland. 1986. Building on Our Strengths. Report of the Royal
Commission on Employment and Unemployment. St. John's,
Newfoundland: Royal Commission on Employment and
Unemployment.

9

Distance and diversity in nonmetropolitan economies

Philip Ehrensaft and Jennifer Beeman

Summary

The post-1945 transformation of Canadian economy and society sorted the population into a new tripartite settlement structure: one third of Canada's population resides in the three major metro areas of Toronto, Montreal and Vancouver; another third resides in medium and small metro areas; and the remaining third is spread across Canada's vast nonmetro hinterland. Predominantly rural counties and townships contain only a small minority of the nonmetro population or even of the total rural population. Rural dynamics are played out in local contexts dominated by small cities and small towns.

Rural economic and social dynamics must be understood as the joint product of the low population which structurally defines rurality and the regional context which shapes the manner in which the consequences of low population density are played out. By context, we mean, in addition to the evident impact of sectoral specialization, the regional location along the new and variegated urban-rural spectrum which has been shaped since World War II. The labour force and demographic dynamics of a rural settlement will vary according to:

- whether it is located in a nonmetro county where the dominant component of the local population is composed of small cities, small towns or villages and dispersed rural residences, or whether the settlement is part of the outer zone of a metropolitan labour force area; and

- whether a nonmetro county is adjacent or not adjacent to a metropolitan area.

The composition and economic welfare of local labour forces vary systematically, though not always in a linear manner, along the new urban-rural spectrum. The Beale code perspective on understanding the new urban-rural spectrum is tested in the Canadian context and found to be a valuable tool for rural and small town policy analysis.

Distance and density count, and they count jointly. Lumping "rurban" and hinterland counties together produces measurements which run the risk of creating averages which poorly reflect conditions in either metro-adjacent or nonadjacent counties. Macro-diversity and micro-specialization in Canada's vast nonmetropolitan hinterland is compounded by the independent effects of the new and variegated urban-rural spectrum.

Table of contents

Distance and diversity in nonmetropolitan economies

Philip Ehrensaft and Jennifer Beeman

1. Introduction

Restructuring of the economic space outside Canada's metropolitan regions proceeded along two dimensions during the post-war decades. First, there was an unprecedented reorganization of the rural and small town labour force. Canada's farm population became a minority of the total rural population during the 1950s. More recently, the proportion of the labour force engaged in goods production—manufacturing and construction as well as primary commodities—has also become a minority of the total labour force in most of Canada's rural counties and townships. The economic diversification of Canada's economic hinterland as a whole, "macro-diversification", has been accompanied by increased specialization of local economies, "micro-specialization".

Second, distance and the urban-rural continuum were redefined by massive highway construction and modern telecommunications. Metropolitan regions, defined by the movements of people back and forth from work, spread out beyond boundaries that were not imagined before World War II. Thirty-five percent of the rural population, as defined by Statistics Canada, is now incorporated in the outer fringes of labour force basins which have total populations of at least 50,000.

The small cities, small towns, and rural regions adjacent to metropolitan regions form a second zone on the urban-rural continuum. This adjacent nonmetro zone is defined by the movement of goods and communications to and from metro regions. These regions are too far to make commuting to metro areas acceptable for most people, but close enough for trucks to economically transport goods to metro centres and close enough to absorb modest long-distance charges for telecommunications.

The economic future of the adjacent nonmetro counties and townships looks promising compared to the third zone of nonmetro regions which are nonadjacent to large urban settlements. For this third zone, distance is a formidable and troubling barrier to economic and demographic viability.

Economic conditions and prospects in the two nonmetropolitan settlement zones have experienced disruptive and deleterious changes during the past decade. Furthermore, these recent changes are probably the harbingers of long-term trends.

During the 1970s, the combination of buoyant prices for primary products, the rural demographic "renaissance", and the favourable performance of small town manufacturing created an optimistic perspective. Part and parcel of this optimism was the predominant view that indirect spillover effects from effective sectoral policies would be the main support for the economic and social viability of nonmetropolitan regions. Explicit rural and small town development policies atrophied at the national level and a similar statement would by and large apply for most provincial governments.

The economic stresses of the 1980s have been associated with negative rather than positive sectoral spillover effects for large fractions of rural and small town Canada. The rural population renaissance has been arrested and it is problematic whether this rural and small town demographic dynamism will, in the absence of policy intiatives, ever return.

Creating new policies to help nonmetro regions restructure their economic base will be difficult without the renewal of a knowledge base that has become rusty, to say the least. Part of this renewal involves making the policy decision to organize existing and inherently rich economic and social data series in the geographically disaggregated form requisite for policy analysis of nonmetropolitan development. A large part of the renewal also involves looking at nonmetro data from a conceptual perspective that takes account of macro-diversification and the reorganization of settlement zones since 1945.

Our objective is to examine the restructuring of nonmetropolitan economies along the joint dimensions of macro-diversification and the new urban-rural continuum. We focus on:

1.   presenting a coding system that reflects the plurality of nonmetro settlement zones and nonmetro economic diversity; and

2.   application of these codes in a cross-sectional analysis of 1986 Census and taxfiler data.

Let us begin with the codes for the settlement zone dimension of nonmetropolitan economic restructuring.

2. Distance and settlement zones: the Beale code approach

Aggregate measures of economic structure, performance and welfare using published data indicate only modest rural-urban differences, despite the popular impression of a crisis in the nonmetropolitan hinterland. This gap is partially rooted in the way "rural" Canada is officially defined and the consequent manner in which "rural" data are collected and analyzed. It is not sufficient to classify the population as rural simply on the basis of having a combination of total population and population density which is less than a specified threshold (in the case of Statistics Canada, less than 1,000 people and a population density less than 400 people per square kilometre).

The regional context of the population in question is equally important in defining the distinct and important varieties of rural demographic structures. By context, we mean the local region in which the settlement is located, the typical units being counties or townships. The labour force and demographic dynamics of a given rural settlement will vary according to:

1. whether the settlement is located in a nonmetro county that is adjacent or not adjacent to a metropolitan area, or is part of the outer fringes of a metro area; and

2. if the settlement is located in a nonmetro county, whether small cities, small towns, or rural settlements are the predominant component in the local demography.

The economic roles, performance and prospects of rural and small town settlements varies systematically with the distance of the host county from metro areas and the rural-urban composition of the host county. This will become clear when we examine labour force and income measures in the different settlement zones. When rural and small town populations are aggregated to the national level and not considered in the context of their regional location, these systematic variations are masked.

Within the post-1945 urban-rural continuum, some nonmetropolitan settlement zones show economic performance and welfare similar to metro areas. This does not necessarily mean that the performance of this nonmetro subgroup is "high" since metro area economies have also faced stresses imposed by continental and international restructuring of production and markets. It does mean a level of performance higher than that of a second subgroup of nonmetro settlement zones where employment and income trends have been distinctly inferior to those of metro regions. When the two subgroups are lumped together, the resultant indices of "modest" metro-nonmetro differences are of limited use for policy analysis in either of the two types of nonmetro regions.

The pioneering effort to take account of rural diversification in an advanced industrial country was initiated by Calvin Beale at the United States Department of Agriculture. Beale developed a system for distinguishing among counties located along different points of the continuum defined by population distance from metropolitan centres and the regional urban-rural mix. This system of classification was based not only on years of examination of rural demographic and economic data but also on the fact that Beale has probably conducted field observations in more of the United States' 2,357 nonmetro counties than any other researcher. Beale's system for classifying and analyzing nonmetropolitan regions has proved useful to so many policy analysts that the settlement classes are commonly referred to as the "Beale codes" (GAO 1989). McGranahan et al. (1986) have synthesized U.S. data to show how social and economic characteristics of local populations vary systematically across Beale code classes.

The major methodological question in employing the Beale codes for rural policy analysis in Canada was not how to draw the boundaries or how to fine tune settlement zone thresholds, but whether the boundaries make analytic sense in a different national context. A number of issues were addressed in applying the Beale codes to the Canadian situation:

1. Have the different settlement histories and political systems in Canada and the U.S. resulted in major differences in social and economic structures such that the Beale codes are of limited applicability here?

Joel Garreau (1982) has identified "Nine Nations of North America". The "nations" which span the formal border are termed, from East to West, "New England", "the Foundry", "the Bread Basket", the "Empty Quarter" and "Ecotopia". For any "nation," the Canadian and U.S. components share many more similarities than would, for example, the Canadian parts of the Bread Basket and New England.

Beale had to develop a coding system that worked both for the northern states which are part of this group of "nations" and the southern states. Codes that worked well for North Dakota or Maine would be expected to work well for Saskatchewan or New Brunswick. They are parts of the same "nation."

2. How does one treat Canada's northern resource hinterland?

Beale's policy codes were created for the 48 contiguous states; Alaska and Hawaii are left out as special cases. Canada's northern hinterland occupies too great a proportion of our land mass and natural resources to leave aside as a residual case. An eleventh northern resource zone was added to Beale's 10 zones. The northern resource zone includes census divisions (CDs) which are entirely or in major part above the following parallels by region: Newfoundland, 50th; Quebec and Ontario, 49th; Manitoba, 53rd; Saskatchewan, Alberta, and British Columbia, 54th; plus the Yukon and Northwest Territories.

3.   Are CDs the appropriate unit to classify in Canada?

In the U.S., counties have a good deal more resources and decision-making power than do counties or CDs in Canada. In both countries, formal powers for allocating powers to local government lie with the state or provincial capitals, but the U.S. system has informally evolved towards a much greater degree of devolution of power to local government. The balance of federal powers is tilted more towards Washington in the U.S. than it is towards Ottawa in Canada. One consequence of this different balance is a practice of direct U.S. federal intervention at the county and municipal level that finds little parallel in Canada.

The political power and importance of county government and federal intervention at the country level results in systematic collection of key data series at the county level. Legislation mandates, for example, that the U.S. federal government publish annual government expenditures by county. Selection of counties as the geographic unit of policy analysis makes eminent sense in the U.S.

By contrast, the greater relative power of Canada's provincial capitals over local government and the greater decentralization of power between Ottawa and the provinces results in a data collection system which is strong at the national and provincial levels or regional aggregates such as the Prairies or Maritimes. Many key data series are simply not available for subprovincial areas and this is especially true for nonmetropolitan areas.

As a practical matter, CDs provide the most useful choice for local policy analysis in Canada. In Central Canada, the Eastern provinces, and British Columbia, CDs are based on the boundaries of politically weak counties. In the Prairies, CDs are more a matter of convenience specified by the provinces. When subprovincial data are available at the level of disaggregation and reliability needed for nonmetro policy analysis, Statistics Canada usually uses CDs as the standard geographic unit. In other cases, different ministries specify their own subprovincial regions, which creates a babel for local policy analysis. More often than not, however, the CD boundaries are a magnet for organizing subprovincial data.

Ease of comparative analysis between nonmetropolitan Canada and nonmetropolitan regions in adjacent U.S. states is another very important reason for selecting CDs as the geographic unit of reference. The number and geographic size of Canadian counties in Central Canada, the East, and British Columbia are similar to adjacent regions across the U.S. borders. The same holds true when comparing Prairie CDs to counties in the adjacent Great Plains states. Beale code classification of Canadian CDs enables comparative analysis with a rich U.S. data set on nonmetropolitan counties.

After consideration of all the factors discussed above, we have adopted the general framework of Beale codes and we have assigned a Beale code to each CD in Canada (see the definitions in Table 1). A list of the Beale code assigned to each CD is available from the authors upon request.

TABLE 1

"Beale codes" adapted for Canadian nonmetropolitan policy analysis

Major metro area

| #0 | Central counties of large metro regions | census metropolitan area (CMA) 1,000,000+ |
| #1 | Fringe counties of large metro regions | CMA 1,000,000+ |

Mid-sized metro

| #2 | Medium metropolitan | CMA 250,000 to 999,999 |

Smaller metro

| #3 | Small metropolitan | CMA 50,000 to 249,999 |

Small nonmetro city zone

| #4 | Nonmetro urbanized, adjacent to metro region | Urban population 20,000 to 49,999 (urban = settlements of 2,500+) |
| #5 | Nonmetro urbanized, not adjacent to metro region | Urban population 20,000 to 49,9999 |

Small town zone

| #6 | Nonmetro, less urbanized, adjacent to metro region | Urban population 2,500 to 19,999 |
| #7 | Nonmetro, less urbanized, not adjacent to metro region | Urban population 2,500 to 19,999 |

Predominantly rural

| #8 | Nonmetro, rural, adjacent to metro region | No places of 2,500+ population |
| #9 | Nonmetro, rural, not adjacent to metro region | No places of 2,500+ population |

Northern hinterland

| #10 | Northern hinterland | Census divisions, entirely or in major part, above the following parallels by region: Newfoundland, 50th; Quebec and Ontario, 49th; Manitoba, 53rd; Saskatchewan, Alberta, and British Columbia, 54th; plus the Yukon and Northwest Territories. |

Source: Adapted from McGranahan 1986.

3. Canada's tripartite population structure

Canada's population is distributed among three basic settlement classes, each with one third of the national population: major metro areas (Beale codes #0 and #1), medium and small metro areas (Beale codes #2 and #3), and nonmetro areas (Beale codes #4 to #10) (Table 2, Figure 1). Consequently, we can speak of a tripartite Canadian settlement structure.

Two alternative and opposing scenarios are possible for the one third of Canada's population which lives in nonmetro areas:

1. the nonmetro population is concentrated in regions that are adjacent to metro regions and an increasing fraction is being incorporated in metro regions as metro boundaries spread out; or

2. the nonmetro population is concentrated in regions that are distant from metro regions, and this is a stable situation linked to the regions's role in Canada's natural resource hinterland.

The present pattern shows a majority of the nonmetro population located in areas which are distant from metro regions. Small nonmetro city and small town CDs that are <u>nonadjacent</u> contain 16% of Canada's population (Beale codes #5 and #7) while similar CDs that are <u>adjacent</u> contain 9% of the population (Beale codes #4 and #6). The adjacent and nonadjacent predominantly rural zones (Beale codes #8 and #9) have very small shares of Canada's total population, each with 1%. When the northern resource frontier is factored in, we see that 20% of Canada's population resides in <u>nonadjacent</u> nonmetro zones (Beale codes #5, #7, #9 and #10). In comparison, 10% of the population lives in <u>adjacent</u> nonmetro zones (Beale codes #4, #6 and #8). Whether this population pattern is stable remains to be observed from an analysis of time series data.

FIGURE 1

Distribution of total population, Canada, 1986

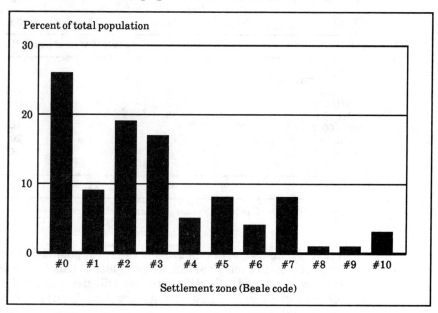

Source: Statistics Canada. Census of Population, 1986.

TABLE 2

Distribution of total population and rural population by Beale codes, Canada, 1986

Population in settlements 2,500 +	Metro	Nonmetro		Total
		Adjacent to metro	Nonadjacent to metro	
(,000)		Beale code #		
1,000 +				
Central zone	0			
Outer zone	1			
250 to 999	2			
50 to 250	3			
20 to 50		4	5	
2.5 to 20		6	7	
< 2.5		8	9	
Remote			10	
(,000)		Percent of total population		
1,000 +				35
Central zone	26			
Outer zone	9			
250 to 999	19			19
50 to 250	17			17
20 to 50		5	8	13
2.5 to 20		4	8	12
< 2.5		1	1	2
Remote			3	3
Total	**71**	**10**	**20**	**100**
(,000)		Percent of rural population		
1,000 +				9
Central zone	3			
Outer zone	6			
250 to 999	7			7
50 to 250	19			19
20 to 50		8	14	22
2.5 to 20		11	20	31
< 2.5		3	4	7
Remote			5	5
Total	**35**	**22**	**43**	**100**

Source: *Statistics Canada. Census of Population, 1986.*

While it is true that over one third of the rural population resides on the outermost zones of metro areas, there is less to this than meets the eye. To be consistent with Beale's data, we will use the 2,500 urban-rural threshold when examining the geographic distribution of Canada's rural population.

When the distribution of the total rural population is observed across Beale code zones, we see that the small metro zone (Beale code #3) is far the modal class for rural residents in the metro areas defined by commuting patterns (Figure 2). Nineteen percent of Canada's rural population is located on the outer portions of smaller nonmetro areas (Beale code #3), nearly as much as the 20% share of Canada's modal rural population class, the nonadjacent small town zone (Beale code #7). The rural portions of smaller metro labour force basins, which often have a quite extensive territory, have different socio-economic characteristics than the rural fringes of Canada's three major cities. One does not have to drive very many miles out of a small metro area like Sherbrooke or Sudbury before encountering a countryside and dispersed settlement patterns that are unambiguously rural.

FIGURE 2

Distribution of rural population, Canada, 1986

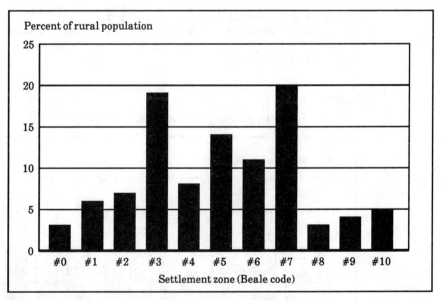

Source: Statistics Canada. Census of Population, 1986.

Some analysts speak of the "rurbanization" of Canada's rural population. In addition to the 35% of the rural population that lives in outer portions of metro areas, another 22 % resides in the nonmetro CDs which are adjacent to these metro areas (Beale codes #4, #6 and #8). One can counter this way of seeing things with the observation that two thirds of Canada's rural population is, after all, located in nonmetro settlement zones (Beale codes #4 to #10). Even the adjacent nonmetro counties are defined precisely because the majority of adult residents are not linked to the metro labour basin in their daily working lives. Furthermore, rural residents in nonadjacent settlement zones (Beale codes #5, #7, #9 and #10) outnumber their counterparts in adjacent nonmetro counties by a ratio of 2 to 1.

4. Labour force composition

4.1 Labour force composition: goods production

A proposition frequently encountered in the U.S. literature on rural and small town economies argues that:

1. there is a trend towards a rising proportion of the labour force in goods production as one moves from the metro to nonmetro settlement zones;

2. goods production is declining in favour of services in advanced industrial economies; and therefore

3. nonmetro counties are more vulnerable to the stresses imposed by contemporary economic restructuring.

Other analysts argue that the purported decline in the role of goods production is more an artifact of the way we have chosen to measure economic activity than a real decline in the importance of producing material commodities.

FIGURE 3

Labour force in goods production, Canada, 1986

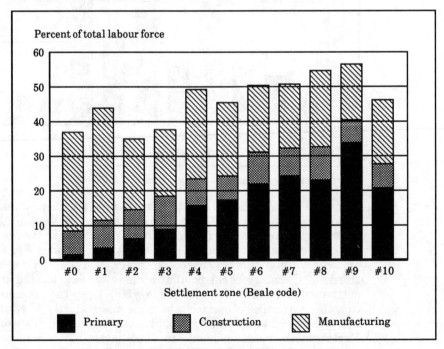

Source: Statistics Canada. Census of Population, 1986.

TABLE 3
Percent of labour force in goods sector by Beale codes, Canada, 1986

Population in settlements 2,500 +	Metro	Nonmetro	
		Adjacent to metro	Nonadjacent to metro
(,000)	Percent in primary sector		
1,000 +			
Central zone	1.4		
Outer zone	3.6		
250 to 999	6.0		
50 to 249	9.6		
20 to 49		15.7	17.3
2.5 to 19		21.9	24.2
< 2.5		22.9	33.8
Remote			20.7
(,000)	Percent in construction sector		
1,000 +			
Central zone	7.1		
Outer zone	8.1		
250 to 999	8.5		
50 to 249	8.8		
20 to 49		7.7	7.1
2.5 to 19		9.2	8.1
< 2.5		9.7	6.6
Remote			6.8
(,000)	Percent in manufacturing sector		
1,000 +			
Central zone	28.4		
Outer zone	32.3		
250 to 999	20.5		
50 to 249	19.3		
20 to 49		25.9	21.0
2.5 to 19		19.1	18.5
< 2.5		22.0	16.1
Remote			18.6
(,000)	Percent in total goods sector		
1,000 +			
Central zone	36.9		
Outer zone	44.0		
250 to 999	35.0		
50 to 249	37.0		
20 to 49		49.2	45.2
2.5 to 19		50.2	50.8
< 2.5		54.6	56.5
Remote			46.1

Source: Statistics Canada. Census of Population, 1986.

In this paper, the size of the goods sector is measured as the sum of the labour force in agriculture, forestry, mining and oil extraction, fishing, and construction. The labour force becomes more concentrated in goods production as one moves from large metro CDs to small town CDs (Table 3, Figure 3). However, the trend is reversed for northern frontier CDs, largely because a smaller proportion of the labour force is engaged in primary production. One explanatory factor is the predominance of capital-intensive mining activities in this settlement zone. If small area value-added data were available, as opposed to labour force data, primary production might be observed to have a greater relative weight in the local economy of remote areas. The labour force trends may also indicate a certain decoupling of the economic dynamism of mineral production and its capacity to generate jobs and support local communities.

The pattern for the overall goods sector incorporates differing patterns among each of the primary, construction and manufacturing sectors:

1. the proportion of the labour force in the primary sector increases as one moves from large metro CDs to small town CDs and, within each class of nonmetro CDs, the primary sector is more important in nonadjacent CDs;

2. the proportion of the labour force in manufacturing generally declines as one moves from major CDs to small town CDs and, within a given class of nonmetro CDs, manufacturing is less important in nonadjacent CDs;

3. the relative weight of manufacturing in the small city, adjacent nonmetro counties approaches that found in the major metro areas, which suggests a spreading of the suburban manufacturing belt to more distant counties;

4. the proportion of the labour force in construction fluctuates inconsistently within a narrow range as one passes along the urban-rural spectrum.

Manufacturing activities are an important component of local labour forces even in the predominantly rural, nonadjacent counties. The type of manufacturing, however, varies considerably as one moves across settlement zones. We classify three types of manufacturing:

1. initial phases in the processing and transformation of raw materials;

2. secondary phases in manufacturing raw materials; and

3. manufacturing activities weakly linked to raw materials, i.e., the major fraction of value-added stems from skilled labour employing advanced technologies.

Examples of initial manufacturing would be a flour mill, lumber mill, or tannery. Examples of secondary manufacturing would be a bakery, furniture factory, or shoe factory. An example of the third class of manufacturing would be the design and construction of a micro-computer. An appendix indicating the methodology and results for classifying manufacturing labour force activities as initial, secondary, or weakly linked to natural resources is available from the authors upon request.

TABLE 4

Percent of labour force in manufacturing, disaggregated by stage of manufacturing[1], by Beale codes, Canada, 1986

		Nonmetro	
Population in settlements 2,500 +	Metro	Adjacent to metro	Nonadjacent to metro
(,000)	Percent in "initial" manufacturing		
1,000 +			
Central zone	14.6		
Outer zone	22.4		
250 to 999	20.0		
50 to 249	42.8		
20 to 49		24.4	44.4
2.5 to 19		39.0	57.4
< 2.5		38.7	69.0
Remote			88.6
(,000)	Percent in "secondary" manufacturing		
1,000 +			
Central zone	38.4		
Outer zone	44.0		
250 to 999	46.8		
50 to 249	29.8		
20 to 49		39.4	32.5
2.5 to 19		33.6	22.6
< 2.5		38.6	19.8
Remote			6.0
(,000)	Percent in "weakly linked" manufacturing		
1,000 +			
Central zone	46.9		
Outer zone	33.6		
250 to 999	32.2		
50 to 249	27.3		
20 to 49		36.2	23.1
2.5 to 19		27.4	20.0
< 2.5		22.7	11.2
Remote			5.4

1. "Initial" manufacturing represents the initial phase in the processing and transformation of raw materials. "Secondary" manufacturing represents the secondary phase in processing raw materials. "Weakly linked" manufacturing represents activities weakly linked to raw materials.

Source: Statistics Canada. Census of Population, 1986.

FIGURE 4
Labour force in manufacturing, Canada, 1986

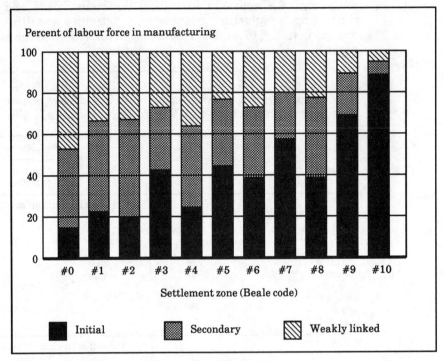

Percent of labour force in manufacturing

Settlement zone (Beale code)

Initial   Secondary   Weakly linked

Source: Statistics Canada. Census of Population 1986.

The intensity of "initial" manufacturing increases from large city CDs to small town CDs <u>and</u> is more predominant in nonadjacent CDs (Table 4, Figure 4). "Secondary" manufacturing varies in intensity among large city CDs and small town CDs but is less predominant in nonadjacent CDs. Manufacturing that is weakly linked to raw materials is less predominant as one moves from large city CDs to small town CDs <u>and</u> is less predominant in nonadjacent CDs. Thus, hinterland manufacturing is largely dependent on the transformation of raw materials. Whether this resouce-linked manufacturing is more or less vulnerable to global economic restructuring than other Canadian manufacturing activities remains to be seen.

4.2   Labour force composition: services

The flip side of the rising fraction of the nonmetro labour force in goods production is the declining proportion involved in services. In addition, the relative weights of different types of services vary across metro and nonmetro CDs.

Transportation, retail trade, and government account for a larger fraction of the services labour force in nonmetro CDs as compared to metro CDs (Table 5, Figure 5). Wholesale trade and the financial sector have greater relative weight in the service sector in metro areas.

TABLE 5
Percent distribution of labour force in services, Canada, 1986

	Metro CDs	Nonmetro CDs
Transportation	20.1	25.4
Wholesale trade	13.3	6.7
Retail trade	31.2	34.2
Finance, insurance, real estate	17.0	7.3
Government	18.4	26.5
Total service sector	**100.0**	**100.0**

Source: Statistics Canada. Census of Population, 1986.

FIGURE 5

Distribution of labour force in services, Canada, 1986

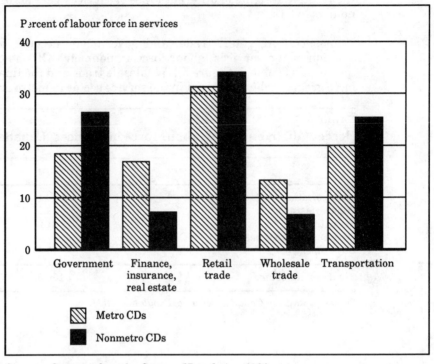

Source: Statistics Canada. Census of Population, 1986.

TABLE 6

Government as percent of total services, by Beale codes, Canada, 1986

		Nonmetro	
Population in settlements 2,500 +	Metro	Adjacent to metro	Nonadjacent to metro
(,000)	Government as percent of total services		
1,000 +			
Central zone	13.1		
Outer zone	15.5		
250 to 999	15.4		
50 to 249	24.4		
20 to 49		20.6	24.6
2.5 to 19		21.3	21.4
< 2.5		20.5	25.8
Remote			26.5

Source: Statistics Canada. Census of Population, 1986.

FIGURE 6

Government as percent of total services, Canada, 1986

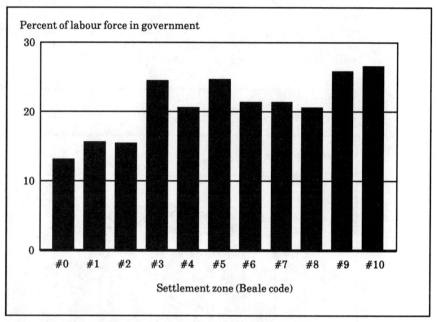

Percent of labour force in government

Settlement zone (Beale code)

Source: Statistics Canada. Census of Population, 1986.

The relative weight of each major service subsector within the total labour force engaged in services was measured by Beale code classes. One example is the changing share of government services in total services as one moves across settlement zones. Major and medium metro CDs have quite low shares of their service labour forces involved in government (Table 6, Figure 6). In contrast, the smaller metro areas exhibit a higher share which also prevails in nonmetro, nonadjacent small city CDs, nonadjacent predominantly rural CDs, and the northern frontier areas.

Note that service sector workers living in CDs adjacent to CMAs are relatively less concentrated in government. They are participating in a wider range of service sector jobs that are probably linked to the capacity of enterprises in adjacent nonmetro counties to produce a variety of goods for metro area markets.

4.3 Dependency ratios by settlement zone

Rurality is frequently associated with high proportions of the population being young dependents and senior citizens. These dependency ratios (the proportion of people under 15 years and 65 years or over) rise as one moves from the metro areas towards the predominantly rural zones (Table 7, Figure 7). However, the nonmetro regions appear to carry a qualitatively similar burden in terms of the dependence by the young and the retired on the adults participating in the labour force.

FIGURE 7
Dependency ratios, Canada, 1986

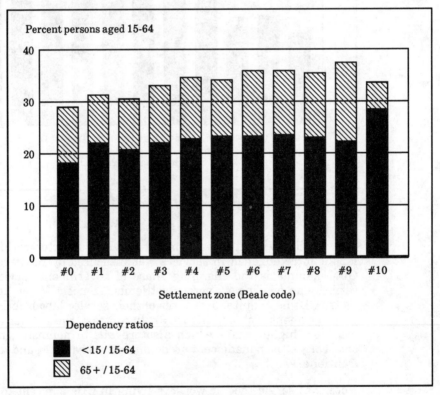

Source: Statistics Canada. Census of Population, 1986.

The most noticeable deviations from cross-regional trends are in the central zones of major metropolitan areas (Beale code #0), which have relatively few people under 15, and the northern resource frontier (Beale code #10), which has a high proportion of young people and a distinctly low proportion of people over 65.

TABLE 7
Dependency ratios, by Beale codes, Canada, 1986

Population in settlements 2,500+	Metro %	Non-metro	
		Adjacent to metro %	Nonadjacent to metro %
(,000)	Population < 15 years / population 15-64 years		
1,000 +			
Central zone	18.1		
Outer zone	22.0		
250 to 999	20.8		
50 to 249	22.0		
20 to 49		22.9	23.3
2.5 to 19		23.4	23.6
< 2.5		23.1	22.4
Remote			28.5
(,000)	Population 65 + years / population 15-64 years		
1,000 +			
Central zone	10.9		
Outer zone	9.2		
250 to 999	9.6		
50 to 249	11.2		
20 to 49		11.6	10.9
2.5 to 19		12.4	12.3
< 2.5		12.4	15.1
Remote			5.0
(,000)	Population < 15 years plus population 65 + years /population 15-64 years		
1,000 +			
Central zone	29.0		
Outer zone	31.3		
250 to 999	30.5		
50 to 249	33.2		
20 to 49		34.6	34.2
2.5 to 19		35.8	35.9
< 2.5		35.4	37.5
Remote			34.0

Source: Statistics Canada. Census of Population, 1986.

The proportion of elderly in the population of predominantly rural nonadjacent counties (Beale code #9) is noticeably higher than the national average. It is important to observe, however, that the proportion of Canada's population living in the highly rural, nonadjacent counties is very small. The rural population in Beale code #9 counties is also a small proportion of Canada's total rural population, as measured by Statistics Canada's present definition of "rural". Thus, most of Canada's rural population resides in regions which do not have a proportion of the elderly which is greatly different from the national, urban-dominated norm.

5. Economic welfare by settlement zone

We use two measurements of economic welfare and the performance of local economies: unemployment rates and the proportion of families reporting low income.

5.1 Unemployment rates

Unemployment rates, as officially defined by Statistics Canada and Employment and Immigration Canada, show a nuanced trend across the urban-rural spectrum (Table 8, Figure 8). Once again, the small city, adjacent nonmetro counties have measured behavior that is closer to the range for major metro areas than for other types of nonmetro counties. This suggests the spatial extension of the metro economies from suburban zones to more distant counties, though in terms of the flow of commodities rather than the flow of the labour force. Also noteworthy is the high rate of employment in the smaller metro areas that frequently serve as the regional centres for resource hinterlands.

FIGURE 8

Unemployment rates, Canada, 1986

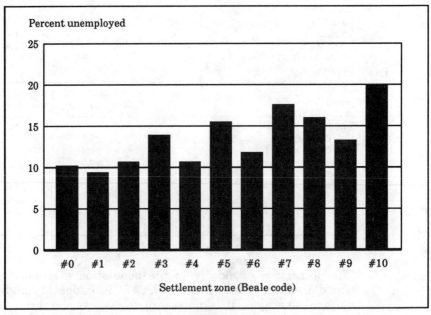

Source: Statistics Canada. Census of Population, 1986.

TABLE 8
Unemployment rates, by Beale codes, Canada, 1986

| Population in settlements 2,500 + | Metro | Nonmetro | |
		Adjacent to metro	Nonadjacent to metro
(,000)	Unemployment rate (percent)		
1,000 +			
Central zone	10.2		
Outer zone	9.4		
250 to 999	10.6		
50 to 249	13.9		
20 to 49		10.7	15.5
2.5 to 19		11.8	17.6
< 2.5		15.9	13.3
Remote			20.0

Source: Statistics Canada. Census of Population, 1986.

Unemployment rates are higher in nonadjacent nonmetro counties compared to adjacent counties, with the exception of the predominantly rural zone. The lower rates in the nonadjacent rural counties could reflect a variety of circumstances, ranging from data errors to the particular circumstances of specific resource subsectors to outmigration or withdrawal from the labour force by discouraged workers. Also of note is the very high 1986 rate of unemployment in the northern resource hinterland, to which we will return shortly.

5.2   Proportion reporting low income

Settlement zone variations in the proportions of economic families[1] reporting low incomes, as defined by Statistics Canada, show incidences of low incomes that are highest in the central zone of major metro areas and nonadjacent small town and rural counties. The variations are within a narrow band and probably result primarily from social program safety nets, as defined and funded in 1986 (Table 9, Figure 9). The lowest incidences of low incomes are in the adjacent small urban nonmetro counties and the suburbs of major metro areas. Adjacent nonmetro counties fared better than metro areas, with the exception of the outer zones of the Toronto, Montreal and Vancouver areas.

---

1.   "Economic family" refers to two or more persons living in the same dwelling and related by blood, marriage or adoption.

TABLE 9

Percent of families below the low income cut-off, by Beale codes, Canada, 1986

| Population in settlements 2,500+ | Metro | Nonmetro | |
		Adjacent to metro	Nonadjacent to metro
(,000)	Percent below the low income cut-off		
1,000 +			
Central zone	22		
Outer zone	17		
250 to 999	20		
50 to 249	20		
20 to 49		16	20
2.5 to 19		18	21
< 2.5		19	21
Remote			17

Source: Statistics Canada. Census of Population, 1986.

FIGURE 9

Incidence of low income, Canada, 1986

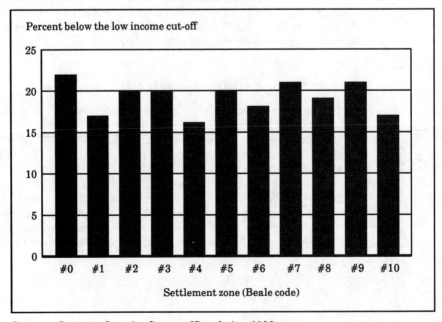

Source: Statistics Canada. Census of Population, 1986.

Both distance from urban centres and population density affect the economic welfare of different settlement zones, as suggested by family income and unemployment rate data. There is a discordance, however, for the northern frontier settlement zone. High rates of unemployment are reported at the same time as low proportions of families with low incomes are reported. Part of this discordance results from the way low income cut-offs are assigned for residents of Indian Reserves.

6.   The diversity of nonmetro economic specialization

The Canadian countryside, as a whole, is characterized by macro-diversity and local micro-specialization. A methodology for capturing and analyzing this joint diversification and specialization has been developed by a research team at the USDA (Bender et al. 1985). On the basis of income tax data, Bender et al. classified nonmetro counties into the following specialized groups:

1.   agriculturally dependent (20% or more of labour and proprietor income from agriculture);

2.   manufacturing-dependent (30% of income);

3.   mining-dependent (20% of income);

4.   government-specialized (25% of 1979 income);

5.   persistent poverty counties (per capita family income in lowest U.S. quintile in 1950, 1959, 1969, 1979);

6.   Federal land counties (Federal land 33% or more of country land area);

7.   retirement destination counties (net 1970-80 immigration of people aged 60 and older was 15% or more of 1980 population aged 60 and older).

The seven nonmetro county dependency (i.e. specialization) types are not mutually exclusive. Twenty-two percent of the counties are in two groups and 6% in three or more groups. Fifteen percent of the nonmetro counties remain unclassified.

Within the Canadian context, it makes more sense to use labour force data as opposed to income data to analyze rural regional economic specialization. The census labour force data for 1981 and 1986 are quite reliable, while subprovincial data on labour and proprietor income by economic sector are problematic. Ross and Green (1985) generated a correlation matrix for alternative specialization criteria which indicated that a classification based on income or labour force variables were very similar.

Previous analysis of the Canadian data suggested that agricultural dependence could be usefully defined on the basis of CDs having 20% or more of their labour force in agriculture. In addition, CDs were classified as being "semidependent" if 8.8% to 19.9% of the labour force was in agriculture. Economic dependence on mining, forestry, fishing, manufacturing or government was indicated on the basis of ranking in the top decile for each sector.

Micro-specialization and macro-diversification of the modern countryside stands out clearly when we look for overlaps in dependence on different economic sectors. A significant minority of nonmetro CDs do have dual specialization, but the general rule is dependence on one sector (Table 10).

TABLE 10

Sectoral dependency of nonmetro census divisions, Canada, 1986

	Dependency of nonmetro census divisions[1]							
	Agri-culture	Agri-culture semi-depen-dent 1	Agri-culture semi-depen-dent 2	Forestry	Mining	Fishing	Maufac-turing	Govern-ment
Solely dependent	30	19	11	23	14	17	15	15
Dual dependency								
Agriculture	..	..	..	0	2	0	0	0
Agriculture semi-dependent[1]	..	..	..	0	3	0	2	2
Agriculture semi-dependent[2]	..	..	..	1	2	0	6	2
Forestry	0	0	1	..	1	0	0	1
Mining	2	3	2	1	..	2	0	2
Fishing	0	0	0	0	2	..	3	4
Manufacturing	0	2	6	0	0	3	..	0
Government	0	2	2	1	2	4	0	..
Number of nonmetro census divisions	32	26	22	26	26	26	26	26

1. Dependency of a nonmetro census division is assigned on the basis of the percent of the labour force in a given industry: agriculture, 20%; agriculture semi-dependent 1, 13% to 19.9%; agriculture semi-dependent 2, 8.8% to 12.9%; forestry, 6.3%; mining, 6.9%; fishing, 3.8%; manufacturing, 26.7%; government, 12.1%. Note that the labour force cutoffs for the latter five industries were chosen so that one tenth of all CDs (i.e. 26 CDs) would be classified to each group.

Source: Statistics Canada. Census of Population, 1986.

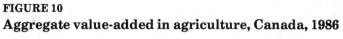

FIGURE 10
Aggregate value-added in agriculture, Canada, 1986

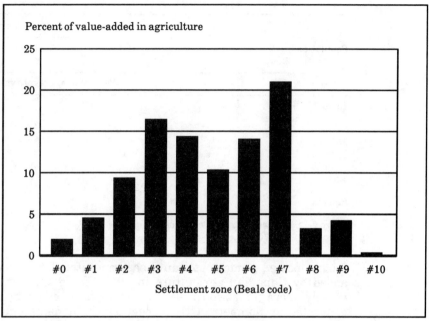

Source: Statistics Canada. Census of Population, 1986.

7.   Agricultural dependence, agribusiness and settlement zones

Cross-classification of CDs along the dimensions of agricultural dependence and Beale code settlement zones reveals the extent to which large stretches of rural and small town Canada are dominated by activities other than agriculture.

There are 80 nonmetro CDs in Canada which are dependent or semidependent on agriculture as opposed to 130 nonmetro CDs where agriculture is a less important or insignificant activity. Even if we subtract the 23 northern frontier counties from the nonmetro group which is not dependent on agriculture (and where it is evident that agriculture is not a viable base for the local economy), this still leaves 107 CDs not dependent on agriculture. This is the spatial dimension of the labour force change where the farm population became a minority of the total rural population during the 1950s and a steadily smaller proportion of the rural population since that time.

TABLE 11

Percent of aggregate value-added in agriculture, by Beale codes, Canada, 1986

Population in settlements 2,500 +	Metro	Nonmetro	
		Adjacent to metro	Nonadjacent to metro
(,000)	Percent of aggregate value-added		
1,000,000 +			
Central zone	2.0		
Outer zone	4.5		
250 to 999	9.3		
50 to 249	16.4		
20 to 49		14.4	10.3
2.5 to 19		14.0	20.9
< 2.5		3.2	4.2
Remote			0.4

Source: Statistics Canada. Census of Agriculture, 1986.

Farms located in metropolitan areas generated 32% of the total value-added by Canadian agriculture in 1985 (Table 11, Figure 10). Conversely, more than two thirds of national value-added by agriculture is generated by nonmetro CDs. Together the nonadjacent and adjacent small town CDs generate 35% of total value-added in agriculture. The contribution of predominantly rural CDs is considerably less, standing at 8%.

When we examine the nexus between settlement zones and agricultural dependence patterns, we find that nondependent CDs (less than 8.8% of their labour force in agriculture) generated 38% of the aggregate value-added by agriculture in 1985. There are many (115) nonmetro non-ag-dependent CDs which generated only 11% of aggregate value-added in agriculture.

The modern agricultural countryside is predominated by small towns and small cities both in the context of land-extensive dryland farming and ranching and in the more land-intensive farming systems outside the Prairies. While an important fraction of the nonfarm economic activities in the ag-dependent and semidependent areas are obviously linked to agricultural production, it appears that an important fraction of nonfarm activities have become decoupled from the agricultural sector.

There is a natural tendency for agriculturally dependent regions and ministries of agriculture to increase backward and forward linkages from farming as a rural development strategy. Parallel statements could be made for mining, forestry, and fishing.

Labour force distributions by industry are one measure of the direct job linkages generated by agriculture beyond the farm gate. However, the agricultural component of activities such as banking or real estate services are not distinguished. On the other hand, the food services subsector, which generates the largest number of agribusiness jobs in nonmetro Canada, is for the most part weakly linked to local agriculture: we are dealing with supermarkets and smaller food retailers who distribute goods which, for the most part, come from outside ag-dependent localities.

FIGURE 11

Nonmetro agribusiness labour force, Canada, 1986

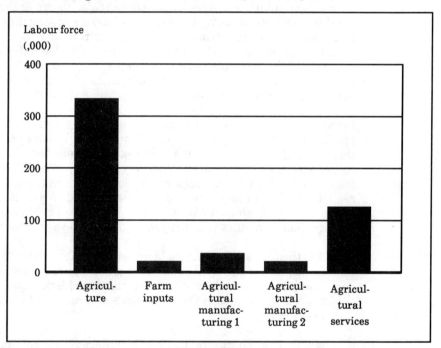

Source: Statistics Canada. Census of Population, 1986.

TABLE 12

Nonmetro agribusiness labour force, Canada, 1986

Agriculture	332,950
Farm inputs	19,470
Agricultural manufacturing 1	36,620
Agricultural manufacturing 2	19,480
Agricultural services	125,110

Source: Statistics Canada. Census of Population, 1986.

In the nonmetro CDs, the measured agribusiness labour force beyond the farmgate is roughly half the level of the nonmetro agricultural labour force (Table 12, Figure 11). The number of jobs generated by these beyond-the-farmgate activities is relatively minor. To the extent the labour force in these industries indicates linkages of agriculture to sectors beyond the farmgate, a rural development strategy to increase backward and forward linkages is open to question.

8.   Conclusion

The post-1945 transformation of Canadian economy and society sorted the population into a new tripartite settlement structure: one third of Canada's population resides in the three major metro areas of Toronto, Montreal and Vancouver; another third resides in medium and small metro areas; and the remaining third is spread across Canada's vast nonmetro hinterland. Predominantly rural CDs contain only a small minority of the nonmetro population or even of the total rural population. Rural dynamics are played out in local contexts dominated by small cities and small towns.

Rural economic and social dynamics must be understood as the joint product of the low population which structurally defines rurality and the regional context which shapes the manner in which the consequences of low population density are played out. By context, we mean, in addition to the evident impact of sectoral specialization, the regional location along the new and variegated urban-rural spectrum which has been shaped since World War II. The labour force and demographic dynamics of a rural settlement will vary according to:

1.   whether it is located in a nonmetro county where the dominant component of the local population is composed of small cities, small towns or villages and dispersed rural residences, or whether the settlement is part of the outer zone of a metropolitan labour force area; and

2.   whether a nonmetro county is adjacent or not adjacent to a metropolitan area.

We have seen how the composition and economic welfare of local labour forces varies sytematically, though not always in a linear manner, along the new urban-rural spectrum. The Beale code approach is a useful instrument for rural and small town policy analysis in Canada.

Distance and density count, and they count jointly. Lumping "rurban" and hinterland counties together produces measurements which run the risk of creating averages which poorly reflect conditions in either metro-adjacent or nonadjacent counties. Macro-diversity and micro-specialization in Canada's vast nonmetropolitan hinterland is compounded by the independent effects of the new and variegated urban-rural spectrum.

Philip Ehrensaft
Jennifer Beeman
Départmente de sociologie
Université du Québec à Montréal
Montréal, Québec H3C 3P8

References

Bender, Lloyd D. et al. 1985. The Diverse Social and Economic Structure of Nonmetropolitan America. Economic Research Service, Rural Development Research Report No. 49. Washington: US Department of Agriculture.

Brown, David L. et al. 1988. Rural Economic Development in the 1980s: Prospects for the Future. Rural Development Research Report No. 69. Washington : USDA,Economics Research Service .

Ehrensaft, Philip and David Freshwater. 1990. Policy regimes and rural development: North America in comparative perspective. Paper presented to the International Symposium on Economic Change and Policies in Rural Regions. Aspen, Colorado: July.

Fuguitt, Glenn, David Brown and Calvin Beale. 1989. Rural and Small Town America. New York: Russell Sage Foundation.

Garreau, Joel. 1982. The Nine Nations of North America. New York: Avon.

General Accounting Office. 1989. Rural Development: Programs That Focus on Rural America and Its Economic Development. Washington: General Accounting Office.

Hady, Thomas F. and Peggy J. Ross. 1990. An Update: The Diverse Social and Economic Structure of Nonmetropolitan America. Washington: USDA, Economics Research Service.

McGranahan, D. et al. 1986. Social and Economic Characteristics of the Population of Metro and Nonmetro Counties, 1970-80. Economics Research Service, Rural Development Research Report No. 58. Washington: USDA.

Ross, Peggy J. and Bernal L. Green. 1985. Procedures for Developing a Policy-Oriented Classification of Nonmetropolitan Counties. Washington: USDA, Economics Research Service.

10

Participation of women in the labour force: a comparison of farm women and all women in Canada

Marcelle Dion and Steve Welsh

Summary

The labour force participation rate for farm women is higher than that of women in the total population. Within the farm population, the participation rate is higher for women living on farms with gross sales above the median (over $30,277 in 1986). In addition to a higher participation rate for women in the farm population, the average number of hours and weeks worked by farm women is higher than the average for women in the total population. Major socio-economic variables explain only a small part of the difference in labour force participation rates between farm women and all women. However, if farm women report a 'farming occupation' or are associated with a larger farm, they are more likely to be in the labour force.

Table of contents

Participation of women in the labour force: a comparison of farm women and all women in Canada

Marcelle Dion and Steve Welsh

---

1.   Introduction

Farm women and non-farm women are increasingly participating in the labour force.   To describe this phenomenon, this report examines similarities and differences between farm women and all women in the labour force.

The data in this study are from the census of population database and the agriculture-population linkage database (a computer linkage of data in the agriculture and population censuses). This base allows one to cross-tabulate the characteristics of the farm population with the characteristics of their farms (See Appendix 1 for data limitations).

2.   A historical comparison

For the historical comparison, the data include all women, 15 years of age or older in the farm and in the total population.

The share of women in the total labour force[1] increased steadily between 1951 and 1986 (Figure 1). The share of women in the labour force also increased in the farm population and the share of women in the two populations have drawn closer together during this period. In 1951, women represented 22% of the labour force, and women represented only 9% of the total farm labour force. By 1986, these proportions had increased to 43% in the total labour force and 37% in the farm labour force.

---

1.   Persons aged 15 years and over who during the week preceding June 3, 1986, were paid workers, were self-employed or were unpaid workers in a family business or farm.

228
Participation of women in the labour force:
a comparison of farm women and all women in Canada

FIGURE 1

Women as percent of total labour force, Canada

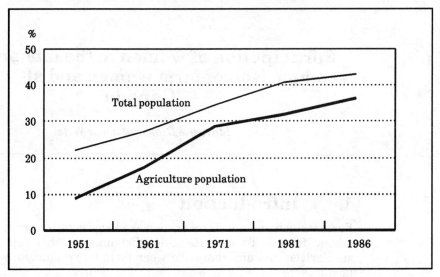

Source: Statistics Canada. Census of Population.

FIGURE 2

Percent of women who are in the labour force, Canada

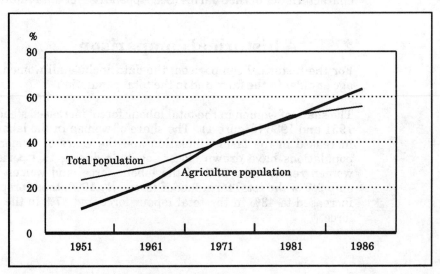

Source: Statistics Canada. Census of Population.

The participation rate is the proportion of women in the labour force in comparison with all women aged 15 years and over in the population. The labour force participation rate for women in each population group has increased over time (Figure 2). Again, we note a rapid increase in the participation rate of women in the farm sector. The percent of farm women who are in the labour force (63%) exceeded the participation rate of all women (56%) by 1986.

3. Labour force participation rates of farm women and all women

For the rest of the study, the universe of women in the farm population includes only the spouses of male farm operators and female farm operators themselves. To compare to the total population, we selected female family heads and the spouses of male family heads. This universe allows us to compare labour force behaviour for women who would be expected to make decisions concerning the management of households and the management of family businesses, including farms.

The participation rates of women in the farm and total populations, are compared through variables such as age, schooling, presence and age of children, family income, and region of residence. Secondly, we will examine the participation rates of women in two subgroups of the farm population in comparison with the total population. Finally, we will discuss data on the average number of hours and weeks worked by these women to better measure their contribution.

3.1 Comparison of the participation rates

We noted above that the labour force participation rate in 1986 was higher for women in the farm population than for all women (Figure 2). This conclusion holds when we restrict the analysis to women included in our study universe. The participation rate of women in our study universe is higher in the farm population (67%) than in the total population (57%) (Figure 3).

Despite the year or variable analyzed, the participation rate of farm women shows the same pattern as for all women but is higher than the participation rate of women in the total population (Figures 4 to 7).

Farm women in all age groups had consistently higher participation rates during 1971-1986 that did all women. In the older age categories in 1971, only 21% of all women participated in the labour force while 35% of farm women still participated. By 1986, about 21% of older women in Canada still participated in the labour force; however, nearly 50% of older farm women were in the labour force (Figure 4)[2].

---

2. Space constraints allow us to present only the graphs for 1986. Graphs depicting the 1971 and 1981 situation are available from the authors upon request.

FIGURE 3

Participation rate of women in the labour force, Canada, 1971-1986

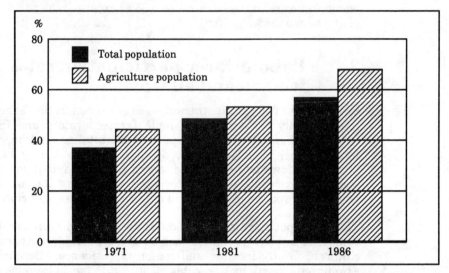

Source: Statistics Canada. Census of Population and Agriculture—Population Linkage.

FIGURE 4

Labour force participation rate of women by age class, Canada, 1986

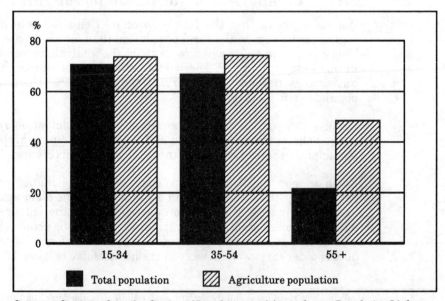

Source: Statistics Canada. Census of Population and Agriculture—Population Linkage.

Across education levels, again a higher percentage of farm women participated in the labour force than did women in general during 1971-1986. The rates between the two populations diverged most among the least educated. Farm women with less than grade 9 had, on average, a 15 percentage point higher participation rate than did all women with a similar education (Figure 5).

FIGURE 5

Labour force participation rate of women by level of schooling, Canada, 1986

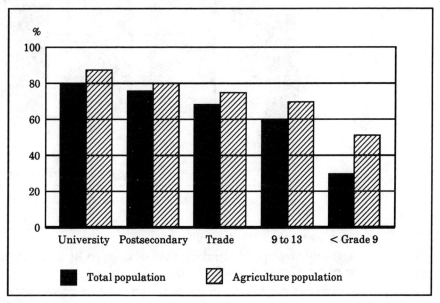

Source: Statistics Canada. Census of Population and Agriculture—Population Linkage.

Regardless of the presence or age of children during 1971-1986, farm women reported higher rates of labour force participation than all women. There was a 10 percentage point difference for women with no children, for women with children older than 15 and for women with children younger than 6 (Figure 6).

Across family income classes during 1971-1986, more farm women participated in the labour force than did women in general except for a slight reversal among high family income women in 1981. At this time, farm women in the $40,000-$50,000 and the over $50,000 family income ranges showed a lower participation rate in the labour force than did women in general. In each of 1971, 1981 and 1986, the labour force participation rate of farm women is similar across all family income classes. For all women, a lower participation rate is associated with a lower family income (see Figure 7 for the 1986 situation).

FIGURE 6

Labour force participation rate of women by presence and age of children, Canada, 1986

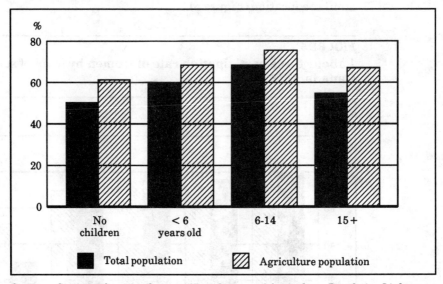

Source: Statistics Canada. Census of Population and Agriculture-Population Linkage.

FIGURE 7

Labour force participation rate of women by class of family income, Canada, 1986

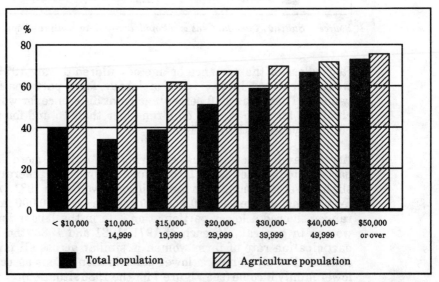

Source: Statistics Canada. Census of Population and Agriculture-Population Linkage.

Several variables (such as occupation, gross or net farm income) could be used to obtain more homogeneous groups within the farm population. For this study, we have chosen the gross income or the value of the sales of farm products, to divide the farm women population into two study groups. The first consists of women associated with farms where the sales are above the median sales of farm products[3]. The second consists of women associated with farms where sales are below the median. Each of these two groups contains about 50% of all the women in the farm population. We chose "the sales of farm products" variable because it could be expected that women would have different economic incentives and possibilities for employment when they were associated with a larger or a smaller farm measured in terms of gross sales.

The participation rate of women in each of the two farm population subgroups is higher than that of women in the total population (Figure 8). We can also see that the participation rate for women on farms with sales above the median is much higher than the rate for women in the other subgroup. Women on farms with sales less than median gross farm sales have labour force participation rates closer to the overall female population. Therefore, we can conclude that the difference between the participation rates depends, in part, upon factors associated with the characteristics of the farm population in general, but also, in part, upon factors related to the characteristics of the two subgroups.

3. The median gross farm sales was $5,560 in 1970, $21,805 in 1980 and $30,277 in 1985.

FIGURE 8

**Labour force participation rate of women showing two
agriculture population subgroups, Canada, 1986**

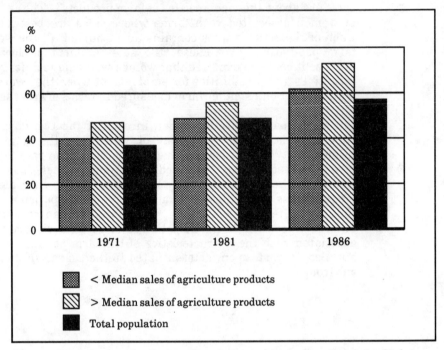

Source: Statistics Canada. Census of Population and Agriculture-Population Linkage.

3.2   Comparison of the number of hours and weeks worked

In addition to participation rates, it is important to consider the number
of hours and weeks worked to confirm our comparisons of the work
activity of farm and all women. In addition to the higher participation
rate of farm women, we find that farm women work more hours per
week. In 1986, farm women averaged 36 hours of work whereas the
average woman in the labour force worked 29 hours (Table 1). Note also
that women on farms with sales above the median worked more hours
than women on farms with sales under the median.

TABLE 1

Average number of hours worked* by women, Canada, 1971, 1981 and 1986

Year	Farm population on farms with gross sales			Total population
	< median	> median	Total	
1971	37.7	39.6	38.8	34.1
1981	31.3	34.5	33.1	30.6
1986	33.0	37.9	35.9	28.6

* Hours worked refer to hours worked in the week before the Census (i.e. the last week of May of the Census year).

Source: Statistics Canada. Censuses of Population and Agriculture—Population Linkage databases for 1971, 1981 and 1986, unpublished tabulations.

Farm women worked, on average, slightly fewer weeks than women in the total labour force in 1971 and 1981, but by 1986 farm women worked more. They worked an average of 41 weeks in comparison with 40 weeks for working women in the total population (Table 2). In general, weeks worked were similar for the two groups of farm women and all women in the labour force.

TABLE 2

Average number of weeks worked by women, Canada, 1971, 1981 and 1986

Year	Farm population on farms with gross sales			Total population
	< median	> median	Total	
1971	35.8	38.0	37.1	38.1
1981	37.9	38.8	38.4	40.3
1986	39.4	41.5	40.6	39.9

Source: Statistics Canada. Censuses of Population and Agriculture—Population Linkage databases for 1971, 1981 and 1986, unpublished tabulations.

4.   Characteristics of women in the labour force

4.1   Demographic characteristics

Farm women tend to be in older age categories (Figure 9). In the younger age class (15-34 years), there is a 10 percentage point lower proportion of farm women than all women.

FIGURE 9
Distribution of women in the labour force by age class, 1986

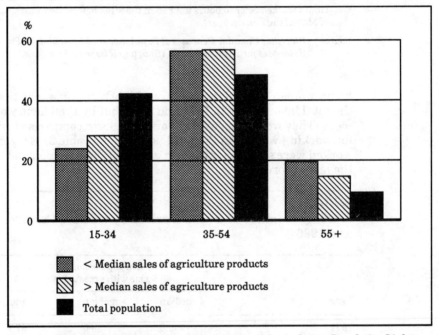

Source: Statistics Canada. Census of Population and Agriculture—Population Linkage.

The distribution of farm women and all women across education classes is very similar (Figure 10).

With the 'presence of children' variable, women associated with farms below the median were more similar to women in the total population than were women associated with farms above the median (Figure 11). Women on larger farms tended to have children aged younger than 6, or between 6 and 14. It is surprising that working farm women tended to have young children.

FIGURE 10

**Distribution of women in the labour force by level of schooling,
Canada, 1986**

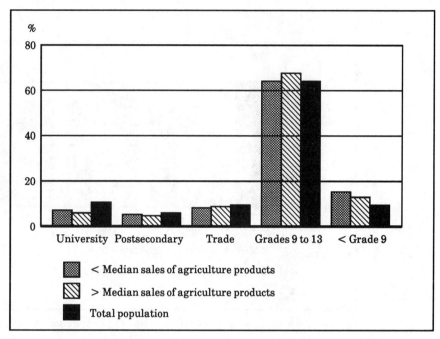

Source: Statistics Canada. Census of Population and Agriculture—Population Linkage.

4.2   Occupation

The working environment offered by the farm would be expected to
influence the labour force participation rate of farm women. In recent
years, farm women have become more involved in the farm business. In
addition, there is a growing determination among farm women to have
their contribution recognized. The distribution of working farm women
according to their occupation should reflect the farm labour supply, and
the involvement of women in farming.

FIGURE 11

Distribution of women in the labour force by presence and age of children, Canada, 1986

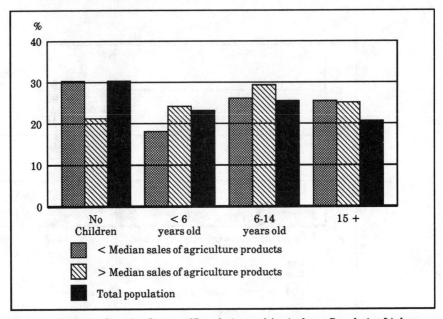

Source: Statistics Canada. Census of Population and Agriculture Population Linkage.

TABLE 3

Distribution of women in the labour force according to their major occupation, Canada, 1971 and 1986

Year	Major occupation		
	Farming	Other than farming	Total
	Percent		
Total population			
– 1971	4.7	95.3	100.0
– 1986	2.6	97.4	100.0
Farm population			
gross sales < median			
– 1971	51.1	48.9	100.0
– 1986	29.1	70.9	100.0
gross sales > median			
– 1971	67.2	32.8	100.0
– 1986	53.0	47.0	100.0

Source: Statistics Canada. Censuses of Population, 1971 and 1986, unpublished tabulations.

Only 3% of working women reported a farming occupation; however, 43% of working women in the farm population reported farming as their main occupation and the proportion increased to 53% for women associated with farms that generated sales above the median (Table 3). Between 1971 and 1986, the decrease in the number of women who reported a farming occupation was mainly attributable to a 20% decrease in the number of farms during the same period, and not necessarily to a decrease in possibilities of employment on the farm. Moreover, for working women reporting a farming occupation there was a marginal increase in the average number of hours (41.9 in 1971, and 42.2 in 1986) and an increase in weeks worked (38 in 1971, and 42 in 1986).

Furthermore, farm women are increasingly working at non-farm occupations. The number of farm women who reported an occupation other than farming increased 76% during 1971-1986. Note, however, that between 1957 and 1980, the share of family non-farm income contributed by women did not increase. Men and women in the farm population increased their work off the farm at about the same rate (Bollman and Smith 1987: Figure 16).

In conclusion, farms that generate sales above the median appear to offer employment possibilities that women in the other groups would not have. Moreover, as the data on occupation show, these women have access to off-farm employment as well.

4.3 Economic characteristics

Financial need is often cited as one reason for farm women to participate in the labour force. Thus, this section of the study concentrates on the analysis of income variables, and, in the case of the farm population, on farm income and expenses.

TABLE 4

Average individual and average family income, Canada, 1986

Group	Average income (women)	Average family income	Contribution in percentage
Total population	10,236	35,706	28.7
Farm population			
– gross sales < median	11,051	36,168	30.6
– gross sales > median	9,801	35,461	27.6

Source: *Statistics Canada. Census of Population and Agriculture—Population Linkage, 1986, unpublished tabulations.*

240
Participation of women in the labour force:
a comparison of farm women and all women in Canada

Among the populations under consideration, few differences exist in the average income of women, the family income, or the significance of women's contribution to family income (Table 4). However, income levels alone do not reflect all of the factors which explain women's labour force participation. The level of family debt and the number of people whose needs must be met by an income may also provide an economic incentive for women to join the labour force. As the debt variable was not available on the census of population database, we decided to use the census of agriculture database and to examine the level of farm debt as an index of the economic incentive that women in the farm population would have to join the labour force.

TABLE 5

Farm economic variables for the two subgroups of the farm population Canada, 1986

Size class of gross farm sales	Average farm sales	Average farm expenses	Average capital	Average farm debt
– gross sales < median	10,605	15,307	189,226	44,157
– gross sales > median	129,733	106,272	565,144	168,206

Source: *Statistics Canada. Agriculture—Population Linkage, 1986, unpublished tabulations.*

FIGURE 12

Labour force participation rate of farm women by size of farm debt, 1986

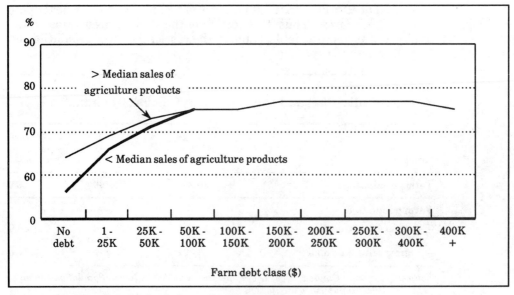

Source: *Statistics Canada. Agriculture—Population Linkage.*

Farms above the median gross farm sales have higher expenses, assets and farm debts, on average (Table 5). The higher the level of farm debt, the higher the participation rate for women[4] (Figure 12). In addition, the participation rates of women living on farms with sales below the median are slightly below the rates of women in the other group and the difference is greatest if the farm has no debt.

5. Conclusion

The main findings from this study follow:

- The labour force participation rate for farm women is higher than that of women in the total population;

- Within the farm population, the participation rate is higher for women living on farms with gross sales above the median (over $30,277 in 1986);

- In addition to a higher participation rate for women in the farm population, the average number of hours and weeks worked by farm women is higher than the average for women in the total population;

- Major socio-economic variables explained only a small part of the difference in labour force participation rates between farm women and all women. However, if farm women reported a 'farming occupation' or were associated with a larger farm, they were more likely to be in the labour force.

---

4. Only a few observations have high debts and low sales because, in most cases, the person has just started farming and has not yet generated the expected level of gross sales. Thus, the line for the smaller farm category in Figure 12 is not shown for debts over $50,000.

These findings are consistent with an American study (Ollenburg et al. 1989) which showed that, in 1985, the individual characteristics of women, such as age, family income, education and the presence and age of children did not play a major role in preventing women from joining the labour force. However, that study went on to suggest that it is necessary to take into account structural factors such as the prices obtained from the sale of farm products, interest rates, the change in the value of farm land, the increase in the cost of products used in farming— to understand the labour force participation of farm women. It would be interesting to measure the impact of these factors in the Canadian context. Some farm women argue that these factors, as well as the scarcity of farm labour, are important elements in their decision to join the labour force.

Marcelle Dion and Steve Welsh
Agriculture Division
Statistics Canada
Ottawa K1A 0T6

Appendix 1

Data limitations

The data used in this study have certain limitations:

1. Tabulations from the census of agriculture or the agriculture-population linkage databases underestimate the number of operators and women who are spouses of operators because the census of agriculture questionnaire has traditionally allowed only one designated operator for each census farm. This situation can be partially avoided by tabulating families on the Census of Population database who do not have a 'census-farm operator' in the family but who have family members with a farming occupation or who have some net farm income.

2. The census of population questionnaire only enumerates the main occupation. Therefore, women who worked on the farm are not included in the estimates if they had a job outside the farm which was their primary job.

3. Regardless of whether people reported a farming occupation or a farming income, only those who were living in the residence of a farm operator were included in the definition of the farm population.

For the 1991 Census of Agriculture, changes have been made in the questionnaire to allow for more than one operator to be reported for a census farm. This change should increase the estimate of the number of operators and allow more women to be recognized as operators. A new question on days of off-farm work for each operator will produce a better estimate of the number of women who are operators and who are employed outside the farm. The changes will also include, in the farm population, a percentage of persons who report having a farming job or farm income, and who have been excluded from the farm population until now.

244
Participation of women in the labour force:
a comparison of farm women and all women in Canada

References

Bollman, Ray D. and Pamela Smith. 1987. The changing role of off-farm income in Canada. Proceedings of the Canadian Agricultural Outlook Conference. Ottawa: Agriculture Canada, 155 -165.

Dominion Bureau of Statistics. 1953. Labour Force—Occupations and Industries, 1951 Census of Canada Series, vol. IV. Ottawa: Ministry of Trade and Commerce.

Dominion Bureau of Statistics. 1965. Labour Force—Occupations, 1961 Census of Canada Series, vol. III. Ottawa: Ministry of Trade and Commerce.

Ollenburg, J. C., S. J. Grana and H. A. Moore. 1989. Labour force participation of rural farm, rural nonfarm, and urban women: an update. Rural Sociology, 54(4): Winter.

Statistics Canada. 1974. Labour Force and Individual Income, (cat. no. 94-704), 1971 Census of Canada Series. Ottawa: Ministry of Industry, Trade and Commerce.

Statistics Canada. 1981. Census of Population, unpublished data. Ottawa: Statistics Canada.

Statistics Canada. 1986. Census of Population, unpublished data. Ottawa: Statistics Canada.

11

Farm family linkages to the non-farm sector: the role of off-farm income of farm families

A.M. (Tony) Fuller and Ray D. Bollman

Summary

Farm business linkages to the non-farm sector have been increasing over time. At one time, the economic welfare of farm families and local service communities was determined primarily by farm business linkages to the non-farm sector. Now, farm family linkages via off-farm capital markets and via off-farm labour markets are increasing in importance.

Canadian farm families receive over one half of their income from off-farm sources. Off-farm investments represent 10% of family income. One third of farm family income is derived from off-farm work. Even for families on the largest farms, over 40% have at least one member working off-farm. Participation in off-farm labour markets is important for a significant number of farm families to achieve a minimum standard of living. In some rural communities, up to 40% of the non-agricultural jobs held by women are held by farm women. The rural labour market is an important option for farm family development and, in this respect, retaining and creating jobs as a rural development strategy is a crucial policy consideration.

Farm families, through farm business links, consumer and social behaviour and especially through labour market and capital market participation, are integral and valuable components of rural community systems across Canada. Policies which support vibrant and healthy rural communities will directly benefit farm families.

Table of contents

Farm family linkages to the non-farm sector: the role of off-farm income of farm families[1]

A.M. (Tony) Fuller and Ray D. Bollman

1. Introduction

Commodities purchased and sold by farm businesses have always provided an important link between the farm and the non-farm sectors. At one time, the economic welfare of farm families was determined primarily by farm business linkages to the non-farm sector: the purchase of farm inputs and the marketing of farm products linked the farm to local agri-business service centres. In recent decades, the family's economic linkage to the non-farm sector has increased in variety and importance. Farm families have increasingly established direct linkages with the non-farm sector in two ways:

a. investment in off-farm capital markets

b. employment in off-farm labour markets.

This paper will document these trends and will comment on them in relation to income stability and the significance of the off-farm sector.

Some of the questions which arise fall into a sequence of steps and propositions:

1. How much do farm families rely on the non-farm rural labour market?

2. Do such linkages have regional variations in Canada?

3. If so, how will changes in farm income and non-farm income levels affect such linkages in different regions?

---

1. The authors wish to acknowledge the contributions to this paper by Philip Ehrensaft and Pamela Smith.

One hypothesis is that in areas where reliance on the off-farm labour market is weak, a downtown in agricultural income would have serious consequences for farm family incomes that would require an "agricultural" response, or drastic measures to improve the off-farm labour market. In areas where there is a high reliance on off-farm labour markets, a downtown in agricultural incomes would cause minor "hurt" to farm families, but a downturn in off-farm labour demand would cause serious income problems for farm families. If these arguments hold true then the fourth and final point of discussion in this paper follows:

4.   Is **rural development** (promotion of non-farm employment opportunities in rural areas) a viable farm policy?

This debate brings farm family income questions firmly into the rural development sphere, a proposition already introduced by Ehrensaft and Bollman (1990) and Fuller et al. (1990).

Farm families, regardless of the definition of a "farm" family, have obtained a larger and larger share of their income from off-farm sources over the last few decades. Although researchers have addressed the issue in academic literature for at least a decade, the idea that off-farm employment is a viable option for farm families has only recently surfaced in the popular farm press.

2.   Farm business linkages to the non-farm sector

Commodities purchased and sold by farm businesses have always provided an important link between the farm and the non-farm sector. In 1989, over 95% of farm production was sold to the non-farm market (Figure 1). The share of production attributable to purchased goods and services has risen to 75%, from 40% in the 1950s (Figure 2). The linkage of farm businesses to off-farm capital markets as measured by the interest paid on borrowed capital has fluctuated dramatically, from 3% of the value of production in 1950 to 13% in 1981 (Figure 3). The linkage of farm businesses to off-farm labour markets as measured by the wages paid to hired labour has varied between 5% and 8% over the past 30 years (Figure 4).[2]

Over time, the business linkage between the farm and the agriculture and food sectors has strengthened, but the linkage between farm businesses and the local community has weakened as many suppliers of farm inputs, including credit and advisory services, as well as commodity markets have moved from locations in small towns to larger centres. Family consumption linkages to the non-farm sectors (e.g. retail services, education and the church) have remained local in scale, but diffused over a set of communities (Fuller et al. 1990; Fuller 1991).

---

2.   This section updates the results in Bollman and Smith (1988).

In effect, the nature of linkages between the farm and the off-farm sector is changing: the farm business linkages are strengthening but are not tied to local services; family consumption linkages remain strong but are increasingly dispersed over a wide set of local communities.

FIGURE 1

Percent of production marketed
99% of production is marketed

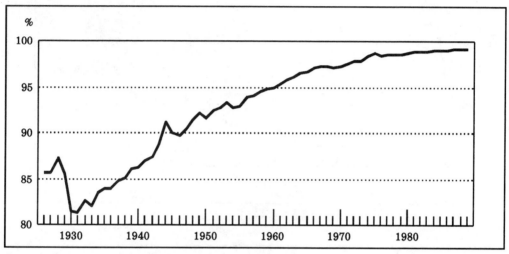

Source: Statistics Canada. Agriculture Economic Statistics, (cat. no. 21-603).

FIGURE 2

Cash inputs as percent of production
72% of production goes to pay cash inputs

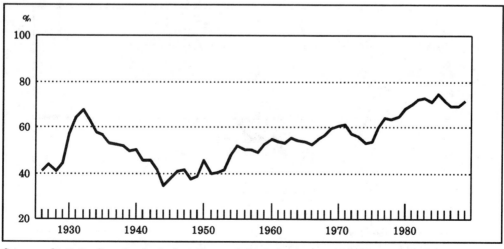

Source: Statistics Canada. Agriculture Economic Statistics, (cat. no. 21-603).

FIGURE 3

Interest paid as a percent of value of production
In 1981, 13% of production value was paid as interest

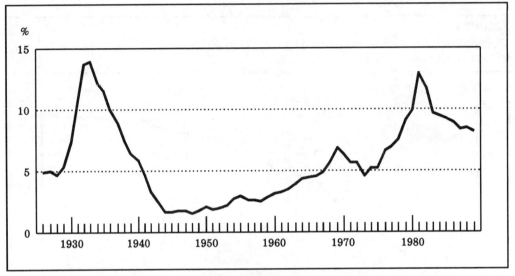

Source: *Statistics Canada. Agriculture Economic Statistics, (cat. no. 21-603).*

FIGURE 4

Wages paid as a percent of value of production
In 1989, 8% of production value was paid as wages

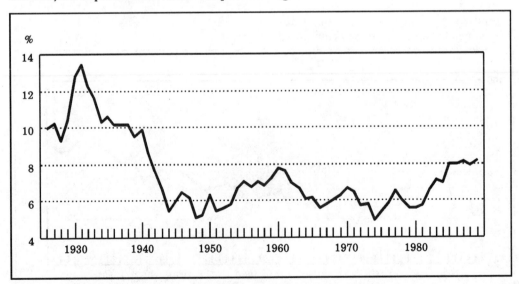

Source: *Statistics Canada. Agriculture Economic Statistics, (cat. no. 21-603).*

3. Farm family linkages to the non-farm sector

The farm family linkage to the non-farm sector will be explored via the medium of income: specifically investment income and income from farm family participation in the off-farm labour market.

FIGURE 5

Off-farm income as a percent of total farm family income
Over half of farm family income comes from off-farm work

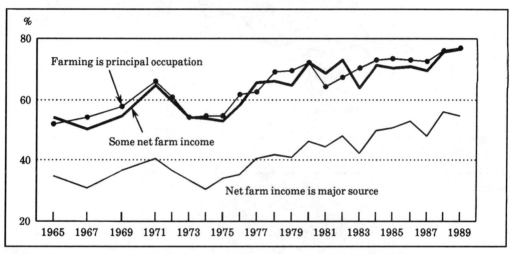

Source: Statistics Canada. Survey of Consumer Finances.

Over time, the share of farm family income from off-farm sources has increased. This conclusion holds regardless of the definition of a farm family. In 1965, between 35% and 54% of farm family income was received from off-farm sources, depending on how a farm family is defined. This increased to between 54% and 77% by 1989 (Figure 5). Canadian farm families have a strong reliance on the non-farm sector for a major share of their income.

3.1 The capital market linkage: off-farm income from off-farm investment[3]

The share of farm family income from returns to financial investments has risen steadily over time. The share peaked at 14% in the early 1980s for two reasons: the commodity price boom of the seventies enabled farm profits to be invested, and high interest rates increased the return on savings. After 1985, the share of family income from return on investments was approximately 10% (Figure 6). Canadian farm families have significant linkages to the off-farm <u>capital</u> market.

---

3.   This section updates the results in Bollman and Smith (1987).

252
Farm family linkages to the non-farm sector:
the role of off-farm income of farm families

FIGURE 6

Family income from investments as a percent of total farm family income
Slight increase in percent of farm family income from investment

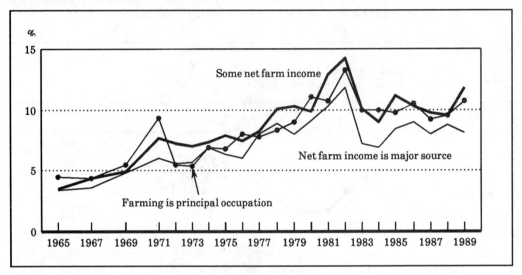

Source: Statistics Canada. Survey of Consumer Finances

3.2   The labour market linkage: off-farm income from off-farm work

3.2.1   Historical Trends, 1941-1989

Since 1941, one third of all census farm operators reported some days of off-farm work (Figure 7). Note that the proportion working full-time off the farm (greater than 228 days) has increased from 4% to 16%. Note also that farms of operators with no off-farm work have produced about 80% of all agricultural production in Canada over the past few decades (Figure 8). The ratio of non-farm earnings to farm earnings has increased as operators on average allocate more days per year to off-farm work **and** non-farm returns have increased relative to farm returns (Bollman and Smith 1987). Data on days of off-farm work refer only to the operator's time. These statistics ignore the contribution of spouses and other family members. However, their share of off-farm income has not increased: non-operators contributed the same proportion of family off-farm income in 1980 as in 1957 (Bollman and Smith 1987).

FIGURE 7
Operator days of off-farm work
60% report no days of off-farm work

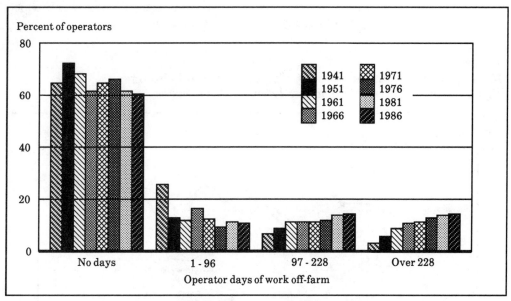

Source: Statistics Canada. Censuses of Agriculture, 1941 to 1986.

FIGURE 8
Aggregate sales by days of off-farm work by operators
80% are by operators with no off-farm work

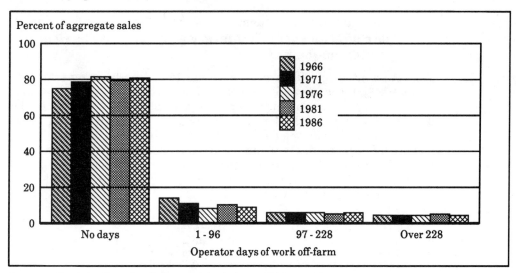

Source: Statistics Canada. Censuses of Agriculture, 1966 to 1986.

Off-farm wage income of all family members, added together, indicates an increased share of farm family income from off-farm work over time. In 1965, between 21% and 36% of farm family income was from off-farm wage income, depending on how a farm family is defined. This increased to between 31% and 51% by 1989 (Figure 9). Canadian farm families have significant levels of income from off-farm work which implies important linkages to the off-farm labour market.

FIGURE 9
Off-farm wage income as percent of total farm family income
Slight increase in percent of farm family income from wages

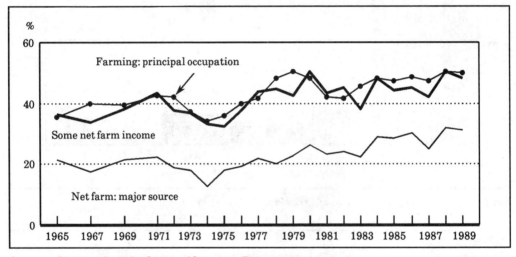

Source: Statistics Canada. Survey of Consumer Finances.

3.2.2   Are apparent off-farm wages really from off-the- farm? An adjustment for "off-farm wages" that may be wage work "on-the-farm"[4]

The contribution of off-farm earnings to total family income may be overstated by the agriculture-population linkage database[5] because structural change in commercial agriculture has led to changes in the way that operators and other family members receive farm enterprise profits. For example, the data on "wages received" may include wages paid by the farm business to family members for work on the farm. We adopt the procedures of Ehrensaft and Bollman (1990) to define and calculate an "agricultural wage income" and a "non-agricultural wage income" (for details, see Appendix I).

---

4.   This section is based on Ehrensaft and Bollman (1990).

5.   The agriculture-population linkage database links the Census of Agriculture and the Census of Population questionnaires for each census-farm operator household. This permits the cross-tabulation of farm and family data. For details, see Freeman (1976) and Beyrouti et al (1989).

3.2.3 The role of "non-agricultural" wage income in total family income

The incidence of off-farm work across the farm (business) size spectrum does not necessarily imply that a small farm <u>causes</u> a high incidence of family participation in off-farm work. Rather, we infer that a trade-off takes place between farm business size and family participation in off-farm work. We think, in general, that the decision to operate a farm of a given size is decided in conjunction with the decision that some family members will work off-farm. Sometimes a small farm "necessitates" some family members to work off-farm, and sometimes off-farm work by some family members "causes" the farm to be of a certain size. However, we think that the amount of off-farm work and the size of farm is determined at the same time. The phase in the family cycle and the motives for holding farm land may be equally as significant as farm size in influencing the off- farm work decision (Fuller 1984).

The adjustments made to wage income to define more accurately "agricultural wage income" and "non-agricultural wage income" (described in Appendix I) are nevertheless biased toward allocating too much wage income to "agricultural wage income". Thus, if we find that "non-agricultural wage income" is a significant contributor to farm family income, we will have greater confidence in our conclusions.

FIGURE 10

Families with off-farm work, 1985
Over 40% on largest farms participate in off-farm work

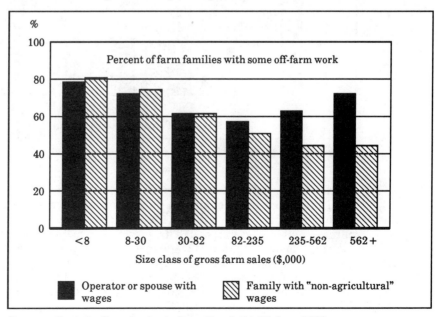

Source: *Statistics Canada. Agriculture-Population Linkage, 1986*

The incidence of some "non-agricultural wage income" is lower for families on larger farms (Figure 10). Nevertheless, there is still a high degree of reporting wage income for families on larger farms. Most importantly, note that after our adjustment for cases where families pay themselves wages for working on their own farms, there remains a significant proportion of families on larger farms who also participate in the off-farm labour market. For families on the largest farms, over 40% of the families participate in the off-farm labour market. Mansfield (1990) has suggested this may indicate the penetration of external capital into agriculture via the ownership of large family farms by professionals and hobbyists.

FIGURE 11

Families attaining low income cut-off via off-farm work, 1985
Farm income is inadequate but farm income plus off-farm work is adequate

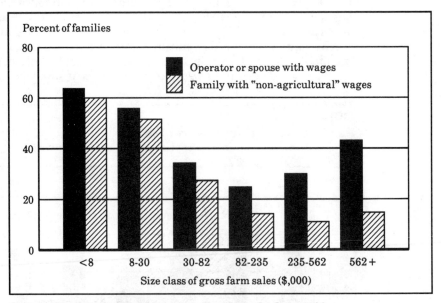

Source: Statistics Canada. Agriculture-Population Linkage, 1986

In addition, a significant proportion of farm families need "non-agricultural wage income" to achieve a minimum standard of living. Statistics Canada's low income cut-off (LICO) may proxy as a measure of a minimum living standard. The proportion of families attaining the LICO via "non-agricultural wage income" is lower for families on larger farms. However, over 10% of the families on the largest farms need "non-agricultural wage income" to attain the LICO. Figure 11 illustrates the importance of family non-agricultural wages in assisting farm families to reach the LICO: this affects over 50% of all families on farms with less than $30,000 gross farm sales.

3.3 Are farm-community links important everywhere?

To what extent do farm families participate in off-farm labour markets in all parts of the country? We wish to investigate the proposition that rural development policy is an effective way to meet the farm family income objective on the farm policy agenda. In testing this and to control for farm size, we selected families on "mainstream" farms[6]. Farm policy appears to be targeted at "mainstream" farms and we found this to be a suitable way to add rigour to our analysis.

We found that only a small share of census divisions[7] (20%) have less than one-half of their "mainstream" farm families participating in off-farm work (i.e. reporting some "non-agricultural wage income"). More importantly, 80% of the census divisions in Canada have over one-half of "mainstream" farm families with some off-farm work. Farm family participation in the labour market **is** important everywhere. The geographic distribution however lacks a specific pattern[8] (Map 1a, 1b)[9]. Census divisions with over 50% of "mainstream" farm families reporting some non-agricultural wages are scattered throughout Canada.

---

6. We adopt the definition proposed by Ehrensaft and Bollman (1990) where "mainstream" farms are defined as farms with gross sales between $30,277 and $235,260 (i.e. between the 50th and 94th percentiles).

7. To be more specific, the sub-provincial areas are "weighting areas" for the agriculture-population linkage database. In general, they conform to census divisions but large census divisions were divided into two weighting areas and census divisions with few farm families are combined with adjacent census divisions.

8. The highest incidence of participation in off-farm labour markets is in areas with only a few "mainstream" farms. These are areas that have poor conditions for agriculture (i.e. northern latitudes, the Canadian Shield) and although the farm may attain the "mainstream" threshold of gross farm sales, the family must rely on non-agricultural wages.

9. We have not shown Newfoundland on our maps to show census division details for Eastern Canada on one page. The data for Newfoundland are available from the authors upon request.

MAP 1a

Mainstream farming families with some non-agricultural wage income

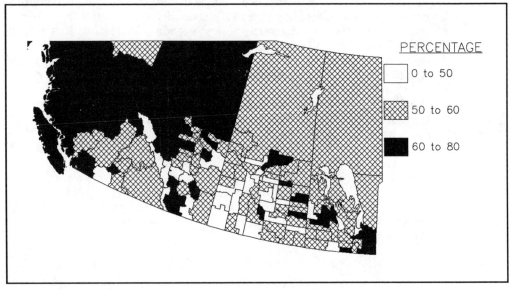

Source: Statistics Canada. Agriculture - Population Linkage, 1986.

MAP 1b

Mainstream farming families with some non-agricultural wage income

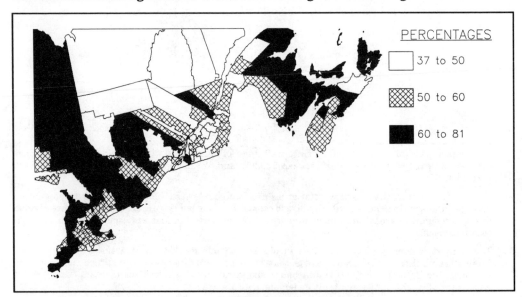

Source: Statistics Canada. Agriculture - Population Linkage, 1986.

The importance of off-farm labour market participation can also be judged by the reliance on "non-agricultural wage income" to attain the low income cut-off. Over one third of "mainstream" farm families require "non-agricultural wage income" to attain the low income cut-off in 10% of census divisions in Canada. In the Prairie provinces, many census divisions show a lower proportion (8% to 15%) of "mainstream" farm families being dependent upon non-agricultural wages to attain the low income cut-off (Map 2a, 2b). In Southern Ontario and the Maritime provinces, the pattern is scattered.

Farm family participation in off-farm labour markets is high in Canada and does not vary much by region, farm business size or type.

4.   The role of off-farm work of farm family members in the off-farm labour market

In discussing the links between farm families and rural labour markets, it is important to emphasize that linkage effects have a two-way impact. Given the considerable involvement of farm families in the off-farm labour market (over 50% of the families of census farm operators have at least one member employed off-farm), the contribution of farm-based labour to the local labour market should be considered. It is not clear whether this aids or detracts from the rural development argument. Wage labour by farm family members takes jobs that otherwise might be occupied by rural non-farm people. On the other hand, some industries and some communities will benefit from the pool of farm labour which has the reputation of permanence and reliability.

As an indicator of the farm family's role in the off-farm labour market, we first identified all individuals with non-agricultural occupations, and we then identified the proportion of these individuals who were members of a farm household.[10]   Nationally, 5% of male non-agricultural jobs and 6% of female non-agricultural jobs are held by individuals residing in a broadly-defined farm household. The proportions are strikingly higher in Prince Edward Island (men 11% and women 13%) and in Saskatchewan (men 14% and women 20%).

The degree to which non-agricultural jobs are held by farm household members is much higher in rural areas. In 12% of census divisions, over 25% of non-agricultural jobs held by women are held by farm women. In some rural areas in Saskatchewan, over 40% of the female non-agricultural jobs are held by farm women (Map 3a, 3b).

---

10. For this calculation, we used an all-encompassing definition of a farm household. Specifically, we have included any household with one individual with some net farm income or with an individual with an agricultural occupation or an individual who is designated as a census farm operator.

MAP 2a

Mainstream farming families who use non-agricultural wages to achieve the LICO

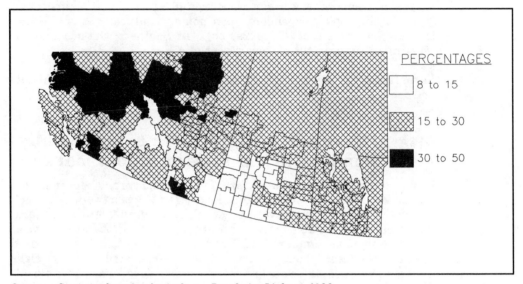

Source: Statistics Canada. Agriculture - Population Linkage, 1986.

MAP 2b

Mainstream farming families who use non-agricultural wages to achieve the LICO

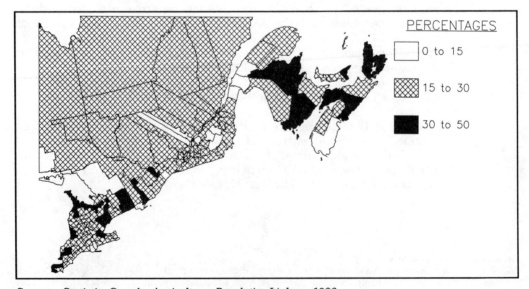

Source: Statistics Canada. Agriculture - Population Linkage, 1986.

MAP 3a

Farm women with non-agricultural occupations as a percent of all women with non- agricultural occupations

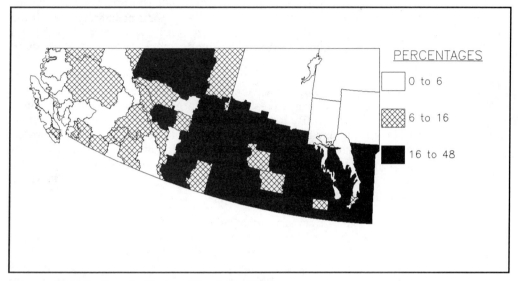

Source: Statistics Canada. Census of Population, 1986.

MAP 3b

Farm women with non-agricultural occupations as a percent of all women with non- agricultural occupations

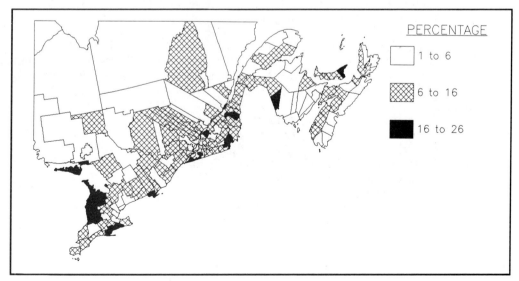

Source: Statistics Canada. Census of Population, 1986.

5.   Conclusion

Farm business linkages to the non-farm sector have been increasing over time. At one time, the economic welfare of farm families and local service communities was determined primarily by farm business linkages to the non-farm sector. However, for the farm family and for the local service community, the relative importance of these business linkages is decreasing. Instead, farm family linkages via off-farm capital markets and via off-farm labour markets are increasing in importance.

Canadian farm families receive over one half of their income from off-farm sources. Off-farm investments represent 10% of family income. One third of farm family income is derived from off-farm work. Even for families on the largest farms, over 40% have at least one member working off-farm. Participation in off-farm labour markets is important for a significant number of farm families to achieve a minimum standard of living. **The maintenance of off-farm job opportunities for farm people is essential.**

Pluriactivity is important everywhere in Canada. In some rural communities, up to 40% of the non-agricultural jobs held by women are held by farm women. The importance of off-farm wage earnings for families on "mainstream" farms has been demonstrated. It suggests that the rural labour market is an important option for farm family development and, in this respect, retaining and creating jobs as a rural development strategy is a crucial policy consideration.

For rural areas with little reliance on off-farm labour markets, a downturn in the agricultural income would demand an "agricultural" sector response or a response to move farm family members into off-farm jobs or to move off-farm jobs to the region.

For areas with a high reliance on off-farm labour markets, a downturn in agricultural income will only cause minor "hurt" to farm families but a downturn in the off-farm labour market will cause a major "hurt" to the family income of farm families.

Farm families, through farm business links, consumer and social behaviour and especially through labour market and capital market participation, are integral and valuable components of rural community systems across Canada. Policies which support vibrant and healthy rural communities will directly benefit farm families. In this sense, rural development policy will make good farm policy.

5.1   Themes for further research

Given the amount and pervasiveness of linkage between the farm
family and the rural labour market four themes emerge for further
research

1. **Farm impacts**

   What are the effects of the linkage between farm families and off-
   farm employment?   For example, is the income earned by
   mainstream farm families used on farm for improvements, debt
   servicing or for farm diversification?

2. **Family impacts**

   What happens to family development and farm organization when
   the farm family's labour is divided between the farm and off- farm
   employment?   And how do changing gender roles in the
   distribution of labour effect family development and farm
   organization?   What are the stress-related behaviours which are
   relieved or created by such emerging work styles?

3. **Rural development**

   If participation in the off-farm labour market is important for
   many "mainstream" farm families and essential for other farm
   families, then barriers to participation (access, distance, child care,
   skills training, literacy and entrepreneurship) need to be
   examined and evaluated for potential program development.

4. **On-farm diversification**

   If off-farm labour participation of farm families takes away rural
   jobs in some areas and reduces farm work, then the prospects for
   starting farm-based businesses need to be examined.   Farm-based
   diversification creates jobs, an extra income flow, absorbs labour
   and may better fit into a farm lifestyle; and yet, farm-based
   businesses are not a tradition in Canada.

Appendix I

An estimate of the "non-agricultural wages" received by farm family members[11]

Net farm income on the census of population questionnaire is an individual's income from an unincorporated farm enterprise. As farms with higher sales levels have adopted an incorporated legal organization to minimize tax obligations and facilitate the inheritance process, profits are taken in the form of dividends, wage payments to family members, and retained earnings[12]. Thus, for families on incorporated farms, some of the reported investment income may flow from dividends paid by the farm corporation.

Wages paid to family members by the farm corporation may represent an important fraction of the farm family members' wages. Unincorporated farms also pay wages to family members. The census of agriculture questionnaire collected information on farm wages paid to family members. The amount of wages received by family members as reported on the census of population, up to the amount of wages paid to family members by the farm[13] as reported on the census of agriculture questionnaire, was defined as "agricultural" wages received by the family.

A.M. (Tony) Fuller
School for Rural Planning
   and Development
University of Guelph
Guelph, Ontario
N1G 2W1

Ray D. Bollman
Agriculture Division
Statistics Canada
Ottawa, Ontario
K1A 0T6

---

11. Excerpted from Ehrensaft and Bollman (1990).

12. The agriculture-population linkage database measures only the income received by individuals. Thus, earnings retained by a corporation are not measured as family income.

13. On some farms, the farm wages paid to the family are greater than the farm family's wage and self-employment earnings. This suggests that farm operators are reporting wages paid to family members residing in other households.

References

Beyrouti, M., M. Dion, and S. Welsh. 1989. Socio-economic Characteristics of the Farm Population, (cat. no 96-114). Ottawa: Statistics Canada.

Bollman, Ray D. 1980. A comparison of the money incomes of farmers and non-farmers. Canadian Journal of Agricultural Economics, Proceedings. August: 48-55.

Bollman, Ray D. 1983. Expanding and declining farm firms: numbers and implications. Canadian Journal of Agricultural Economics, Proceedings. 31: 134-42.

Bollman, Ray D. 1989. Who receives farm government payments? Canadian Journal of Agricultural Economics, 37(3): 351-378.

Bollman, Ray D. and Pamela Smith. 1987. The changing role of off- farm income in Canada. Proceedings of the Canadian Agricultural Outlook Conference. December: 155-166.

Bollman, Ray D. and Pamela Smith. 1988. Integration of Canadian Farm and Off-farm Markets and the Off-farm Work of Farm Women, Men, and Children. Working paper no. 16, Analytical Studies Branch. Ottawa: Statistics Canada.

Conseil national du Bien-être social. 1987. Les seuils de pauvreté de 1987. Ottawa: Gouvernement du Canada.

Culver, David, Monica Tomiak and Ray D. Bollman. 1991. High and low margin prairie grain and oilseed farms. Canadian Farm Economics, 23(1).

Ehrensaft, Philip. 1987. Structure and Performance in the Canadian Beef Sector. Ottawa: Farm Development Policy Directorate, Agriculture Canada.

Ehrensaft, Philip, and Ray D. Bollman. 1983. The industrial organization of modern agriculture. Canadian Journal of Agricultural Economics, 31: 122-133.

Ehrensaft, Philip, and Ray D. Bollman. 1990. The microdynamics and farm family economics of structural change in agriculture. Proceedings of the United States Bureau of the Census Annual Research Conference. Washington, D.C: 85-126.

Ehrensaft, Philip, Pierre LaRamee, Ray D. Bollman and Frederick H. Buttel. 1984. The microdynamics of farm structural change in North America: the Canadian experience and Canada-USA comparisons. American Journal of Agricultural Economics, 66(5): 823-828.

Ehrensaft, P. and R. D. Bollman. 1985. The farm management input and structural change in modern agriculture. Proceedings of the Canadian Agricultural Outlook Conference, December. Ottawa: Agriculture Canada, 156-166.

Fitzpatrick, J. M. and C. V. Parker. 1965. Distribution of income in Canadian agriculture. Canadian Journal of Agricultural Economics, 13(2): 47-64.

Freeman, W. G. 1976. An introduction to the agriculture-population linkage program. Canadian Farm Economics, 2(1): 9-16.

Fuller, A.M. 1984. Part-time farming: the enigma and the realities. Research in Rural Sociology and Development, volume 1, Focus on Agriculture: 187-219.

Fuller, A.M. 1991. Multiple job-holding among farm families in Canada. In Multiple Job-holding Among Farm Families, edited by M. C. Halberg, Jill Findeis and Daniel A. Lass. Ames: Iowa State University Press, 31-44.

Fuller, Tony, Philip Ehrensaft and Michael Gertler. 1990. Sustainable rural communities in Canada: issues and prospects. In Sustainable Rural Communities in Canada, edited by Michael E. Gertler and Harold R. Baker. Saskatoon: Agriculture and Rural Restructuring Group.

Jones, Wayne. 1989. Notes, Presentation to the Manitoba Institute of Agrologists. Winnipeg: April 7.

Kulshreshtha, Surendra N. 1965. Considerations involved in developing a valid comparison of farm and non-farm incomes in Canada, 1926-1961. Unpublished PhD Thesis. Winnipeg: University of Manitoba.

Kulshreshtha, Surendra N. 1966. An approach to develop comparisons of farm and non-farm incomes in Canada. Canadian Journal of Agricultural Economics, 14(1): 61-74.

Kulshreshtha, Surendra N. 1967. Measuring the relative income of farm labour, 1941-1961. Canadian Journal of Agricultural Economics, 15: 28-43.

Mansfield, Lois. 1990. A macro-scale analysis of hobby farming in southern Ontario. Unpublished M.A. thesis. Guelph: University of Guelph.

Porteous, W. L. 1974. Outlook for Canadian farm income levels. Proceedings of the Canadian Agricultural Outlook Conference, December. Ottawa: Agriculture Canada, 114-119.

Salant, Priscilla, M. Smale and W. Saupe. 1986. Farm Viability: Results of the USDA Family Farm Surveys. Rural Development Research Report No. 60, July. Washington: U.S. Department of Agriculture, Economic Research Service,

Shaw, Paul. 1979a. A note on shifts in parity, poverty, and sources of farm family income in North America. Economic Development and Cultural Change, 27(4): 645-652.

Shaw, Paul. 1979b. Canadian farm and non-farm family incomes. American Journal of Agricultural Economics, 61(4): 676-682.

Shaw, Paul. 1979c. Canada's Farm Population: analysis of income and related characteristics, Ottawa: Statistics Canada.

Gull Lake, Saskatchewan

12

The changing rural environment: a look at Eastern Ontario's Jock River basin

Douglas F. Trant

Summary

The Jock River basin has undergone many changes during the past two centuries. Stream hydrology has been significantly altered making the river more sensitive to stagnation and bacterial build up. Statistical records show that over the last twenty years population has tripled, and that use of land has intensified significantly. Fertilizer and pesticide inputs, which have high environmental impact, have increased as well.

The changing rural environment: a look at Eastern Ontario's Jock River basin[1]

Douglas F. Trant

Introduction

The rural environment[2] in Canada has seen more changes in the 20th century than it has since the last ice age. Most of these changes have been caused by a growing human population. One hundred years ago, Canada had a population of 5 million. Today, the population exceeds 26 million. At the same time, global population has grown exponentially, from under 1 billion in 1890 to over 5 billion today. Increasing population has placed increasing demands on the rural environment to feed people and to support their economic livelihoods by providing the essential raw materials for a modern, urban society. For the time being, the rural environment has sustained increased demands for food and natural resources.

Natural resource consumption continues to grow in Canada. Canadians are consuming more water, minerals, forest products, and land resources than ever before (Statistics Canada 1986). For example, a century ago the energy demand of Canadian society was 300 teraJ (300 trillion joules), most of which came from renewable sources. Today, total energy demand is in excess of 8,000 teraJ, and most of this comes from non-renewable sources. On a per capita basis, Canadians consumed 60 MJ (60 million joules) per person in 1890. By 1990 the average Canadian was consuming 300 MJ (Statistics Canada 1986). The impact of energy development on the rural environment range from the creation of reservoirs for hydro-electricity generation to potential global climatic changes caused by energy based carbon dioxide emissions.

---

1. I would like to thank all of Statistics Canada's Environment and Natural Resources Section staff for their critical review of this paper. In particular, I would like to thank staff members Murray Cameron and Hélène Trépanier for their suggestions and contributions to the research which supports this study.

2. For the purposes of this paper, the rural environment is defined as everything within the boundaries of Canada that is not part of the urban environment. This definition includes such things as land, water, forests, minerals, soils, mountains, wildlife and even air.

Another example of increasing natural resource consumption comes from agriculture where loss of fertile land and land degradation pose a serious problem. Agriculture ranks only behind tundra and forests in terms of occupied Canadian land area. In 1890, 5 million ha (hectares) were cultivated to provide food for 4.8 million people. Today, most of the suitable agricultural land is being cultivated amounting to some 47 million ha. Since 1890, the number of hectares cultivated per capita has doubled going from 1 ha per capita to almost 2 in 1990.

At the same time crop yields per hectare have more than doubled for most crops because of improvements in cultivation techniques and developments in genetic research. The impacts of agriculture on the rural environment have evolved since World War II, with the development of highly productive, capital-intensive, labour substituting technology (Dumanski et al. 1986). Modern agricultural practices contribute to Canada's large food surplus. In 1987, Canada produced a crop surplus sufficient to feed 325 million people (World Food Council 1988).

Productivity has a price, though, and much of the productivity gain has been achieved at considerable cost to the environment and the natural fertility of many soils (Dumanski et al. 1986). As resource demands from the rural environment increase, the question of long term sustainability arises. Measuring resource flows and subsequent sustainability are challenges that will have to be met if we are to maintain current living standards and provide for future generations.

The consumption habits of an increasing population are important determinants of rural environmental quality. Over the last century Canadians have been enjoying a steadily rising standard of living which is reflected by an increased per capita consumption of goods and services (Statistics Canada 1983, 1990b). Rising living standards have, however, environmental costs. The solid waste problem is an example. Goods consumption and subsequent waste production have increased to the point where many waste storage sites are reaching capacity sooner than expected. Most urban waste sites are located in the rural environment. Unfortunately, solid waste is often poorly catalogued: we do not know what has been dumped at each site, or how wastes will interact with the environment at each disposal site. Unanswered questions such as these make it difficult to determine the actual state of the environment.

Today, the main challenge facing the rural sector is to provide food and resources for Canada's population at sustainable rates. This challenge is threatened by problems such as continued soil erosion, declining soil fertility, monoculturing, the toxic material build up, and arable land loss to urban uses. Obtaining relevant information for analysis is essential to solving both large and small environmental problems.

Finding applicable information is often most easily accomplished at a local level. The familiarity and concern that people have with their immediate surroundings provides a wealth of knowledge that is often hidden to larger scale studies. The remainder of this paper will explore environmental issues in a small area only. That area is Eastern Ontario's Jock River basin. The main objectives of this paper are to develop and analyze a river basin profile using detailed local information from Statistics Canada databases.

The Jock River case study

The Jock River is a major tributary of the Rideau River which flows from the Rideau Lakes to the city of Ottawa, where it meets the Ottawa River (Map A). The Jock River basin has been mainly farmland since it was cleared of forests in the early 1800s. Today, while still predominantly agricultural, the Jock River basin is being urbanized as Ottawa's rural-urban fringe expands from the city's central core. The Jock River basin is shared by 4 municipalities: Goulbourn, Nepean, Rideau and Beckwith. For some time now residents and users of the Jock River basin have been aware of water quality problems which make the Jock unusable for recreational activity. Weed growth makes the river unnavigable in summer months, swimming is a thing of the past, fishing is successful only in early spring and the river, as source of potable water, would prove quite hazardous.

MAP A
Jock River Basin

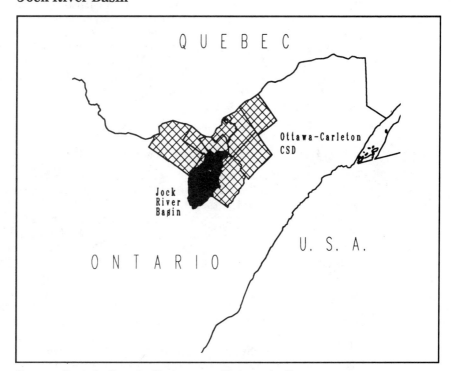

Source: Statistics Canada. Environmental Information System.

In 1989 concerned citizens formed a committee, "The Friends of the Jock River". Preliminary results from an environmental monitoring program in the summer of 1990 showed the river to be polluted. Phosphorus levels as well as bacteria levels were well above provincial guidelines.

Statistics Canada's Environment and Natural Resources Section is providing data to this group to help it identify potential environmental impacts in the Jock River watershed. The Environment and Natural Resources Section operates and maintains a large geographically referenced database known as the Environmental Information System (EIS) which can be used to analyze environmental problems on various scales ranging from large national studies to assessing local watershed concerns. The system is particularly useful for re-aggregating data to spatial units which will provide the necessary foundation for analysis. Watersheds are a good example of these spatial units, where impacts within a river system transcend traditional political boundaries, and it becomes essential to know about activities throughout the catchment area.

Methodology

Much of the research in this study employed Geographic Information System (GIS) technology to develop a detailed statistical profile of the river basin. A Rideau Valley Conservation Authority watershed map was used to capture a digital picture of the river and its catchment area. This was accomplished by digitizing the watershed boundaries and creating a computer map which could then be selectively combined with the information layers in the EIS. These information layers provided data on physiography, climate, soils, population, labour force characteristics, agricultural activity, and manufacturing establishments throughout the basin.

Jock River hydrological background

Annual hydrological discharge profiles provide information about the water flow characteristics of a river throughout the seasonal drainage cycle. To determine the factors behind the visible decline in Jock River water quality, an analysis of the discharge profile is necessary (Figure 1). To summarize, the Jock River is characterised by low summer flow and high spring discharge. Daily Jock River discharge readings have been kept by Environment Canada since 1969. From these records the average peak discharge (110.1 m³/s—March 30) is 1,310 times greater than the average low discharge (0.084 m³/s—July 15). The hypothetical forested discharge curve on graph 1 represents the same volume of water but shows the effects of a greater proportion of forest cover. For comparison, the Bow River in Alberta has a maximum discharge only 38 times larger than the minimum discharge. The high spring run-off volumes on the Jock River cause

erosion problems along the river banks, while in contrast, the low
summer flow contributes to stagnation and nutrient build-up. Reasons
for high spring run-off and low summer flow in the basin can be
attributed to human activity in the basin. The Jock River's discharge
pattern has changed over time as vegetative cover and drainage
conditions have changed (Figure 2).

FIGURE 1
Jock River discharge rates (m³/s)

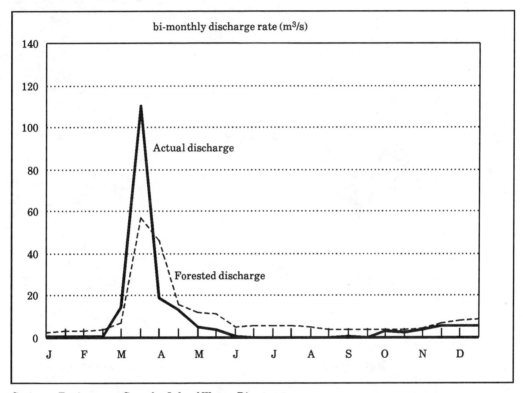

Source: Environment Canada. Inland Waters Directorate.

Unfortunately, historical discharge records do not go back to the pre-
agricultural era when the basin was under natural forest. Typically,
the removal of forested land increases the run-off rate in a river basin
because forests intercept and store a great deal of moisture both in the
trees themselves and in soils beneath the forest. In contrast, tilled land
does not store water as readily because tilled land is exposed to direct
sunlight and is frequently cultivated which brings soil moisture to the
surface to be evaporated. Spring snow is also not protected by tree
cover so it melts and runs-off more quickly under tilled conditions.
Agricultural land is often artificially drained to allow earlier spring
planting and moisture level control. Artificial drainage lowers soil

moisture which reduces the flow of water to the river in dry months such as August, when ground water is the major source of water for the river. In 1986, some 6,890 ha of agricultural land in the Jock River basin were artificially drained. This amounts to more than 12% of the river basin area, and represents a substantial alteration of natural drainage patterns.

FIGURE 2
Jock River hydrology

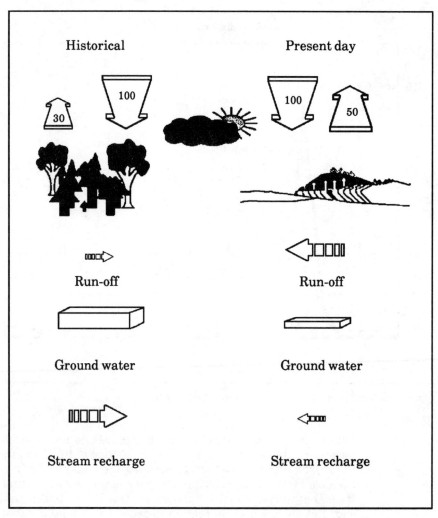

Physiography, climate and soils

Access to Agriculture Canada's Land Potential Database (LPDB) is available through Statistics Canada's EIS. This database contains details on Canadian land potential at a scale of 1:5,000,000. The results from overlaying the Jock River digital map and the LPDB are briefly described as follows. The Jock River basin consists of two soil types: an Orthic Melanic Brunisol, and a Humic Gleysol. These are young soils which have developed under a forested environment. The brunsolic soil is the better drained soil of the two. Fertility of these soils is variable, but in the Jock River basin, fertility is moderate to high. These soils developed primarily from glacial till and lacustrine deposits.

The climate in the basin is one of cold winters and warm summers with moderate precipitation throughout the year. The average minimum monthly temperature occurs in January with a temperature of -16°C, and the average monthly maximum temperature occurs in July with a temperature of 26.3°C. Average rainfall is 370.8 cm per year, the wind speed averages just over 3 m/s, and the growing season length in the basin is 148 days. Given the physical properties alone, the area has only a slight chance of water erosion. However, cultivation practices and field slopes have significant local effect soil erosion.

Socio-economic conditions

Historical data from the EIS were used to analyze trends that might affect Jock River environmental quality. The Jock River catchment area is 56,552 ha, and in 1971, this area was divided into the following major land use categories: 65% agriculture, 10% urban/transportation, 10% wetland, 15% forest. By 1986, the agricultural land area had declined to 55% and the majority of this land use change was from agriculture to urban uses (Table 1).

TABLE 1
The Jock River watershed, 1971-1986

	1971	1986	% change
Land use			
Watershed area (ha)	56,552	56,552	
Farmland area (ha)	35,461	30,850	-13.0
Cropland area (ha)	12,845	15,075	17.4
Wide-row monoculture area (ha)	687	1,820	164.8
Chemicals			
Chemical expenses ($1971)	33,330	75,526	126.6
Chemical expenses per cropland hectare	2.59	5.01	
Population			
Urban population	2,122	10,187	380.1
Rural population	4,873	10,508	115.6
Total population	6,995	20,695	195.9

Source: Statistics Canada. Environmental Information System.

Agricultural practices in the basin have significant impact on environmental quality. Agriculture affects vegetative cover, soil quality and basic stream hydrology. These factors determine the physical and chemical inputs to the river system via run-off and ground water flow. Chemical expense data (constant 1971 dollars) shows more than a doubling of expenditures on pesticides in the watershed over the 1971-1986 study period (Map B). Other data indicate intensified land use. Actual cropped area increased from 12,845 ha to 15,075 ha by 1986. Crop output potential has gone up in the basin despite the decline in agricultural land area. Fertilizer application rates have doubled during the study period, going from 1,600 t (tonnes) in 1971 to 3,300 t in 1986 (Map C). (Data for 1971 were derived from fertilizer expense data).

MAP B

Jock River basin agricultural pecticide application rates, 1971 to 1986

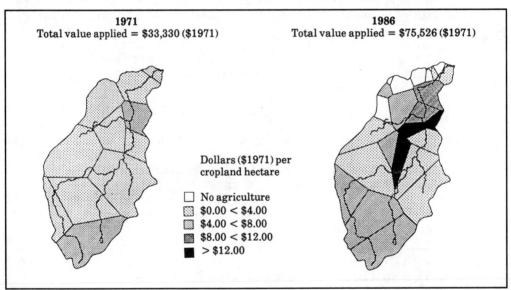

1971
Total value applied = $33,330 ($1971)

1986
Total value applied = $75,526 ($1971)

Dollars ($1971) per cropland hectare

- No agriculture
- $0.00 < $4.00
- $4.00 < $8.00
- $8.00 < $12.00
- > $12.00

Source: Statistics Canada. Environmental Information System.

MAP C

Jock River basin fertilizer application rates, 1971 to 1986

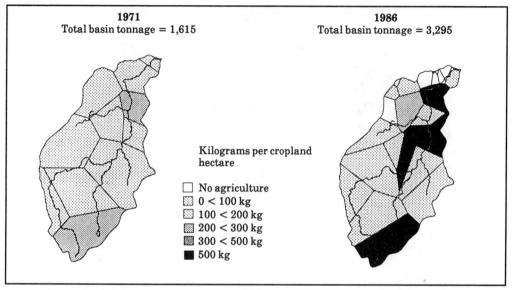

1971
Total basin tonnage = 1,615

1986
Total basin tonnage = 3,295

Kilograms per cropland hectare

☐ No agriculture
▨ 0 < 100 kg
▨ 100 < 200 kg
▨ 200 < 300 kg
▨ 300 < 500 kg
■ 500 kg

Source: Statistics Canada. Environmental Information System.

MAP D

Jock River basin wide-row monoculture trend, 1971 to 1986

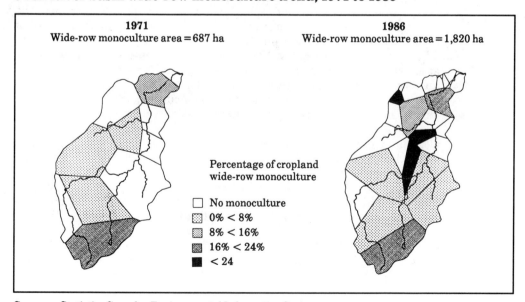

1971
Wide-row monoculture area = 687 ha

1986
Wide-row monoculture area = 1,820 ha

Percentage of cropland wide-row monoculture

☐ No monoculture
▨ 0% < 8%
▨ 8% < 16%
▨ 16% < 24%
■ < 24

Source: Statistics Canada. Environmental Information System.

MAP E
Jock River basin population density changes, 1971 to 1986

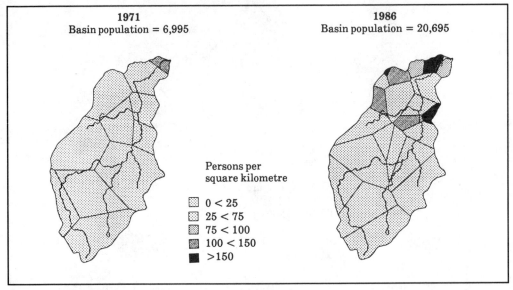

Source: Statistics Canada. Environmental Information System.

Land management practices in the Jock River valley were tested using the Agricultural Practices Impact Model APIM[3]. Results indicate that high stress monoculture cropping practices were on the rise over the study period. Wide-row monoculture, the practice of planting wide-row crops year after year, occupied 5% of total crop area in 1971 rising to 14% of total crop area by 1986 (Map D). Wide-row monoculture is associated with high run-off and subsequent soil erosion, as well as high levels of pesticide and fertilizer inputs. The spatial correlation between fertilizers, pesticides, and wide-row monoculture is evident by comparing maps B, C and D, where these activities coincide.

Census of population figures indicate that the urban population has grown by 380%, from 2,122 in 1971 to 10,187 by 1986. Rural population has also increased from a low of 4,873 in 1971 to over 10,500 by 1986, bringing the total population in the catchment area to some 20,695 (Map E). This population trend is expected to continue as urban development proposals for both Nepean and Goulbourn are implemented.

3.   For a description, see Trant (1990).

The Environment and Natural Resources Section has developed a set of environmental interaction classes which are used to classify manufacturing establishments. These classes indicate whether an industry has high, medium or low impact potential on the environment. The industrial data from the 1986 Census of Manufacturers indicates that there are 9 manufacturing establishments in the Jock River basin. Most of these industries are in the low impact category with little effect on the environment. One could conclude that manufacturing had little overall environmental impact in the basin and that stresses in the area must be primarily from human settlements and agricultural activity.

Conclusion

The Jock River basin has undergone many changes during the past two centuries. Historically limited statistical records show that over the last 20 years, population has tripled. The use of land, the main natural resource in the basin, has intensified significantly. Fertilizer and pesticide inputs, each having high environmental impact, have increased as well.

Immediate solutions to prevent further water quality deterioration are available but may pose some difficulty in implementing. Solutions put forward include conservation education, technological improvements for fertilizer, chemical waste handling and tree planting along the river bank to prevent further erosion. These measures will not return the river to its original pristine state, but should improve it so that people can once again use it.

Douglas F. Trant
Environment and Wealth Accounts Division
Statistics Canada
Ottawa, Ontario
K1A 0T6

References

Dumanski, J., D. Coote, G. Luciuk and C. Lok. 1986.
Soil conservation in Canada. Journal of Soil and Water
Conservation, 4(41): July-August.

Environment Canada. 1981. Historical Streamflow Summaries,
(cat. EN36-418). Ottawa: Government Publishing Centre.

Statistics Canada. 1983. Historical Statistics of Canada, Second
Edition. Ottawa: Statistics Canada.

Statistics Canada. 1986. Human Activity and the Environment,
(cat. no. 11-509E). Ottawa: Statistics Canada.

Statistics Canada. 1990a. Measuring environmental stress on
agricultural land using the agricultural practices impact model
(APIM). Internal working paper by D. Trant and H. Trépanier,
Environment and Natural Resources Section, Feb. 1990. Ottawa:
Statistics Canada.

Statistics Canada. 1990b. National Income and Expenditure
Accounts, Annual Estimates 1978-1989, (cat. no. 13-201).
Ottawa: Statistics Canada.

Statistics Canada. 1990c. Postcensal Annual Estimates of Population
by Marital Status, Age, Sex and Components of Growth, for
Canada, Provinces and Territories, June 1, 1989, (cat. no. 91-210).
Ottawa: Statistics Canada.

Trant, Douglas F. 1990. Estimating agricultural soil erosion losses
from census of agriculture crop coverage data. Working Paper no.
27, Analytical Studies Branch. Ottawa: Statistics Canada.

World Food Council. 1988. Growing hunger amidst food surpluses.
WFC/1988/2. New York: United Nations.

13

Health of the rural population: selected indicators

Russell Wilkins

Summary

Life expectancy at birth was almost 3 years greater in metropolitan areas with a million or more persons (Toronto, Montreal and Vancouver) compared to municipalities with fewer than 1,000 persons which were not part of larger urban agglomerations. Also, the smaller the community, the higher the infant mortality rate. In the smallest community size group, the infant mortality rate was 43% higher than in the largest metropolitan areas. Age-standardized death rates for all accidents, poisoning and violence were 63% higher in the smallest community size group (in this case, all communities with a population of fewer than 2,500 persons) compared to the largest community size group (with at least 100,000 persons).

Disability rates were higher in smaller community size groups, but the highest rates were in the next-to-smallest size group (1,000-9,999), rather than in the smallest size group.

Belle-Anse, Quebec

Health of the rural population: selected indicators

Russell Wilkins

Introduction

The best known and most generally useful health indicators are based on vital statistics records of births and deaths, census population data, disability and risk factor data from health surveys, and to a lesser extent, hospital morbidity and medicare utilization data.

Rural and small town mortality

The Canadian Centre for Health Information in Statistics Canada publishes summary data on births and deaths by Census Division (Statistics Canada, Cat. No. 84-204) and by Census Subdivision (Statistics Canada, Cat. No. 84-542)[1]. Health and Welfare Canada and Statistics Canada used these data to prepare a three volume atlas of mortality (Health and Welfare Canada and Statistics Canada 1980). For each county and urban agglomeration (including many smaller agglomerations), the atlas shows age-standardized death rates for various age groups and for many causes of death. A new atlas of mortality is currently in preparation (Health and Welfare Canada and Statistics Canada 1991).

The vital statistics by local area have also been analyzed by grouping rural municipalities and urban agglomerations by community size (Wilkins and Adams 1983; Basavarajappa and Lindsay 1976). They showed that life expectancy at birth was almost 3 years greater in metropolitan areas with a million or more persons (Toronto, Montreal and Vancouver) compared to municipalities with fewer than 1,000 persons which were not part of larger urban agglomerations (Figure 1). In each of the community size groups of intermediate size (1,000-9,999, 10,000-99,999 and 100,000-999,999), life expectancy was close to the Canadian average—higher than the smallest size group, but lower than the largest.

---

1. Most detailed tables of health statistics are now published as Supplements to <u>Health Reports</u> (Statistics Canada, cat. no. 82-003).

FIGURE 1

Life expectancy at birth, Canada, 1975-1977

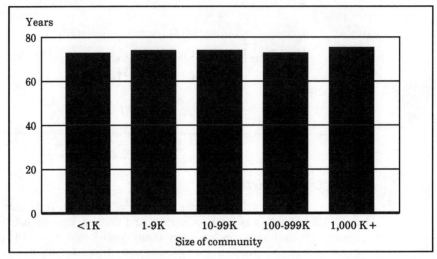

Source: Wilkins and Adams. 1983.

The smaller the community, the higher the rate of infant mortality (Figure 2). In the smallest community size group, the infant mortality rate was 43% higher than in the largest metropolitan areas.

FIGURE 2

Rate of infant mortality*, Canada, 1975-1977

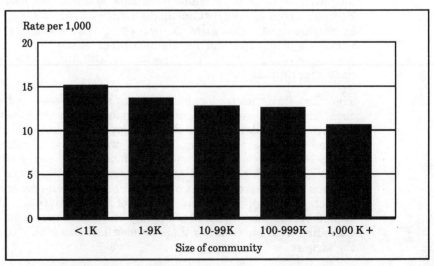

* Note: Based on life probability of dying.

Source: Wilkins and Adams. 1983.

Age-standardized death rates for all accidents, poisoning and violence were 63% higher in the smallest community size group (in this case, all communities with a population of fewer than 2,500 persons) compared to the largest community size group (with at least 100,000 persons) (Figure 3). Communities in the two next lowest size groups (between 2,500 and 30,000 persons) experienced accidental death rates 27% higher than that of the largest size group.

FIGURE 3

Age standardized death rate from all accidents, Canada, 1970-1972

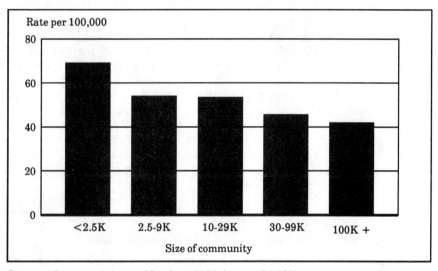

Source: Basavarajappa and Lindsay. 1976. (cat. no. 84-533).

Occupational health studies

Another way to identify persons more likely to live in rural and small town Canada is through information on usual occupation (such as farming, mining, logging or fishing). This information is available for survey and census data but is not usually available for health and vital statistics records. However, the British Columbia death records have been coded to occupation for the 1950 to 1978 period and Gallagher et al. (1986) have prepared an analysis of mortality by occupation. More recently, as part of a collaborative study with Health and Welfare Canada, the Canadian Centre for Health Information has coded by occupation all deaths which occurred to residents of Canada in 1986, except for deaths which occurred in Québec, where data on usual occupation is not reported on death certificates.

A wide variety of occupational and environmental health studies have been carried out using the Canadian Mortality Data Base, and more are expected using the Canadian Births Data Base which is currently under consideration. The examples of such studies to which Martha Fair (chapter 14, this volume) has drawn our attention represent but a few of the many possibilities for enhancing the value of existing data through record linkage of health-related data sets.

Native health

The health of Canada's Indian and Inuit populations have been analyzed by Medical Services Branch (1988) and Hagey et al. (1989).

Disability by community size group

Mortality data relate to length of life, while disability data are more closely related to quality of life. The Canadian Health and Activity Limitation Survey defined "disability" to include any health-related activity limitation (Statistics Canada 1988c). We defined "dependency" to be the need for assistance for another person for self care, mobility, shopping, meal preparation or housework. Disability rates were higher in smaller community size groups, but the highest rates were in the next-to-smallest size group (1,000-9,999), rather than in the smallest size group (Figure 4). Dependency rates had a generally similar pattern as for disability, except the rates for the smallest size group were only marginally higher than those of the largest size group. These rates were not age-standardized.

FIGURE 4

Disability and dependence, Canada, 1986

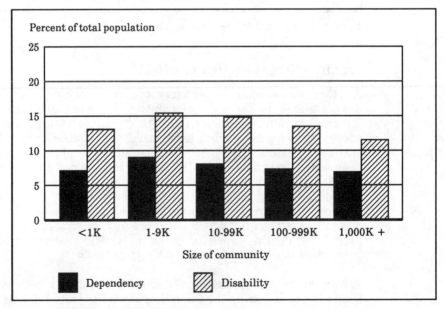

Source: *Wilkins and Adams. 1990.*

Conclusion

To summarize, rural and small town Canada has a lower life expectancy at birth, a higher infant mortality rate, higher death rates from accidents and higher disability and dependency rates. The Canadian Centre for Health Information at Statistics Canada can provide published and unpublished health information for rural communities in Canada.

Appendix I

Availability of health indicators for rural and small town Canada

The best known and most generally useful health indicators are based on vital statistics records of births and deaths, census population data, disability and risk factor data from health surveys, and to a lesser extent, hospital morbidity and medicare utilization data. Except for health survey data which are based on too small a sample size, most of the data which underlie the key health indicators are available coded to the county and/or municipal level. Even when county or municipal codes are not available, postal codes of residence usually are. Either of these is sufficient to distinguish rural and small town populations from the rest of Canadians, at least in a rough sort of way. Another way to identify persons more likely to live in rural and small town Canada is through information on usual occupation (such as farming, mining, logging or fishing), but except for survey and census data, this information is not usually available for health and vital statistics records.

The studies summarized in this paper have grouped local areas into broad categories based on size prior to the analysis of the data. However, many other groupings are possible. The sample design of the 1986 Health and Activity Limitation Survey was intended to provide statistically meaningful estimates of the presence or absence of any disability, by gender and broad age group, for each of 236 subprovincial areas (including, for example, 22 in Alberta, 16 in Saskatchewan, and 3 in the Northwest Territories). Public use microdata files are available for results at the national and provincial levels. Results for northern areas are on separate files. In addition, results at the subprovincial area level can be obtained by special tabulation from the Statistics Canada Disability Database Program.

Data on disability and behavioural risk factors from the Quebec Health Survey of 1987 are available for each of 30 community health department districts. A geographic analysis of Quebec Health Survey data based on even smaller areas has recently been published in the form of an atlas (Pampalon et al. 1990). Similar data from the 1990 Ontario Health Survey will also be available by health district.

Finally, the 1986 Census of Population long questionnaire which was
enumerated for 20% of the households contained questions on activity
limitations and handicaps which were used primarily to identify an
enriched sample for interviewing by the Health and Activity Limitation
Survey. However, the results of the census questions in terms of
presence or absence of any activity limitation in adults have been found
to compare well to the results of the same questions on the Health and
Activity Limitation Survey. If needed, special tabulations of the census
disability questions can be obtained on a cost-recovery basis for any
standard or user-defined areas or target populations. Special
tabulations of any other census variables, as well as semi-custom
tabulations intended to identify target populations for health and social
services, can also be obtained on a cost-recovery basis.

Russell Wilkins
Canadian Centre for Health Information
Statistics Canada
Ottawa K1A 0T6

References

Basavarajappa K.G. and J. Lindsay. 1976. Mortality Differences in Canada 1960-1962 and 1970-1972. (cat. no. 84-533). Ottawa: Statistics Canada.

Gallagher R.P., W.J. Threlfall, R.P. Band, J.J. Spinelli, and A.J. Coldman. 1986. Occupational Mortality in British Columbia 1950-1978. (cat. no. 84-544). Ottawa: Statistics Canada.

Hagey N.J., G. Laroque, and C. Mcbride. 1989. Highlights of Aboriginal Conditions 1981-2001. Part I: Demographic trends. Part II: Social conditions. Part III: Economic conditions. Quantitative analysis and socio-demographic research, working paper series 89-1, 89-2, 89-3. Ottawa: Indian and Northern Affairs Canada.

Health and Welfare Canada and Statistics Canada. 1980. Mortality Atlas of Canada. (cat. no. H49-6/1-1980). 1: Cancer. 2: General mortality. 3: Urban mortality. Ottawa: Minister of Supply and Services Canada.

Health and Welfare Canada and Statistics Canada. 1991 General mortality.patterns and recent trends. Mortality Atlas of Canada. Volume 4 (cat. no. H49-6/4-1990). Ottawa: Supply and Services Canada.

Medical Services Branch. 1988. Health Status of Canadian Indians and Inuit: Update 1987. Ottawa: Indian and Northern Health Services, Health and Welfare Canada.

Pampalon R., D. Gauthier, G. Raymond, and D. Beaudry. 1990. La Santé la Carte. Une exploration géographique de l'enquête santé Québec. Atlas. Québec: Les Publications du Québec.

Statistics Canada. 1988a. Births and Deaths. Vital Statistics, 1: 1986. (cat. no. 84-204). Ottawa: Statistics Canada.

Statistics Canada. 1988b. Principal Vital Statistics by Local Areas 1986. (cat. no. 84-542). Ottawa: Statistics Canada.

Statistics Canada. 1988c. User's Guide. The Health and Activity Limitation Survey. Ottawa: Disability Database Program, Statistics Canada.

Wilkins R., and O.B. Adams. 1983. Healthfulness of Life. Montreal: Institute for Research on Public Policy.

Caraquet, New Brunswick

14

Health of the rural population: occupational mortality patterns

Martha Fair

Summary

Increasing population mobility complicates the task of pinpointing public health trouble spots. Examining the health status of occupation groups is one way to assess the health of rural populations. For example, among Saskatchewan farm operators, a correlation has been noted between acres sprayed with herbicides in 1970 and non-Hodgkin's lymphoma (a form of cancer). Across Canada, the incidence of heart attacks, or acute myocardial infarction (AMI), varies substantially. Incidence rates for fatal and non-fatal AMIs are higher in Nova Scotia than in Saskatchewan. In 1977, the proportion of fatal episodes was higher in Nova Scotia than in Saskatchewan with the greatest difference in mortality occurring in deaths before hospitalization. A mortality study of Ontario miners indicates a higher rate of lung cancer deaths among Ontario uranium miners compared to the Ontario male population.

Health of the rural population: occupational mortality patterns

Martha Fair

Introduction

Current widespread demands for information on the well-being of rural people coincide with an increased population mobility that greatly complicates the task of pinpointing public health trouble spots. Moreover, concern now centres on diseases that are delayed in their expression (often by as much as two or three decades after the environmental insult to health that caused or contributed to their development). Two typical questions arise. What are the effects of pesticides and sprays on human populations? Are there excess cancers among particular occupational groups such as miners, fishermen and farmers?

Canadians are a mobile population. For persons aged 5 and older, 1986 Census data indicated that about 45% had moved since the 1981 Census. The detailed breakdown is as follows:

- 56% lived at the same residence;
- 24% lived at a different residence, but within the same municipality;
- 14% lived in a different municipality, but within the same province or territory;
- 4% lived in a different province; and
- 2% lived outside Canada.

Methods for assessing health in rural populations could be improved by exploiting existing administrative and survey data files, organizing files by individual longitudinal histories, and using the new generalized system developed at Statistics Canada plus national files such as the Canadian Mortality Data Base. Three ongoing collaborative cost-recovery studies illustrate how Statistics Canada information is used for health studies. This paper summarizes the published early results of these studies.

Summary of results

A study funded by Health and Welfare Canada of about 326,000 Canadian male farm operators enumerated in the 1971 Census of Agriculture examines the mortality patterns of farm operators in relation to farm practices and a variety of socio-economic variables. The prime concern, which has been suggested by previous studies of farmers, is the association between pesticide use and certain cancers. Preliminary results for the province of Saskatchewan have already been published (Wigle et. al. 1990). Although a Saskatchewan study group showed no excess mortality for any particular cause of death—including cancers like non-Hodgkin's lymphoma—a significant correlation was noted between the risk of developing non-Hodgkin's lymphoma and acres sprayed with herbicides in 1970, as well as with dollars spent on fuel and oil for farm purposes that same year.

The Canadian Farm Operators' cohort group was assembled using the generalized iterative record linkage system (Hill 1981) and five major databases: the 1971 Farm Register, the 1981 Farm Register, the 1971 Census of Population, the 1971 Census of Agriculture, and the Census of Agriculture Longitudinal file. The study group was then linked to the Canadian Mortality Data Base (Smith et. al. 1982) to determine mortality patterns. The methodology and techniques used in this study have been described in detail in a paper published in Health Reports (Jordan-Simpson et. al. 1990).

In Canada, cardiovascular diseases are the leading cause of death and of potential years of life lost. Persons with cardiovascular diseases are the major users of health care services in Canada. Ischemic heart disease (IHD) accounts for 60% of cardiovascular deaths. Currently, IHD mortality rates differ substantially across the country. In general, rates are higher in eastern than in western Canada. Nova Scotia, for example, has a relatively high IHD mortality rate while Saskatchewan has one of the lowest in the country. Rates within single provinces may also vary.

Past attempts to explain the risk factors that cause the sizeable differences in IHD mortality rates have been hindered by limited information. For example, the incidence of IHD is not readily available and community registries to generate and validate these data have been proposed but are expensive and require long observation periods. However, hospital-based data and mortality data are readily available in machine-readable form for Canada. Using Nova Scotia and Saskatchewan data, a feasibility study was conducted to determine whether using existing information and record linkage techniques to estimate the incidence of IHD would be cost effective. Nova Scotia and Saskatchewan are at the extreme ends of the national mortality experience for IHD. Most of the differences in the incidence of acute myocardial infarction were attributable to the compound effect of a generally higher attack rate and a higher case fatality rate. The reasons for differences found in deaths prior to formal admission to hospital are unexplained to date and require further investigation. (Nova Scotia-Saskatchewan Cardiovascular Disease Epidemiology Group 1989). Further work is in progress to extend the period and the regions being investigated.

A variety of radiation studies were conducted in Canada (Fair 1989) to determine the long-term effects of radiation on the health of specific groups. Some of the populations currently under study include uranium miners, radiation workers, and persons who received low doses of radiation during medical treatment or screening (e.g. mammography).

Rural areas proposed for waste management sites may also be investigated to obtain baseline data.

A mortality study of Ontario miners indicates a higher rate of lung cancer deaths among Ontario uranium miners compared to the Ontario male population. It also shows that exposure to radon progeny was the likely cause of such deaths (Muller et. al. 1989).

Conclusion

Existing administrative and survey records have been successfully linked to produce epidemiological data on the well-being of specific populations. For example, as an occupational group, farmers experience low overall mortality. However, specific groups of farmers have been reported to be at increased risk of developing specific cancers such as non-Hodgkin's lymphoma.

It is important to identify high risk populations to enhance preventive and control measures. Evaluation of cardiovascular health in the community, including an assessment of time trends as well as regional and provincial differences, is possible using routinely collected administrative data. This has been proven using Nova Scotia and Saskatchewan data relating to acute myocardial infarction. The time period and the regions investigated should be extended, paying special attention to deaths prior to formal hospitalization.

Martha Fair
Canadian Centre for Health Information
Statistics Canada
Ottawa, Ontario
K1A 0T6

References

Fair M.E. 1989. Radiation studies in Canada. the national files
and facilities necessary. In the Workshop/Symposium on Radiation
Protection: Past and Future edited by D.J. TerMarsch and D.K.
Myers DK. Chalk River: Chalk River Nuclear Laboratories.

Hill, T. 1981. Report from general systems. Generalized Iterative
Record Linkage System: GIRLS. Ottawa: Statistics Canada.

Jordan-Simpson D.A., M.E. Fair and P. Poliquin. 1990.
Canadian farm operators study: methodology. Health Reports,
(Cat. no. 82-003) 2(2): 141-156.

Muller, J., R. Kusiak, and A.C. Ritchie. 1989.
Factors Modifying Lung Cancer Risk in Ontario Uranium Miners
1955-1981. Toronto: Ontario Ministry of Labour (OMOL), Ontario
Workers' Compensation Board of Canada.

Nova Scotia-Saskatchewan Cardiovascular Disease
Epidemiology Group. 1989. Estimation of the incidence of acute
myocardial infarction using record linkage: a feasibility study in
Nova Scotia and Saskatchewan. Canadian Journal of Public
Health, 80: 412-417.

Smith, M.E. and H.B. Newcombe. 1982. Use of the Canadian
Mortality Data Base for epidemiological follow-up. Canadian
Journal of Public Health, 73: 39-46.

Wigle, D.T., R.M. Semenciw, K. Wilkins, D. Riedel, L. Ritter,
H.I. Morrison and Y. Mao. 1990. Mortality study of Canadian
male farm operators: non-Hodgkin's lymphoma mortality and
agricultural practices in Saskatchewan. Journal of the National
Cancer Institute, 82: 575-582.

15

Population, income and migration characteristics for urban/rural areas and farm/non-farm families in Saskatchewan

Bruce Meyer

Summary

The number of rural and farm families in Saskatchewan declined between 1982 and 1987. At the same time, the number of urban families grew by 8%.

Self employment farm income represented 26% of the total income of farm families in 1987. Employment income from sources other than self employment farming was more important to farm families in 1987 than it was in 1982. Median income for farm families was higher than for rural families but lower than for urban families.

The highest rate of migration was for individuals living in rural areas in 1982. Least mobile were residents of 1982 farm family units. Rural residents also had a tendency to move further when they moved, either to an urban area within Saskatchewan or outside the province.

The 1982 median incomes for migrant taxfilers in urban, rural and farm family units were lower than their non-migrant counterparts. The median incomes for all three migrant groups rose faster than for their non-migrant counterparts.

Table of contents

Population, income and migration characteristics for urban/rural areas and farm/non-farm families in Saskatchewan

Bruce Meyer

1. Purpose

The Saskatchewan economy is going through a restructuring resulting, in part, from the difficulties in the agricultural sector. This paper will document some of the socio-economic effects of this restructuring on individuals and families living in rural areas. Population, income levels, sources of income and migration patterns are examined. The three major axes of analysis are urban/rural, farm/non-farm and gender.

A secondary objective of the paper is to demonstrate the analytical potential of a data set developed from taxation records by Statistics Canada. These data, known as tax family data or T1 Family File (T1FF) include matched taxfiling family members and imputed dependants. These population based data have been created for several years such that cross section, time series and longitudinal analyses are now possible.

2. Method and definitions

The principal data source is personal income tax records. On the basis of information contained in the taxation records, it is possible to match taxfilers to create families and to impute non-taxfiling family members.

Records can be linked from one year to another. Based on the address information contained in the records, it is possible to determine whether an individual has moved during the intervening period. The income tax records for 1982 and 1987 were used for migration estimates between 1983 and 1988[1]. The migration methodology is summarized in Appendix I.

---

1. The migration estimates are one year later than the taxation year since the mailing addresses on the tax form are normally effective about April of the year after the taxation year.

Families consist of a husband and a wife, a single parent or a common law couple with or without their single children[2]. Individuals not classified as belonging to a family are considered to be unattached individuals[3].

A family is considered to be a farm family if one or both adult members of the family have reported gross self employment income from farming[4]. The family unit[5] is classified as urban or rural based on the postal code of the family mailing address[6].

3. Background

The gross domestic product (GDP) for Canada, in current prices, was 49% higher during 1985-1989 than it was during 1980-1984. Nominal output in Saskatchewan increased 23% during the same time (Table 1). The slower growth in the Saskatchewan economy resulted in this province's share of national GDP being reduced from 4% in 1980-1984 to 3% in 1985-1989.

TABLE 1

Gross domestic product ($million)

	Annual average		Change(%)
	1980-1984	1985-1989	
Canada	**373,228**	**557,369**	**49.3**
Saskatchewan	14,625	18,033	23.3

Source: Statistics Canada. Provincial Economic Accounts. (cat. no. 13-213).

The accrued net income of Canadian farm operators from farming increased an average of 39% during 1985-1989 compared to 1980-1984. The comparable figure for farm operators in Saskatchewan was 12% (Table 2).

---

2. Unlike the census family, where children can be any age, tax family children have been arbitrarily defined as less than 30 years old.

3. Some non-family persons may, in fact, live in households with other relatives. Examples include a child over thirty years of age living with his/her parents and an elderly individual living with his/her married child.

4. Gross self employment income does not include incorporated self employment income.

5. The term family unit is used to describe families and non-family persons.

6. Postal codes are assigned by Canada Post to assist with mail delivery. The code identifies individual block faces in urban areas with door to door delivery and identifies post office areas in rural communities. The second digit of the postal code is zero for rural areas and any other number for urban areas. Suburban service and rural route delivery are considered as urban delivery using this criterion. Individual postal codes can be aggregated into larger areas, known as Forward Sortation Areas (FSAs). The first three characters of the postal code represent the FSA.

For both Canada and Saskatchewan, the growth in accrued net income of farm operators from farming was about 10 percentage points lower than the growth in GDP. The accrued net income of farm operators from farming represented 6% of GDP in Saskatchewan during 1980-1984. It fell to 5% of provincial GDP during 1985-1989. On the other hand, accrued net income of farm operators from farming represented less than 1% of Canadian GDP in both periods.

TABLE 2

Accrued net income of farm operators from farming ($million)

	Annual average		
	1980-1984	1985-1989	Change (%)
Canada	3,369	4,283	39.0
Saskatchewan	852	954	12.0

Source: Statistics Canada. Provincial Economic Accounts. (cat. no. 13-213).

The low growth in incomes from farming is having a more dramatic effect on individuals and families than is immediately suggested by the data. Trends towards increased farm sizes and increased mechanization translate to less employment for a given level of output[7]. Saskatchewan agricultural employment dropped by 5,000 from 1980 to 1990 (Statistics Canada 1989a, 1991b). The decline in agricultural employment has a deleterious effect on the entire rural community. Traditional economic estimates suggest that every time eight farm families leave the land, one business in a nearby agricultural service community will be lost (Annis 1989).

After the Northwest Territories, Saskatchewan had the highest rate of net population loss because of interprovincial migration (Statistics Canada 1991a). During 1984-1989, migration caused a net population loss of 36,625 representing close to 4% of the 1984 population estimate for Saskatchewan (Statistics Canada 1988a, 1991a).

In summary, Saskatchewan has had slower than average economic growth during 1985-1989 compared to the previous five year period. The self-employed farm sector has been hard hit, experiencing only a modest growth in nominal output during 1985-1989. The province has experienced a high level of net outmigration and low population growth.

---

7. Bollman and Ehrensaft (1988: 44) have documented that, between 1936 and 1981, the number of Prairie farms were cut almost in half, the average farm size more than doubled and the number of individuals employed per farm had not changed.

The T1FF data are used to analyze these results in more detail. The paper examines population changes, the relative levels of income for urban/rural/farm families and how the sources of their income have changed. Migration analysis focuses on rural/urban movements within and outside Saskatchewan.

4. Results

4.1 Population

When the number of families and unattached individuals living in urban areas, rural areas and those engaged in self-employed farming are examined, some trends are clearly evident (Table 3):

a.   the highest population growth was in urban areas;

b.   the number of families and unattached individuals engaged in farming has declined;

c.   the number of unattached individuals grew more rapidly than the number of families (part of this may result from an increase in the number of people filing for the Federal Sales Tax Credit);

d.   rural and farm families are distinct populations. Although not shown in the table, over 50% of rural families have no self employment farm income[8];

e.   rural populations have remained stable. This may mask differential population growth rates, with a "rurbanization"[9] effect taking place in rural areas near urban centres;

f.   self employment farming is an occupation dominated by individuals in families.

TABLE 3
Number of family units

	Families			Unattached individuals		
	1982	1987	Change (%)	1982	1987	Change (%)
Farm*	67,875	64,675	-4.7	15,475	15,175	-1.9
Rural	119,050	118,175	-0.7	46,025	46,975	2.1
Urban	127,150	137,500	8.1	59,000	72,825	23.1

*   Included in urban/rural totals

Source: Statistics Canada. Unpublished tabulations from the T1 Family File.

8.   It was reported in Statistics Canada (1987: Table 1) that 19% of Saskatchewan farm operators did not reside on their farms and a further 6.5% resided on their farms for less than 9 months a year. In 1987, 18% of Saskatchewan taxfilers with gross farm income had an urban mailing address.

9.   Gilson (1990) uses this term to describe the growing rural populations near urban centres, where commuting to an urban job is a frequent practice.

4.2   Income by source and gender

4.2.1   Introduction

In 1987, Saskatchewan taxfilers reported $11 billion in income. Taxfilers in farm families reported 20% of this total while taxfilers in non-farm families reported 61% of the total. The remaining 18% was reported by unattached individuals. Women reported 33% of the total (Table 4).

4.2.2   Families

Net self employment income from farming represented 26% of the 1987 total income of farm families (Table 4). It represented 33% of the income reported by men in farm families and 7% of the income reported by women. Although not shown in Table 4, net self employment income decreased by 17% from 1982 to 1987. This resulted in net self employment income from farming's decline from 32% in 1982 to 26% in 1987 of total income reported by farm family taxfilers.

TABLE 4

Aggregate income by source and gender for farm and non-farm families, Saskatchewan, 1987

	Total income (1987) ($,000)			% Distribution		
	Male	Female	Total	Male	Female	Total
	Farm families					
Wages and sal.	555,983	419,017	975,000	33.8	67.0	42.9
Self emp.-farm	543,123	40,390	583,513	33.0	6.5	25.7
Self emp.-other	69,931	13,042	82,973	4.2	2.1	3.7
Investment	205,849	90,026	295,875	12.5	14.4	13.0
Pension	127,360	34,005	161,365	7.7	5.4	7.1
Unemployment	25,821	14,209	40,030	1.6	2.3	1.8
Fam. allow.	19,827	6,665	26,492	1.2	1.1	1.2
Other	97,780	7,915	105,695	5.9	1.3	4.7
Total income	**1,645,674**	**625,269**	**2,270,943**	**100.0**	**100.0**	**100.0**
	Non-farm families					
Wages and sal.	3,512,035	1,676,472	5,188,507	74.6	78.3	75.8
Self emp.-farm	0	0	0	0.0	0.0	0.0
Self emp.-other	291,058	55,611	346,669	6.2	2.6	5.1
Investment	270,997	173,898	444,895	5.8	8.1	6.5
Pension	428,871	114,171	543,042	9.1	5.3	7.9
Unemployment	99,666	73,666	173,332	2.1	3.4	2.5
Fam. allow.	48,662	32,905	81,567	1.0	1.5	1.2
Other	55,354	15,237	70,591	1.2	0.7	1.0
Total income	**4,706,643**	**2,141,960**	**6,848,603**	**100.0**	**100.0**	**100.0**

Source: Statistics Canada. Unpublished tabulations from the T1 Family File.

Off farm employment accounted for 47% of total farm family income
(wages and salaries and other self employment income). For men, off-
farm employment income accounted for 38% of total income, and for
women, it accounted for 69% of total income. Off-farm employment
income as a percentage of total income increased 10 percentage points
during the period, from 37% in 1982 to 47% in 1987.

Investment income, as a percentage of total income, was twice as
important to farm families as non-farm families. This may reflect, in
part, the high capital cost of running a farm and the uneven nature of
income receipts. It may also indicate less use of pension plans and a
greater requirement to save for old age. Other income, which includes
capital gains, RRSP income and net rental income, is also more
important to farm families than to non-farm families. The prevalence of
"other income" may reflect the need to rent or sell some assets to
maintain the financial viability of the farm.

Pension income (Canada Pension Plan (CPP), Old Age Security (OAS)
and private pension income) represented 7% of the income for farm
families and 8% for non-farm families. The age profile of individuals in
farm families (11% age 65 and over) compared to non-farm families (7%
age 65 and over) suggests that farm families have to take more
individual initiative to provide for later years.

Wages and salaries account for a much higher proportion of income for
non-farm families (76%) than for farm families (43%). Non-farm
families receive proportionately less income from investments and from
other incomes (including net rental income and capital gains).
Although women report less than half as much income as men, the
distribution of income by source is much more similar for men and
women in non-farm families.

4.2.3   Unattached individuals

Nearly 120,000 unattached individuals in Saskatchewan filed 1987 tax
returns. Of these, 13% reported self employment farm income and were
defined as farmers. They accounted for 15% of the income reported by
unattached individuals.

Self employment farm income accounted for 31% of the income of
unattached farmers. Other employment income (including wages and
salaries, and other self employment income) represented a further 21%
of the total income. The other important income sources were
investment (27%), pension (14%) and other (6%) income (Table 5).

TABLE 5

**Aggregate income by source and gender for farm and non-farm
unattached individuals, Saskatchewan, 1987**

	Total income (1987) ($,000)			% Distribution		
	Male	Female	Total	Male	Female	Total
	Unattached farmers					
Wages and sal.	49,388	9,035	58,423	20.9	11.9	18.7
Self emp.-farm	82,753	14,247	97,000	35.0	18.8	31.1
Self emp.-other	4,660	804	5,464	2.0	1.1	1.8
Investment	59,969	24,344	84,313	25.4	32.0	27.0
Pension	23,318	20,032	43,350	9.9	26.4	13.9
UIC	3,355	231	3,586	1.4	0.3	1.1
Fam. allow.	9	5	14	0.0	0.0	0.0
Other	12,761	7,273	20,034	5.4	9.6	6.4
Total income	**236,213**	**75,971**	**312,184**	**100.0**	**100.0**	**100.0**
	Unattached non-farm individuals					
Wages and sal.	633,765	443,946	1,077,711	72.9	52.3	62.7
Self emp.-farm	0	0	0	0.0	0.0	0.0
Self emp.-other	32,477	9,479	41,956	3.7	1.1	2.4
Investment	78,601	164,241	242,842	9.0	19.4	14.1
Pension	81,283	200,106	281,389	9.3	23.6	16.4
UIC	43,475	11,509	54,984	5.0	1.4	3.2
Fam. allow.	110	448	558	0.0	0.1	0.0
Other	14,592	18,434	33,026	1.7	2.2	1.9
Total income	**869,927**	**848,163**	**1,718,090**	**100.0**	**100.0**	**100.0**

Source: Statistics Canada. Unpublished tabulations from the T1 Family File.

Employment income represented 65% of the total income for unattached
non-farm individuals.   The other important sources were pension
income (16%) and investment income (14%).

Pension income is more important to unattached women than it is to
unattached men. For instance, 26% of the income for unattached farm
women is from pension income compared to 10% for unattached farm
men. This is explained by the fact that 62% of the unattached farm
women are aged 65 or over compared to 24% of the unattached farm
men.

The major differences in income by source for both farm and non-farm
unattached individuals compared to their family counterparts is a
greater reliance on investment and pension income and less reliance on
income from employment.

The changes in income by source for farm family persons from 1982 to 1987 extended to unattached farmers, but the changes were less pronounced. For unattached farmers, income from farming decreased from 36% of total income to 31% while off-farm employment income increased from 17% to 21%.

4.3 Median incomes

When the median incomes for urban, rural and farm families and unattached individuals for 1982 and 1987 are tabulated, the data lend themselves to the following observations (Table 6):

a.   incomes of farm families were higher than those for all rural residents but lower than for urban residents[10];

b.   incomes of unattached farmers were higher than incomes for either urban or rural unattached individuals;

c.   median income for urban families was higher than the median income of rural or farm families and grew faster;

d.   incomes for unattached individuals remained stable during 1982-1987. The changing mix of unattached taxfilers is, in part, responsible. Since 1986, additional low income individuals have been filing for the refundable Federal Sales Tax Credit thereby preventing measuring median incomes from rising more quickly.

TABLE 6

Median income of families and unattached individuals, Saskatchewan, 1982 and 1987

| | Median income (current $) | | | | | |
| | Families | | | Unattached individuals | | |
	1982	1987	Change (%)	1982	1987	Change (%)
Farm*	25,800	28,800	11.6	14,300	14,700	2.8
Rural	22,600	25,700	13.7	11,300	11,500	1.8
Urban	31,500	36,300	15.2	14,200	14,400	1.4

*   Included in urban/rural totals

Source: Statistics Canada. Unpublished tabulations from the T1 Family File.

10. The median incomes for farm family units do not necessarily provide a good indication of the economic viability of farming. Bollman, Smith, and Tomiak (1988) analyze farm economic viability in relation to returns to both equity and labour. Auer (1989: 70) claims, that after allowances for capital costs, net farm operator incomes are 60% to 70% of net incomes per worker employed in other sectors of the economy.

When the median incomes of male and female taxfilers in both farm and
non-farm and family and non-family situations are compared, the
following are noteworthy (Table 7):

a.   the median incomes of men in farm and non-farm families were
      between two and three times higher than the median incomes of
      women in families;

b.   less difference exists for the median incomes of unattached men
      and women. In fact, the median incomes for unattached farm
      women were higher than their male counterparts in both 1982
      and 1987. The differences in the age structure of males and
      females in this category are responsible: males tended to be
      younger while females were older;

c.   the fastest growing incomes were for women in families;

d.   males in farm families had the slowest growing incomes;

e.   women in farm families had the lowest incomes.

TABLE 7

**Median income of individuals by family status, farm and non-
farm status and by gender, Saskatchewan, 1982 and 1987**

	Median total income (current $)		
	1982	1987	Change (%)
Taxfilers in families			
Farm			
Male	19,700	20,200	2.5
Female	6,600	9,100	37.9
Non-farm			
Male	23,200	26,200	12.9
Female	8,200	10,300	25.6
Unattached individuals			
Farm			
Male	13,600	14,300	5.1
Female	16,200	15,900	-1.9
Non-farm			
Male	13,300	13,700	3.0
Female	12,300	12,400	0.8

Source: Statistics Canada. Unpublished tabulations from the T1 Family File.

310
Population, income and migration characteristics for urban/rural
areas and farm/non-farm families in Saskatchewan

4.4 Migration[11]

Coincident with Saskatchewan's slow economic growth is the low rate of population growth. One response to economic disadvantage is to relocate. This section will examine the characteristics of migrants and non-migrants and the migration patterns for farm and non-farm rural residents. The key factor in defining migration was whether a person lived in a different community in 1988 than in 1983[12].

Overall, 20% of the population were defined as migrants. The majority, 79%, were defined as non-migrants. No migration status was determined for the remaining 1% of individuals.

Given the different size of urban and rural communities, the rates of migration for urban and rural residents may not be directly comparable. Nevertheless, 18% of Saskatchewan's urban dwellers in 1983, for whom a migration status could be determined, had moved to a different community by 1988. The migration rate for rural residents was 23%. Individuals in farm family units are more stable in terms of geographic location. Only 14% of farm family members migrated during the reference period.

For all three cases in 1982 (urban, rural and farm), the median incomes of migrants were lower than the median incomes of their non-migrant counterparts. However, all three migrant groups made relative income gains by 1987, compared to their non-migrant counterparts. Although the income patterns for urban and rural migrants vis-à-vis non-migrants also apply to farm migrants, the differences are much smaller (Table 8).

---

11. The analysis in this part of the paper is for individuals only. It is difficult to follow migration patterns by family, given the volatility of family structures over time. The urban, rural and farm classifications assigned to individuals are assigned on the basis of their 1982 family situations.

12. This is explained more fully in Appendix I.

TABLE 8

Migration rate and change in median income of migrants and non-migrants, Saskatchewan, 1983

		Farm*	1983 Rural	1983 Urban
Migrants				
Population (1)		31,125	94,500	75,200
1982 Taxfiler median income	($)	11,300	9,700	12,200
1987 Taxfiler median income	($)	13,400	14,600	17,100
(%) Change in median income		18.6	50.5	40.2
Non-migrants				
Population (2)		199,100	321,950	344,150
1982 Taxfiler median income	($)	11,900	11,700	15,800
1987 Taxfiler median income	($)	13,500	13,200	19,800
(%) Change in median income		13.4	12.8	25.3
Migration rate (1)/((1)+(2))	(%)	13.5	22.7	17.9

*   Included in urban/rural totals.

Source: Statistics Canada. Unpublished tabulations from the T1 Family File.

Rates of migration by age and gender for farm family members in 1982 are shown in Table 9[13]. The possible reasons for migration are many: marriage, postsecondary education, medical necessity, economic opportunity elsewhere, lifestyle or retirement. However, this table provides an indication of the characteristics of individuals who are potentially leaving farming and farm communities. As noted above, the rate of migration is low for individuals in farm family units. This is as expected, given the location-specific nature of self employment farming.

Rates of migration for males (13%) and females (14%) are almost the same. The highest rates of migration are for males and females who were in the 18-24 age group in 1982. What is significant is that more than two thirds of this youth group have remained in the same community. The higher rate of migration for young women may reflect that farming remains a male dominated occupation or that women have a greater propensity to relocate to their husband's community at the time of marriage.

---

13.   The migration rate for those under 18 years of age is understated because some children who were not taxfilers in 1982 would have left home by 1987. The methodology used does not capture these cases.

TABLE 9

Individuals in 1982 farm family units, Saskatchewan

	Migrants (1)	Non-migrants (2)	Migration rate (1)/((1)+(2)) (%)
Males			
< 18	4,625	33,950	12.0
18-24	4,100	10,725	27.7
25-44	3,975	25,950	13.3
45-64	2,825	27,250	9.4
65 +	925	9,050	9.3
Total	**16,450**	**106,925**	**13.3**
Females			
< 18	4,400	31,800	12.2
18-24	3,550	7,175	33.1
25-44	3,600	24,400	12.9
45-64	2,525	23,050	9.9
65 +	625	5,775	9.8
Total	**14,700**	**92,200**	**13.8**

Source: Statistics Canada. Unpublished tabulations from the T1 Family File.

Migration patterns for rural residents are shown in Table 10. This table
is divided into members of farm family units and members of non-farm
family units[14]. Members of rural farm family units are much less likely
to migrate than non-farm rural residents and even when they do
migrate, they stay much closer to home. The most popular location for
rural farm migrants is another community in the same rural forward
sortation area (FSA). Rural non-farm migrants, on the other hand, are
most likely to move to an urban centre within Saskatchewan, and
failing that, to leave the province. Migration within the same rural
FSA is the least likely to be motivated by economic reasons. If this
migration is excluded, then the rate of migration for non-farm rural
residents is 24%. The comparable migration rate for members of farm
family units is 9%.

---

14. The data for members in farm family units are slightly different than above, since this table is
restricted to individuals who were rural residents in 1983.

TABLE 10

Migration patterns for 1983 rural residents

	Farm	Non-farm
Total population	**192,325**	**223,975**
Non-migrants	165,800	156,150
Migrant same FSA	10,225	14,375
Migrants other rural in Saskatchewan	4,225	12,100
Migrants urban in Saskatchewan	7,700	24,275
Migrants outside Saskatchewan	4,375	17,075
Mrate1*(%)	13.8	30.3
Mrate2**(%)	8.5	23.9

*   All migrants/total population.

**   All migrants except migrants in the same FSA/total population.

Source: Statistics Canada. Unpublished tabulations from the T1 Family File.

Relationships between migration rates by rural FSA for farm and non-farm individuals and their median incomes were very weak. Either motivations stronger than economic circumstances affect the decision to migrate or to not migrate, or some minimum level of economic well-being is required before migration becomes a viable option.

The net flows show that there were fewer farm families and fewer unattached farmers in Saskatchewan in 1987 than in 1982. The net flow is the difference between the number of individuals entering[15] farming and the number leaving. The gross flows are shown in Table 11. The total 1982 population in farm family units which could be linked to 1987 was 230,200. Of these, 196,350 or more than 85% were still in farming in 1987, but self employment farm income represented a smaller proportion of their total income. There was a total of 22,025 individuals who were members of farm family units in 1987 but who were not members of farm family units in 1982.

15. Individuals "entering" farm family units between 1982 and 1987 were taxfilers in 1982 and 1987 and were classified in a farm family in 1987 but not in 1982.

TABLE 11

Individuals remaining in, leaving and entering farm family units

Farm family members	Individuals	Median income 1982 (current $)	Median income 1987 (current $)
1982 and 1987	196,350	11,600	13,500
1982 only (leavers)	33,850	10,600	16,000
1987 only (entrants)	22,025	13,200	15,500

Source: Statistics Canada. Unpublished tabulations from the T1 Family File.

Taxfilers who left farming had a lower 1982 median income than taxfilers who remained in farming. However, the decision to leave farming was a good decision economically as by 1987, the median income of taxfilers who left farming was 19% higher than the median income of taxfilers who remained.

New entrants to farming had higher incomes than those who remained in farming, both before they entered and once they were members of farm families.

5.   Conclusion

The family data derived from personal income tax records show a decline in the number of rural and farm families in Saskatchewan between 1982 and 1987. At the same time, the number of urban families grew by 8%. For unattached individuals, the largest growth was in urban areas and rural areas experienced modest growth. The number of unattached farmers declined slightly.

Self employment farm income represented 26% of total farm family income in 1987. Employment income from sources other than self employment farming was more important to farm families in 1987 than it was in 1982.

Median income for farm families was higher than for rural families but lower than for urban families. Unattached farmers had median incomes higher than either urban or rural unattached individuals.

The highest migration rate was for rural individuals. Least mobile were farm family residents. Rural residents also had a tendency to move further when they moved to an urban area in Saskatchewan or out of the province.

The 1982 median incomes for migrants in urban, rural and farm family units were lower than their non-migrant counterparts. The median incomes for all three migrant groups rose faster than for their non-migrant counterparts.

Appendix I

Migration methodology

The starting points for the migration estimates were the 1982 and 1987 T1FF family files. These files contain data on taxfilers and dependants aggregated into husband and wife, single parent, and common law family classifications as well as for non-family persons.

One record per taxfiler was created for each year. The key information was the Social Insurance Number (used for linking records from 1982 to 1987) and the address information (used for determining migrant and non-migrant status). Data on non-taxfiling dependants were associated with each taxfiler. If both the husband and wife in a family were taxfilers, an allocation routine was used to assign non-taxfiling children to their parents' records. These records are called taxfilers and dependants (TFDs). The one exception to this process is for non-taxfiling spouses. If a Social Insurance Number could be determined for the non-taxfiling spouse (taxfilers are asked for the SIN of their spouse), then a TFD was created for the non-taxfiling spouse.

The 1982 Saskatchewan T1FF contains 927,984 records. As well, 601,876 TFD records were created which included 918,490 individuals. The remaining 9,494 individuals were dropped because either it was indicated on their tax return that they were deceased or because they indicated that they were bankrupt and the address appeared to be a third party commercial address.

Although the address information contained a postal code, automated postal coding software was used to assign postal codes. Use of the automated postal coding software ensured that the same postal code was assigned to both the 1982 and 1987 TFD, provided that the addresses were the same.

The 1982 TFDs for Saskatchewan were matched to 1987 T1FF data from across Canada and to individuals filing Canadian tax returns from other countries. A total of 547,544 TFDs were matched, representing 91% of the 1982 Saskatchewan TFDs and 92% of the individuals.

The determination of migrants and non-migrants was based on a comparison of the postal codes from the 1982 and 1987 TFDs. Individuals on a TFD were classed as non-migrants as follows:

a.   the postal codes from the matched TFDs were the same and rural;

b.   the postal codes from the matched TFDs were urban and were within the same city. This means, for instance, that a person who moved from one part of Saskatoon to another would be classed as a non-migrant;

c.   either the 1982 or 1987 postal code had an urban commercial delivery mode and the other postal code was from an immediately surrounding rural forward sortation area. Empirical research showed that the urban addresses in these situations were frequently post office boxes.

High flows were detected between some postal codes. These flows may be caused by a realignment of postal delivery services rather than relocation of the individuals involved. These cases were classed as uncertain non-migrants. There were other cases of very high flows to or from some urban postal codes. These may be tax discounter addresses. These cases were also classed as uncertain non-migrants.

If no postal code was returned from the automated postal coding software, then the original family postal code on the record was used. The same process logic as above was used. The only difference was that when the original family postal code was used, it was compared to both the original and automated postal code from the other year. If either code met the non-migrant conditions, then individuals on that TFD were classed as non-migrants.

If no postal code was available from the matched 1987 TFD, then the record was classified as an uncertain non-migrant.

All records not classified as either non-migrants or uncertain non-migrants were classified as migrants.

Overall, 90% of the original 1982 TFDs were classified either as migrants or non-migrants. This represents 99% of the 1982 TFDs which were matched to 1987 TFDs. There were 4,820 1982 TFDs (1%) which were deemed to be uncertain non-migrants. For TFDs classified as migrants or non-migrants, migrants represented 21% of the total and non-migrants represented the remaining 79%.

Bruce Meyer
Small Area and Administrative Data Division
Statistics Canada
Ottawa, Ontario
K1A 0T6

References

Annis, Robert. 1989. Strategic Planning for Rural Development.
Brandon, Manitoba: Westarc Group Inc.

Auer, L. 1989. Canadian Prairie Farming, 1960-2000 — An Economic
Analysis. Ottawa: Economic Council of Canada.

Bollman, Ray D., and Philip Ehrensaft. 1988. Changing farm size
distribution on the Prairies over the past one hundred years.
Prairie Forum, 13(1): Spring.

Bollman, Ray D. 1991. Efficiency aspects of part-time farming.
In Multiple Job-holding Among Farm Families , edited by
M.C. Hallberg. Ames, Iowa: Iowa State University Press.

Bollman, Ray D., Pamela Smith and Monica Tomiak. 1988.
Farm financial stress and the ability of a farm to sustain a family.
Paper presented to the VII World Congress for Rural Sociology.
Bologna, Italy: June.

Canada Post. 1988. Canada's Postal Code Directory. Ottawa:
Canada Post Corporation.

Employment and Immigration Canada. 1989. Saskatchewan
Medium Term Economic and Labour Market Outlook, 1989/90-
1994/95. Regina: Employment and Immigration Canada,
Economics, Planning and Analysis Division.

Gilson, J. C. 1990. Rural tradition and a changing society.
Prairie Forum on Rural Development: Selected Readings.
Brandon, Manitoba: Westarc Group Inc.

Revenue Canada—Taxation. 1988. Farming Income Tax Guide
and General Tax Guide. Ottawa: Revenue Canada.

Statistics Canada. 1982. Agriculture: Saskatchewan. In the 1981
Census of Canada series (cat. no. 96-909). Ottawa: Statistics
Canada.

Statistics Canada. 1987. Agriculture: Saskatchewan. In the 1986
Census of Canada series (cat. no. 96-910). Ottawa: Statistics
Canada.

Statistics Canada. 1988a. Postcensal Annual Estimates of
Population by Marital Status, Age, Sex, and Components of
Growth for Canada, Provinces and Territories, June 1, 1988,
(cat. no. 91-210). Ottawa: Statistics Canada.

Statistics Canada. 1989a. Labour Force Annual Averages, 1981-1988,

318
Population, income and migration characteristics for urban/rural
areas and farm/non-farm families in Saskatchewan

(cat. no. 71-529). Ottawa: Statistics Canada.

Statistics Canada. 1989b. Provincial Economic Accounts: Annual Estimates 1976-1987, (cat. no. 13-213). Ottawa: Statistics Canada.

Statistics Canada. 1991a. 1984-1989 Migration Estimates, Table C. Unpublished Tabulations from the T1 Family File. Ottawa: Statistics Canada, Small Area and Administrative Data Division.

Statistics Canada. 1991b. Labour Force Annual Averages 1990, (cat. no. 71-220). Ottawa: Statistics Canada.

Statistics Canada. 1991c. Provincial Economic Accounts: Preliminary Estimates 1989. (cat. no. 13-213p). Ottawa: Statistics Canada.

16

Rural deprivation:
a preliminary analysis of census and tax family data

Bill Reimer, Isabelle Ricard, and Frances M. Shaver

Summary

Average incomes are lower in rural areas than in both small and large urban areas. However, a lower proportion of rural households live below Statistics Canada's low income cut-off (LICO) than do households in other areas. This lower proportion results partly from the adjustment to LICO for lower living costs in rural areas. The rural LICO is approximately 26% lower than for metropolitan centres.

As well, the low proportion of rural households below the LICO is attributable to people living in non-farm households. The incidence of households below the LICO is as high on farms as it is in the most deprived areas of the country. Small communities (less than 5000 persons) also have a higher level of deprivation than do larger urban areas. Although rural poverty and deprivation appear to be lower overall than urban poverty, a number of high-risk groups face particular problems in rural areas:

- households with no wage income
- people older than 65
- households in Newfoundland, New Brunswick, and Quebec
- farm households
- families in which women are the only taxfilers
- families with only one adult income earner
- families with many children

The analysis of poverty and deprivation is easiest when using economic indicators. However, this biases the research away from the social and political aspects of deprivation.

Table of contents

Rural deprivation:
a preliminary analysis of census and tax family data[1]

Bill Reimer, Isabelle Ricard, and Frances M. Shaver

1.   Introduction

Statistics Canada estimates that 28% of rural families and 13% of rural unattached individuals live below the low income cut-off (Ross and Shillington 1989) yet few studies have focused on this problem. In addition, small community studies and census data from other countries indicate that, although the causes may be similar, the experience of poverty in rural areas is considerably different than in urban regions. This study will present a preliminary analysis of census and taxation data to identify the distribution and major characteristics of deprivation.

Research on rural deprivation in Canada is frustrated by the limitations on relevant census data. Published data provide an indication of the proportion of rural individuals and families for several geographical regions as well as information on the proportion below the low income cut-off (LICO) living in rural regions, but there is virtually nothing beyond this type of information. Producing the relevant tabulations are an expensive proposition under the current policy.

In addition, most of the easily available census data contains a bias toward the economic and individual aspects of rural deprivation. Indicators of health, education, recreation, and culture resources are not easily integrated into standard population information. To do so increases the cost in terms of time and money, discouraging analysis beyond incomes, individuals and families.

1.   The authors wish to thank the Small Area and Administrative Data Division of Statistics Canada and the Agriculture and Rural Restructuring Group for their financial support.

2.   Analysis of census data

This section is based on custom tabulations from 1986 Census of Population data, since the combined characteristics of "low income" and "rural" were not available in published media.

The Statistics Canada LICO is used to identify economically deprived households in rural Canada. Family expenditure data indicate that rural families, when ranked in terms of the threshold of expending 62% of their income on food, clothing and shelter, cross this threshold at lower levels of family income (Wolfson and Evans 1990). Thus, the rural LICO is approximately 26% lower than for metropolitan centres. This calculation has been challenged in a number of ways (CCSD 1984), but we have accepted it for our preliminary analysis since it provides the most convenient access to census data.

2.1   Urbanization class

The proportion of rural households below the LICO is lower than in both small and large urban regions (Figure 1). This difference conceals several important variations, however, because the LICO is adjusted for differing areas of residence and family size. The low proportion of rural households below the LICO is attributable to people living in non-farm households (Figure 2). The incidence of households below the LICO is as high on farms as it is in the most deprived areas of the country. Small communities (less than 5,000 persons) also have a higher level of deprivation than do larger areas.

FIGURE 1

Percent of households below LICO, Canada, 1986

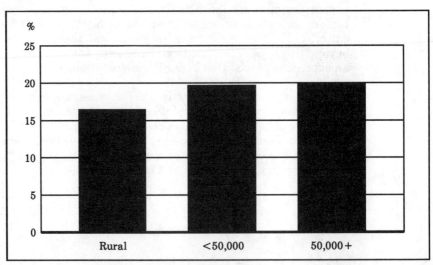

Source: Statistics Canada. 1986 Census of Population.

FIGURE 2

Percent of households below LICO, Canada, 1986

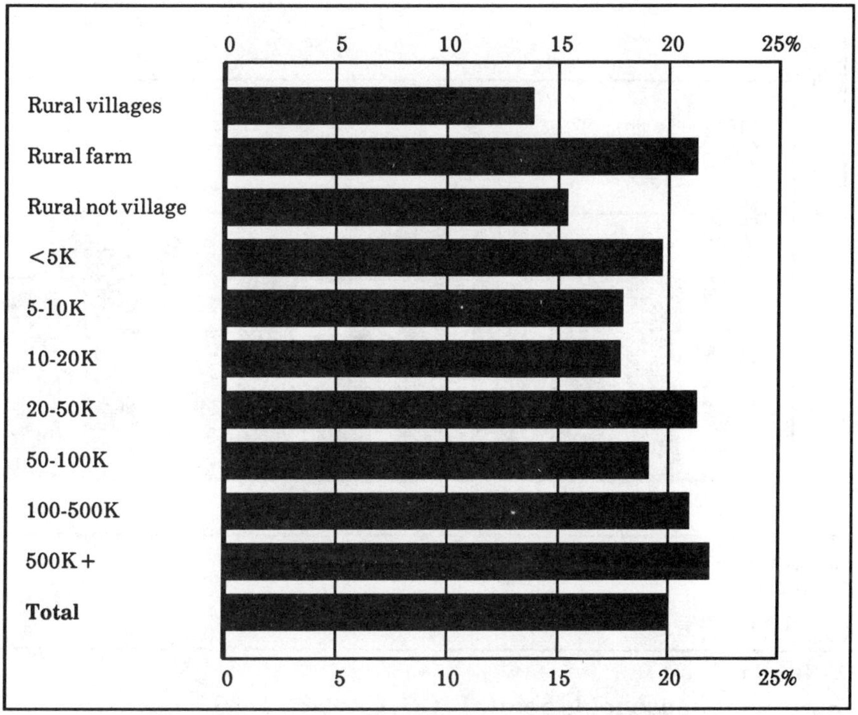

Category	Percent
Rural villages	
Rural farm	
Rural not village	
<5K	
5-10K	
10-20K	
20-50K	
50-100K	
100-500K	
500K +	
Total	

Source: Statistics Canada. 1986 Census of Population.

2.2   Province

The incidence of low income in rural households varies considerably among provinces (Figure 3). The highest proportions are in Newfoundland, New Brunswick, and Quebec; Ontario's incidence is uniquely low. This pattern follows the incidence of low income for all households, although the relative incidence of low incomes for rural versus all households is reversed in Newfoundland and Alberta (Figure 4)[2].

---

2.   Both Newfoundland and Alberta have a relatively low incidence of low income in regions under 50,000 population (Figure 5).

FIGURE 3

Percent of rural households below LICO, Canada, 1986

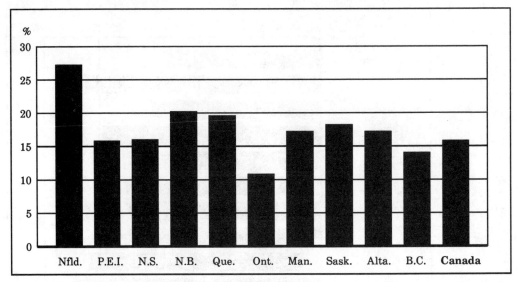

Source: Statistics Canada. 1986 Census of Population.

FIGURE 4

Percent of households below LICO, Canada, 1986

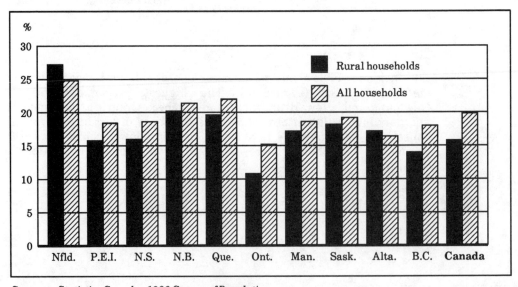

Source: Statistics Canada. 1986 Census of Population.

To assess the importance of the size of the area of residence and of the province on the level of low income, we conducted a multiple regression analysis of the data, using census subdivisions as our basic unit of observation[3]. This analysis makes clear that the province is much more significant for explaining the differences in low income than the size of the area of residence (Figure 5).

FIGURE 5

Percent of households below LICO, Canada, 1986

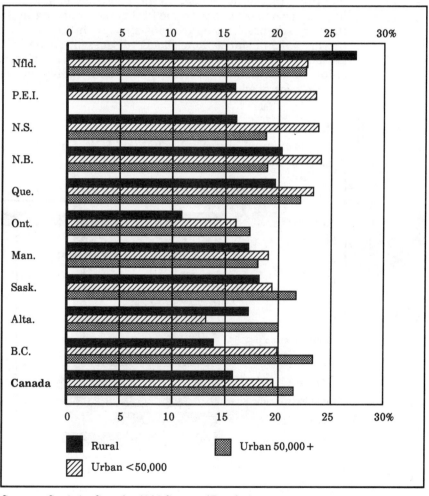

Source: Statistics Canada. 1986 Census of Population.

---

3.   The size of the area of residence and the province were transformed into dummy variables.

2.3   Industry

The industrial base of a region is likely to affect the extent of poverty in a number of different ways. Wages vary considerably from one industry to another as does vulnerability to market variations. In addition, the number of jobs as well as the duration of those jobs will affect the level and security of income.

To assess the effect of the type of industry on the incidence of low income, we examined the industry of employment of the first person identified in the household[4]. The incidence of low income is clearly highest for households with the first person working in the agricultural industry (Figure 6): a figure consistent with the high incidence of low income within farm households discussed earlier. Considerable variation exists between the other industrial categories, suggesting the value of additional exploration of their individual effects on the organization of poor households.

FIGURE 6

Percent of rural households below LICO, Canada, 1986

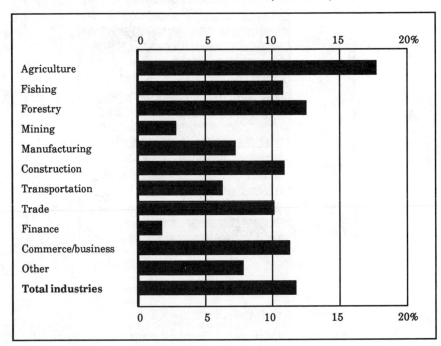

Source: Statistics Canada. 1986 Census of Population.

---

4.   The costs of processing prevented us from identifying the highest income earner.

Despite this variation, regression analysis revealed that controlling for industry levels had little effect on the ability to predict variations in incidence of low income households in the provinces. Sixty-seven percent of the variation of low income households was explained by provincial variations, even when controlling for industries.

2.4   Sources of income

An examination of the major source of income for households shows considerable variation in the level of deprivation associated with these different sources (Figure 7). By far the highest incidence of low income is found in households where family allowances are the major source of income. We can conclude that a significant number of children are represented in these households.

FIGURE 7

Percent of rural households below LICO, by major source of household income, Canada, 1986

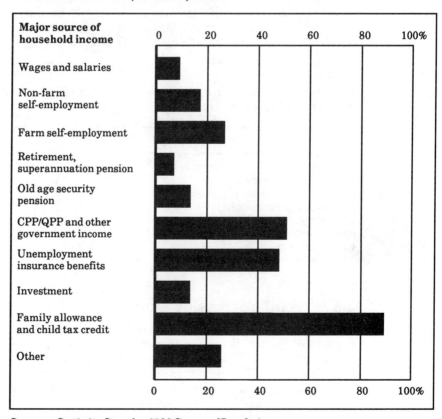

Source: Statistics Canada. 1986 Census of Population.

The high incidence of low income among households receiving pensions or old age assistance indicates that age plays an important role in rural poverty. This is consistent with data from urban areas, but has special significance for rural areas since a disproportionate share of the aged live in rural areas.

The impact of employment is clear from this data. The incidence of low income is high in those households were unemployment insurance is a major source of income and it is low where wages are a major source.

Once again, we conducted a regression analysis to examine the relative impact of sources of income and the province on the incidence of low income. This analysis revealed very little change in the ability to predict low income using provincial differences when the sources of income were controlled.

A regression analysis of industries and the sources of income revealed that they provided a good deal of predictive power. The wage income had the greatest impact on the level of low income, reducing it considerably (Table 1). The two pension variables were next, each increasing the chance of the household being in the low income group. Four other variables were significant: commerce (reducing), UIC (increasing), forestry (increasing), and finance (reducing).

TABLE 1

Beta coefficients for industries and sources of income on incidence of low income

Stepwise regression, multiple R^2 = .73	
Wage income	-.52
Old age pension income	.38
Canada-Quebec pension	.36
Commerce, business industry	-.26
UIC income	.25
Forestry industry	.15
Finance industry	-.13

2.5   A full regression model

To introduce controls on all of the variables examined, we constructed a regression model using provinces, industries of employment, and sources of income. The resulting predictive power of the model was very high (Table 2). The importance of the industry of employment was overshadowed by the other two variables: wages and pension income. None of the variations in industry were significant, so they do not appear in the final model.

TABLE 2

**Beta coefficients for provinces, industries, and sources of income
on incidence of low income**

Stepwise regression, multiple $R^2 = .81$	
Wage income	-.51
Old age pension income	.49
Newfoundland	.38
Quebec	.35
Canada-Quebec pension	.33
New Brunswick	.20
Farm self employment	.14
Alberta	.13
Ontario	-.12

NOTE: B.C., Other industries, and Other sources of income are the reference categories
for the dummy variables.

The results of this analysis confirm the importance of a closer
examination of the relationship between low income and wage
employment, the proportion of older people in rural areas, farming, and
several of the provinces. Within the context of these variables, it
appears that the differences in industries are less important for
explanatory purposes.

3.   Analysis of taxation data

In this section we examine the characteristics of the rural poor through
the use of the tax family data for Quebec. The examination was limited
to Quebec for cost reasons since much of the analysis was exploratory.

Rural taxfiler families were identified by the second character in their
postal code (rural = 0). According to Canada Post, a rural area is one of
less than 5,000 delivery points with no municipal plans for growth
above that figure within the next five years.

Families were identified by a six-step procedure. Spouses were matched
by social insurance number and then by name and postal code[5]. Any
filing children were then included in the family.   This procedure
produced four types of families. The next step was to match common-law
spouses using the address, postal code, and age difference of the filers.
The final step was to impute non-filing children in the family by the use
of child tax exemptions, child tax credits, family allowance income,
child care expenses, and additional exemptions as declared on the tax
return of the parent or parents.

---

5.   Unlike census data, the possibility exists for spouses to report different addresses. For example, in
0.4% of the Québec rural families, one spouse gave an urban address.

The characteristics of the families identified by these procedures resemble those in the census data. Tax family data covered 94% of the population enumerated in the 1986 Census. The coverage varies by province, from 92% in Prince Edward Island and British Columbia, to 101% in Manitoba. It also varies by age, offering a good coverage of the population younger than 65, from 92% among those aged 60-64, to 101% among those younger than 30. Comparatively, about 68% of the enumerated population aged 65 and older was covered by the tax family data. The coverage of the elderly population is expected to improve since 1985 following the introduction of the Federal Sales Tax Credit. The coverage ratio for husband-wife families is 94% while that for lone-parent families reaches 109%. For non-family persons, the coverage ratio is 92% (Bergeron 1988).

Income was defined by combining the appropriate sources of income reported on the income tax return to approximate the census definition. A comparison of the income reported by the tax family data compared to other sources of information showed very good results, with a coverage ranging from .95 to 1.04 for the provinces (Bergeron 1988: 57). An examination of individual sources of income showed considerable variation. Low income groups were under represented simply because they were less likely to file tax returns. The median total family income has a coverage ratio of 102% for husband-wife families, 71% for lone mother families, and 91% for lone father families (Bergeron 1988: Tables 91, 104, 105).

In general, the tax family data must be used with caution when analyzing rural deprivation. It under estimates the number of poor and elderly people, the very young, and lone mother families. For this reason, it has limited value when estimating the size of these groups. However, its utility increases when proper standardization techniques are used, as in the examination of variation in deprivation within the groups. It also has the advantage of providing annual information so that short-term changes can be explored.

3.1   Gender differences

Women are more likely to report a low income status compared to men. According to the taxfiler data for Quebec, 29% of all rural females live below the LICO compared to 22% of males. If we consider single-parent and single person families, we find 57% of all single parent and single person families headed by a female live below the LICO compared to 34% of similar families headed by men (Figure 8). The difference between men and women increases dramatically for single-parent families: 67% of single-parent families with female heads live below the LICO, whereas only 21% of single-parent families with male heads live below the cut-off.

FIGURE 8

Percent of single-adult families below LICO, Quebec, 1987

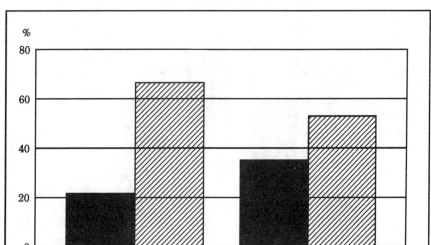

Source: *Statistics Canada. Small Area and Administrative Data Division, Taxfiler T1
Family File (T1FF).*

3.2   Family structure

An examination of the full range of family types confirms that single-
parent families are particularly vulnerable to income problems. These
families are most likely to be in the low income group followed by single
persons and families where only one spouse filed an income tax form
(Figure 9). Both common-law families, and husband-wife families with
dual incomes are less likely to be within the low income group.

These figures confirm the importance of wage labour for reducing the
chance of economic deprivation. The chance of falling within the low
income group when there is only one income earner in the family is
sufficiently high for us to consider the two-earner household essential
for economic health within the family.

FIGURE 9
Percent of families below LICO, Quebec, 1987

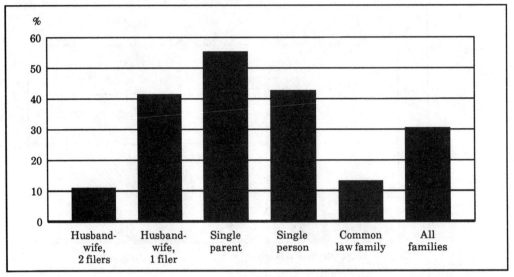

Source: *Statistics Canada. Small Area and Administrative Data Division, Taxfiler T1 Family File (T1FF).*

3.3   Number of children

The number of children in the family has a curvilinear relationship with the likelihood of low income. Two-filer families with no children are more likely to be within the low income group than families with 1, 2, or 3 children (Figure 10). However, with more than 3 children, the proportion of low income families increases. These figures are affected by the variation in low income cut-offs by family size, but the extent of this effect has not been investigated.

When we separate the families by type, it becomes apparent that the most significant factor for low income is gender. Both single parent and two parent families are more likely to have low incomes if the female is the sole taxfiler. For all combinations the pattern is the same: the greater the number of children, the more likely that the family will be in the low income group.

FIGURE 10
Percent of 2-parent families below LICO, Quebec, 1987

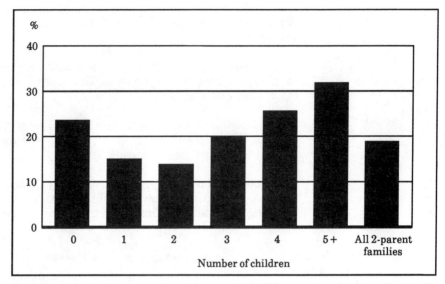

Source: Statistics Canada. Small Area and Administrative Data Division, Taxfiler T1
            Family File (T1FF).

4.   Conclusion

A number of general conclusions are possible from this preliminary
analysis. Although rural poverty and deprivation appear to be lower
overall than urban poverty, a number of high-risk groups face
particular problems in rural areas. Initially, we can identify these
groups as follows:

- households with no wage income
- people older than 65
- households in Newfoundland, New Brunswick, and Quebec
- farm households
- families in which women are the only taxfilers
- families with only one adult income earner
- families with many children

During the next stage of our research, we will focus on these groups but
expand our definition of deprivation beyond the narrow economic one.
Research into the independent impact of certain factors affecting
poverty requires data which permit multivariate analysis to allow the
analyst to control for the impact of other factors that may be important.

Limitations in our analysis reflect limitations in Statistics Canada data. Some of these limitations are:

- Published data are difficult to analyze in cases where the analyst wishes to impose several conditions on the data (eg. rural plus low income). The special tabulations required to do this are expensive.

- It is expensive and difficult to conduct multivariate analysis to introduce controls on the data. This limits the possibilities of explanatory analysis.

- Since some data are only available for large geographical regions, the risk of error is increased when inferring to individuals, families, or households.

- The analysis of poverty and deprivation is easiest when using economic indicators. However, this biases the research away from the social and political aspects of deprivation.

Bill Reimer, Isabelle Ricard, and Frances M. Shaver
Department of Sociology
Concordia University
Montréal, Québec
H3G 1M8

References

Beaudin, Arnold, Réjean Chamard, Eric Gervais, and Daniel Lalande. 1990. La pauvreté au Québec: situation récente et évolution de 1973 à 1986. and up-to-date calculations from Direction de la Recherche, Ministère de la Main d'Oeuvre, de la Sécurité du Revenu et de la Formation professionnelle. Québec: Gouvernement du Québec.

Bergeron, Louis. 1988. Tax Family data. A Comparison to Other Data. Ottawa: Statistics Canada, Small Area And Administrative Data Division.

CCSD (Canadian Council on Social Development). 1984. Not Enough: The Meaning and Measurement of Poverty in Canada. Ottawa: Canadian Council on Social Development.

Ross, David P. and E. Richard Shillington. 1989. The Canadian Fact Book on Poverty - 1989. Ottawa: The Canadian Council on Social Development.

Statistics Canada. 1987. Income Distribution by size in Canada, (cat. no. 13-207). Ottawa: Statistics Canada.

Statistics Canada. 1988. Québec: Part 2, Volume 1 of 2. In the 1986 Census of Canada series—Profiles, (cat. no. 94-110). Ottawa: Statistics Canada.

Wolfson, M. C. and J. M. Evans. 1989. Statistics Canada's low income cut-offs: methodological concerns and possibilities. Discussion paper. Ottawa: Statistics Canada, Analytic Studies Branch.

17

The distribution of federal-provincial taxes and transfers in rural Canada

Brian B. Murphy

Summary

Despite the lack of specific consideration of rurality in the tax-transfer system, the 1990 tax-transfer system actually imposes lighter tax burdens and significantly more cash transfers to rural residents than to urban residents mainly because of federal programs. With the exception of social assistance, rural Canadians as a group receive higher transfers in every transfer category, especially unemployment insurance and payments for children. Provincial tax and transfer programs, despite their formal relationship to federal taxes, tend to impose a much more consistent burden across urbanization class because they have a higher proportion of regressive commodity taxes.

Many factors give rise to lower income tax liabilities and higher sales tax payments in rural Canada. Families living in rural communities tend to have slightly lower incomes, less employment income and more farm income, larger family sizes and older families than their urban counterparts. They spend a greater proportion of their income on food, electricity, home heating fuels, and automobiles and less on rent, hotels and restaurants and personal business. They show higher rates of self employment and unemployment.

The evolution of the tax-transfer system between 1984 and 1990 does not change the relative balance between urban and rural Canadians vis-à-vis the burden of net taxes and transfers on individuals and families. It has however shifted rural Canadians on average from net gainers from the system to net contributors to the system.

Table of contents

The distribution of federal-provincial taxes and transfers in rural Canada

Brian B. Murphy

1.   Introduction

In Canada, the federal and provincial governments levy significant income taxes and pay substantial cash transfers to families and individuals. Particular taxation provisions and transfer programs are highly interconnected and in effect form a single tax-transfer system. Embodied in this system are judgements about fair treatment of families and individuals in different circumstances. These judgements rarely consider degree of urbanization; but rather, are the implicit outcomes of historical processes of political debate and compromise.

This paper examines the program specific and cumulative impact of the tax-transfer system on Canadian families. Emphasis is placed on the differences between families living in rural and urban areas. No major government programs are based explicitly on urbanization. The taxes paid to governments and transfer benefits received from them are determined by the rules of the tax-transfer programs. These rules are applied to individuals with a variety of individual and family characteristics. The characteristics are not evenly distributed across urbanization classes and give rise to differing mixes of taxes and transfers as well as differing overall tax-transfer burdens.

The study first outlines the various types of programs in the tax-transfer system. This is followed by an examination of the characteristics of families and individuals which determine their taxes and transfers across urbanization categories. Next, the distribution of specific tax-transfer elements and the overall system as legislated in 1990 is examined. Finally, at an aggregate level, the 1990 system is contrasted with the tax-transfer system as legislated for 1984.

2.   Public sector taxes and transfers

The system of federal and provincial taxation has three main kinds of
taxes borne directly by households: personal income taxes, sales or
commodity taxes, and payroll taxes. Households additionally pay many
other forms of taxes to governments (e.g. property taxes, utility taxes
and various licence fees). These other sub-provincial taxes, while likely
to vary between rural and urban centres, have not been included in this
analysis because of insufficient data. In general, they would tend to
result in higher tax burdens in urban areas and reinforce the general
findings of this study.

In 1990, personal income tax accounted for about 60% of all direct
federal and provincial taxes paid by households. An individual's tax
liability is largely determined by the level and sources of income as well
as by family situation.

Commodity or sales taxes are also levied by both levels of government
and accounted for about one quarter of direct federal and provincial
taxes in 1990. Different goods and services are taxed at different rates.
As such, the proportion of a household's income spent on sales taxes will
depend on the amount and relative mix of goods purchased. These
taxes, to the extent that they are levied at intermediate levels in the
production process, are assumed to fully shift to consumers.

Payroll taxes are collected from employment earnings. The major such
taxes are contributions to fund the unemployment insurance program
and the Canada Pension Plan. Individuals' level of earnings as well as
their employment status are taken into account when determining the
amount of their payroll taxes.

The federal and provincial governments provide substantial cash
transfers to households in Canada; over $50 billion in 1990. These
transfers may be classified into three main groups: employment related
programs, means-tested programs, and demogrants.

Employment related programs are the largest group and accounted for
about 40% of all government cash transfers to households in 1990.
There are three programs in this group, unemployment insurance, the
Canada Pension Plan and the Quebec Pension Plan (CPP/QPP).
Individual unemployment benefits are paid to the unemployed
depending on the level of earnings and work history within the past two
years. Self-employed persons are not eligible for benefits. As such, a
region's aggregate unemployment benefits will be largely determined
by the unemployment rate.   Retirement benefits from the Canada
Pension Plan are based on an individual's lifetime earnings history as
well as the age when benefits commence. The aggregate Canada
Pension Plan receipts in a given region will be determined mainly by
the size of the elderly population.

340
The distribution of federal-provincial
taxes and transfers in rural Canada

Means-tested transfer programs take into account the financial resources (usually income) of a family when determining benefits. They include social assistance, the guaranteed income supplement (GIS) for OAS beneficiaries and the spouses allowance (SPA). The child tax credit and federal sales tax credit are also considered means-tested transfer programs in this analysis. In 1990, these programs accounted for almost 30% of federal-provincial cash transfers to households. Means-tested programs largely depend on family income; the lower the income the higher the benefits. Social assistance benefits also take into account a wide variety of other factors, such as asset levels and specific expenditure requirements in determining benefit levels.

Demogrants are cash transfers based solely on the demographic characteristics of individuals once they are deemed Canadian residents. There are two such programs in Canada, Family Allowances and Old Age Security (OAS). Benefits are determined by age: younger than 18 for Family Allowance or older than 65 for OAS.

3.   Data and methods

The analysis uses the Social Policy Simulation Database and Model, a micro-simulation model publicly available from Statistics Canada. The SPSD/M is a micro-computer product designed to analyze the financial interactions between governments and the household sector in Canada (See Bordt et al. 1990; or Wolfson et al. 1990 for a description of the SPSD/M). The SPSD/M calculates the taxes and transfers of a sample of individuals and aggregates them to represent the Canadian population. Using the rules of the 1990 tax transfer system, the simulated incidences of taxes and transfers are examined.

The SPSD/M is based on the Survey of Consumer Finances and as such on the Labour Force Survey sampling frame. Consequently, the definition of rural is the Labour Force Survey definition; non-self reporting enumeration areas. Towns of several thousand people may thus be considered rural, as may the fringes of large urban centres. Furthermore, the Labour Force Survey frame does not include large geographical areas of rural Canada. Excluded from the frame are the Yukon and Northwest Territories as well as persons living on reservations. These areas are, however, sparsely populated and their omission does not greatly affect the overall results. The final breakdown of the Canadian population may be seen in Table 1. Note that rural Canada under this definition is the second largest group with over 1.5 million families. Almost 50% of the population is in large urban centres.

TABLE 1

Census families by urbanization class, Canada, 1986

	Census families	
Urbanization class	(,000)	(%)
500,000 and over	5,119	49.0
100,000 - 499,999	1,085	10.4
30,000 - 99,999	1,218	11.6
Urban under 30,000	1,416	13.5
Rural	1,618	15.5

Source: Statistics Canada. Social Policy Simulation Database/Model.

The analysis is based on census families including "families" of size one. They are defined as legal or common-law husband and wife couples, or single adults and their never married children. This is the family definition used in the determination of most taxes and transfers.

Microsimulation allows us to answer certain hypothetical questions in the absence of current data. For example, the rules and regulations of the tax-transfer system are known in 1990. However, because of delays in survey collection and processing, no current data are available to describe the population on which that system actually operated. Therefore, microsimulation is used to apply the rules of the 1990 tax-transfer system to the population as it was in 1986; the most current data available at the time of this study. Similarly the rules of the tax-transfer system in 1984 will be applied to the identical 1986 population.

To reiterate, all figures expressed in this study are in constant 1986 dollars. The descriptive label of 1990 applied to distributions should be interpreted as the 1990 system of taxes and transfers applied in 1986.

This paper addresses three central questions: If the 1990 tax and transfer system were in place in 1986, what would the distribution of tax-transfer expenditures be in rural versus urban Canada? How would this compare to the 1984 system as it would have applied in 1986? In terms of disposable income, would changes affect the position of rural versus urban Canadians?

4. Determinants of taxes and transfers

The distribution of individual and family characteristics across the urbanization continuum are used to determine taxes and transfers. The major determinants are income, family characteristics, expenditure patterns, labour force status, and other geographic factors.

4.1   Income

Personal income taxes, payroll taxes and cash transfers have a
progressive structure; higher income individuals receive fewer transfers
and pay more taxes as a percentage of their income. Thus systematic
differences in income distributions across urbanization levels would
give rise to differential taxes and transfers. Figure 1 shows the
distribution of income for five different urbanization classes. The top of
each box corresponds to the income of the families at the 75th percentile.
So, for example, 75% of Canadians living in large cities have total
incomes less than $48,000. The mean is indicated by the star. The
dashed lines are set at the levels of rural areas to facilitate comparisons.

FIGURE 1

Distribution of census family income, Canada
(1986 $, 1990 transfer system)

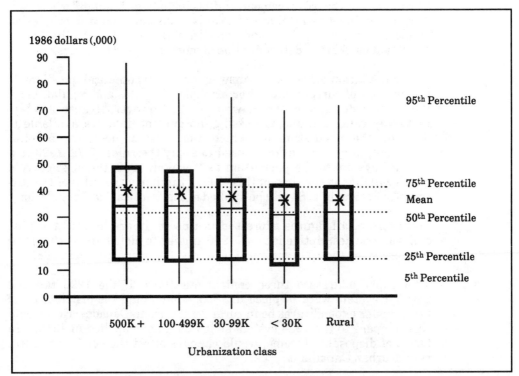

Source: *Statistics Canada. Social Policy Simulation Database/Model.*

The distribution of total income does not vary a great deal across five
different urbanization categories (Figure 1). By examining the dashed
line for the 25th percentile (the poorest 25% of census families) we see
virtually no difference across urbanization categories with a slight
exception for towns under 30,000. In other words, the poorest 25% of

families make less than $13,000 to $14,000 regardless of the size of urban or rural centre where they live. Average incomes vary by only a few thousand dollars across urbanization classes.

It is only in the high end of the income distribution that there is a significant difference in the distribution. Comparing urbanization classes at the 95th percentile, the richest 5% of rural families require a total income in excess of $70,000 while the richest 5% of metropolitan Canadian families require a total income of almost $90,000. On average rural Canadian families have less income than urban Canadians and this results mainly from the influence of higher incomes among "rich" Canadians in urban areas.

The source of income affects tax-transfer liabilities and benefits as well as the level of income. Certain types of employment earnings, investments and transfers are subject to different rules in the tax system. Table 2 shows the composition of income from various sources as a percentage of total income. For example, wages and salaries represent 70% of total income in large urban centres but only 59% in rural areas; an 11 percentage point difference. However, rural families have a larger share of total income from self employment in both the farm and non-farm components. This narrows the gap in overall employment earnings to 6.5%. Net employment earnings receive the same treatment for purposes of personal income taxes.

Government transfers represent a higher percentage of total income for rural families. On average 17% of rural income comes from government transfers compared to 10% for urban areas. The gap of 7 percentage points approximately offsets the gap in earned income. Not all government transfers are taxable and therefore tax liabilities will be greater on average in large urban areas. Investment income shows a "U" shaped curve. The investments in more rural areas are retirement pensions and annuities while large centres experience more interest and dividend income. Other income shows no definite trend.

TABLE 2

Census family income composition, Canada, 1990

Income composition (%)	Urbanization class					
	500K plus	100K-499K	30K-99K	30K and less	Rural	Canada
Wages	70.2	72.8	69.9	65.1	58.6	68.2
Self employment						
Non-farm	4.8	3.0	3.3	3.6	5.7	4.5
Farm	0.2	0.1	0.2	0.4	4.4	0.8
Investments	10.3	8.9	8.7	9.8	10.6	9.9
Transfers	10.2	11.6	13.2	16.7	17.1	12.5
Other	4.3	3.6	4.7	4.4	3.6	4.1
Head's percent of total income	81.2	82.0	81.1	80.7	78.8	80.8
Average number of earners	1.2	1.2	1.2	1.1	1.3	1.2

Source: Statistics Canada. Social Policy Simulation Database/Model.

The degree to which a family's income is split among different family members will also affect tax liabilities. Because individual earners can each claim personal deductions, families with split incomes will experience lower marginal tax rates on average. No real difference exists in the average number of earners per family and a slight difference exists in the proportion of total family income attributable to the head between urban and rural families (Table 2). For example, on average the total income of the head of rural families accounts for 79% of total family income compared to 81% for urban families. As such, rural families have their incomes slightly more evenly distributed among family members. This will in part reflect the rules for income splitting for self-employed farm income. The net effect is one of reducing the tax burden for rural families.

4.2   Family characteristics

Many federal transfers and tax credits are based on the numbers and ages of children. Some provinces (notably Quebec) have strong pro-natalist tax-transfer policies which favour families with a large number of children (Wolfson and Murphy 1990). On average, families living in rural areas have two thirds again as many children as urban families (Table 3). This will result in more transfer payments per family under the family allowance program and the child tax credit. It also allows more tax credits per family for dependant children and potentially more child care expense deductions.

TABLE 3

**Census family characteristics by urbanization class,
Canada, 1986**

	Urbanization class					
	500K plus	100K-499K	30K-99K	30K and less	Rural	Canada
Average size	2.23	2.36	2.38	2.39	2.82	2.37
Average number of kids	0.51	0.62	0.61	0.64	0.86	0.61
% Families with eldest under 25	10.0	10.6	10.2	8.1	5.0	9.0
25-44	44.2	41.9	41.9	38.3	41.4	42.5
45-64	27.5	28.2	28.7	28.2	31.5	28.4
65 and over	18.3	19.3	19.2	25.4	22.1	20.1

Source: Statistics Canada. Social Policy Simulation Database/Model.

Rural families, or at least the married couples in them, tend to be older
(Table 3). The eldest member of a census family is either the head or the
spouse. Only 5% of rural families have all members younger than 25
compared to twice that percentage in large cities. At the other end of
the scale, 22% of rural families have the eldest member older than 65
compared with 18% in large urban centres. Note that the highest
percentage of old families is 25% in urban centres under 30,000. This
blip in the trend may result partially from the sparseness of medical and
other services in rural areas required by the elderly. These
demographics will result in higher average payments of transfers to the
more rural elderly (OAS/GIS/CPP) and lower tax liabilities (because of,
for example, the age exemption).

4.3   Expenditure patterns

The amount of sales taxes a family pays will depend, in part, on the
relative mix of commodities purchased; some commodities having
higher sales tax rates. For example, the effective retail equivalent sales
taxes (the average amount of expenditures collected under a specific
tax) on tobacco in Newfoundland in 1986 was 127% while the
comparable number for federal import duties was less than 5% in all 40
expenditure categories. Federal commodity tax rates do not vary
significantly across urbanization classes (less than 0.5% except for
excise taxes at almost 1%).

Different provinces have different rates of sales taxes. Provincial retail
equivalent rates vary more across urbanization, up to two percentage
points. Rates for gasoline and tobacco are higher in rural areas while
amusement taxes and liquor taxes are higher in urban areas.

In most spending areas rural Canadians do not significantly differ from
their urban counterparts in terms of relative commodity mix of
purchases (measured as average percent of household expenditure
devoted to certain commodities). The commodities which do display a
difference of over half a percentage point across urbanization classes are
shown in Table 4.

TABLE 4

**Household expenditures as percent total expenditure,
Canada, 1990**

Expenditure category	Urbanization class				
	500K plus	100K-499K	30K-99K	30K and less	Rural
Food	12.5	13.1	13.6	14.4	15.4
Housing					
Imputed rent	13.5	16.3	15.2	14.8	16.7
Paid rent	6.4	5.1	5.3	5.2	2.4
Electricity	2.0	2.2	2.3	2.5	2.8
Other fuels	0.6	0.9	1.1	1.2	1.3
Transportation					
Automobiles	6.2	6.2	6.3	6.0	6.6
Gasoline	3.4	3.4	3.7	3.8	4.1
Inter-city	2.5	2.4	2.2	2.2	1.9
Hotel and restaurant	7.6	7.4	7.0	6.6	6.2
Personal business	5.6	5.8	5.8	5.2	5.3

Source: Statistics Canada. Social Policy Simulation Database/Model.

The largest differences are found in food, a low tax item, and rents.
Rural families have a higher proportion of homeowners and thus the
lower percent expenditure on rents. Recall, however, that property
taxes are not included in the analysis. While the lower taxed food is a
higher percentage of rural spending the higher taxed items of energy
and transportation are also high proportional expenditure items. While
there are offsetting items there is no clear indication from these
expenditure patterns what the net effect will be on urban versus rural
Canada.

4.4   Labour force status

Labour force status has a significant effect on the net burden of the tax-transfer system on households. The payroll taxes and income taxes on employment earnings are borne by members of the labour force while over $10 billion of transfers are distributed to the unemployed. We have already seen a significant difference in the levels of wages as a percentage of total income in Table 2 from 70% in large cities to 59% in rural areas. The labour force participation numbers for 1986 follow this pattern and show 71% of urban individuals aged 15-64 are employed compared to 61% of rural individuals. This will increase the taxation of urban families.

The unemployment rate has a twofold effect on aggregate payments of unemployment insurance. The more unemployed the higher the number of beneficiaries. But the unemployment rate in a region will determine the maximum benefits available; more benefits being paid in high unemployment regions of the country. Table 5 shows the annualized unemployment rates by province and class of urbanization in 1986, the rates used for the analysis. Some urbanization classes are absent from the table because of the confidentiality measures of the SPSD/M from which these data are drawn. The clear trend is toward higher unemployment rates in rural areas. The Prairie provinces are the only significant exception.

TABLE 5
Annualized unemployment rate by province and urbanization, Canada, 1986

Urban class	Province									
	Nfld	P.E.I.	N.S.	N.B.	Que.	Ont.	Man.	Sask.	Alta.	B.C.
500,000 +	—	—	—	—	10.8	7.5	8.5	—	12.1	13.2
100,000	—	—	—	—	12.6	10.5	—	9.0	—	—
30,000	—	—	11.5	10.0	14.5	10.0	—	10.8	10.2	14.3
<30,000	15.5	12.8	13.2	14.4	15.9	12.0	8.4	7.9	8.9	17.0
Rural	29.7	12.8	15.2	19.9	16.3	10.3	7.4	6.5	10.1	19.1

Source: Statistics Canada, 1986. Social Policy Simulation Database/Model.

Several other factors which vary by urbanization can in part determine taxes and transfers. Different provincial tax-transfer systems will apply to areas with various concentrations of rural population. However, the bulk of the provincial systems of taxation are determined by the federal system and as such provincial differences will not be pronounced. Certain other measures of the tax-transfer system will vary but these make up a very small proportion of the overall tax-transfer system and are not explicitly considered. (For example, the northern deduction largely will benefit rural families).

5.   Incidence of taxes and transfers in 1990

Table 6 shows taxes paid as a percentage of total income by type of tax, level of government and urbanization class. As such, it presents a measure of the relative burden of taxation. For example, on average, Canadians living in rural areas spent 17% of their total income on federal income, sales and payroll taxes compared with 18% in large urban centres; a 1 percentage point difference. As we would expect from the preceding discussion, the burden of federal taxation decreases steadily from urban to rural Canada because of the progressive rate structure, lower percentage of earned income, higher proportion of transfer income, and greater children's benefits. Federal sales taxes are higher in rural Canada mainly because of higher energy and transportation costs. Higher unemployment rates translate into lower unemployment insurance contributions. The slightly higher CPP/QPP contributions reflect the higher percentage of self employment income. Self-employed persons contribute twice as much as employees who have their contributions matched by their employers.

TABLE 6

Taxes as percent of total income by urbanization class, Canada, 1990

	Urbanization class					
	500K plus	100K-499K	30K-99K	30K and less	Rural	Canada
Federal	**18.7**	**18.4**	**18.3**	**17.6**	**17.4**	**18.2**
Income tax	12.0	11.6	11.4	10.6	10.2	11.4
Sales tax	4.4	4.4	4.5	4.7	4.9	4.5
Payroll (UI)	1.2	1.3	1.3	1.2	1.1	1.2
Payroll (C/QPP)	1.1	1.1	1.1	1.1	1.2	1.1
Provincial	**12.1**	**12.1**	**11.3**	**11.2**	**11.1**	**11.8**
Income tax	7.8	7.4	6.8	6.6	6.5	7.3
Sales tax	4.2	4.6	4.5	4.6	4.6	4.4

Source: Statistics Canada. Social Policy Simulation Database/Model.

Provincially the story is different. Provincial taxes show about half the increase that federal taxes do between rural and urban areas. The income taxes follow the same general pattern as the federal taxes to which they are tied. However, they represent a smaller proportion of total taxes and the progressive rate structure is offset by the regressive provincial sales taxes.

Federal transfers account for a much larger share (16%) of rural residents' total income than of urban residents' total income at 9% (Table 7). In other words, rural families receive on average over three-quarters again as much of their income in federal transfers than their counterparts in large cities. Much of the difference is accounted for by the unemployment insurance program, 3% in absolute terms or over twice as much as urban centres as a percent of total income. Children's benefits (family allowances and the child tax credit) as a percent of total income are 1% higher in rural areas than in urban areas because rural families have more children on average and lower average incomes. This rural-urban difference represents a doubling of average benefits (as a percent of total income) for rural families compared to urban families.

TABLE 7

Transfers as percent of total income by urbanization class, Canada, 1990

	Urbanization class					
	500K plus	100K-499K	30K-99K	30K and less	Rural	Canada
Elderly	4.5	5.3	5.9	8.1	6.9	5.5
OAS	2.0	2.3	2.5	3.6	3.1	2.5
GIS/SPA	0.7	0.9	1.1	1.7	1.7	1.0
C/QPP	1.8	2.0	2.3	2.7	2.1	2.0
Children	0.8	1.0	1.1	1.3	1.9	1.1
Unemployed	2.2	2.3	3.1	4.1	5.1	2.9
Assistance	0.8	0.9	1.0	1.0	0.9	0.9
Other	0.7	0.8	0.9	1.0	1.2	0.9
Federal total	**9.0**	**10.3**	**12.0**	**15.5**	**16.0**	**11.3**
Provincial	**1.3**	**1.5**	**1.4**	**1.6**	**1.5**	**1.4**

Source: Statistics Canada. Social Policy Simulation Database/Model.

The elderly transfer programs as a whole are 2.4 percentage points higher in rural areas than in large urban centres, from 6.9% to 4.5%. However, in urban centres under 30,000, the urbanization class with the highest percentage of elderly families, the percent of income from OAS/GIS/SPA and the CPP/QPP rises to over 8%. Of the three individual elderly programs, the CPP/QPP shows the least variation. The expected increase in relative rural benefits is offset by differences in regional employment rates and average wages as CPP/QPP benefits are determined based on average annual earnings. Should these latter factors be even across urbanization classes the variation should be closer to the roughly 1% difference in OAS resulting from age composition differences. The social assistance payments are roughly even across urbanization classes.

Provincial transfer payments do not vary significantly by urbanization. These payments are largely made up of social assistance payments as well as some children's benefits.

Figure 2 compares the combined effect of taxes and transfers, (the net "burden" of the tax-transfer system) by urbanization and income. The horizontal axis divides the population according to deciles (ten groups of equal size arranged by ascending income). The vertical axis shows average taxes minus transfers as a percentage of total income. There are five lines plotted on the graph, one for each urbanization category. Where the lines are below the "0" line parallel to the horizontal axis, on average families receive more transfers than they pay in taxes. So, for example, the poorest 10% of families living in large urban centres receive on average about half of their total income in transfers from the federal and provincial governments. Or at the other end of the graph, the richest 10% of Canadians in all urbanization groups pay on average between 25% and 30% of their total income in federal and provincial taxes.

FIGURE 2

Net impact of tax-transfer system by income decile group, Canada, 1990

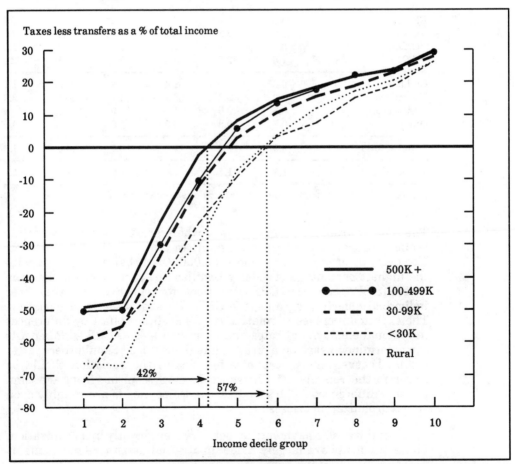

Source: *Statistics Canada. Social Policy Simulation Database/Model.*

The general slope of the five curves shows the progressive structure of
the tax-transfer system; families with higher incomes pay a greater
percentage of their incomes in taxes. About 42% of the poorest families
living in large cities receive more transfers than they pay in taxes
(Figure 2). The comparable number for rural families is 57%, a
significant gap of 15% of families. Also note that the bottom 10% of
rural families receive, on average, over 70% of their income from
transfer payments. With minor exceptions rural families across all
income classes have a lower net burden and the difference narrows the
higher the income class. Note the fanning out of the difference between
urban and rural from high to lower income Canadians.

Figure 3 separates the influence of the federal and provincial
governments on the overall net burden. The majority of the pro-
gressivity results from the federal system. Also the difference in net
impacts between urban and rural families is mostly attributable to the
federal system (mainly because of transfers in the lower decile groups).
Note that for federal taxes and transfers, 72% of rural families are in a
net gain position compared with just over 50% for families in large
urban centres. This is a 7% larger gap than for the combined systems in
Figure 2. The corresponding provincial number shows about 25% of
families in a net gain position.

FIGURE 3

Net impact of tax-transfer system by income decile group, Canada, 1990

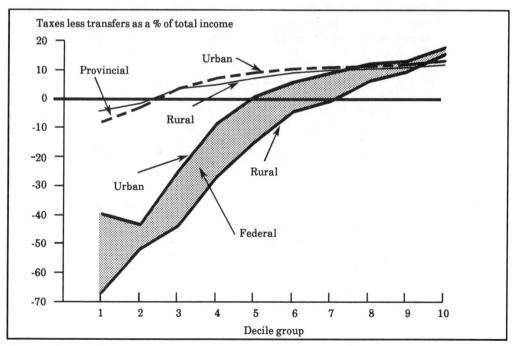

Source: *Statistics Canada. Social Policy Simulation Database/Model.*

A close examination also shows that for provincial net balance, rural families are in a worse position than their urban counterparts in the bottom three decile groups; a reversal of the dominant federal trend. The predominance of regressive sales and commodity taxes at the low end of the income distribution is responsible. At the bottom decile, this gap represents close to 5% of income.

6.   Tax-transfer changes, 1984 to 1990

The Canadian tax system has undergone significant change between the 1984 and 1990 tax years. The wide range of changes included enrichment of the GIS, Phase I of tax reform, partial de-indexation of the income tax system, redesign of the child benefit system, "repayment of social transfers" which apply to family allowances and old age security (the so-called clawbacks), changes to the unemployment insurance program, and many changes in commodity taxation. This analysis, as stated earlier, compares the tax-transfer systems in place in calendar year 1984 with those in place in 1990. Note that the differences are therefore not solely attributable to changes introduced by the Conservative government. An analysis restricted to Progressive Conservative changes since 1984 was performed in Grady (1990). Many of the changes to the system have had immediate effects while others will take time for their full impact to be realized; in particular, the partial de-indexation of the tax system (Murphy and Wolfson 1991).

The following list gives a sense of the range of income and payroll tax changes and transfer changes by indicating some of the adjustments to the tax system which have been incorporated into the analysis.

Taxes
Repayment of Social Transfers (OAS/FA)
High income surtax
Introduction of minimum tax
Increased tax on dividends
Increase in disability deduction
Increase in child care expense deduction
Partial de-indexation of tax system
Lifetime capital gains exemption
Exemptions to credits and rate modification
Increase in inclusion rate for capital gains
Reduction of dividend gross-up and tax credit
Elimination of investment income deduction
Elimination of employment expense deduction
Family Allowance reported by higher income spouse

Transfers
GIS Enrichment
Partial de-indexing of FA & Child Tax Credit
Increase in Child Tax Credit
Reduction of Child Tax Credit threshold
Modification of child exemption-credit
Child Tax Credit supplement
Extension of Widowed Spouses Allowance
Introduction and enhancement of refundable sales tax credit
Unemployment insurance benefits-contributions
Increase in CPP/QPP contribution rates

Many changes to the commodity tax system occurred from 1984 through 1990. This analysis accounts for numerous increases in excise duties on tobacco, alcohol, gasoline and communications as well as increases in the manufacturers sales tax, the airport tax and a new tax on telecommunication services. Because of insufficient data, some changes were excluded from the analysis. These omissions include extensions of the federal sales tax to confectioneries, soft drinks, health foods, pet foods and insulation, and several exemptions and special provisions. These omissions have only a small effect on both the aggregate and distributional results.

7.   Impact of tax changes, 1984 to 1990

None of the changes during 1984-1990 were specifically targeted at the rural population. This analysis is not concerned with the individual effects of specific measures. Rather, the aim is to ascertain whether the overall structure of taxation in rural versus urban areas has changed as a consequence of the cumulative effect of the changes.

FIGURE 4
**Net impact of tax-transfer system by urbanization class, Canada,
1984 and 1990**

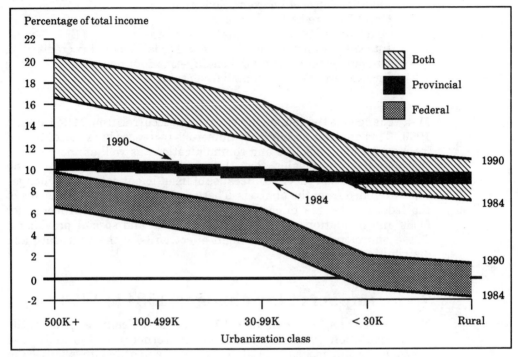

Source: Statistics Canada. Social Policy Simulation Database/Model.

The changes introduced have not significantly altered the relative
positions of urban versus rural families. This is expected since most
changes were made to the tax system and the transfer system is largely
responsible for the better net position of rural versus urban families.

On average, families in large cities paid just over 20% of their total
income in federal and provincial taxes in 1990. Rural families paid
about half that amount (11%). In 1984, the corresponding figures were
16.5% in urban centres and again about half, or 7.5%, in rural areas.
The findings are the same for both levels of government. The striking
feature is the overall rise in the net burden of taxation; almost 4
percentage points average increase in the portion of income devoted to
taxes. The structure of this increase was itself progressive (Grady
1990), and thus the relative positions of rural and urban Canadians
stayed the same. Note however, that the magnitude of the increase for
federal taxes and transfers made an accounting change to rural
Canadians. Under the 1984 tax-transfer system, rural Canadians on
average received almost 2% of total income as transfer payments.
Under the 1990 tax-transfer system, the same families on average were
paying 2% of that same income in taxes.

8.   Conclusion

Despite the lack of specific consideration of rurality in the tax-transfer
system,   the 1990 tax-transfer system actually imposes lighter tax
burdens and significantly more cash transfers to rural residents than to
urban residents mainly because of federal programs.   With the
exception of social assistance, rural Canadians receive higher transfers
in every transfer category, especially unemployment insurance and
payments for children. Provincial tax and transfer programs, despite
their formal relationship to federal taxes, tend to impose a more
consistent burden across urbanization classes because they have a
higher proportion of regressive commodity taxes.

Many factors give rise to lower income tax liabilities and higher sales
tax payments in rural Canada. Families living in rural communities
tend to have slightly lower incomes, less employment income and more
farm income, larger family sizes and older families than their urban
counterparts. They spend a greater proportion of their income on food,
electricity, home heating fuels, and automobiles and somewhat less on
rent, hotels and restaurants and personal business. They show higher
rates of self employment and unemployment.

The evolution of the tax-transfer system between 1984 and 1990 does
not change the relative balance between urban and rural Canadians
vis-à-vis the burden of net taxes and transfers on individuals and
families. It has, however, shifted rural Canadians on average from net
gainers from the system to net contributors to the system.

Brian B. Murphy
Analytical Studies Branch
Statistics Canada
Ottawa, Ontario K1A 0T6

References

Bordt, Michael, Grant Cameron, Stephen Gribble, Brian Murphy, Geoff Rowe, and Michael Wolfson. 1990. The social policy simulation database and model: an integrated tool for tax/transfer policy analysis. Canadian Tax Journal, 38(1): 48-65.

Grady, Patrick. 1990. The distributional impact of the federal tax and transfer changes introduced since 1984. Canadian Tax Journal, 38(2): 286-297.

Murphy, B.B., and M.C. Wolfson. 1990. When the baby boom grows old: impacts on Canada's public sector. Paper presented to the United Nations Economic Commission for Europe, Seminar on Demographic and Economic Consequences and Implications of Changing Population Age Structure. Ottawa: September.

Statistics Canada. 1990. SPSD/M version 4.1 documentation. Reference Manual. Ottawa: Statistics Canada.

Wolfson, M.C., and B.B. Murphy. 1990. The role of equivalence scales in Canadian public policy. Paper presented to the Séminaire de l'Association Européenne pour l'Étude de la Population sur «Familles et niveaux de vie : observations et analyse». Barcelona: October.

Wolfson, Michael, Stephen Gribble, Michael Bordt, Brian Murphy, and Geoff Rowe. 1990. The social policy simulation database and model: an example of survey and administrative data integration. Survey of Current Business, 69(5): 36-40.

18

Social indicators from the General Social Survey:
some urban-rural differences

Douglas A. Norris and Kulbir Johal

Summary

Time use patterns are similar among rural and urban populations. Urban victimization rates are higher for most types of crime and from most age-gender groups. Urban residents indicated more fear of crime and were more likely to perceive crime as higher and increasing in their neighbourhoods. Ownership and use of home computers is substantially higher in urban areas. Rural residents have lower levels of education, are more likely to indicate dissatisfaction with their education and are less likely to plan to pursue further education. Participation in volunteer groups was slightly higher in rural areas but rural-urban differences varied widely by type of organization. Participation was higher in rural areas for religious, community or service-oriented organizations but lower than in urban areas for cultural, business, sports-related and political groups.

Table of contents

Social indicators from the General Social Survey:
some urban-rural differences

Douglas A. Norris and Kulbir Johal

1.   Introduction

Labour market and income-related issues are generally well documented for rural Canada. Less attention has been paid to issues of health, education, justice or culture. The purpose of this paper is to compare selected social indicators for urban and rural Canada.

2.   Background

Statistics Canada's social statistics program provides information on the demographic and social characteristics and conditions of Canadians. The census of population, held every five years, is the cornerstone of the social statistics program, providing benchmark information on the demographic, social and economic conditions of the population and the basis for future sample surveys. The geographically comprehensive nature of the census yields a rich source of social data and Bollman and Biggs (1992) use census and other data to provide a detailed portrait of rural and small town Canada.

In addition to the census, household surveys provide another source of social data. While household surveys have long been an important part of the social statistics program, the regular survey program has historically been directed mainly at labour market and income-related issues, not to areas such as health, education, justice or culture. To partially fill this data gap, Statistics Canada established a General Social Survey (GSS) program in 1985.

This paper illustrates the potential use of the GSS for providing social indicators for urban and rural Canada. The aim is to provide indicators that are not available from other data sources, not to review all the topics covered by the GSS.

3. Data source

The GSS is an annual survey which, over five years, covers a range of topics. Core topics are repeated every five years to monitor temporal changes in the living conditions and well-being of Canadians. Five core topics are covered by the GSS:

1. Health
2. Time use
3. Personal risk (accidents and criminal victimizations)
4. Education and work
5. Family and friends

The GSS is conducted using random digit dialing telephone methodology and the target population is the non-institutional population aged 15 or older living in the 10 provinces. One individual is randomly selected as a respondent from each household contacted and the base sample size for each survey is 10,000 persons. In some surveys, the sample size was increased for certain regions and age groups. For a detailed description of the GSS, see Norris and Paton (1990).

While the sample size for the GSS yields fairly detailed national data, more limited data can also be produced for sub-national areas. Because of the random digit dialing telephone methodology, sub-national areas must be delineated using a combination of telephone exchanges and postal codes collected routinely in each survey. Where available, the postal code is the primary geographic indicator and postal codes can be mapped to more standard geographic areas by using the Statistics Canada postal code conversion file. In particular, for most GSS cycles the postal code was used to delineate census metropolitan areas (100,000 and over) census agglomerations (10,000—99,999) and the rural and smaller urban areas. Note that using postal codes to delineate these three areas has some limitations. However, the resulting data are thought to provide a good indication of urban-rural differences.

This presentation will focus on several topics covered in the GSS for 1986 (Time use), 1988 (Personal risk) and 1989 (Education and work).

4. Time use

Information on how people spend their time is a central component of social statistics. While money provides an integrating unit for understanding the economic system, time performs a similar integrating role for understanding our social system. The GSS time use survey measured a "24 hour time budget" generally for the day preceding the interview. Respondents provided information on each primary activity that day, the start time and duration of each activity, and associated information on where the activity took place and whom the respondent was with at the time (e.g. spouse, children, friends). These data measured how often people participate in activities such as paid work, household work, cultural events, television viewing, and time spent on these activities.

The GSS classified daily activities into nearly 100 individual categories and these can be grouped into 10 major activity groups. Major activity groups fall into three broad categories: productive activities (including both paid and unpaid work), free time and personal care activity (mostly sleep). The average time spent in each of the groups provides an indicator of the time use of a population group and allows for comparisons between groups.

TABLE 1

Average time spent for each activity* by urban-rural location, Canada, 1986

	Total	Census metropolitan areas (100,000+)	Census agglomeration (10,000-99,999)	Rural/ small urban (<10,000)
		Hours per day		
Employed work	3.6	3.8	3.6	3.1
Domestic work	1.8	1.6	1.7	2.1
Primary care of children	0.4	0.4	0.4	0.4
Shopping and services	0.9	0.9	0.9	0.9
Education	0.8	0.9	0.9	0.6
Organizational, voluntary and religious	0.3	0.2	0.3	0.3
Entertainment (attending)	1.3	1.3	1.3	1.4
Sports and hobbies	0.8	0.7	0.8	0.9
Media and communication	3.2	3.2	3.2	3.2
Personal care (including sleep)	11.0	11.0	11.0	11.1
Total	**24.0**	**24.0**	**24.0**	**24.0**

*   Activities are groups of activities related to the topic listed.

Source: Statistics Canada. 1986 General Social Survey, unpublished data.

Overall there are no major urban-rural differences in time use (Table 1). However, the time spent on paid work decreases with urban size from 3.8 hours per day for persons in census metropolitan areas (CMAs) to 3.1 hours for those in rural areas, perhaps reflecting differences in labour force participation rates. Time allocated to unpaid domestic work is actually higher in rural areas (2.1 hours) than in CMAs (1.6 hours). Time spent on sleep and other personal care activities and the balance of time (free time) is about the same in all areas.

5.   Criminal victimization

In early 1988, the GSS surveyed the topic of personal risk including both criminal victimizations and accidents. Traditionally, information on these topics has been derived from administrative sources such as police statistics and hospital records. However, these data provide very little information about the victim and, in addition, many crimes (the GSS estimates more than half) and accidents are not reported to authorities.

362
Social indicators from the General Social Survey:
some urban-rural differences

The personal risk survey asked respondents about criminal victimizations and accidents experienced during 1987. Data were also collected on several lifestyle measures—such as alcohol consumption and frequency of night outings—and were correlated with criminal victimizations and accidents. For each reported crime or accident, data were collected on the nature of the incident, the resulting activity restriction, medical attention and financial loss. In addition, respondents were asked to report perceptions of crimes and accidents and precautions taken to prevent these events.

Sacco and Johnson (1989, 1990) have analyzed GSS victimization data including urban-rural differences and these results are taken from their studies. For this survey, areas were identified as urban or rural by the second digit of the postal code.

TABLE 2
Rates of victimization per 1,000 persons or per 1,000 households by urban-rural location, Canada, 1987

Offence type	Total	Urban	Rural
Total personal incidents	**143**	**158**	**114**
Personal theft	59	70	46
Total violent	83	88	68
Robbery	13	14	–
Assault	68	72	56
Total household incidents	**216**	**252**	**146**
Break and enter	54	64	32
Motor vehicle theft	51	59	36
Household theft	48	54	35
Vandalism	63	76	42
Personal incidents			
Males			
All ages	148	155	135
15 - 24	335	322	354
25 - 44	149	154	118
45 - 64	44	64	–
65 +	–	–	–
Females			
All ages	138	161	93
15 - 24	287	306	277
25 - 44	167	190	77
45 - 64	47	61	–
65 +	–	–	–

– Rate cannot be reliably estimated.

Source: Sacco and Johnson (1989, 1990).

Victimization rates are higher in urban areas for all types of crime (Table 2). Urban-rural differences are larger for household crimes and the largest difference was for break and enter crimes where the urban rate was twice the rural rate.

Personal victimization rates are inversely related to age and in nearly all cases rates are higher in urban areas. However, for males aged 15-24, personal victimization rates are higher in rural areas.

TABLE 3

Selected measures of perceptions of crime and adoption of defensive behaviour by urban-rural location, Canada, 1988

	Total	Urban	Rural
		Percent	
Perceptions of crime			
Level of crime in neighbourhood higher compared to other areas	8	10	4
Level of crime increased in last year	20	23	16
Feel unsafe walking alone at night in neighbourhood			
Total	25	28	18
Males	11	12	8
Females	39	42	28
Crimes reported to police	40	42	34
Adoption of defensive behaviour			
Changed activity	25	27	22
Changed telephone number	5	5	3
Installed security hardware	23	26	14
Took self-defense course	3	3	2

Source: Sacco and Johnson (1989) and Statistics Canada. 1988 General Social Survey, unpublished data.

Selected indicators of perception of crime were also obtained. Fear of crime is substantially higher for females than for males but for both sexes levels of fear are higher in urban areas (Table 3). Urban residents are also more likely than their rural counterparts to perceive levels of crime higher in their neighbourhood than elsewhere and to feel crime is increasing.

The GSS also surveyed responses to crime. In urban areas 42% of crimes were reported to police compared to 34% in rural areas (Table 3). Urban residents were also more likely to adopt defensive behaviour particularly when it came to installing security hardware. In urban areas, 26% of respondents had installed security hardware in 1987 compared to 14% of rural residents.

6.   Education and volunteer work

The 1989 GSS was developed around three main themes that reflect
fundamental changes in Canadian society: patterns and trends in work
and education; new technologies and human resources; and work in the
service economy. The survey collected data on many dimensions of work
and education. Here, only a few are considered: in particular, knowledge
and use of computers, satisfaction with education, educational
intentions and volunteer work.

Historically, educational levels were higher in urban areas than in
rural areas. Bollman and Biggs (1992) provide a number of measures of
urban-rural differences in education including several measures of
literacy as derived from a recent survey of literacy. The 1989 GSS
provides data on another dimension of education, computer literacy.

TABLE 4
Selected indicators of computer literacy, satisfaction with education and plans for future education by urban-rural area, Canada, 1989

	Total	Census metropolitan area (100,000+)	Census agglomeration (10,000-99,999)	Rural/ small urban (<10,000)
		Percent		
Taken computer course				
All ages	31.5	36.3	28.4	21.0
15 - 19	63.4	68.4	61.4	50.9
20 - 24	52.7	57.5	52.4	35.0
25 - 44	35.8	40.6	32.5	23.8
45 +	13.5	16.2	10.2	9.7
Able to use computer				
All ages	47.3	53.3	42.4	34.6
15 - 19	82.3	85.9	74.2	78.8
20 - 24	66.0	70.4	69.1	47.3
25 - 44	58.2	63.9	53.3	44.7
45 +	21.9	26.7	17.1	14.1
Computer at home				
Household income:				
Total	19.4	22.1	17.2	13.9
less than 30,000	10.0	11.9	9.8	6.6
30,000 - 59,999	21.9	22.8	21.9	19.3
60,000 or higher	36.2	37.6	37.5	25.0
Satisfied with education	72.9	74.4	72.3	69.5
Plans to pursue additional education in next 5 years	24.4	26.4	25.5	18.4

Source: Statistics Canada. 1989 General Social Survey, unpublished data.

From looking at patterns of computer use and training, and ownership of a personal computer, it appears urban dwellers—residents of census agglomerations (CAs) and census metropolitan areas (CMAs)—are more computer literate than rural residents. Rural residents are less likely to have taken computer courses or to use computers than urban residents, and the differences are more pronounced when age is taken into account (Table 4). Computer training and use are more prevalent among the younger age groups across all sectors. However, even in the 15-19 and 20-24 age groups, the rural sector shows significantly smaller (10-15%) proportions with computer training compared to the CA and CMA categories. Similar patterns exist for the ability to use a computer.

Rural residents are also less likely to have a personal computer at home than CA and CMA residents. This pattern holds even when accounting for household income strongly influencing home computer ownership. One of the most striking differences is in the $60,000 and over annual income group. About 25% of rural residents in this income group own a personal computer compared to 38% of both CA and CMA residents. A similar pattern emerges when education levels of personal computer owners are examined. For example, 36% of people in CMAs with a university education own a computer, compared to 27% in rural areas. CMA residents with less than a high school education are also more inclined to own a computer (16%) than their non-CMA (11%) and rural (11%) counterparts. While the differences in home computer ownership between rural and urban residents are not great, they still emerge even when accounting for income and education levels.

The GSS also asked about satisfaction with education and plans for future educational training. In rural areas, 70% of the population were satisfied with their education compared to 74% in CMAs (Table 4). When asked about plans for the future, 18% of the rural population indicated they intended to pursue further education sometime in the next five years compared to 26% in CA and CMA areas.

Another topic covered in the 1989 GSS was participation in volunteer activities. More specifically, respondents were asked if they had taken part in various volunteer activities over the past 12 months.

TABLE 5

Participation in organizations in last 12 months by urban-rural location, Canada, 1988

	Total	Census metropolitan areas (100,000+)	Census agglomeration (10,000-99,999)	Rural/ small urban (<10,000)
		Percent		
All organizations	55.7	54.8	57.1	57.0
Charitable, service or volunteer	41.3	40.2	42.6	43.2
Neighbourhood, community or school related	37.9	36.8	36.6	41.7
Religious or church related	27.8	25.4	29.6	32.7
Social, cultural or ethnic group	27.4	28.5	28.2	24.1
Sports or athletic	44.2	46.0	42.3	40.9
Business, professional or work related	23.6	26.4	22.3	17.1
Political organizations	9.8	9.8	10.6	9.2

Source: Statistics Canada. 1989 General Social Survey, unpublished data.

Overall participation in the organizations was about the same in rural (57%) and in CA areas (57%) and these were higher than the rates in CMAs (55%) (Table 5). However, the participation rates and the urban-rural differences vary widely by type of organization.

Comparing only rural and CMA areas, participation rates are higher in rural areas for charitable, service or volunteer organizations (43% vs. 40%), neighbourhood community or school related organizations (42% vs. 37%), and church related organizations (33% vs. 25%). On the other hand, participation is lower in rural areas for social, cultural or ethnic organizations (24% vs. 29%) sports or athletic groups (41% vs. 46%) business or professional groups (17% vs. 26%) and political organizations (9% vs. 10%).

7. Conclusion

This paper has delineated urban-rural differences on a range of social topics using the General Social Survey (GSS). While the GSS sample size is not large enough to permit a detailed analysis of urban-rural differences, it does allow for broad urban-rural comparisons. However, in using the GSS to make urban-rural comparisons, limitations of urban-rural delineations based on the postal code should be kept in mind.

The GSS covers a wide range of topics and only a few were considered here. The data showed urban and rural areas to be fairly similar in time use patterns. Urban victimization rates were higher for most types of crime and for most age-gender groups. Consistent with this, urban residents indicated more fear of crime, and were more likely to perceive crime as higher and increasing in their neighbourhoods. Ownership and use of home computers were substantially higher in urban areas. Consistent with lower levels of education, rural residents were less "computer literate", more likely to indicate dissatisfaction with their education, and less likely than their urban counterparts to be planning to pursue further education. Overall, participation in volunteer groups was slightly higher in rural areas than in CMAs, but urban-rural differences varied widely by type of organization. Participation was higher in rural areas for religious, community or service oriented organizations but lower than in urban areas for cultural, business, sports related and political groups.

Douglas A. Norris, Kulbir Johal,
Housing, Family and Social Statistics Division
Statistics Canada
Ottawa, K1A 0T6

References

Bollman, Ray D. and Brian Biggs. 1992. Rural and small town Canada: an overview. Chapter 1, this volume.

Norris, D. and D. Paton. 1990. Canada's General Social Survey: five years of experience. Paper presented at 1990 Annual Meeting of American Statistical Association. Anaheim, California.

Sacco, V. and H. Johnson. 1989. Patterns of Criminal Victimization in Canada. General Social Survey Analysis Series, (cat. no. 11-612E, no. 2). Ottawa: Statistics Canada.

Sacco, V. and H. Johnson. 1990. Urbanization and criminal victimization. Paper presented at 1990 Annual Meeting of Canadian Sociology and Anthropology Association. Victoria, B.C.

Moosonee, Ontario

19

The Aboriginal socio-economic situation: a rural-urban comparison

Andrew J. Siggner

Summary

A review of major demographic, social and economic characteristics indicate that Aboriginal peoples still lag behind the non-Aboriginal population. The gap tends to be more pronounced in rural Indian reserves and in the other rural areas of Canada as compared to urban areas. For the Aboriginal population living on reserves, 45% aged 15 or older have less than a grade 9 education. Among Aboriginals with postsecondary qualifications and living on reserves, the heaviest concentration is in applied technologies and trades. The average income of Aboriginals and non-Aboriginals is higher in urban areas than on reserves; however, moving from the smallest urban areas (less than 10,000 population) to the largest urban areas (100,000 +), the gap between Aboriginals' and non-Aboriginals' average income widens.

Table of contents

The Aboriginal socio-economic situation: a rural-urban comparison

Andrew J. Siggner

1. Introduction

When I agreed in the Spring of 1990 to address this topic, little did anyone realize what a summer it was going to be in this country vis-à-vis Aboriginal people. However, as I began putting my thoughts together, I asked myself, from a statistical perspective was the situation at Kahnesatake (Oka, Québec) and Kahnawake (Mercier Bridge, Montréal) that unpredictable? The answer, I concluded, was "no".

The demographic characteristics to potentially set the stage for such discontent have been in place for the Aboriginal population and, in particular, for the First Nations, since the 1960s. At that time, their birth rate peaked and was equivalent to many Third World countries. The generation of Aboriginal children born in the 1960s are now the young adult population that is forming new families, looking for improved education, looking for jobs, and needing housing. According to the 1986 Census, the young adult population aged 15-24 residing on Indian reserves represented 22% of the total on-reserve population (Figure 1). This compares to 16% in the same age group for non-Aboriginals in Canada. In addition, those younger than 15 represent 38% of the on-reserve population and will continue to add to the young adult population as they age.

The following presentation will describe the rural and urban situation of Aboriginal people in 1986 according to selected demographic, social and economic indicators.

FIGURE 1

Population on reserves by age and gender, Canada, 1986

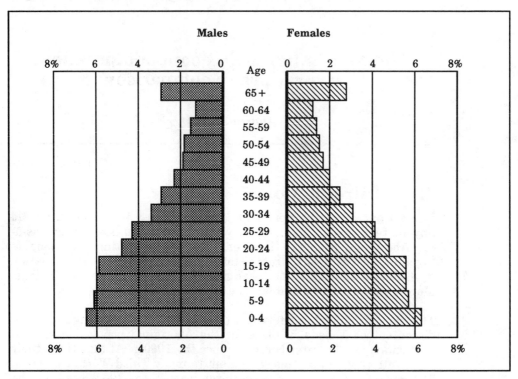

Source: Statistics Canada. 1986 Census of Population.

2.   Data sources and definitions

The data on Aboriginal people are from the question on the 1986 Census of Population on ethnic or cultural origins. Respondents were asked to identify their origins which included three Aboriginal categories: North American Indian, Métis and Inuit. Unlike previous censuses, the 1986 Census encouraged people to mark as many origins as they felt applied to them. In 1981, multiple responses were not encouraged. Consequently, persons reporting Aboriginal origins increased from 490,000 in 1981 to 711,720 in 1986. Such an increase was not simply a result of demographic growth, but was also a reflection of the change in the question wording between the two censuses. We discovered in 1986 that 48% of the 711,720 persons with Aboriginal origins reported mixed origins; for example, combinations of North American Indian and non-Aboriginal origins such as French or Scottish.

For the purpose of this paper, an Aboriginal person is anyone who reported an Aboriginal origin as a single or multiple response on the 1986 Census form. While there are important socio-economic differences among the various Aboriginal groups as well as between those giving a single versus multiple origin response, this paper focuses on the total Aboriginal population.

3. Geographic distributions

The Aboriginal and non-Aboriginal population is composed of the following five geographies:

- Rural reserves
- Rural non-reserves
- Urban areas less than 10,000
- Urban areas 10,000 - 99,999
- Urban areas 100,000+

Rural reserves include Indian reserves and settlements as designated under the Indian Act of Canada, and some additional Indian communities in the Northwest Territories, Yukon, Alberta and Saskatchewan as of June 1986. Indian reserves within urban areas were included in the urban categories. The population in such reserves is small (7,400).

Note that about 136 Indian reserves were incompletely enumerated in the 1986 Census with an estimated population of about 45,000 representing about 20% of the on-reserve population.

In 1986, 55% of Aboriginals resided on Indian reserves, in other rural areas, or in communities of less than 10,000, while 31% lived in large urban areas of 100,000 and over (Figure 2). This contrasts with about 32% among non-Aboriginals in rural areas or urban areas of less than 10,000 and 54% in urban areas of 100,000 and over.

FIGURE 2

Aboriginal and non-Aboriginal population by urbanization class, Canada, 1986

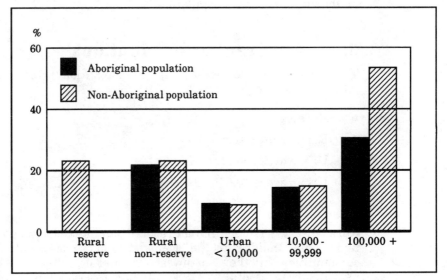

Source: Statistics Canada. 1986 Census of Population.

4.   Demographic characteristics

Rural Indian reserves have the largest share (37%) of their population in the younger than 15 age group (Figure 3). In the largest urban areas, the share of the Aboriginal population younger than 15 drops to 32%, but this contrasts with about 21% younger than 15 among non-Aboriginals.

Note the higher percentage of Aboriginals aged 25-34 in the largest urban areas (22%) compared to only 14% on rural Indian reserves. This likely reflects the migration of young Aboriginal people to the cities.

5.   Mobility characteristics

Mobility is measured by the percent of the population aged 5 and older which migrated to a different community from the one they lived in five years previously. Among Aboriginals living in urban areas (with a population of 10,000-99,999), nearly 32% were migrants, while only about 9% were migrants among Aboriginals living on rural Indian reserves (Figure 4). About 42% of non-Aboriginals living on rural Indian reserves were migrants. These would tend to be nurses, teachers and police stationed there.

FIGURE 3

Age distribution in selected areas, Canada, 1986

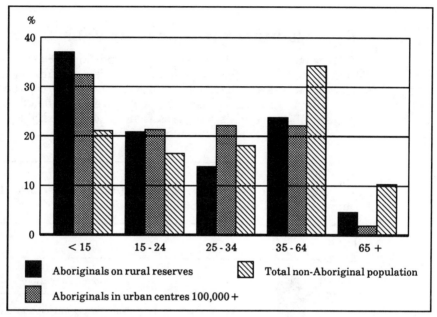

Source: Statistics Canada. 1986 Census of Population.

FIGURE 4

Aboriginal and non-Aboriginal population older than 5 who were migrants, Canada, 1986

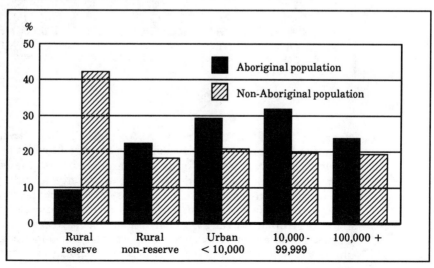

Source: Statistics Canada. 1986 Census of Population.

Norris (1988) found that among Aboriginal migrants, 49% were moving among urban areas during 1981-1986. About 20% were moving from rural to urban areas, while an equivalent percentage (21%) were moving in the opposite direction.

6.   Education characteristics

A large percent of Aboriginals aged 15 and older have less than grade 9 education (Figure 5). The highest percent occurs on rural Indian reserves where 45% have less than grade 9. The percent decreases from rural areas to urban areas. In urban areas of 100,000 or more, the percent of Aboriginals with less than grade 9 is slightly lower (13%) than that of non-Aboriginals (about 15%).

FIGURE 5

Aboriginal and non-Aboriginal population older than 15 with less than grade 9, Canada, 1986

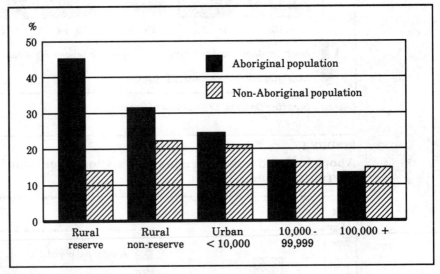

Source: Statistics Canada. 1986 Census of Population.

Nearly 14% of rural on-reserve Aboriginals had trades or other postsecondary, non-university schooling (Figure 6) while only about 1% had a university degree (Figure 7). In other areas, the percentage of Aboriginals with trades and other non-university schooling rises from 19% in rural non-reserve areas to almost 27% in urban areas of 100,000 or larger. The percentage of Aboriginals with a university degree also increases from just over 2% in rural non-reserve areas to over 6% in the largest urban areas. However, the percentage of non-Aboriginals with university degrees is at least double that of Aboriginals in all rural and urban areas.

FIGURE 6

Aboriginal and non-Aboriginal population older than 15 with trades and other non-university training, Canada, 1986

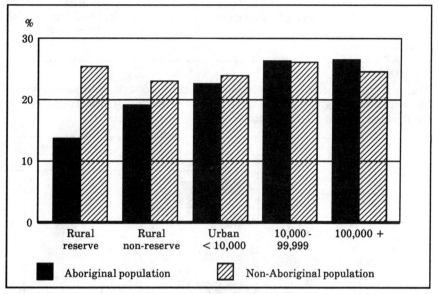

Source: Statistics Canada. 1986 Census of Population.

FIGURE 7

Aboriginal and non-Aboriginal population older than 15 with university degree, Canada, 1986

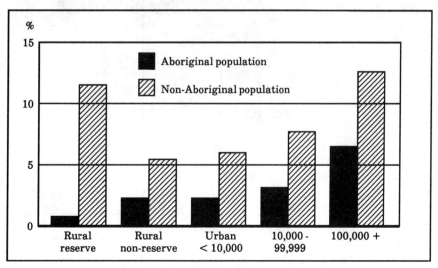

Source: Statistics Canada. 1986 Census of Population.

As government program responsibilities are acquired by Aboriginal communities, and in particular, by Indian communities, they will need the skill pool or human resources to manage these programs. About 18% of Aboriginals with postsecondary qualifications concentrated in the business field (commerce, management and business administration) compared to 23% in the general population of Canada. Only 6% of on-reserve Aboriginals studied in health professions compared to 12% in the general population (Figure 8).

FIGURE 8

Major field of study for persons older than 15 with postsecondary qualifications: comparison of the Aboriginal population on-reserve and the total population, Canada, 1986

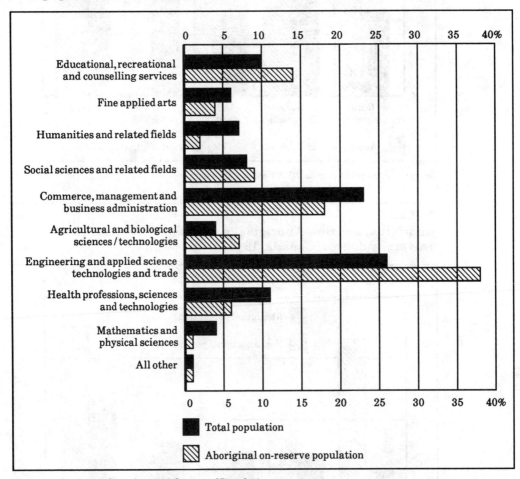

Source: Statistics Canada. 1986 Census of Population.

The heaviest concentration among on-reserve Aboriginals with post-secondary qualifications is in applied technologies and trades (38%).

7.   Employment by industry

Across all geographic areas, the Aboriginal population seems
concentrated in the tertiary sector which includes employment in the
service industries, government services (such as community and Indian
band councils), communications, and health and social services among
others (Figure 9).

FIGURE 9

Aboriginal population older than 15, by industry, Canada, 1986

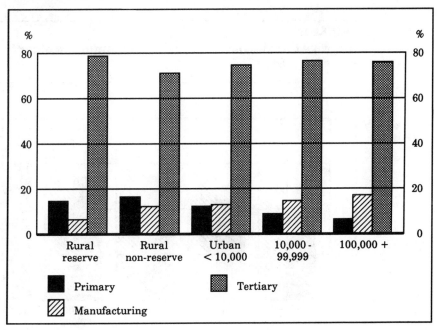

Source: *Statistics Canada. 1986 Census of Population.*

Involvement in the primary and manufacturing sectors is significantly
lower. For example, about 15% of the Aboriginal labour force on rural
Indian reserves is engaged in the primary sector comprised of hunting,
fishing, trapping, farming, logging and mining industries. However,
this figure does not reflect the Aboriginal people who hunt, fish and trap
for subsistance or as part of their traditional activities.

8.   Income characteristics

The average income of Aboriginals living in all geographic areas is lower than non-Aboriginals in those areas (Figure 10). On rural Indian reserves the average income in 1986 was just over $9,000 per year from all sources (including transfer payments). In middle-sized urban areas the average income among Aboriginals was $13,500 per year, rising to about $14,700 in the largest urban areas. However, the gap in the average income between Aboriginals and non-Aboriginals living in urban areas was greatest in urban areas with 100,000 population and over.

FIGURE 10

Average total income of Aboriginal population older than 15, Canada, 1986

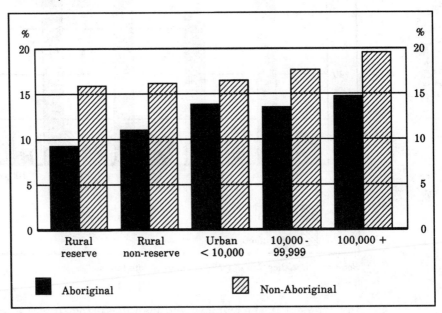

Source: *Statistics Canada. 1986 Census of Population.*

9.   Conclusion

In conclusion, these major demographic, social, and economic characteristics indicate that Aboriginal peoples still lag behind the non-Aboriginal population. The gap is more pronounced in rural Indian reserves and in other rural areas of Canada compared to urban areas. The 1991 Census and a postcensal Aboriginal Peoples Survey (scheduled for September, 1991) should allow for greater insight into Aboriginal conditions across Canada. The census information will show how conditions have changed over time and whether the gap between Aboriginal and non-Aboriginal conditions has closed. The Aboriginal Peoples Survey will provide a broader range of information on social, health, cultural, schooling, economic and housing issues facing Aboriginal peoples on and off reserves.

Andrew J. Siggner
Aboriginal Data Unit
Statistics Canada
Ottawa, Ontario K1A 0T6

References

Norris, M. J. 1988. The demography of Aboriginal people in Canada, (revised February, 1989). Paper presented to the National Symposium on Demography of Immigrant, Racial and Ethnic Groups in Canada. Winnipeg: August 26-27 .

Statistics Canada. 1989. A Data Book on Canada's Aboriginal Population from the 1986 Census of Canada. Ottawa: Statistics Canada, Aboriginal Data Unit.

Statistics Canada. 1990. A Profile of the Aboriginal Population Residing in Selected Off Reserve Areas, 1986 Census. Volumes 1 and 2. Ottawa: Statistics Canada, Aboriginal Data Unit.

Trinity, Newfoundland

20

Small-area, socio-economic profiles: a case study of Fogo Island, Newfoundland

Ken Donnelly

Summary

Although Fogo Island is performing up to the provincial and national standards of quality of life, it is weak in the employment and income sub-indices. These factors are probably related to the single-industry or single-resource dependency structure of its economy and are less severe than the data indicate because of the presumed lower costs of living.

Numbers and averages alone cannot give an accurate portrait of the island. Many hard-to-measure factors must be added to the equation. On Fogo Island, the way of life of the community rather than inputs and outputs determines its socio-economic strengths and weakness. Data are important but they tell only a partial story.

Table of contents

Small-area, socio-economic profiles: a case study of Fogo Island, Newfoundland

Ken Donnelly

1.   Introduction

To prepare for and adjust to major economic change, communities need to identify and assess information to initiate long-term economic planning.   The report, "Canada's Single Industry Communities: A Search for a New Partnership" (Canada Employment and Immigration Advisory Council 1988) recommended that the federal government assist in identifying information for economic planning.

To meet this objective, the federal government helped to produce a **Small Area Data Guide,** described in Appendix 1. This paper will use the **Guide** to prepare a socio-economic profile of Fogo Island, Newfoundland.

Fogo Island is situated off the northeastern coast of Newfoundland. An assessment of socio-economic strengths and weaknesses may assist the Gander Community Futures Group and the residents of Fogo Island to form and direct their development.

2.   Demography

Although Fogo Island has been settled for almost 300 years, the population has increased little during this time (Table 1). The increase is certainly small (3.8%) compared to the natural population increase of the second quarter of the twentieth century where population growth in Newfoundland and Labrador was 43%.

TABLE 1

Comparison of population growth rates of Fogo Island and
Newfoundland and Labrador, 1874-1986

	Newfoundland and Labrador	Percent growth	Fogo Island	Percent growth
1874	161,374		3,500	
1935	289,588	79.5	3,970	13.4
1956	415,074	43.3	4,120	3.8
1961	457,853	10.3	4,470	8.5
1976	557,725	21.8	3,851	-13.8
1981	567,681	1.8	4,028	4.6
1986	568,349	0.1	4,201	4.3

Sources: Dewitt (1969: 6).

Historical Statistics of Newfoundland and Labrador (1988: A-1).

Roy and Lambert (1980: 5).

Statistics Canada. (cat. no. 94-102).

Of particular interest is the difference in growth rates during the 1960s
and the first half of the 1970s. During this time, Fogo Island faced the
prospect of resettlement and began its co-operative. Newfoundland's
population grew 22% between 1961 and 1976—quite surprisingly in
light of the stories of a failing fishery and the mass migration westward.
Fogo Island's population, however, declined by 14% during these years
of change—likely a result of voluntary resettlement.

Recent figures show a reversal in historical trends. Census data show
that Fogo Island's growth rate was higher than the Province's in the
1980s. Between 1976 and 1981, Fogo Island's population grew 4.6% to
4,028 people and by 1986, it grew 4.3% to 4,201 people. In comparison,
the Province's growth rate was only 1.8% during 1976-1981 and 0.1%
during 1981-1986.

Historically, most communities on Fogo Island had one predominant
religion, as did most Newfoundland outports. This arose from the
settlement patterns (small bays and inlets were settled by people
originating from the same area of Europe, often of the same family) and
was perpetuated by natural geographic isolation and, until recently, a
lack of adequate physical infrastructure. Many of these single-religion
communities remain today. A notable example is the Community of
Tilting which is predominantly Catholic (Table 2).

TABLE 2

Distribution of population by religious affiliation, 1981

	Catholic	United church	Anglican	Other protestant	Other
			Percent		
Fogo	32	20	49	5	1
Jba	29	13	48	4	0
Seldom	0	42	32	26	0
Tilting	99	0	1	0	0
Other	24	18	43	10	0
Fogo Island (subtotal)	32	19	40	8	0
Newfoundland and Labrador	36	18	27	17	1
Canada	47	15	10	15	11

Source: Statistics Canada. (cat. no. 93-x-937).

3.   Socio-economic indicators

The average incomes on Fogo Island are lower than the provincial averages and significantly lower than the national averages both for males and females (Table 3). Family incomes are also lower; over 50% of families have incomes of less than $20,000, and very few families report incomes of more than $50,000 a year. However, incomes in traditional communities such as Fogo Island cannot be compared in dollar terms to other areas because of the differential factors of lifestyles, customs and traditions.

TABLE 3

Average income of individuals and families, 1986

	Individuals with income			Percent with family income	
	Males	Females	Family	< $20,000	>$50,000
Fogo	14,640	7,566	24,783	51	6
Jba	10,946	7,687	19,382	68	5
Seldom	12,786	5,061	18,911	63	4
Tilting	8,824	7,431	24,509	47	5
Other	11,508	5,748	19,159	54	3
Newfoundland Labrador	**17,582**	**9,876**	**28,880**	**40**	**12**
Canada	**23,265**	**12,615**	**37,827**	**26**	**24**

Source: Statistics Canada. (cat. no. 94-102).

Most Fogo Islanders build their homes and do most of their own maintenance and repairs. As well, most people harvest and burn firewood for fuel, provide some of their food through hunting, fishing, gathering berries and growing garden plots and participate in the informal economy (bartering goods and services among neighbours). Consequently, it costs less cash to live on Fogo Island than in the rest of Canada or in many of the urban areas of Newfoundland.

Fogo Island's unemployment rate is significantly higher than the Newfoundland average and almost four times the Canadian average (Table 4). The high unemployment rate reflects the economy's reliance on a single resource industry. The percentage of the labour force that is female on Fogo Island is only slightly lower than elsewhere in Canada.

TABLE 4
Labour force characteristics, 1986

	Fogo Island	Newfoundland and Labrador	Canada
Males			
Number in labour force	1,020	145,575	7,441,170
Percent of labour force	62	59	57
Unemployment rate	36	25	9
Females			
Number in labour force	635	101,520	5,608,690
Percent of labour force	38	41	43
Unemployment rate	44	27	11

Source: Statistics Canada. (cat. no. 94-102).

4. Performance indicators

To analyze Fogo's socio-economic strengths and weaknesses, we adopt a method proposed by Lamontagne and Tremblay (1989). They analyzed 54 different socio-economic indicators grouped into four indices: performance, capacity, vitality and policies. Together these indices give comparative socio-economic strengths and weaknesses by answering the following questions:

1   is the economy doing a good job of providing the region's inhabitants with opportunities for a better life (example: job security)?

2   are the enterprises located in the region vital to its growth and survival?

3   what is the economy's capacity to sustain growth and expand opportunities?

4   what local initiatives have been taken to encourage socio-economic growth and development?

Some indicators were inappropriate for the Fogo Island study. The entire vitality index, for example, reflects the importance of entrepreneurship in small and medium business which is not valid for a small single industry area such as Fogo. Only 22 of the 54 indicators are suitable.

However, these indicators were sufficient for a reasonable analysis of Fogo Island's socio-economic strengths and weaknesses. Because of space limitations, I have picked the performance index to illustrate this study's work. The performance index measures the residents' opportunity to better their living and working conditions. It combines the more traditional indicators of employment and income with the sub-indices of equity and quality of life.

Fogo Island has a consistently poor showing in employment (Table 5). The high unemployment rate and the decline in employment may be the result of a non-diversified economy and the fishing industry crisis.

TABLE 5

Performance index: employment

		Fogo Island	Newfoundland and Labrador	Canada
Employment growth, 1981-1986				
Number of jobs		-110	-2,920	534,300
Growth rate	(%)	-9.9	-1.6	4.8
Participation rate, 1986				
	(%)	55.4	59.2	66.5
Unemployment rate, 1986				
	(%)	39.3	25.6	10.3

Source: Statistics Canada. (cat. no. 94-102 and 93-x-937).

The participation rate is the ratio between the size of the labour force and the size of the population eligible to work. The lower rate on Fogo Island shows that a higher percentage of those who could work are not even looking for work. The low participation rates could result from feelings of helplessness and despair or from women deciding not to enter the workforce—a common practice among more traditional, rural communities.

The income indicators show Fogo Island well under the provincial and national averages (Table 6). This may be attributed to the lower cost of living on Fogo Island based on lifestyles and the importance of the informal economy. Despite its poor performance on the income index, Fogo Island appears to be prosperous; houses are well-kept and contain all of the modern conveniences. Most Islanders own late model cars or pick-ups, and personal effects such as clothing and furniture are generally new and of considerable quality. Thus, it is apparently possible to live well on less money on Fogo Island.

TABLE 6

Performance index: income

	Fogo Island	Newfoundland and Labrador	Canada
Earned income per capita, 1986			
($)	5,697	8,234	12,303
Income growth, 1981-1986			
($)	1,538	2,588	3,865
(%)	37.0	45.8	45.8
Percent with family income < $20,000			
(%)	58.2	39.8	25.6
Percent of families on social assistance, July, 1990			
(%)	14.4	16.0	N/A
Percent of families with low incomes, 1986			
(%)	26.8	21.5	14.3

Source: Statistics Canada. (cat. no. 94-102 and 93-x-937).

Fogo Island's results for the quality of life index are consistent with those for Newfoundland and Canada (Table 7). The number of social workers per capita is slightly higher on Fogo Island, but this probably results from geography rather than caseload. Similarly, the amenities capacity index shows Fogo Island with more doctors but fewer hospital beds and few hospital employees per capita compared to the provincial average (Table 8).

TABLE 7

Performance index: quality of life

	Fogo Island	Newfoundland and Labrador	Canada
Infant mortality rate, 1986 (%)	.00	.85	.79
Number of social workers per capita, 1988	.05	.03	.04

Sources: Statistics Canada. (cat. no. 84-542).

Health and Welfare Canada. 1990.

TABLE 8

Capacity index: amenities

	Fogo Island	Newfoundland and Labrador	Canada
Physicians per 1,000 residents, 1988	.70	.16	2.00
Hospital employees per 1,000 residents, 1985	10	16	12
Hospital beds per 1,000 residents, 1985	4	6	7
Number of libraries per 1,000 residents, 1987	.24	.19	.25
Number of movie theatres per 1,000 residents, 1987	.00	.03	.03

Sources: Statistics Canada. (cat. no. 82-232, 87-204, 87-205).

Health and Welfare Canada. 1990.

5.   Summary

The performance index shows that although Fogo Island is performing at the provincial and national standard of quality of life, it is weak in the employment and income sub-indices. These factors are probably related to the single-industry, single-resource structure of its economy and are less severe than the data indicate because of the presumed lower costs of living.

Often the reality of Fogo Island is such that numbers and averages alone cannot give an accurate portrait. Many hard to measure factors must be added to the equation. On Fogo Island, the total way of life of all the community members rather than inputs and outputs determines its socio-economic strengths and weakness. Data are important but they can only tell a partial story. Finally, many of the indicators in the Lamontagne and Tremblay study are not suitable for small resource-based areas.

Ken Donnelly
Labour Market Services
Employment and Immigration Canada
Ottawa, K1A 0J9

References

Dawe, Shirley P. 1990. Fogo Island, Newfoundland: A Portrait of
the Island and its People. A paper prepared for Employment and
Immigration Canada.

Dewitt, Robert L. 1969. Public Policy and Community Protest:
The Fogo Case Study. Newfoundland Social and Economic
Studies, No. 8. St. John's, Newfoundland: Memorial University of
Newfoundland, Institute of Social and Economic Research,

Canada Employment and Immigration Advisory Council. 1988.
Canada's Single Industry Communities: A Search for a New
Partnership. Ottawa: Supply and Services Canada.

Health and Welfare Canada. 1990. Health Personnel in Canada:
1988. Ottawa: Supply and Services Canada.

ICURR (Intergovernmental Committee on Urban and Regional
Research). 1991. Small Area Data Guide. Toronto: ICURR.

Lamontagne, Francois and Christyne Tremblay. 1989.
Development Indices: A Québec Regional Comparison. Local
Development Paper No. 14. Ottawa: Economic Council of Canada.

Newfoundland. 1988. Historical Statistics of Newfoundland and
Labrador. St. John's: Newfoundland Statistics Agency.

Newfoundland. 1989. Annual Survey of Development Associations:
1987 - 1988. St. John's: Department of Development.

Newfoundland. 1990. Education Statistics: Elementary - Secondary.
St. John's: Department of Education.

Roy, Michael A. and Raymond A. Lambert. 1980. Forest Resource
Inventory: Fogo Island, Newfoundland. St. John's: The Atlantic
Centre of the Environment in co-operation with the Extension
Service, Memorial University of Newfoundland and the
Newfoundland Department of Forestry.

Statistics Canada. 1983. Census Divisions and Subdivisions:
Selected Social and Economic Characteristics, (cat. no. 93-x- 937).
Ottawa: Statistics Canada.

Statistics Canada. 1987. Hospital Annual Statistics: 1984 - 1985,
(cat. no. 83-232). Ottawa: Statistics Canada.

Statistics Canada. 1987. Census Divisions and Subdivisions:
Newfoundland, Part 1, (cat. no. 94-101). In the 1986 Census of
Population Series. Ottawa: Statistics Canada.

Statistics Canada. 1988. Census Divisions and Subdivisions:
Newfoundland, Part 2,(cat. no. 94-102). In the 1986 Census of
Population Series. Ottawa: Statistics Canada.

Statistics Canada. 1988. Principle Vital Statistics by Local Areas,
(cat. no. 84-542). Ottawa: Statistics Canada.

Statistics Canada. 1989. Work Injuries: 1986 - 1988,
(cat. no. 72-208). Ottawa: Statistics Canada.

Statistics Canada. 1990a. Public Libraries in Canada: 1987,
(cat. no. 87-205). Ottawa: Statistics Canada.

Statistics Canada. 1990b. Film and Video in Canada: 1987 - 1988,
(cat. no. 87-204). Ottawa: Statistics Canada.

Appendix 1

Small Area Data Guide

Why the guide?

The **Small Area Data Guide** (ICURR 1991) is in part, a response to the report on "Canada's Single Industry Communities: A Search for a New Partnership" (Canada Employment and Immigration Advisory Council 1988). The report focused on the need for small communities, specifically those whose economic livelihood is dependent on one major industry, to prepare for and adjust to major economic change. One of the key recommendations of the report was that the federal government provide assistance to these communities in identifying and accessing information to initiate long-term economic planning.

After careful consideration as to the best means of providing this assistance, Employment and Immigration Canada established a Steering Committee composed of representatives from the Canadian Association of Single Industry Towns, the Canadian Federation of Independent Business, the Federation of Canadian Municipalities, and the Industrial Developers Association of Canada to develop the **Small Area Data Guide.** The Committee contracted the work to the Communications Division of Statistics Canada. The team leader was Victoria Crompton.

To ensure that the **Guide** would meet the needs, not only of small communities but of a variety of other potential users as well, the Committee carried out a comprehensive user consultation program to determine the scope and format of the **Guide**. Included in this consultation process were municipal, provincial and federal government departments, educators, librarians and the private sector users such as the Chambers of Commerce.

Principal function

The **Small Area Data Guide** is not a database. It was developed to fulfil two principal functions:

i.   to help you quickly and easily identify what types of statistical data are available for different geographic areas within each province and territory; and

ii. to direct you to where you can actually access the data you need.

Format

The **Guide** is a single publication with chapters for each province and territory. Federal and provincial/territorial data sources are integrated in each chapter.

This integration of federal and provincial data sources for each province and territory is, we feel, the most "user-friendly" presentation. At the same time, having all provinces and territories under one cover makes it easy for the user to access information from other provinces as well.

The **Guide** will also be available on diskette.

The data sources

The **Small Area Data Guide** indexes subprovincial sources of statistical data from the federal and provincial/territorial governments that are publicly available, whether in published or unpublished format. As a rule, only the primary data sources, those responsible for producing the data, are cited in the **Guide**. In some instances, therefore, there may be additional, or secondary, sources for the data that are not cited. Appendix A of the **Guide** has samples of data sources generated by municipalities themselves. There are no references to private sector data sources.

Geography

The first thing you must do is determine the geographic area that you wish to look up. If you are unfamiliar with the geographic levels in the **Guide**, Part II of the Introduction provides a glossary of terms and abbreviations for your reference.

The next step is to identify which geographic levels you want. If you are researching a specific municipality such as Yorkton, Saskatchewan, you will begin with the section on municipalities, which provides data sources available for all incorporated cities, towns, villages, Aboriginal territories and settlements. If you are unsure whether a municipality is incorporated, you can quickly consult the alphabetic listing of municipalities in Part IV of the Introduction.

In addition to the section on municipalities, you may also want to consult the section on census divisions which may provide you with some additional data sources, aggregated for the entire census division of which the municipality is part. Similarly, for municipalities that are components of larger urban areas (e.g. Saint Boniface, Manitoba), either census agglomerations (CA) or census metropolitan areas (CMA) (e.g. Winnipeg), even more data sources may be available. To determine whether a particular municipality falls within one of these larger urban areas, check the list of CMAs and CAs and their component municipalities in Part IV.

If you are interested in data sources for areas within a municipality, neighbourhood or market area, you can refer to the sections on enumeration areas, postal areas and census tracts for key sources of submunicipal data. The annotated listing of geographic reference documents in Part IV will direct you to the necessary sources for maps and other reference tools.

If the area you are researching is an unincorporated place or place name, data sources may still be available. You will need to identify the specific postal areas, enumeration areas or census tracts for your area of interest and track the data sources for those geographic levels. For assistance, consult the listing of geographic reference documents in Part IV.

Variables

Now that you have found the geographical level, what kind of data sources are available? The data sources are ordered alphabetically by variable or type of data. For each variable six essential fields of information are provided:

1. **Source:** the name of the government department or ministry that produces the data;

2. **Title:** the title of the document or data base which contains the data;

3. **Format:** whether the data is available in a publication, from a data base, or in some other form.

4. **Frequency:** how often the data is updated e.g. annually, quarterly, monthly;

5. **Contact:** who to contact for more specific information about the data or about accessing the data; and

6. **Special notes:** additional information about the data or its geographic availability.

21

The economics of rural-urban integration: a synthesis of policy issues

L.P. Apedaile

Summary

The debate over sustainable rural economies and subsidies to rural enterprises of agriculture, fishing, mining and forestry and to rural governments and institutions is a debate over the validity of a separate rural rationale for income redistribution. The focused issue is efficiency of the rural system to achieve a purpose. But the larger issue is the social willingness to pay for the goods and services produced by rural enterprises based on an ongoing judgement of their importance in both the public and the private interest and on the social standards for well-being of all citizens, both rural and urban, in a nation.

The fundamental roots of rural economies require that rural households be continuously cross-subsidized with non-resource employment income, or with income transfers to the rural system from the urban system.

A means of determining prices for rural goods and services possessing the status of public good, produced in the national interest, would go a long way to resolving problems of rural income distributions and subsidies.

As long as countries set standards for the social and economic well-being of rural people, and have the political will to redistribute income and wealth, rural areas will require different income transfer programs than urban households or corporations.

Prince Albert, Saskatchewan

The economics of rural-urban integration: a synthesis of policy issues[1]

L.P. Apedaile

"Ever since the dawn of civilization, people have not been content to see events as unconnected and inexplicable. They have craved an understanding of the underlying order in the world." (Stephen Hocking 1988)

Does rural matter?

A growing body of evidence indicates that rural and urban economic systems are integrating (Fuller et al. 1990). Past dependency of urban growth upon the rural hinterland may have been reversing for several decades (Beckman 1970). The commerce of rural towns is becoming largely disassociated from their agricultural economy (Stabler 1985; Lerohl et al. 1989). Farm family incomes are similar to urban family incomes (Bollman and Smith 1987). Agriculture is a minor economic activity in rural places (Fuller et al. 1990). All evidence points to substantive changes in the rural economic system over the post war decades (Federal/Provincial Rural Development Committee 1990).

The rural economic system fulfils national and global purpose as well as its own. The system is complex and organic. It produces the basic ingredients for such staples as food manufacturing, metals, electricity, fuel and paper. The rural system also produces public goods including national defence, the rural domain and management of the ecosphere for future generations. Other outputs such as cereals may possess the dual identities of private and public goods. Rural products have been viewed through history as a base for influence in world affairs and a source of political stability within countries.

---

1. The author wishes to acknowledge the contribution of Le Laboratoire d'Études Comparées de Systèmes Agraires, Le Département de Systèmes Agraires et de Développement, L'Institut National de la Recherche Agronomique, all at Montpellier; Department of Rural Economy, University of Alberta; the helpful insight of Steven Schilizzi, Wictor Adamowicz, Dhara Gill, Craig McKie and Pierre Osty; and to Ray Bollman for his stimulating critique of the logical arguments.

The consequent problem for rural places is that their output is perceived as being subject to market forces when in reality a substantive portion of that output may be regarded as a public good. Valuation of public goods depends on political processes to determine their prices. Trying to force public goods through private markets as the basis for rural factor incomes may account for many of the rural policy contradictions and the consequences in rural places.

Consider three fundamental points. Rural economic improvements are only possible when producing things which are valued. Second, the rural economic system is an aggregation of systems and is only a part of a global system made up of the national and international economies. Third, closing the rural system with political actions such as stabilization programs, safety nets and restrictive trade practices that are incompatible with efficiency criteria inhibits the rural system's ability to achieve its purposes. Upon these three points rest the solutions and opportunities in rural development problems.

Arguments follow that the action-feedback relationship of rural activities and functions relative to those outside the rural system create development problems unique to the rural economy. It is further argued that the milieu of the rural system contains norms of behaviour, memory, technology and learning distinct from those of urban systems. The underlying malaise of rural life is the sense of disorder and lack of understanding about where events are leading people. The heterogeneity of values generated by the integration of rural and urban system milieus conflicts with longstanding features of the rural system, contributing to disorder and uncertainty.

The paper begins with a systems model of the rural economy as a framework for exploring the nature of rural economic realities. Sections follow to cast the notions of rural well-being and of rural inputs markets into this framework and to propose further consideration of institutional pricing, markets, structural change, terms of trade, consumer behaviour and capital formation. The next section is included to underscore the fundamental requirement that rural economic life depends on producing goods and services which are saleable at prices which cover costs and provide a standard of living that matches the vision of rural people. The paper then offers some observations about the expectations for rural policy from a rural point of view on rural-urban integration. The paper ends with guidelines to reduce the dependency of rural economies on policies which distort markets for their products.

A rural systems model

The systems framework

The rural economic system may be modelled in a purposeful organic systems framework (Anderson et al. 1988; Arthur 1990; Hirschleifer 1978). It consists of activities, performing functions which achieve certain purposes. The system is self-regulated by system decision units (SDUs). These SDUs are both empowered and constrained by the system milieu. This milieu is the collection of rules and regulations, written and unwritten, which govern the behaviour of the system. The milieu contains the memory of historical events and emotions, the technologies and know-how, the learning processes at work for the system and the vision of the future held collectively within the system. The system has a boundary to distinguish events where the SDUs have control and where neighbouring systems have control. The neighbouring systems constitute the environment of the system. The environment includes parts of the biosphere and other ecospheric systems as well as human systems (Figure 1).

FIGURE 1

Holistic framework for rural economic system synthesis

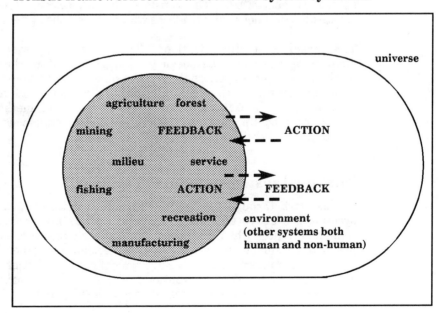

The rural system is part of an aggregation of systems, just as it also includes other systems. The actual definition and separation of the rural system within the aggregation is determined by the problem at hand. In this paper the boundary definition is broad because the complexity of the rural aggregation of systems is at issue. It is no longer sufficient to be a proficient cattleman, a skilled grain grower, an efficient sawmill operator or to provide top quality servicing of equipment, health or commercial needs in rural places. Marketing and political skills, personnel management, safety awareness, financial structuring and global understanding are some of the complexities in the opening rural systems of today.

The rural system relates to its environment through direct and indirect actions and feedbacks originating within the system and its environment. The actions and feedbacks do not appear to be mechanical; but rather, organic and process driven. Thus the system is in co-evolution with its urban and other systems in its environment (Le Moigne 1983). Actions and feedbacks work through flows of energy or energy proxies, acting in response to economic, political and social signals such as prices, sanctions and rewards.

There is considerable debate, of course, about the role of governments and markets in achieving order and stability in this process. Varying perceptions of driving forces are the source of debate. They lead to ideological premises for models of rural development. The systems model attempts to put ideology aside. The model identifies technology, purpose of the system, the environment and democracy, as the four powerful influences on the rural economy, whether internally or externally generated. The constant flux in actions and feedbacks constitutes the checks and balances which control the system.

The model is a simplification. The most usual way of further simplifying the model has been to disaggregate it in the manner of disciplinary science. Alternatively, the model may be made simpler by assuming linear mechanical relationships/responses to actions and feedbacks, or by excluding time. These issues of method and the theoretical modelling of rural systems are addressed in a separate work (Apedaile and Schilizzi 1991).

The rural system as a human system

Let us work through the model with added detail. Rural economic systems are above all, human systems. They are characterized by human activities which transform natural resources into intermediate products for further processing by other economic systems. Forestry, agriculture, mining and fishing are typical rural activities. These are carried out by human interventions in the ecosphere, principally the biosphere. Humans are an integral part of the biosphere.

These activities contribute to the multiple human purposes of the system and to the operational needs of the system. In the first category of purposes are Descarte's primary qualities of human intentionality, namely income and wealth, security and self-worth, quality and meaning of life. In colloquial terms, these reduce to three purposes: providing food, fibre and other primary goods; providing social and economic well-being for rural inhabitants; and managing the ecosphere for the benefit of future generations (Apedaile and Schilizzi 1991). Their rankings may differ over time and according to whether the point of view is internal or external. The second category of purposes are more technical. They include stability and order of the system, vitality, flexibility in co-evolution with the environment, and survival of the system. The functions of the system include control and self-regulation, development and selectivity in response to environmental signals and forces.

The concept of system decision units [SDUs] is used to reflect the breadth and variety of rural decision-making. For example, SDUs include farms, other firms, households and their various institutional aggregations such as unions, chambers of commerce, commodity associations, churches, municipal councils and sports teams.

Rural SDUs are a reflection of their milieu. The rural milieu is composed of cultural practices rooted in agrarian tradition, and a moral and ethical consensus about acceptable behaviour by SDUs. Historical experience, such as the great depression, constrains behaviour. Technological knowledge and technical know-how enables expansionary behaviour. The collective vision of the future held by the system participants stimulates creative behaviour. The integration of the rural and urban milieus confuses the guidelines for rural behaviour by blurring the ground rules for change itself.

The rules and expectations regarding the processes of change in the milieu, apply to learning, amending consensus, sanctioning deviations from the norms, redesignating priorities and revising the purpose and objectives of the system. These processes are normally under the control of the rural system and thus are to be distinguished from those of other systems in its environment. Nevertheless, the milieu, like the system itself, is to varying degrees subject to the milieus of other systems in various hierarchical configurations such as those which enact national laws and enter into international accords.

Features of the rural economic system

The fundamental function of a rural economic system is to generate value-added from its resources, in either households or larger firms. The combination of labour, land and equipment is the source of improved standards of rural living and for achieving other economic purposes in the system. The outputs of the activities chosen to fulfil this function must be valued, that is, they must satisfy a demand or need for which people are willing to pay.

The rural economic system is composed of the same economic activities and functions as other economic systems. These are production, allocation, distribution of earnings, investment, savings, consumption and capital formation. The system also redistributes earnings by post-market actions often carried out by families and other rural social institutions. Governments also redistribute rural earnings through regulations, pricing, unemployment insurance, grants to companies, social assistance, health care, taxes and subsidies.

The unique rural context of these activities may be summarized in the following seven features of the rural economic system. These are grouped as features of the system, features of the boundary between the system and other systems and features of the environment.

- System feature: dependence on the ecosphere, and the significant proportion of intermediate natural resource [ecosphere] based goods in the private product mix.

- System feature: the structure of earnings relating rents, capital earnings, wages and profits.

- System feature: the significant proportion of public [unpriced] goods in the product mix, and the possibility that a single good such as wheat may embody both a priced private component and an unpriced public component.

- System feature: the cost structure of production typified by extended technological economies of size for industrial manufacturing and diseconomies for artisan enterprises including much of agriculture and fishing.

- Boundary feature: the significant transfer costs which distance the rural economy from markets and political institutions and therefore, from participation in price and policy determination.

- Boundary feature: monopsonistic tendencies in many commodity market structures.

- Environment feature: global substitution of industrial goods for natural resources into production processes including displacement of labour, synthetic vegetable oils and sweeteners, and synthetic fibres and coverings.

These seven economic features are the underlying realities of the rural economy responsible for day-to-day symptomatic realities. These features are responsible for endemic economic weakness and instability in the rural economic system. Development of the rural system requires that these features and the relationships among them be addressed. However, the lack of understanding of the whole system and the consequent lack of attention to the complexity has instigated instead, urban to rural income transfers to bridge the shortfalls between achievement and purpose of the rural system. The distinct rural milieu has traditionally contained processes to cope with this weakness. When these processes are subjected to urban integration and income transfers, they may become less able to cope in the future. The perception of not being able to cope reinforces opportunism, and gives voice to demands for government assistance to rural economies.

Structure, well-being and markets: How they fit

predominance of natural resource-based production: a system feature

Rural economic systems for the most part remain resource-based. Resource-based economies are characterized by a secular decline of real prices, and supply and price instability (Boothe 1990). The renewable resource sectors of agriculture, forestry and fishing are subject to the uncertainty of the ecosphere not controlled by humans, such as the weather and insects. Industrial technology has intensified biospheric production processes to the known limits, in some cases, beyond the speed that habitat can regenerate. Thus over-fishing, timber clear-cutting and intensive cropping may be transforming once-renewable resources into irreversibly depleted resources.

The non-renewable resource sectors, such as mining, oil and gas, have always been temporary activities in the rural economic system. They offer no long term basis for sustaining the economy beyond the exhaustible supply of raw material or its technological usefulness. Only technological invention which enables reprocessing of waste material or delayed implementation of resource-saving technologies could extend the economic life of those sectors. Declining productivity as resource extraction moves on to marginal stocks leads to high cost uncompetitive enterprises and reduced output contributing to economic decline of rural systems. These sectors are joined in their decline by agriculture, forestry and fishing when their rate of resource extraction exceeds the rate of renewal.

Predominance of resource-based activities brings further vulnerability to the rural system as it integrates with urban systems. Urban concerns over the rural 'environment' (the ecosphere) are felt by farmers in industrialized countries. For example, in Europe changing regulations and new costs are being imposed on rural activities by urban interests. Pressure on agriculture is mounting so rapidly that a representative of Bretagne agriculture warns the public in an unusual advertisement for Le Monde, that without farmers nature's 'garden' would go to weeds (Rocher 1990). The new costs include deferred production, delayed approval of chemical inputs, restrictions on technical practices, and capital expenditures for pollution control devices. These costs occur in specific countries and therefore introduce unevenness within the global market. These costs hasten the global substitution of industrial facsimiles for wood fibre, animal and fish proteins, vegetable oils, metals and petroleum products. Public safety concerns have similar effects.

The structure of earnings: a system feature

The structure of earnings is the proportional share of outlays to equity holders from revenue, through payments or retentions for industrial inputs, wages, rents, capital earnings and profits. Earnings structure is often expressed in simpler terms as the ratio of residual claims on income relative to primary claims. Inputs requiring cash payment are primary claimants against earnings. Wages for employees and especially organized labour are also a primary claim on earnings. Conversely, wages in household economies for self-employed workers are a residual. Rents, returns to capital and profits are also residuals compressed between primary claimants and primary commodity prices. The distribution of earnings by source is one determinant of the rural income distribution by size and of rural-urban income differences. Income distributions are important determinants of economic growth in rural development.

The impact of earnings structure on future growth of rural economic enterprises is relayed through the ownership structure of inputs. The higher the debt to equity ratio with well developed capital markets, the greater may be the amount of capital controlled by rural SDUs. However the extent to which equity is alienated from rural enterprises is also greater as is the shift of the capital share of earnings out of the rural economy in the form of debt servicing. The other determining factors to the earnings structure are the proportion of factors in rural enterprises and their relative productivities.

Historically, rents and wages have been the two shares of rural earnings receiving the greatest attention by economists (Ricardo 1951). Rents are the reward for land and natural resource ownership. Wages are the reward for labour. The family farming system combines the two. Peasant farming systems usually involve separate land ownership and labour, even though labour may be organized in family units. Rents—from current earnings used to pay taxes and from capitalized future streams of earnings influencing property tax assessments—are the principal base for financing rural local government except in the case of poll taxes or local income taxes. The expectation of a continuing stream of rents is theoretically the basis for financing further land ownership and land improvements. The rural economy is weakened when rentiers such as retired farmers leave the rural community and other absentee landowners claim the rents from farm operators and spend these earnings on consumption or invest them in non-rural enterprises. Multinational resource extraction firms which extract the rent component of total earnings for urban or foreign investments or shareholder dividends also weaken the growth rate of rural economies.

The share of earnings attributable to capital formation, risk taking and management is the basis of financing new capital and technological advance, and preventing obsolescence. This share of earnings is an important incentive to entrepreneurial initiative and the willingness to accept risk in implementing new ideas and making investments. In subsistence parts of rural economies, less capital makes uncertainty more relevant than risk. In commercial industrialized agriculture, forestry, mining and fishing, the rewards to capital and risk accrue to the equity holders. As in the case of urban or foreign rentiers, urban and foreign equity holders may not reinvest in rural enterprises, and entrepreneurial initiative may not focus on rural growth opportunities when resources deplete or diversified corporate interests offer higher rates of return.

A restructuring of earnings occurs when the mix of factors in production activities changes and when the equity holders change their allegiance to non-rural economic interests. As rural enterprises industrialize, capital, industrial inputs and debt financing substitute for land and labour. Thus the wage and rent shares of total earnings are reduced. When both of these sources of earnings are combined in household firms, they are residual to those of other claimants and likely to be lower than the marginal value product of the labour and land in the rural enterprise. Rural economic systems tend to have higher proportions of household or family units than do urban systems. The consequence is weaker growth potential in rural places.

The restructuring of earnings affects family businesses more than it does other firms. The combined wages, rents, returns to capital and profits form the basis of household revenue and of resilience of family businesses to uncertainty arising within and outside the system. Resiliency is reduced as non-rural primary claims against earnings increase, especially when foreign government support programs and concessions on environmental issues drive commodity prices down.

The main disciplinary force driving technological advance, efficiency and productivity in rural enterprises is a technology which enables urban or foreign firms to sell their products at lower cost than rural firms. By choosing to retain traditional ways of farming, mainstreet business or grain handling, as examples, households and firms choose to accept reduced residuals as wages, rents, returns to equity capital and to risk-taking, as the cost of remaining competitive and staying in the market. Ironically, both progressive industrializing firms and those choosing slower technological paths of development are faced with restructured earnings; the former as a consequence of being progressive and the latter as a requirement of staying in business. However productivity gains, if captured in income, may allow progressive firms to maintain land and labour input levels.

The restructuring of rural earnings tend to contribute to the order of larger economic systems at the expense of instability and stagnation of rural economic systems. The earnings structure problem is a major reason for rural self-employed families to attempt to expand output as prices decline and to cross-subsidize enterprises with pluriactivity. The earnings structure problem is also one of the main reasons for interest in value added industry and diversification for rural development. As the proportion of earnings retained as a residual within the rural

408
The economics of rural-urban integration:
a synthesis of policy issues

economy diminishes, and the share of this residual attributable to agricultural wages increases, so economic flexibility is lost. The rural economy tends to revert from the Jeffersonian ideal of self-reliant firms owned and operated by rural people accumulating wealth, to the status of Chayanov's peasant economy where family enterprise is shaped by a balance between satisfaction of family needs from labour income and the drudgery of work (Chayanov 1986).

Public/private structure of output: a system feature

The output mix of private and public goods is undergoing restructuring. In Canada, agriculture was the lead sector in the settlement of most rural areas. However, an important consequence of agriculture was the strategic occupation and control of Aboriginal territory for economic gain and to ward off pressure from the United States. This settlement had the nature of a public good benefitting the nation, but the private cost was borne heavily by the Aboriginal peoples and by the homesteaders.

In contemporary times, private enterprise in rural systems continues to produce public goods such as countryside amenities to urban visitors, maintenance of the ecosphere and the social values outlined by Penn (Penn 1979). The costs of these goods and services are borne by rural tax bases, and depending on the particular assessment and rate structures in each area, by farmers and other owners of natural resources. There is little or no acceptable means to recover these costs from urban users of the amenities or from urban governments. Economic difficulties for rural economies increase as the tax base is restricted when public goods are underpriced in public income transfers and as public goods become an important component of the total output of rural economic systems relative to marketable products.

An interesting case arises when the same commodity produced in the rural economy has both private and public qualities. Suppose, for example, that wheat is valued as a political bargaining chip as well as a marketable commodity. Then part of the value of wheat to a nation derives from prevailing market forces and part from the strategic degrees of freedom it provides to government in both foreign and domestic policy.

A country that cannot feed itself, trade notwithstanding, is weak in a showdown and in the long run is sensitive to domestic instability and to fickle popular loyalty to its institutions. As evidence, consider the concessions to ideological norms in China's household responsibility reforms in the late 1970s in response to the domestic food crisis after the Cultural Revolution (Apedaile and Calkins 1989). Note the rapid dissolution of Soviet central power in 1990 as queues for food grew. Consider also the international political clout of the United States because of their export enhancement program employed in 1990 as a lever in the Uruguay round of the GATT negotiations and coincident with the Persian Gulf crisis, despite historically low world stocks of cereals.

One could argue, following this line of reasoning, that because it lacks an oil surplus to assist less developed countries hurt by rising oil prices, that it is in the U.S. national interest to induce farmers to maintain renewable cereal output as an alternative form of aid. Food and fuel are the two major claimants against foreign exchange for many of these countries. Higher oil prices place heavy demands upon delicate foreign exchange situations for countries already involved in difficult structural debt adjustments promoted in part by U.S. influence in the IMF and the World Bank. Surplus food gives the United States an opportunity to secure political support in the United Nations for its Gulf or other global policies. Wheat prices to U.S. farmers are supported in 1991 at about twice the Canadian level.

Food self-sufficiency in the narrow sense of food security and the broad sense of international bloc power also motivates European policy. The current ascendancy of public good status for wheat relative to its misleadingly more obvious status as a private good may be one reason for the margin over world prices that governments are willing to pay their wheat producers. Export subsidies and food aid in the form of wheat promote changes in tastes and preferences away from indigenous cereals in developing countries thereby generating dependence on industrialized wheat exporting countries. Governments of less developed countries which cannot afford to pay the public good value in cereals, often subsidize consumers to maintain political stability in urban places at the expense of their rural economies. The same governments often secure rural acquiescence to this policy with poor education, inadequate amenities, fragmentation of rural leadership, promotion of authoritarian religious fundamentalism and rural impoverishment through inequitable land tenure.

The dependency of rural economies on political processes to price their output increases with environmental concerns and with the long term decline in real market prices. Distinctly public rural output, with no private value, holds national importance, but principally for urban societies. This importance appears to be growing, placing increased value on maintaining the ecosphere and on assuring a pleasing rural countryside for recreation and leisure in regions with denser populations. The share of these public goods and services in the rural output mix appears to be increasing as the private value of goods such as agricultural and forest commodities stagnates or declines in the long run. Social pressure to extend production processes such as free range for animals and to reduce clear-cutting reinforce the effects on rural incomes of the secular decline of primary product prices in real terms.

The consequence of the increasing public good component of rural output is an increasing reliance on income transfers from urban sources to the rural system. The price for public 'amenities' produced by the rural economy is determined outside the rural system by political processes upon which rural SDUs have declining influence. A tendency toward public good status for rural outputs reduces the self-regulative capability of the rural system, serving to diminish the distinction between that system and the urban system.

Cost structure of production: a system feature

Long run economies of size appear to characterize production of natural resource commodities. This cost structure is typical of industrial processes. However, independent family firms may experience diminishing returns for several reasons. These firms specialize in artisan activities requiring several sequential time-sensitive technical processes. Family firms face apparent capacity constraints limited access to land, financing and management capability because they cannot or are not motivated to outbid other uses under prevailing policies and technologies. The reasons for diminishing returns also include the agrarian milieu. Social penalties on success, and thin, inefficient labour, capital and land markets also limit expansion of output and of pluriactivity to finance expansion. Lack of personnel management skills, and high transfer costs relative to those of urban or corporate competitors limit expansion of rural economic capacity and markets.

Consequently small firms are vulnerable to lower cost competition whenever technologies within their market area permit some firms to capture economies of size. The virtual disappearance of small dairies and cheese plants from rural places is an example. The only way for high cost firms to meet the competition is to shift their short run cost structure with its rapidly increasing marginal cost, down the long run industry cost curve while reducing the slope of its marginal cost. Such a shift requires all the characteristics of the professionalizing firm (Arkleton Trust 1989; Apedaile 1990). The shift to lower cost also requires more technical skill and new technology as witnessed by changes over the past decades in poultry, dairy, sawmill, grain handling and cattle feedlot operations. Vulnerability arising in the cost structures of rural firms is an outcome of technological advance.

Several features of technological change led Beckman, in a 1970 paper presented to the Canadian Council on Rural Development, to conclude that constant or increasing economies of size promote locational concentration of enterprises. By resorting to comparative statics, Beckman observes that dispersion of firms in space is only compatible with assumptions of perfect competition. Monopolistic competition or oligopolistic market structures emerge and dispersion is reduced when technology reduces transportation and variable costs. Firms tend to expand output and to seek additional market share to maximize profits by lowering prices. This behaviour contributes to overproduction and to supply-pressure in markets. The process takes into account the adoption of similar technology by competitors and is less sensitive to retaliation, the less concentrated the market.

Beckman's analysis addresses manufacturing firms. Natural resource firms have fewer options to differentiate products or expand market shares. Thus they are in a reactive posture to lower cost, labour saving or product changing technologies. Short run problems with higher fixed costs are associated with capital augmenting technologies (Beckman 1970). Faced with labour saving technologies, family firms face three options: underemployment, expansion of other fixed inputs such as land and machinery to use the fixed family labour base, or diversification of employment within the family firm or outside the family. In the case of cost reducing technology, family firms initially have to reduce their residual claim to revenue which triggers change or exit. Given the specialization of family resource-based firms in primary commodities or artisan products and the associated technologies, changing the form of the product is not usually an option.

The cost structure of transformation activities affects the development of the rural system through its influence on feedbacks among the parts of the system. Cost economies appear to be associated with substitution of inputs produced on specialized production lines for inputs fabricated in-house. Cost economies are also associated with indeterminate optimum levels of production and market volumes which periodically exceed demand, and greatly exceed the requirements of a single rural place let alone the needs of a single rural firm. As firms adopt cost reducing technologies and in the long run overcome other constraints on size, their feedbacks and actions with other parts of the rural economic system through economic multipliers diminish, reducing the dynamic coherence of the rural system. The system becomes increasingly integrated to urban systems progressively losing its self-regulating capability. Thus decisions to finance economic expansion and judgements on intergenerational trade-offs related to the exploitation of the ecosphere are less and less the domain of rural SDUs as they become increasingly subject to urban norms and visions.

Distance and remoteness: a boundary feature

The measure of remoteness of rural places is the transfer cost between rural SDUs and the geographical and institutional pricing points, for products used and produced in rural systems. These costs include transport, communications, storage, handling, product deterioration and transit damage, thin markets, deferred payments, verification, human relationship building and political influence. These costs reduce the competitive position of rural firms and depress the standard of living of rural households.

Transfer costs distort markets and reduce the mobility of the three principal inputs to rural development: labour, capital and financing. In cases where transfer costs actually separate the markets for these inputs geographically, rural factor markets may be so undeveloped that they fail to allocate resources within the rural economic system. Labour remains underemployed on farms or in households and capital assets deteriorate for lack of a market. Similarly, land, improvements and leases are difficult to trade. Pluriactivity by family firms is inhibited by poorly developed labour markets and the costs of displacement from home to work (Arkleton Trust 1989). Impeded mobility introduces inefficiency and reduced well-being into the rural system. Transfer costs tend to close the system thereby reducing its vitality.

Rural systems close as transfer costs increase because these costs impede transactions and generate inflexibility in the action/feedback responses of the rural system to events in its environment. Co-evolution is impeded. The rural system loses vitality with its incapability to respond to signals. The system also loses a degree of self-regulation as actions originating within its environment transform market and political signals into imposed forces requiring compliance by the rural SDUs.

Reduced transfer costs are the main source of advantage in economic agglomeration. Thus periurban rural systems have better growth and incomes than more distant rural places (Fuller et al. 1990). Governments and firms attempt to reduce transfer costs by upgrading roads, telecommunications, and by locating government regulatory agency offices in rural places. However often there are insufficient economic benefits to justify necessary and lumpy investments. Political justification may also be weakened by a heavy concentration of public benefits to a small proportion of the population. Thus investments in rural infrastructure often involve substantial financial transfers from middle and lower income urban tax payers to rural income elites, or the cross-subsidization of rural operations by companies, such as banks, from urban revenue.

Monopsonistic tendencies in commodity markets: a boundary feature

In his analysis of the impact of science and technical change on the location of economic activities, Beckman also emphasized the influence of prevailing market structure (Beckman 1970). Natural resource-based commodities beginning with agricultural commodities are produced by many firms and purchased by progressively fewer firms through a process of assembly, handling and transportation. By its very nature this assembly process is monopsonistic with fewer buyers at each stage reflecting the increasingly industrial nature of the technology used as the commodities move to final demand.

Each input is priced within its own market, such as diesel fuel for trains, enzymes for baking and cash registers for supermarkets. However the primary commodity in different physical forms in space and time is priced as a final good, with some exceptions, at the wholesale and retail levels. This pricing process extracts the residual value created by each lower assembly process and ultimately the primary production enterprise which is located in rural places. The same process in reverse works with consumer and intermediate goods coming in to rural places, extracting the full or greater than full marginal utility, in the case of consumer goods, or marginal value product for intermediate goods. In this manner, monopsonistic tendencies in primary commodity market structures exacerbate adverse terms of trade for rural primary products.

Adverse terms of trade reduce the ability of rural firms to finance technological advance thereby inhibiting modernization and access to economies of size relative to urban competitors. A persistent lag in technical and technological progress reinforces the income effect of declining terms of trade, particularly for self-employed family firms. Their short run in terms of fixed costs is longer than the short run of larger multiplant firms, especially transnationals. Transnationals can close or open production lines for multiproduct firms and plants in a shorter period than family and natural resource-based firms in response to global signals and forces. Alternatively when large firms are linked to natural resources through leases with governments, they can negotiate adjustments to address declining terms of trade. They may employ transfer pricing strategies to avoid taxation, subsidize losses, or to extract wealth which would otherwise be available for financing rural diversification.

The rural reality of monopsonistic tendencies in the assembly process for primary commodities appears to be enabled by technology and motivated by rent seeking. Any market concentration enables a degree of autonomy in price setting described as what the market will bear. When firms in rural space do possess market power, they are usually in a position to transfer the erstwhile benefits to urban centres from their rural sites. The progressive integration of rural economic systems with urban systems would not appear to change this reality for rural stakeholders unless these are shareholders in urban enterprise.

Global substitution of industrial for primary goods: an environment feature

The integration of the rural system with urban systems results, in part, from the technical and economic substitution of industrial goods for primary goods. Substituting urban behaviour norms relative to energy use is part of the integration. On a global scale, industrial components of production processes are slowly displacing natural resources. The consequent weakening of demand for natural resources helps to keep their prices low relative to other inputs.

The substitution of industrial edible oils, proteins and fibres for oilseeds, maize, soybeans, livestock products and forestry products may continue for some time. This substitution drives part of the structural change from small family firms specializing in natural resource goods to large corporate firms specializing in industrial goods. This economic restructuring advances the integration of rural and urban systems.

Rapid increases in the price of energy caused by international events
would reduce substitution of industrial goods for natural resource goods
because the price of industrial goods would increase relative to natural
resource goods. With present low real energy prices, industrial goods
are being substituted for natural resource goods.

In the long run increasing energy prices would spur the development of
alternative energy such as wind, solar, nuclear and fusion. These
energies cannot be made into food substitutes because they lack
hydrogen, carbon and nitrogen. Thus, in the event of a rapid
changeover to alternative energy sources for fuels before the depletion
of petroleum reserves, relatively cheap industrial substitutes for
proteins and fats in foods and for fibres could persist for some time.

It would seem that food energy, among all other private outputs of the
rural system, may be an exception to the substitution process. However
the price effect of substituting industrial goods for feed grains, and of
low cost healthy industrial fats, sweeteners and proteins for those
combined with high energy cereals in human diets could eventually
diminish the demand for grains.

Industrial processes, especially those implementing new product
technologies, have allowed urban places to grow without hinterlands in
the traditional sense (Fuller et al. 1990). This decoupling, or closure of
the urban system, resulted from trade and increased mobility of
financial services, management and information. All of these reduce
urban reliance on rural goods and services. Even television, videos,
commercial sport and groomed urban parks substitute for rural
recreation. Thus the urban economy not only displaces rural
commodities but becomes more independent of rural inputs and growth
as technical and industrial progress continues.

Rural-urban integration from the rural perspective

The rural perspective originates with rural SDUs and individuals. The
context is their sense of dependency and opportunism regarding the
imposition by non-rural systems, including government, of rules and
regulations upon their system milieu. Rural institutions such as farm
organizations, rural municipality and county councils, rural
electrification associations, chambers of commerce and political
constituencies, also hold an interest. These individuals and institutions
comprise the rural stakeholders. There are other stakeholders within
the systems environmental to the rural system.

From the rural perspective, social and economic well-being is
consistently ranked first among the three primary purposes of the rural
system. It is the principal motivation for SDUs. The seven distinctive
features of rural economies outlined earlier are perceived by rural
residents to jeopardize this well-being. Rural people and their
representatives focus their attention on this one of the three purposes,
their social and economic amenities, incomes and wealth.

Now however, urban stakeholders are recognizing that their interests in the other two purposes of sustainable production and sound management of the ecosphere may be in jeopardy from the public policies to achieve the rural social and economic objectives. There is also concern about the feedbacks by the rural economic system in response to actions originating in their environment. In particular, the long term secular reduction of rural resource rents and their extraction through uncompetitive market structures, may be promoting exploitation of the ecosphere by intensive industrial transformation technologies.

Equally important, but not well recognized, is the effect of integrating the rural and urban systems on the flexibility of the rural system as it relates to its environment. Flexibility to respond to ecospheric and economic shocks may be reduced by integration, in spite of increasing technical flexibility associated with the higher capital/labour ratios of industrial processes. The reason is reduced financial flexibility from high recurrent costs payable to primary non-rural claimants, and increasing proportions of fixed obligations in the cost structure. Since these circumstances are driven by the dual cost structure of sectors characterized by rural household enterprises, by technology and by the preoccupation of policy makers with income transfers, financing the technological advances contains elements of self defeat. Inflexibility is problematic because of the distinctive features of rural resource-based economies, namely persistent adverse and unstable terms of trade, periodic ecospheric disasters and the public good context of primary goods and services.

These features also affect the operating status of the rural economic system. Recall that vitality, stability, order and self- regulating control using action and feedback underlie the behaviour of a system as it evolves. Recall also that closing the system to its environment permits entropy-type processes to hamper system operations. The tendency for firms, institutions and states to falter, decay and decline has long been a preoccupation (Hirschman 1970). The rural economic system is subject to these tendencies whatever its particularities.

The rural economic system is also integrating its milieu with that of urban systems. Integration alters the vision and raises the expectations for social and economic objectives. Integration also introduces heterogeneity into the milieu resulting in social tensions, reduced perseverance and discipline, loss of memory about how to cope with ecospheric uncertainties, ambiguity in extra-legal enforcement of behaviour norms, sense of structural disorder and reduced control over system activities. An example of these changes is reduced strength in the links among farmers, business people and labour as new alliances emerge with urban counterparts and interregional lobby interests. These changes are in marked contradiction with the less changeable features of the system.

SDUs in the process of integration have had to violate the norm in the rural milieu of full-time employment and business commitment to product lines, to cross-subsidize commitments to unprofitable resource-based activities with pluriactivity. Pluriactivity at the level of the household firm involves vertical integration, and labour, financial and inputs markets. The prospects for these improve with integration of rural and urban milieus. At the corporate level, mergers and takeovers to diversify resource-based holdings enable a pluriactivity of a different sort. Thus sustaining primary resource-based rural enterprises of all sizes appears to require income supplements generated elsewhere.

Pluriactivity is not the same as diversification. The cost structure of primary production requires specialization by SDUs to maximize the contribution of such enterprises to income. However the rural system holistically must diversify its mix of specialized economic activities to provide the opportunity for family pluriactivity. The contradiction arises in the generality of this conclusion because of the place specificity of natural resources and ecospheric conditions. Isolated mining, fishing and forestry places have all the qualitative features of rural systems and in some cases may even be urban in the context of population density and their milieu. However, they are the least integrated with urban economic systems. Their household SDUs are least able to cross-subsidize incomes with pluriactivity.

The interaction of rural-urban integration, rural features and milieu appear to result in data illusions which may mask the actual signals to rural SDUs and to policy makers. Average farm family income after expenses is approaching parity with urban family incomes without considering consumption in kind (Bollman and Smith 1987). However in 1986, 46% of farm family income was from off-farm sources. If average urban family income having wages as the main source is considered as a standard for comparison, net farm family income derived from equity in land and capital as well as from wages from agricultural activities is about half the standard. The correct signal from the data is that the Canadian agricultural sector evaluated against its output of private goods is failing markedly to achieve its social and economic purpose.

Canadian agricultural SDUs have responded to this signal with partial exit in the form of pluriactivity and with lobbying in seeking corrective income transfers through government. That agricultural SDUs have pursued means of cross-subsidizing their agricultural activities does not alter the reality of thin margins and an inadequate growth in the size of agricultural enterprises in response to industrial technology. Government policies to correct these problems have failed to disassociate subsidies from production creating social losses in the form of inefficiencies. Reactive designs of input and output subsidies which transfer too little too late may have allowed deterioration to proceed too far to enable politically acceptable correction of the fundamental issues. The consequence is that the political direction of lobbying may be misguidedly perpetuating an illusion that the transfers are successful corrective devices.

Conclusion

This paper presented several hypotheses. The first is that understanding the underlying order of the rural economic system and its place among other systems is a precondition to steering the development of that system, whether from within or from without.

The second is that rural-urban integration alters the system milieu and facilitates pluriactivity but does not alter the underlying features of the resource-based economy. Rural stakeholders are in jeopardy as the milieu of the rural system becomes less suited to dealing with the realities for economic activities based on natural resources.

The third general hypothesis is that these underlying features ensure a perpetuation and even a worsening of the economic performance of the ecosphere-related activities of the system over time. These hypotheses are thought to be consistent with economic development theory and revealing of fundamental policy flaws.

Seven unchanging features of the rural economic system are the basis for the symptoms describing the state of the rural system explored here. The first feature is the dependence of rural enterprises on the ecosphere, with a significant proportion of intermediate natural resource-[ecosphere] based goods in the private product mix. The second feature is the changing structure of earnings relating rents, capital earnings, wages and profits. As the proportion of retained rents and capital earnings declines relative to wages imputed to family labour, many rural households return to peasant status with incomes confined to basic needs and limited accumulation of wealth.

The third feature is the significant proportion of unpriced public goods in the rural product mix. The fourth feature is the contradiction between the cost structure of production associated with available technology typified by extended economies of size, and the diminishing returns found in many rural enterprises. The fifth feature is the significant transfer cost which distances the economy from markets and price determination. The sixth feature is monopsonistic tendencies in many commodity market structures. And the seventh feature is ongoing global substitution of industrial goods for natural resources into production processes resulting in the displacement of labour and capital from rural enterprises. Rural primary products for food processing are also replaced by synthetic vegetable oils, proteins, sweeteners and synthetic fibres.

The trends and events in rural economies have been summarized in the findings of the Adaptive Planning Committee of the American Agricultural Economics Association [AAEA]. The agricultural economy is increasingly integrated into the general and international economies. Traditional agricultural programs are under attack as environmental and consumer interests grow in strength. Rural communities are identifying more and more with their surrounding regional economies rather than with local extractive industries. Agribusiness is increasingly conducted by multiproduct firms (AAEA Adaptive Planning Committee 1990).

The integration of the rural system into urban systems transfers control to urban institutions from rural institutions and their arms within urban governments. Integration is changing the rural milieu and dissipating its learning through migration. Increased heterogeneity of vision introduces new variables into objective functions and requires new processes to reconcile priorities. This change, though uncomfortable in the disruption of routine and the challenge of undemocratic ways, wherever these persist, may have a positive long run effect on the erstwhile rural people. This effect is generated by improving business and employment alternatives, by reducing the costs of exit, and by reducing conflicts between rural and urban objectives.

The first conclusion is that the fundamental roots of the distinctive features of rural economies require a perpetual within-household cross-subsidization of resource-based enterprises with non-resource employment income, or income transfers to the rural system from the urban system.

The second conclusion is that a means of determining prices for rural goods and services possessing the status of public good, produced in the national interest, would go a long way to resolving problems of rural income distributions and subsidies.

The third conclusion is that as long as countries set standards for the social and economic well-being of rural people, and have the political will to redistribute income and wealth, there will be a need for income transfers designed differently to the programs of income and wealth redistribution existing within urban household and corporate systems.

The implications arising from these systems hypotheses and the ensuing conclusions may be condensed into six principles to guide rural policy. Distinguish the public from the private components in the goods and services produced by the rural economic system. Reward rural resources according to the social value of the public goods. Maintain policy distance between the recompense for public goods and services, and the decision-making about the production of private goods. Employ supply management in cases where the public interest is associated with private goods through a dual public-private identity. Use income transfers, including taxes and subsidies, to compensate for situations where market outcomes are inconsistent with social objectives.

Communicate further residual deficiencies with information signals to individuals and governments that will facilitate adjustment or timely exit, leading if necessary, to a return in some rural places to an ecosphere with few humans.

The debate over sustainable rural economies and subsidies to rural enterprises of agriculture, fishing, mining and forestry and to rural governments and institutions is a debate over the validity of a separate rural rationale for income redistribution. The focused issue is efficiency of the rural system to achieve its purpose. But the larger issue is the social willingness to pay for the goods and services produced by rural enterprises based on an ongoing judgement of their importance in both the public and the private interest and on the social standards for well-being of all citizens, both rural and urban, in a nation.

L.P. Apedaile
Department of Rural Economy
University of Alberta
Edmonton, Alberta
T6G 2E1

References

American Agricultural Economics Association, Adaptive Planning Committee. 1990. Your association, the AAEA beyond the year 2000. Memorandum to Members. AAEA Newsletter, 12 (4): July/August.

Anderson, P.W., K.J. Arrow, and D. Pines. 1988. The Economy as an Evolving Complex System. Redwood City, California: Addison Wesley Publishing Company.

Apedaile, L.P. 1990. The Restructuring of European Agriculture: Implications for Canadian Agriculture. Department of Rural Economy Staff Paper No. 90-04. Edmonton: University of Alberta.

Apedaile, L.P. and P. Calkins. 1989. Development theory and Chinese agricultural development. Canadian Journal of Agricultural Economics, 37(5): 953-974.

Apedaile, L.P. and S.G.M. Schilizzi. 1992. [Forthcoming] La Méthode du Modele Systémique et la Conception du Développement Agricole: Avec Application à la Camargue. Montpellier: LECSA/SAD/INRA, Études Systémiques.

Apedaile, L.P. and W.S. Zhang. 1988. Family farms: prospects for agricultural development in Canada and China. In China's Rural Development Miracle, edited by J. W. Longworth, International Association of Agricultural Economists. St. Lucia: University of Queensland Press.

Arkleton Trust. 1989. Appraisal of the Factors Which Influence the Evolution of Agricultural Structures in the Community and Contribute to the Efficiency of the Common Agricultural Policy at the Regional and Farm Level. Preliminary report. Inverness, Scotland: Arkleton Trust (Research) Ltd.

Arthur, W.B. 1990. Positive feedbacks in the economy. Scientific American, 262(2): 92-99.

Beckman, M.J. 1970. The impact of scientific and technical change on the location of economic activities. Unpublished Paper. Ottawa: Canadian Council on Rural Development.

Bollman, R. and P. Smith. 1987. The changing role of off-farm income in Canada. Proceedings of the Canadian Agricultural Outlook Conference. December: 155-166.

Boothe, Paul. 1990. Public Sector Saving and Long Term Fiscal Balance in a Resource-based Economy: Alberta 1969-1989. Department of Economics Research Paper No. 90-13. Edmonton: University of Alberta.

Chayanov, A.V. 1986. In The Theory of Peasant Economy, edited by D. Thorner, B. Kerblay and R.E.F. Smith. Madison:The University of Wisconsin Press.

Federal/Provincial Committee on Rural Community Development. 1990. Committee Report. Toronto: Ministry of Agriculture, Economics and Policy Coordination Branch.

Fuller, A., P. Ehrensaft and M. Gertler. 1990. Sustainable rural communities in Canada: issues and prospects. In Sustainable Rural Communities in Canada, edited by M. Gertler, and H.R. Baker. Saskatoon: Canadian Agricultural and Rural Restructuring Group.

Hayami, Y. 1989. Community, market and state. Elmhurst Memorial Lecture. In Agriculture and Governments in an Interdependent World, edited by A. Maunder and A. Valdés. Proceedings of the XXth International Conference of Agricultural Economists in Buenos Aires. Dartmouth: International Association of Agricultural Economists, 3-14.

Hirschman, A.O. 1970. Exit, Voice and Loyalty: Responses to Decline in Firms, Organizations and States. Cambridge, Mass.: Harvard University Press.

Hirshleifer, J. 1978. Competition, cooperation and conflict in economics and biology. American Economic Review, 68(2): 238-243.

Hocking, S.W. 1988. A Brief History of Time. London: Transworld Publishers Ltd.

Le Moigne, J.-L. 1983. La Théorie du Système Général. Deuxième Edition. Paris: Presses Universitaires de France.

Lerohl, M.L., L.P. Apedaile, E.W. Tyrchniewicz and M.L. Nakamura. 1989. Impact of Changes in Method of Payment of the Crow Benefit on Grain Handling and Transportation Efficiency in Alberta. Edmonton: University of Alberta, Department of Rural Economy.

Li, Y. and L.P. Apedaile. 1988. A simulation of the effects of technology transfer in cereal production. Canadian Journal of Agricultural Economics, 36(3): 473-488.

Marten, G.G. 1988. Productivity, stability, sustainability, equitability and autonomy as properties for agroecosystem assessment. Agricultural Systems, 26: 291-316.

Penn, J.B. 1979. The structure of agriculture: an overview of the issue. In Structure Issues of American Agriculture, edited by B. Bergland. Agricultural Economic Report 438. Economics, Statistics and Co-operatives Service. Washington: United States Department of Agriculture.

Ricardo, D. 1951. On the Principles of Political Economy and Taxation, edited by P. Sraffa. Cambridge: Cambridge University Press.

Rocher, Y. 1990. [La Gacilly, Bretagne] Publicité. Le Monde, Mercredi, 3 octobre: 40.

Stabler, J.C. 1985. Trade Centre Viability in the Prairie Region, 1961-1981. Marketing and Economics Branch Working Paper 8/85. Ottawa: Agriculture Canada.

Kenora, Ontario

22

Does rural matter?

Craig McKie

Summary

The intrinsic community based values of rural life were once based on personalism. There still is more to rural life than simply an alternative place to conduct business. Not surprisingly, rationalizing services in rural areas threatens the very fabric of this endangered social milieu. The fundamental values of social and community life in rural areas are changing as these communities are drawn into the distribution networks of the modern state. This is happening at a time when agrarian society is becoming increasingly attractive to disgruntled urban residents seeking change.

Rural does matter. It means going without certain goods and services that are taken for granted in large cities. However, rural communities still provide an attractive alternative lifestyle for Canadians. This lifestyle is perhaps best understood by people still residing in rural areas.

Does Rural Matter?

Craig McKie

At the outset I would like to state that in the early 1990s in Canadian society, rural residence continues to matter both positively and negatively. First of all, the distinction between urban and rural residents, using the conventional Statistics Canada definition of urban versus rural residence[1], serves as an important distinguishing dimension on many social statistical measures. Secondly, and in a more personal sense, it matters to rural residents who continue to value the style of life and the social institutions which are characteristic of rural areas, and also to urban residents who in large numbers idealize the rural lifestyle as an attractive alternative to urban living[2]. Thirdly, the urban core in Canadian society continues to grow as a result of both immigration and internal migration to a few large urban concentrations. As the density of rural populations diminishes relative to that of urban populations, electoral representation based roughly on population density also matters for rural residents.

As a sociologist with an urban perspective, my attention has been drawn to the rapidity of the rural-to-urban transition in Canada in concert with other demographic trends. The collapse of the large agrarian plurality, a plurality which existed in most Western nations at the turn of the century, has proceeded with a vengeance in Canada, particularly since the Second World War. The number of farms has declined rapidly including a large number of farms that were once going economic concerns. The resulting change in the economic character of the rural population from farming-related in the main to clearly farm-unrelated has been striking (McSkimmings 1990).

---

1. Conventionally, Statistics Canada defines urban v. rural residence as follows: urban areas are continuously built-up areas having a population concentration of 1,000 or more and a population density of 400 or more per square kilometre. To be considered continuous, a built-up area must not have a discontinuity exceeding two kilometres. Rural areas are those lying outside urban areas.

2. For a visual display of "Preferred Residential Location" see Figure 7 in Bollman and Biggs, chapter 1 of this book.

Notwithstanding my urban point of view, having lived many years in rural Ontario, I do have views on what has happened to the texture of rural life in my lifetime.

The title of this paper, "Does rural matter?" is an attempt to tap the sometimes intangible social consequences of the demographic, social and economic transformations in Canadian society in our lifetimes. These transformations have shattered what little remains of 19th century agricultural and small town Canada and replaced it with a more urbanized Canadian society centred around three growth nodes: the greater Toronto region, the lower Fraser valley of British Columbia, and the greater Montreal region.

As the three major cities and their smaller municipal counterparts grow, they expand into surrounding green areas, assimilating satellite cities and the remnants of small towns, and turning most of what they engulf into dormitory sprawl at the expense of agricultural lands and towns. In the process, the character of rural society is dramatically altered.

FIGURE 1

Population of 10 largest census metropolitan areas in 1986

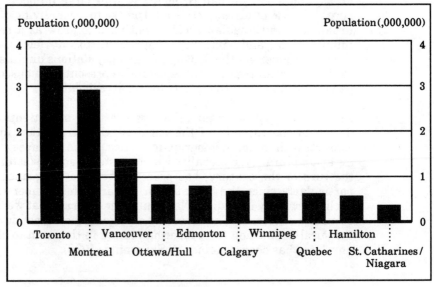

Source: *McKie and Thompson. 1990.*

During the 1980s, the rate of population growth in Canadian urban areas was five times that of rural areas (Akyeampong 1990: 23). The proportion of the Canadian population living outside cities of 500,000 or more persons has fallen from about 82% in 1940 to less than 55% today; and that decline is accelerating gradually and has never reversed since

1940 (Kettle 1990a). One projection shows the proportion of rural residents dropping to approximately 25% by the year 2020 (Kettle 1990b).

A number of conclusions about this trend seem obvious: (1) mechanization has made many rural workers redundant, (2) the logistics of food distribution have improved vastly and are urban-based, (3) the ethnic origins of urban residents, reflecting postwar immigration patterns, dictate distinctive subcultural consumption patterns involving foreign goods, and (4) skilled labour finds optimal rewards in cities.

Of the three conurbations, south-central Ontario—the greater Toronto region—clearly stands out in polar opposition to rural Canada in its population characteristics (it has been a magnet for post-war immigration and it has a different ethnic mix), its economic strengths, its investment in public transit infrastructure, its participation in forming global information-based trading arrangements, and its pivotal position in the Canadian public information system that apparently will form the basis of tomorrow's service-centred employment structure.

How this came about is a long and tortured tale of political economy. It is not a uniquely Canadian story; it is happening worldwide. For instance, in 10 years, Mexico City will have as many citizens as Canada does today. Sao Paulo in Brazil and Tokyo will not be far behind. The present reality of social change is such that a few urban areas seem poised to dominate the population profile of this country, as major cities will in others. These conurbations may come to dominate the social and economic agenda, and the content of public communications, as they now do the financial institutions and manufacturing enterprises of the nation. In 1950, there were just seven cities in the world with a population in excess of 5 million. By the year 2000, there will be 60 such cities (Cahill 1990).

Little on the horizon will stop the growth of these great urban complexes. The future of rural areas, of farm and forest, or small town Canada, or of life at the margins seems clouded. A number of secular trends combine to reinforce this transformation:

1. the aging Canadian population (giving rise, among other things, to extraordinary new centralizing pressures on the health care system as demand increases, and on the retirement income system as well);

2. an incipient shortage, especially in urban areas, of highly educated young workers;

3. a need to retrain a large portion of the adult work force, especially literacy training;

4. the migration of the highly educated to urban centres of employment both in and out of the country;

5.   the growing reliance on service-based employment and information processing occupations in the labour force.

In this context, the answer to the question: "Does rural matter?" seems to evoke the response **yes of course it matters**. At its worst, rural means structural disadvantage and marginalization. At best, it still means less of virtually everything except perhaps solitude, a state desired by many. Rural life is important in many ways not easily documented: the amorphous lifestyle, cultural, and individual liberty factors which define the quality of life.

When I first considered the question of lifestyle differences between urban and rural Canada (McKie 1968), even then it was difficult to find material dimensions of difference. Household possessions and tools: refrigerators, televisions, automatic washers, telephones—the signs of Canadian domesticity—were the pervasive pattern. On this dimension (household capital goods) there was little difference between urban and rural households.

What I missed then was the pattern of service delivery, or more generally, the availability in rural areas of services which have come to be standard features of urban life in Canada, the urban amenities.

TABLE 1
Selected characteristics of urban and rural households for 1986

		Urban	Rural
Number of households	('000)	7,297	1,552
Average household size	(persons)	2.6	3.0
Average number of earners	(persons)	1.5	1.5
Average age of head	(years)	46	49
Average annual household income before tax	($)	36,690	30,830
Average annual household expenditures	($)	36,240	30,180
Proportion of households owning home	(%)	55	85
Proportion of households owning at least one car or truck	(%)	77	89

Source: *Statistics Canada. Perspectives on Labour and Income (cat. no. 75-001E: Autumn 1990).*

Setting aside the romanticism and idealism sometimes directed towards earlier eras, many differences in contemporary service delivery do matter because the differences are undesirable and discrepant for rural residents. Many services characteristic of urban life are not (or are no longer) delivered in rural areas. Information is less available. Lesser degrees of availability affect the choice of major newspapers, national radio service, postal services, and cable television. Municipal services are also less available. These include responsive policing, the full range of emergency and chronic care medical services, the full range of consumer goods and services (which are more expensive and choice-constrained in rural areas), and the full range of educational services (such as specialist courses in electronics, data processing, and telecommunications technology). These tend to be unavailable in rural areas. Urban amenities such as neighbourhood swimming pools and tennis courts, and full service libraries are not generally available either.

FIGURE 2

How a typical household's dollar was spent in 1986

The most prominent differences between urban and rural household expenditures were for taxes, shelter and transportation

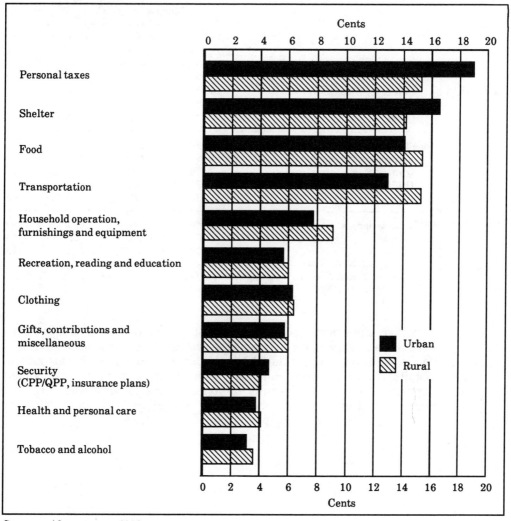

Source: Akyeampong. 1990.

Rural residents in Canada must spend a higher proportion of smaller incomes on food, transportation, household operation, recreation, reading and education, clothing, health and personal care, and tobacco and alcohol. They only spend less on personal taxes and shelter, the former as a partial result of significantly lower incomes in rural areas and the latter as a result of lower property values (Akyeampong 1990: 25). These patterns have not changed since a measurement in 1978.

TABLE 2

Average annual expenditures of urban and rural households on selected items in 1986

	Expenditures		Proportions	
	Urban $	Rural $	Urban %	Rural %
Food	5,090	4,640	100.0	100.0
Purchased from stores	3,740	3,740	73.4	80.7
Purchased from restaurants	1,320	870	26.0	18.8
Other	30	30	0.6	0.5
Shelter	5,980	4,280	100.0	100.0
Rented accommodation	1,990	460	33.3	10.7
Owner-occupied accommodation	2,570	2,230	43.0	52.0
Utilities	1,050	1,300	17.5	30.4
Other accommodation	370	290	6.2	6.9
Transportation	4,660	4,630	100.0	100.0
Private	4,190	4,430	90.0	95.7
Public	470	200	10.0	4.4

Source: *Statistics Canada. Perspectives on Labour and Income (cat. no. 75-001E: Autumn 1990).*

Further, since more people live in urban areas, rural political concerns are less well represented because the system of ridings is partially based on population. Also related to population density is the amount of capital in rural areas, and the prevalence of modern employment options. This pattern results in young people leaving rural areas to obtain good employment or advanced education, thus increasing the mean age of the remaining population.

TABLE 3

Average annual expenditures of urban and rural households in 1987, 1982 and 1986*

	Urban			Rural		
	1978 %	1982 %	1986 %	1978 %	1982 %	1986 %
Average annual expenditures on:	100.0	100.0	100.0	100.0	100.0	100.0
Food	16.8	15.0	14.1	18.2	16.4	15.4
Shelter	16.8	17.9	16.5	14.8	15.8	14.2
Household operations	3.8	4.3	4.2	4.3	4.8	4.9
Household furnishings and equipment	4.3	3.5	3.5	4.8	4.0	4.2
Clothing	7.2	6.1	6.3	7.2	6.0	6.4
Transportation	12.3	11.6	12.9	16.3	14.3	15.3
Health Care	1.9	1.9	1.8	2.1	2.0	2.2
Personal care	1.7	1.8	1.9	1.6	1.8	1.9
Recreation	5.1	4.6	5.0	4.9	4.8	5.4
Reading materials	0.6	0.6	0.6	0.5	0.5	0.6
Education	0.7	0.7	0.9	0.5	0.5	0.6
Tobacco and alcohol	3.3	3.3	3.1	3.2	3.4	3.5
Security (CPP/QPP, insurance)	4.4	4.4	4.5	3.6	4.0	4.1
Gifts and contributions	2.5	2.8	2.5	3.0	3.5	2.8
Personal taxes	16.1	18.3	19.0	12.4	15.5	15.3

* Shares for 1978 and 1982 may not exactly correspond to those previously published because of slight changes in measurement concepts.

Source: Statistics Canada. Perspectives on Labour and Income (cat. no. 75-001E: Autumn 1990).

The picture of rural Canada is one of low population densities supporting less dense social networks, fewer services of lesser quality and range, lower wages, fewer employment opportunities, and a sparser social life in general. The much talked about "electronic cottage", the work-at-home hypothesis based on computers and telecommunications, might well fit into this pattern but there seems little evidence of this phenomenon in Canada yet. Indeed, the possession of home computers is highest in the most densely urbanized provinces. For example, 1.7 million adult Ontario residents out of about 10 million Ontarians of all ages had access to a home computer in 1989 (Lowe 1990: Chapter 4, Table 9).

From a socio-economic viewpoint, the grand political coalition of farmers and industrial workers characteristic of the first decades of this century has disappeared. Both groups are in numerical decline. As Peter Drucker the American organizations theorist wrote, "neither 'farmer' nor 'labor' has the numerical strength or the political importance to be an 'economic estate' any more in any developed country" (1989: 23). The remnants of these once powerful social formations are not socially or behaviourally distinct anymore: there is no fully articulated "rural society" in Canada—even on the simplistic dimension of kitchen machinery—and there hasn't been since the 1960s. Its residues now constitute simple rural destitution, especially for registered Native peoples living on reserves.

Drucker also says farmers have "the highest degree of computer literacy of any occupational group in the world" (1989: 24-25), a possible overstatement, but nevertheless suggestive that domestically and occupationally, the distinction between farm, factory, and office is largely intangible today. More generally, occupation in 1990 is not as suggestive of distinctive lifestyle as it once clearly was. Socio-economic status has become equivalent to purchasing power, pure and simple.

Service levels matter in rural residence. They are inferior to those in urban areas and are a direct consequence of low population densities. It is uneconomic or indeed impossible to replicate urban service levels in a rural context and this discrepancy is, in my view, increasing. With the demographic transition to an older society on average (as much as a quarter of Canada's entire population will be older than 65 in the third decade of the next century), services to the elderly come into sharp focus. Chronic hospital care and long term care services, specialized housing for the elderly, the infirm and the disabled (remembering that the proportion of age groups who are disabled rises steadily with age), food delivery to those no longer able to drive, reconstructive dental services rather than the cavity-filling needed by a young population will have to be addressed. These services are exceedingly difficult to provide to an elderly population, and especially so if it is geographically dispersed.

Circumstances therefore dictate the concentration of elderly citizens near service nodes; and the more esoteric the service required, the more likely it will be in a large urban setting. The Princess Margaret cancer treatment facility in Toronto is a good example of this. Patients from all over Ontario attend this clinic. Travel is a large complicating factor.

There is virtually nothing we can collectively do about this aging process nor about the change in service profiles it will stimulate. Centralization of expensive specialist services will of necessity take place in urban contexts. The pressure for the aged to move close to these services will become intense.

Alternative models

Are we locked into this unfolding pattern? Perhaps not. The "electronic cottage" scenario previously mentioned offers an alternative. Other countries provide examples of the revivification of small towns. For instance, high speed train service (fast by Canadian standards though still considered inadequate by locals) between London and Manchester meant that the mill villages of Yorkshire and Lancashire were repopulated by residents who work as far as 250 miles away while maintaining permanent village residences.

Yorkshire mill village cottages, priced at a pittance in the 1960s, now sell for $200,000, mainly to professionals who work in another region. Installing modern telecommunications equipment in the cottages may well induce these neo-villagers to spend more time in their cottage offices. But even if they worked permanently from these remote residences, they would remain functionally part of the great urban labour force of southern England.

Repopulation of rural areas **can** take place if a high quality transportation service is constructed and maintained between conurbations and residential villages and hamlets. The small northern hill towns in the Yorkshire dales were the birthplace of the industrial revolution. As the economic climate changed, they fell into long term disuse, depopulation, and decay but have rebounded in a new form as the homes of urban professionals.

It is indeed possible to imagine a parallel process in Canada. The telecommunications facilities exist today and if the necessary transport facilities were installed, such towns in Canada might once more become attractive dwelling areas. I suppose that the King City, Orangeville, Barrie, and Stouffville areas surrounding Toronto might serve as Canadian examples, or the small towns of the upper Fraser river valley in British Columbia such as Rosedale and Harrison Lake.

Tourism in the once heavily forested areas of Canada is an attractive alternative as well. A seasonal population can also revivify such areas. This is difficult, however, if the area has been clear-cut logged and left to languish. Again transportation seems to be a key variable, particularly where weekend residency is involved.

Conclusion

The intrinsic and intangible community-based values of rural life revolved around personalism—the provision of services by identifiable human beings in post offices, co-ops, and stores that assumed not merely social roles but rather a social identity which transcended the cash nexus. They became, and perhaps are, the custodians of the emotional heart of small communities, overlaying transactions with friendship and camaraderie now clearly threatened by closures and reductions of the service web in rural Canada. For people living in isolation, the social content overlaying cash transactions is very important. Rationalization of services in rural areas appears to threaten the very basis of social life. Discontinuing services such as passenger rail, the rural post office, or the grocery store forces not only a change of transportation and communications patterns but may also force a social milieu to grow sparser.

The fundamental values of social and community life in rural communities as they were lived and experienced in the late 19th century in this country are changed as these communities are drawn into the distribution networks of the modern state. This occurs even as the conditions of the vanishing agrarian society become more attractive to disgruntled urban residents looking for a change (or a novel theme park experience). Yes, I conclude, rural matters. It means sacrificing the availability of goods and services readily found in large cities. This is the price of rural existence. But perhaps, despite the obvious disadvantages facing rural residents, rural life still provides an attractive and enhanced community attachment for contemporary Canadians in some limited fashion best understood by those still resident in rural areas.

Craig McKie
Housing, Family and Social Statistics
Statistics Canada
Ottawa K1A 0T6

References

Akyeampong, Ernest B. 1990. Consumer spending in urban and rural Canada. Perspectives on Labour and Income, Autumn: 23-29.

Cahill, Jack. 1990. The future of greater metro. Toronto Star, Section B1: October 17.

Drucker, Peter. 1989. The New Realities. New York: Harper & Row.

Kettle, John. A. 1990a. Can the rural exodus be reversed? FutureLetter, June 1.

Kettle, John. A. 1990b. Can the rural exodus be reversed? Part 3. FutureLetter, September 1.

Lowe, Graham. 1991. Work and Education in Canada: Highlights from the 1989 General Social Survey. Ottawa: Statistics Canada.

McKie, Craig. 1968. The rural family in Canada. In The Family in the Evolution of Agriculture, edited by E. Kasirer. Ottawa: The Vanier Institute of the Family.

McKie, C. and K. Thompson, ed. 1990. Major centres getting larger. Canadian Social Trends. Toronto: Thompson Educational Publishing Co.

McSkimmings, Judie. 1990. The farm community. Canadian Social Trends, Spring: 2-23.